THE REVOLUTION WITHIN

Stanford Studies in Middle Eastern and
Islamic Societies and Cultures

THE REVOLUTION WITHIN

Islamic Media and the Struggle for a New Egypt

Yasmin Moll

STANFORD UNIVERSITY PRESS
Stanford, California

Stanford University Press
Stanford, California

© 2025 by Yasmin Moll. All rights reserved.

No part of this book may be reproduced or transmitted in any form or by any means, electronic or mechanical, including photocopying and recording, or in any information storage or retrieval system, without the prior written permission of Stanford University Press.

Library of Congress Cataloging-in-Publication Data

Names: Moll, Yasmin, author.
Title: The revolution within : Islamic media and the struggle for a new Egypt / Yasmin Moll.
Other titles: Stanford studies in Middle Eastern and Islamic societies and cultures.
Description: Stanford, California : Stanford University Press, 2025. | Series: Stanford studies in Middle Eastern and Islamic societies and cultures | Includes bibliographical references and index.
Identifiers: LCCN 2024050353 (print) | LCCN 2024050354 (ebook) | ISBN 9781503638358 (cloth) | ISBN 9781503642416 (paperback) | ISBN 9781503642423 (ebook)
Subjects: LCSH: Religious broadcasting—Egypt. | Religious broadcasting—Islam. | Mass media—Religious aspects—Islam. | Islamic renewal—Egypt. | Islam and politics—Egypt. | Egypt—History—Protests, 2011–2013.
Classification: LCC BP185.75.E3 M65 2025 (print) | LCC BP185.75.E3 (ebook) | DDC 253/.780962—dc23/eng/20241121
LC record available at https://lccn.loc.gov/2024050353
LC ebook record available at https://lccn.loc.gov/2024050354

Cover design: Michele Wetherbee
Cover image: Karson Schenk
Typeset by Newgen in 10.5/14.4 Brill

Contents

Note on Transliteration and Translation vii
Preface ix

Introduction 1

Part I
1 Calibration 49
2 Innovation 89
3 Moderation 129

Part II
4 Impact 171
5 Coexistence 213

Epilogue 253

Acknowledgments 265
Notes 269
Index 327

Note on Transliteration and Translation

I have used a modified version of the *International Journal of Middle East Studies* system to transliterate both Modern Standard Arabic and the colloquial Egyptian Arabic spoken in Cairo. I have omitted all diacritical marks except for ' to signify the Arabic letter *ayn*, and ' for the hamza (glottal stop). Following colloquial Egyptian pronunciation, I have used the hard g for the letter *jim*, and ' for the letter *qaf*. When available, I have used the English transliteration of Arabic names used by the individuals concerned themselves—for example, Amr Khaled—and have omitted diacritical marks for all personal names—for example, Emad. Place names are rendered as they are spelled in English within the country. For ease of reading, I have pluralized some Arabic words by adding an "s" (e.g., shaykhs not *shuyukh*, nadwas not *nadawat*). All translations from Arabic are my own unless otherwise indicated.

Preface

"You can't write about that."

I was at the annual meeting of the American Anthropological Association and had just finished telling a colleague over lunch about being harangued for not wearing a headscarf on the way to my neighborhood grocery store in Egypt one afternoon during my fieldwork. "Enjoy your hair while you can," a middle-aged man had jeered as I walked past him. "Tomorrow, God willing, we will be in power and it will be all over for you." He was wearing an ankle-skimming white shirtdress and skullcap and had a chest-long beard with a shaved moustache, the conventional visual markers of Salafi piety. While my colleague was visibly upset on my behalf, she was also worried about the possible public harms of not keeping my experience private.

The interaction I shared with her occurred a few months after the 2011 revolution toppling Egypt's autocratic president Husni Mubarak. In the competitive democratic interlude that briefly followed, many Salafi revivalists abandoned their long-standing doctrinal repudiation of party politics and formed several of their own: *Hizb al-Nur*, "The Party of Light," *Hizb al-Asala*, "The Party of Authenticity," and *Hizb al-Fadila*, "The Party of Virtue." While they differed in their campaign strategies and policy proposals, the Salafi parties shared a clear political theology: To be a polity pleasing to God, the Egyptian state would have to better enforce divine commands. As the Salafi preacher turned presidential hopeful Shaykh Hazem Abu Isma'il explained, the hijab was not a matter of personal freedom but of public morality. If elected, he had an obligation to ensure that women in Egypt met their own obligations of bodily modesty.[1] In the meantime, some Salafi-identifying groups had mounted a grassroots effort to "encourage good, forbid evil," citing the Qur'anic verse 3:110 in justification.[2] Women across the country reported being reprimanded by moral vigilantes for their dress or being in public without a "male guardian."[3]

In sharp contrast to my academic colleague's reaction, when I shared my own passing experience with such vigilantism with several of my fieldwork interlocutors in Islamic television, none urged me to refrain from writing about it. One of them, Madame Nawal, was particularly indignant on my behalf, even though she herself had on different occasions tried to gently persuade me to don the hijab. My street encounter was in her estimation a troubling indication of how the exclusivist claims of Salafism to religious rectitude and purity could quickly become coercive. She was old enough to vividly remember the violence of Islamic militants seeking to overthrow the government in the late 1980s and '90s, when foreign tourists were gunned down, Christian-owned stores smashed, novelists deemed blasphemous stabbed, and acid thrown on unveiled women's faces.[4] The revolution's emerging power struggles were inextricable, in her view, from this painful past. Already, Salafi preachers had framed a vote for the candidates they endorsed as a "vote for Islam" and sneered that Egyptians who felt otherwise were free to leave the country. While critical of secularism, self-identified pious Muslims like Madame Nawal were also critical of the claims emanating from many within the Islamist camp that opposing their political agenda amounted to being "against religion." Such a conflation not only betrayed Islamic theological ideals of coexistence and pluralism, but also the revolutionary promise of dignity, freedom, and justice unleashed in Tahrir Square, the ethical epicenter of the 2011 uprising. From this perspective, my experience with the offended Salafi man was not an idiosyncratic interaction but indicative of a much wider battle in which the authoritative definition of the "Islamic" was ineluctably intertwined with the political and ethical shape of the "New Egypt."

My American colleague, a self-identified atheist born into a Muslim family, had different histories and power dynamics in mind than Madame

Nawal when she urged me to refrain from writing about being heckled in the name of Islamic piety. She did not doubt my own experience of such chastisement and as a feminist was disturbed by it. Nevertheless, she felt that including such encounters in my ethnography would only give fodder to a pervasive and normalized Islamophobia in the United States, where we both worked and lived. Following the attacks of 9/11, Salafism crystallized as the target of damaging "counter-extremism" policies both domestically and globally. Salafi Muslims became the abject Other in Western media and policy discourses, which saw their version of piety as a path to terrorism. More broadly, under such secularist scrutiny, adopting pious norms that run counter to a conception of religion as a matter of private, interior faith is deemed problematic. This includes within the liberal academy, with its long-standing dismissal of conservative religious groups as the "repugnant other."[5] And since the highly particular assumptions of the secular liberal West continue to masquerade as universal in and out of the academy, my most urgent task as an anthropologist of Islam was surely to critique secularism at home by means of the Islamic tradition.

My colleague's reaction exemplifies what Sherry Ortner has memorably called "the problem of ethnographic refusal." Ethnographic refusal is born of an "impulse to sanitize the internal politics of the dominated," to not give fodder to those doing the dominating.[6] It eschews a focus on the internal struggles and power dynamics of subordinated groups (e.g., Salafis, but also Muslims more generally) in favor of a critique of the powerful external forces they are resisting (e.g., Euro-American policymakers, but also more broadly the imperial ambitions of secular power). In this view, ethnographic research centering on how many pious Egyptians were themselves repelled by Salafism could be too easily co-opted by external critics as confirmation of Islam's fanatical intolerance against which their own enlightened secular liberalism was the only antidote. Moreover, while violence in the name of Islam invariably receives prominent coverage, no comparable attention is paid to Western states' devastating violence against Muslims worldwide in the so-called war on terror. The critical and ethical move as an anthropologist, then, was not to provincialize Salafism, but to provincialize secularism.

This has become a key move within the anthropology of Islam since Talal Asad's canonical theorization of Islam as a "discursive tradition" with distinctive temporalities and assumptions, norms and sensibilities.[7] While the idea of Islam as a discursive tradition aimed to methodologically account for Islam's internal diversity, much of the work informed by it approaches the study of Islam as most valuable for providing "a counter to the triumphalist history of the secular."[8] Along these lines, Saba Mahmood influentially made the widespread secular feminist repugnance toward the Salafi piety movement she studied in Egypt an object of inquiry. The anthropological stakes of the "politics of piety" of her field-defining oeuvre include, above all, to illuminate the aporias of secular liberalism, "to take the resources of the Islamic tradition and question many of the liberal political categories and principles for the contradictions and problems they embody."[9] In much of the critical scholarship inspired by this aim, whether we are learning about Islamic states or Islamic subjectivities, the emphasis is on provincializing their secular correlates.[10]

When I started this project in 2010, I also expected to focus on Islamic television as a site of contestation of the liberal "secular" sensibilities of mainstream media. Instead, I quickly learned that my interlocutors in Islamic media were even more concerned with how to counter Salafi sensibilities to ensure that the Islamic Revival to which they had committed their professional and personal lives would continue to flourish and attract new adherents. For even as "contemporary Islamist activists identify secular liberalism as a powerful corrosive force within Muslim societies,"[11] many of them also pinpointed Salafism as harmful to Muslims. I would be repeatedly struck during my fieldwork by the repugnance my pious interlocutors evinced toward what they deemed the intolerant exclusivism of Salafi sensibilities and to the ways that its "unrealistic" constraints challenged the Islamic tradition Salafi adepts claimed to best embody. The pervasiveness of this critique is frequently missed by secular-identifying progressive Egyptians, who invariably downplay the internal differences of the Islamic Revival in their own critique of its prescriptive ambitions.[12] It is also overlooked by scholars who critique the Asadian emphasis on pious self-cultivation for marginalizing the ambivalent pursuits and fragmented everyday lives of Muslims who "do not simply want to be good Muslims."[13] For my interlocutors in Islamic television, what was at stake was the very meaning of what makes a Muslim, in the eyes of God, "good." And in that definitional contest they felt an ethical call to provincialize Salafism as much as secularism.

My aim in this book is to take seriously this call by examining how it shaped the praxis and ethos of new forms of Islamic media in Egypt at the cusp of revolution. I wrote it out of the conviction that an ethnographic emphasis on the widespread internal contestation over the substantive definition of "piety" enables a more granular understanding of the highly differing investments Muslims bring to the Islamic tradition. In turn, as we shift our attention from unsettling the assumptions of our secular readers to taking seriously the efforts of our pious interlocutors to unsettle each other, we attain new analytical insights into Muslim piety as a constellation of highly variable norms, dispositions, and practices in which the boundaries of the "secular" and the "religious" are continually affirmed as crucial even as they are continually contested, adjudicated, and redrawn. Instead of following the well-trod path of staging the assumed radical alterity of the Islamic tradition as a transformative challenge to "our" own secular liberal imaginaries, I decided to attempt a thicker ethnographic account of how, why, and to what ultimate ends pious practitioners contest each other's theological imaginaries and the ways in which such internal critiques matter for understanding the promises and unraveling of Egypt's revolutionary movement beyond the usual binary of secularist versus Islamist power struggles. Doing so, I believe, provides a way to still provincialize the universal claims of secular liberal power while remaining attuned to the situated reasonings, predicaments, and contradictions of those who define themselves against such power while simultaneously expressing aversion to each other. I also believe that to take these internal contestations seriously is to approach Islam as it most matters to my pious interlocutors: as God's final guidance to all of humanity.

Recently, some anthropologists have called for taking God seriously as a "social actor" while remaining methodologically indifferent to the question of God's existence.[14] Such an ethnographic stance contrasts with theology, where there is little room for indifference to the ontological status of God on the part of the analyst. Unlike theologians, as anthropologists we routinely proceed as if God did not matter analytically, as if the divinely mandated relations of obligation that bind us to each other and to this earth should not shape social scientific ways of knowing. While as teachers and researchers we welcome religious perspectives in our classrooms and may privilege them in our ethnographies, in common with other disciplines in the global Western academy we seldom explicitly make religious warrants the basis of either our pedagogy or our theorizing. As anthropologists of religion, then, we are not really looking from the inside out, or at least not from the same inside as our pious interlocutors, even if our personal religious lives overlap significantly with theirs.

By contrast, even when we question secular suppositions, we only do so from the secular presupposition of divinity as unnecessary to the labor of analysis. This holds even when the ethnographic terrain for this analytical labor is a theistic tradition. This is less a point about insider-outsider positionality and more about how the telos of critique is inextricable from the shared premises that make arguing with something possible in the first place. For revivalists this would include recognition of divine agency in human history and acknowledgment of divinely defined limits to human action, even as their internal critiques seek to ascertain what those limits are and what modes of being they authorize. Put simply, when we study Islam anthropologically, Islam is not, in that process, our tradition, even when we are Muslim anthropologists. Our critical engagement with it is not an internal, normative one, one conducted within that tradition's own sources of authority and appeal. If we seek to be morally responsible in our analysis, we can argue *about* the Islamic tradition, but not *with* it, to repurpose an important Asadian provocation.[15]

In researching and writing this book, I became convinced that the best way to take God seriously as an anthropologist is to pay attention to how my interlocutors themselves do so, to trace ethnographically *the social life of theology* as a dynamic and vibrant space of critical contestation. Islamic media preachers and producers who are themselves wary of the creep of secularism into the nooks and crannies of everyday life nevertheless critique Salafism as promoting an "unnatural," "unrealistic," and ultimately "repellent" religiosity ill-suited to Muslim flourishing in the contemporary period. This does not mean that they discount Salafism; rather, they take it seriously in what for them is the most important way: theologically, as a rival foray into God-talk with significant consequences for the kind of life, individual and collective, believers aspire to.

Contests over what makes media "Islamic" are particularly revealing of these rival theologies, not least because of their shared assumption that media-making is an object of divine interest and declaration. Set against the fractures of the Islamic Revival at a tumultous time of radical change, these theologies shape the means and ends of the politics of piety with stakes much higher than our own: attaining God's loving pleasure in this world and the next. This book shows how that quest inspired a revolution.

THE REVOLUTION WITHIN

Introduction

ON AN APRIL AFTERNOON IN 2012, I WAITED FOR REEM—A LOQUACIOUS, outgoing woman in her late twenties—outside a busy cultural center in an upscale neighborhood of Cairo. Reem and I first met in Qur'anic recitation lessons almost two years earlier when I moved back to Egypt to start my fieldwork on Islamic television preaching.[1] That month we had made plans to attend together the Islamic television preacher Mustafa Hosny's seminar at the Sawy cultural center, where he was to discuss the country's upcoming presidential election, anticipated to be Egypt's first free and fair one. The election was a gift of the 2011 revolution, a largely peaceful uprising that toppled the authoritarian regime of Husni Mubarak in the regional mass protest wave dubbed "the Arab Spring."

Reem wasn't one of the thousands of Egyptians who converged on Tahrir Square when demonstrations broke out across the country on January 25. Instead, like millions, she participated in the revolution through its mass mediation, clicking between the Arab and foreign news channels from the moment she woke up until late into the night. Throughout the eighteen days of marches, street battles, demands, and negotiations that it took for Mubarak to resign on February 11, Reem may have been in her living room, but her heart, exhilarated and exhausted, was in the Square. Reem also kept a loose tab on the stances of the Islamic television preachers whose programs she avidly watched. This wasn't because she needed them to tell her what to think about the revolution, but because she needed to know what she should think about *them*: backing Mubarak landed their programs on her "will-never-watch-again" list; backing the protesters ensured her continued attention. She was pleased that Hosny, by far her favorite preacher, had come out in support of the uprising.

Hosny is one of Egypt's New Preachers, along with Moez Masoud and Amr Khaled. When I started research in 2010, the New Preachers were among the most visible and talked-about Islamic media figures in the Arab world and among Muslim communities worldwide. Their television programs attracted on average 15 million viewers per broadcast; their Facebook pages were the most popular of all pages in the region with almost 20 million subscribers combined; and their YouTube platforms were among the ten fastest growing channels in Egypt. Together, the New Preachers have produced some of the most innovative Islamic media of the last two decades, drawing on genres such as dramatic serials, music videos, and American-style televangelism to create religious media at once edifying and entertaining. In doing so, they straddled differing standards of moral probity, commercial success, and sensuous pleasure as their programs expanded what counts as "Islamic media" and why. Indeed, they are called the "new preachers," *al-duʿah al-gudud*, precisely because their preaching styles were unprecedented within Egypt's half century of Islamic Revivalism.

The New Preachers' viewers were predominantly women like Reem—young, educated, middle-class professionals who felt a sense of intimate familiarity toward these three men: *they speak our language, they know our problems, they understand us, they even dress like us!* viewers would invariably enthuse to me in interviews. By contrast, Salafi television preachers made the viewers I came to know "emotionally distressed," "uneasy," even "traumatized." This had to do with their message—*this is forbidden, that is forbidden, everything is forbidden except what we say*—and their delivery—*they scream, they shout; they point their fingers and wag them at us*. When people told me this, they would invariably adopt a gruff tone, frown fiercely, and scrunch their noses. Salafi preaching—its content and form—was repellent (*munaffir*) for many of my interlocutors like Reem.

Such comparative evaluations of different kinds of preachers by regular viewers of Islamic media became sharper after the 2011 revolution. Like so many Egyptians more than a year and a half after the uprising, Reem was fearful and no longer so optimistic about the possibility of a New Egypt. The topic of Hosny's seminar that April promised some relief. He would be speaking about the ethical criteria against which all presidential candidates should be assessed. Reem had not yet decided whom to vote for and was hoping that what she would hear today would help her figure out how to pick a candidate. At the same time, she appreciated that the New Preachers, unlike their Salafi counterparts, were not publicly backing specific candidates. This did not make the former less political than the latter, in her opinion. For Reem, Salafi programs were problematic not because they "mixed" religion and politics—a nonsensical metaphor since religion governed everything, including political practice—but rather because they "exploited religion" to partisan ends. By contrast, she felt that Hosny's programs addressed the revolutionary politics of the moment without ulterior motives.

I had gone to enough seminars by the New Preachers at the Sawy center to know that it would be hard to find each other among the eager, jostling attendees, and so I asked Reem to meet me outside an adjacent mosque, whose walls were plastered with the campaign flyers of presidential hopefuls. The Muslim Brotherhood candidate's posters competed for space on the gray stone walls with the socialist candidate's, while those of a former general in the running seemed to stare down those of another old regime insider. The single poster of a human rights lawyer in the running felt forlorn, overshadowed by its well-funded competitors.

A taxi pulled up in front of me, and Reem stumbled out from the backseat as she peered frantically into her purse for the fare money. "Sorry, so sorry!" she waved at me in English, while simultaneously paying the driver and adjusting the edge of her headscarf back over her hairline. The taxi zoomed off, a campaign sticker looking back at us from the car's rear window. We rushed inside, scanning the space for seats.

At exactly 4:30 p.m., Hosny walked up onto the stage, relaxed in a white polo shirt and jeans, his head ritually shaved from his recent pilgrimage to Mecca. After some light banter and greetings, Hosny launched into his main topic: the political exemplarity of Umar ibn al-Khattab, a close

Companion of the Prophet and the second of the Four Rightly Guided Caliphs, who died by an assassin's hand in 644 CE. For many Sunni Muslims, Umar, who acquired the moniker Commander of the Faithful during his lifetime, was a paradigmatically "Islamic" leader: powerful yet humble; ambitious yet incorruptible; just yet merciful; and, perhaps most importantly, politically astute without being religiously manipulative. To illustrate the texture of Umar's governance, Hosny narrated a series of telling incidents, interspersing these stories with allusions to other, less common exemplars: James Madison, the fourth president of the United States, who was deeply concerned with the moral discipline of civic character (*tarbiyat al-muwatin*); and Aristotle, that great philosopher of ancient Greece, who argued that one role of the state was to train its citizens in the virtue of freedom. These were the political ethics Hosny felt Egyptians needed at this critical juncture.

The stories that Reem enjoyed the most, however, were those about Hosny's own life. He told us that evening about the time he felt self-important while at a conference abroad as people opened doors for him and chauffeured him around. He neglected his family in favor of the thousands attending his religious lessons, perversely turning his *daʿwa*, preaching, into a *shahwa*, an illicit desire. Power can be consuming, its pursuit addictive. We should be careful to choose a candidate who is indifferent to power's lure, a president who wants to serve, not rule. A man just like Umar, he advised.

The question-and-answer part of the seminar was long. During it, God and country jostled for attention with the more quotidian concerns of Hosny's youthful fans. The queries, written on small scraps of paper and collected by the volunteers, seemed endless: *How can I motivate myself to study for my exams? How can I perform my prayers regularly? Should I marry a man who is suitable but much younger? My mother regularly insults me in front of others, what can I do? How can I feel closer to God?*

Reem also had a question, one scribbled hastily in a notebook in the cab, the page now neatly torn out and folded to hand to one of the volunteers. Approaching thirty, she was alarmed that there were still no marriage prospects in sight. While she enjoyed her job as an elementary teacher, she also yearned to get married and have children of her own. She wanted Hosny to make a supplication for her, to beseech God to grant her a righteous husband, a man just like him. In the meantime, did the preacher have any advice on how she could manage her growing anxiety about being single?

The pieces of paper piled up on the podium. The preacher assured us that he would answer our questions, all of our questions. But first let us talk about Egypt.

This is a book about the New Preachers and their Islamic media: about how they came to be, about who and what made them possible, and about why they mattered to millions of Egyptians coming of age at a time of revolution. Between 2010 and 2013 I conducted ethnographic fieldwork in Cairo at the world's first Islamic television channel, called Iqraa. The channel was founded in 1998 by a Saudi billionaire businessman with the mission of promoting a "moderate Islam," *Islam wasati*, as a media bulwark against both secular Westernization and religious dogmatism. My research focused on the efforts to create novel forms of Islamic media by the New Preacher Mustafa Hosny, then on the channel's staff, and his media team. Six months into my fieldwork the 2011 uprising occurred. I watched as debates about innovations in Islamic media production became linked to broader debates about the shape of a New Egypt. Through their new Islamic media, my interlocutors aimed to cultivate on a mass scale the pluralism, solidarity, and coexistence that marked Tahrir Square, the ethical epicenter of Egypt's revolution. The New Preachers are typically disparaged as neoliberal apologists by leftists, as stealth Islamists by liberals, as secret liberals by Islamists, and as Westernizing sellouts by Salafis. In this book, I show how for many young Egyptian Muslims the New Preachers radically refigured both what it means to be pious and what it means to be revolutionary at a crucial moment in the country's history.

Coming of age in the Arab world's most populous country, Egypt's rapidly growing youth population had faced what appeared in the decade before the revolution to be a bleak future: a growing gap between rich and poor, university degrees that led to unemployment for the middle class, chronic corruption and police violence, acrimony between Muslims and Christians, dissent and expression curtailed in the name of security and moral propriety, air that was toxic to breathe and food that was harmful to eat, even if you could afford it. For men, the soaring price of real estate made the dream of moving out of childhood bedrooms and starting families fantastical; for women, sexual harassment made the simple task of commuting to work an ordeal of mind and body. Meanwhile, the sound of the Qur'an was so ubiquitous it hardly registered, the music videos of bodies gyrating to the beat were tastelessly predictable, and the news about invasions, occupations, and bombings of Arab neighbors were feeding anger about Western hypocrisy and avarice and a sense of helplessness. The hours, days, months, years of one's life piled up with nothing to show for them. Enter the New Preachers, intent on capturing the attention of Egypt's Muslim youth. In return, they offered millions of viewers a new sense of self-worth and purpose, an Islamically grounded ethic of engagement that positioned them not as passive victims of their circumstances but as catalysts of change. Most important of all, the New Preachers presented them with an Islamic piety predicated on pleasure, not punishment; on love, not judgment.

Egypt's "culture wars" have long been analyzed along a broad secular versus religious polarity.[2] In the former camp are said to be liberal and progressive intellectuals, artists, and activists championing diversity, creativity, and autonomy through an epistemology of truths as multiple, partial, and contextual. In the latter camp are Islamists and Islamic revivalists promoting discipline, continuity, and authority through appeal to divine revelation. Many ethnographic accounts of Egypt take seriously how one camp distinguishes itself from the other, showing on the one hand how Islamic pietists, preachers, and lawyers seek to counter secular conceptions of the self, the senses, and the state,[3] or, on the other, how secular-oriented intellectuals, artists, and activists compete against Islamists for symbolic and institutional space.[4] Importantly, as Gregory Starrett notes, each of these groups see themselves as "embattled minorities with respect to the other."[5] The sense of being under siege by "the other side" increased dramatically with the 2011 revolution, making the secular versus religious divide even more central to scholarship on Egypt.

This book has a different focus. It shows that, far from being exclusively definable along a secular versus religious axis, the culture war's major fault lines are replayed *within* the Islamic Revival. This finding surprised me. I started fieldwork at Iqraa expecting to investigate how the New Preacher Hosny and his production team aspired to create media to counter the mainstream entertainment industry. Instead, I quickly discovered they were more concerned with undermining Salafi preaching media. To be sure, Iqraa producers considered much of the media broadcast on the region's satellite channels to be Islamically incorrect and morally deplorable.[6] For them, however, this kind of media flourishes not because of its intrinsic pull but because there are not many entertaining yet ethical alternatives. Importantly, they similarly attributed the popularity of Salafi media within the piety movement to the lack of high-quality alternatives. From this perspective, Iqraa, unlike Salafi channels, appreciated that Islamic media encompasses yet also exceeds religious programs aimed at correcting doctrinal understanding or enjoining ritual observance. And unlike mainstream television channels, Iqraa understood that divine parameters of permissibility and prohibition matter to creative media. In this production space, Islamic media could be at once edifying and entertaining, morally serious and visually dazzling. For Iqraa's producers and viewers alike, the channel was a pioneer of new forms of Islamic media within what has over the past twenty years become a crowded and contentious Islamic television field on satellite. This ambition called for a new kind of preacher promoting an alternative sense of piety.

In the late 1990s, when the New Preacher Mustafa Hosny was in his early twenties, it felt like being religious meant that one "couldn't have an ordinary life—it meant having to cancel out 99 percent of your life," he told me. Hosny and his producers at Iqraa define "ordinary life" (*al-hayah al-'adiya*) largely through participation in the leisure activities available to middle-class urban youth: going to the cinema, spending time at the beach in the summer, playing backgammon in coffee shops, listening to music while cruising. The Salafi preachers popular at the time—the "cassette shaykhs," Hosny called them, referring to the medium on which he like so many of his generation first encountered them—promoted as pious a sensibility that shunned such activities as morally corrupting. These preachers had become virtually synonymous with the Islamic Revival. From Hosny's perspective, this conflation proved problematic, because the norms Salafi revivalists propagated were incorrect, unnatural even. Such an evaluation differs from that of some Egyptians outside the piety movement, who view Salafi norms as aspirational even while bemoaning their own incapacity to fulfill them. It also diverges from the critiques of both secular nationalists and political

Islamists in Egypt, who disparage the piety movement's focus on ritual practice. Like their Salafi counterparts, the New Preachers do understand ritual worship—praying and fasting, for example—as an essential component of creating the capacity for virtue. For them, as for Salafi preachers, religion demands above all an embodied discipline.

The problem, as Hosny saw it, was that Salafism's pious promoters and secular critics alike conflate its particular norms and lifeworlds with Islamic piety itself. By upholding as "Islamic" fanatical ideas and practices, by forbidding what God actually permits, by fostering a holier-than-thou attitude, Salafism made secular lifeways *more* attractive and repelled "ordinary youth" (*al-shabab al-'adi*) from piety. Salafism, my interlocutors lamented, led to social alienation, existential burnout, and an enclave mentality, and missed what godliness actually demands: a continual commitment to helping people find ways to be pious within the everyday idioms and rhythms of the present worlds they inhabit, not in the annihilation of these worlds. Consequently, what the *da'wa* movement needed was nothing less than a "reconstruction of what piety looks like" (*'iyadat siyaghat shakl al-tadayyun*), as Hosny often put it. His mission as a preacher was to reclaim piety from its conflation with "certain shaykhs and certain appearances." This involved reenvisioning both the content and form of Islamic media.

My interlocutors on Hosny's production team at Iqraa disparaged Salafi television channels as confirming secular stereotypes of Islamic media, and by extension of Islamic piety itself, as irrelevant and boring. In contrast to the "direct *da'wa*" of Salafi television, with its monotonous rehearsal of *God-said, the Prophet-said*, theirs would be a "dazzling *da'wa*" that drew on the conventions of popular entertainment forms, from music videos to reality shows to dramatic serials. This novel strategy of Islamic publicity was challenged by Salafi *da'wa* practitioners, who vociferously repudiated entertainment forms precisely for the "dazzlement" that they engender[7] and judged the New Preachers as stealth secularizers, charging that their *da'wa* smuggles Western sensibilities into the Islamic Revival in the guise of promoting piety. Such challenges matter greatly to Islamic television preachers and their pious viewers, who spend much more time debunking each other than they do secular Egyptians. Taking these differences seriously offers new insight into the social life of theology as a terrain of critical contestation.

The Revolution Within argues that contestations over the forms of Islamic mediation enact distinctive imaginaries of what makes a form of life virtuous, a person pious, a sensibility ethical, a public godly. Far from constituting a coherent counterpublic defined by an internally stable opposition to secular publics and subjects, participants in the Islamic Revival draw the boundaries of the "religious" and the "secular" in radically different ways. These differences point to incommensurable theologies of the Islamic tradition. For the New Preachers, remaining Islamic is predicated on continual change, on constant transformation based on a view of Islam as a realistic religion attuned to changing human realities. Innovation is not a rupture of tradition, but rather its continuation in new form for new generations of Muslims. For Salafi preachers, remaining true to Islam requires mimetic fidelity to its original form as embodied by the Prophet and first generations of righteous ancestors. Their theology refuses not just the substance of change but the very notion of change as intrinsic to Islam. Their preaching media provides a counter to secular Westernization by cultivating a pious public "pure" from outside influences. By contrast, as this book shows, the New Preachers, their producers, and their viewers aimed to subvert from within not only the substance of the Salafi counterpublic—its sensibility, sociability, protocols of address, topics of concern—but the very premise of a counterpublic as a pious ideal. A counterpublic can never, from their vantage point, be Islamic. After 2011, they also deemed the ethos of the counterpublic antithetical to the revolutionary.

Inspired by the protests that toppled neighboring Tunisia's autocratic regime a couple weeks earlier, on January 25, 2011, thousands of ordinary Egyptians took to the streets in a "Revolution against Torture, Poverty, Corruption, and Unemployment."[8] After eighteen days of mass mobilizations across Egypt, Mubarak resigned and handed power over to the armed forces. In June 2012, Mohamed Morsi, a leader in the Muslim Brotherhood, Egypt's largest opposition group, was elected president. Popular discontent with the group's year in power again led to mass protests in the summer of 2013, precipitating the coup that ended the country's brief experiment with competitive electoral politics.

Scholarly and media accounts of this tumultuous period between 2011 and 2013 conventionally frame its struggles as primarily between secularists and Islamists, between those committed to a principled separation of religion from politics and those who see no distinction between the religious and the political.⁹ This leaves out the more complex and contingent stances of many Egyptians active in the country's decades-long Islamic Revival, like the television producers at Iqraa. My interlocutors resolutely opposed secularism's demarcation of religion as a matter of private, inner conscience. Instead, they were committed to the idea of Islam as a "comprehensive religion" (*din shamil*) informing all aspects of life, including political life. Yet most of them were as critical of the Muslim Brotherhood as they were of Salafi groups, judging both to be exclusionary and authoritarian in their insistence on conflating pious commitment with unquestioning support for their particular agenda. These groups' narrative that whoever opposed them was actually "opposing Islam" was one my revivalist interlocutors found infuriating. In this conflation, Islamists and Salafis not only betrayed Islamic ideals of coexistence and engagement but also the revolutionary promise of dignity, freedom, and justice unleashed in Tahrir Square.

In the months after the uprising, I observed how the directors, editors, scriptwriters, and researchers on Hosny's media team at Iqraa aspired to create media that would promote Tahrir's revolutionary ethos in a pious register. They framed the nation's fraught transitional period as not merely a political crisis but more fundamentally an ethical one. For my revivalist interlocutors, the revolution was as much about cultivating particular ways of thinking, feeling, and doing as it was about the downfall of a particular regime. And the conflicts that followed the fall of the regime were not only about what kind of polity Egyptians wanted—"Islamic," "secular," "civil," or something beyond or in between—but more fundamentally about what kind of people they wanted to be. For them, as for so many, Tahrir Square brought out the best in them. In Tahrir, Egyptians unified across differences of religion, class, gender, and ideology with extraordinary results. The challenge was how to transform "the spirit of Tahrir" from exceptional to everyday.

Iqraa producers' reconceptualization of Islamic media as an agent of revolutionary change was predicated on a form of piety rooted in social engagement and solidarity. This task of becoming other-oriented began with the self. One of the first programs by a New Preacher after the revolution, a program by Moez Masoud titled *Thawra 'ala al-Nafs* (*The Revolution Within*), addressed this idea directly. The premise of the program was that even though Egyptians succeeded in overthrowing an "external corrupt system," they still needed to internalize the revolution, to embody its ethics in their interactions with each other. Structural transformation, to be sustainable and successful, must be shored up by the everyday actions and ethical commitments of those making up the body politic. Furthermore, New Preachers like Masoud believed their programs could be catalysts for the mass cultivation of the more ethical New Egypt prefigured in Tahrir by going beyond the divisive rhetoric of "us-the-saved" versus "them-the-damned" of Islamists and secularists alike. They would do so through creating media that celebrated in both form and content the idea of a shared space, of coexistence, as itself at once religious and revolutionary, as a radical middle path beyond well-worn binary paths.

This book is ethnographically grounded in an extraordinary moment in Egyptian history, a moment of widespread hope that new, better ways of collective living and relating were just on the horizon. As I write this, more than a decade after "the end" of the revolution, Egypt's affective landscape is significantly different from that time. One aim of this book is to show that understanding Egypt's revolution ten years after the toppling of Mubarak requires understanding what Egyptians who were committed to the success of a "New Egypt" imagined as standing in its way. *The Revolution Within* demonstrates how the dilemmas of ethical practice in a diverse society—which turn on questions of pluralism and polarization, contestation and consensus—shaped the Islamic Revival's internal differences, and their debate on-screen and off, revolutionizing many ordinary Egyptians' sense of what counts as Islamic piety, of what is pleasing to God. By refusing as false a binary of structural reform versus individual change, of power versus virtue, the New Preachers as "unlikely" revolutionaries alert us to the world-making, collectively attuned capacities of the social life of theology. The revolution, with a capital R, depends on a "revolution within."

THE WORLD'S FIRST ISLAMIC TELEVISION CHANNEL

Iqraa, the world's first self-declared Islamic television channel, was founded in 1998 by a Saudi media mogul. Headquartered in Jeddah, the channel has had an important production and administrative unit in Cairo from the start. This unit played a key role in launching the transnational television careers of the New Preachers Amr Khaled, Moez Masoud, and Mustafa Hosny and was the main site of my fieldwork in 2010–2013. Islamic preachers have appeared on state-run television since the early 1960s, when Egypt set up its first broadcast station. The country's media ministry mollified religious objections to this new medium through assurance that scholars from al-Azhar—"instead of those mosque preachers who sometimes present Islam incorrectly"—would have their own programs for Qur'anic interpretation and that the daily calls to prayer would interrupt scheduled broadcasts.[10] One of those Azhari preachers was Shaykh Sha'rawi, whose televised weekly mosque sermons and other programs garnered him a level of popularity that remains undiminished even after death.[11]

In the mid-1990s, regulatory changes made possible the private ownership of television channels on satellite signals, ending the state's monopoly on the medium. The proliferation of satellite channels that followed was hailed by many Middle East Studies scholars as the harbinger of a more liberal future. This was dubbed the "al-Jazeera effect," after the Qatari-based channel whose pan-Arab aspirations for democratic dissent and political pluralism were memorably represented in the slogan "The opinion . . . and the other opinion." In offering Arab television audiences the opportunity to watch politicians, activists, and intellectuals from a wide variety of backgrounds and ideologies—Islamists and secularists, Israeli officials and Hamas militants—express their views and debate each other live on-air, the news channel was lauded by academics as "at the forefront of a revolution in Arab political culture."[12] One longtime chronicler of the channel even argues that "a clear path can be found from al-Jazeera's founding in 1996 to the events of the Arab Spring in 2011."[13]

Iqraa was the al-Jazeera of Islamic television. Just as al-Jazeera gave a platform to multiple perspectives in an effort to counter the power of governments to shape narratives around current events, Iqraa offered an inclusive platform for Islamic theologians, preachers, and even ordinary Muslims from a wide variety of orientations across the Arab world to get their messages across with much less interference than on state-owned terrestrial channels.[14] Indeed, many older employees at the channel were on unpaid permanent sabbaticals from state television and appreciated Iqraa not only for its comparatively better pay but for its freer conditions to create the content they wanted. As I detail in chapter 3, the broadcast of Sunni revivalism's diverse, often mutually antagonistic, doctrinal, and ideological gamut—of Sufis and Salafis, of oppositional Islamists and government-affiliated shaykhs—was central to how Iqraa, like al-Jazeera, branded itself as "the middle ground" of competing views. Significantly, Iqraa's sense of moderation was theologically elaborated, as it sought to normatively transform the ethos of the Islamic Revival from an intolerance of disagreement to an embrace of interpretive pluralism as godly.

Nevertheless, while observers positively linked current events–oriented channels like al-Jazeera to the raising of revolutionary consciousness and anti-authoritarianism, they invariably framed *da'wa*-oriented channels like Iqraa as antithetical to the democratic dreams of the Arab Spring. During my research, I affiliated with Cairo University's Faculty of Media. The dean was candid when we met, criticizing state media coverage of the blatantly rigged 2010 parliamentary elections. Remaining cordial, he also bluntly dismissed my chosen topic of Islamic television channels with an impatient wave of his hand. "Those channels are all the same," he said. "Just a bunch of shaykhs talking about the same things over and over. They have made religion a business while not contributing anything interesting from a media perspective." He rehashed the familiar framing of the Islamic satellite television sector as a Wahhabi "cultural invasion" fueled by Saudi petrodollars. In this telling, dedicated Islamic channels like Iqraa are merely the result of Gulf oil boom domination of pan-Arab satellite television and a symptom of the neoliberal commodification of religion.[15]

Many ordinary Egyptians agreed with this negative assessment, disparaging Islamic television preachers as opportunistic novices who lack the credentials to expound on religion. They weren't trained theologians, but former accountants, salesmen, and artists. Such criticisms predated the 2011 revolution but increased in volume and intensity after it. From 2010 to 2013, I clipped hundreds of editorials and articles from newspapers, both governmental and oppositional, condemning Islamic television preachers as money-grubbing charlatans who might also be treasonous collaborators working for foreign powers. This newspaper coverage—along with dramatic serials, films, and novels—lambasted Islamic television preachers as instrumentalist and insincere, as *tuggar din*, merchants of religion.[16] Indeed, when preachers made headlines, it was usually because their incomes had been deemed too high. What business does a person who calls himself a guide to God's straight path have making "so much" money, critics wondered? After the revolution, television preachers also made headlines when they were deemed to be "exploiting" religion for partisan gain. Friends and family would contrast the turpitude of satellite television preachers to the rectitude of their neighborhood mosque preacher toiling in obscurity to make ends meet as he brought God's words to the faithful without seeking recompense or influence.

This book goes beyond these conventional narratives about Islamic satellite channels and preachers through fieldwork with Iqraa's producers and viewers. For almost three years, I conducted research at the channel's Cairo branch, working alongside translators, editors, directors, and others as I observed and participated in trainings, meetings, focus groups, brainstorming sessions, studio recordings, and on-location shoots. My research also included talking to dedicated viewers (many of whom I met at the New Preachers' in-person gatherings) and spending time with them across different spaces, from cafes to Qur'anic recitation classes to malls. Many of the people I came to know, whether on the production or audience side of Islamic television, shared in the widespread concern that Salafi satellite channels were broadcasting harmful content that inflamed religious strife and made living across differences less possible. But instead of banning such channels, they proposed to counter them through reimagining Islamic media, and with that, Islamic piety itself. As I detail in chapter 1, Iqraa's structure as a privately owned channel presented both ethical opportunities and challenges to Islamic television producers, calling for the calibration of various forms of capital through attention to divine dictate, to God as the ultimate owner of all things. The solution to the problem of novice "satellite shaykhs" was more godly channels, not fewer.

"RELIGION IS MEDIA"

This is a book about the making of Islamic media but, crucially, it is not just about the content of this media. It is also about how Islam came to be thought of *as* media. Emilio Spadola has called attention to how the conceptualization of Islam as a communicative "call" reveals the ways in which for many Muslims "local discourses and acts of religious selfhood and social life are explicitly bound up with changing discourses and acts of media."[17] In Islamic television production, these two domains are entwined on several levels, from the ethical to the epistemological. Since the late nineteenth century, many Islamic theologians have been ascertaining the permissibility of mass media technologies, from the telegraph to the radio, and urging their adoption for *daʿwa*. For example, the prominent turn-of-the-century Islamic reformist Rashid Rida embraced the new media of his time as a force for Islamic renewal. Rida even argued that the Prophet Muhammad would have used a phonograph to record his recitations of the Qur'an had one been available; if new media technologies served beneficial ends, their use was sanctioned by Islam.[18] In the postcolonial period, however, a new, more radical idea of the relation between Islam and media emerged. In his posthumously published *Media at the Dawn of Islam*, Abd al-Latif Hamza, a pioneering scholar of mass communication in the Arab academy, argued that the Qur'an was "God's newspaper" (*sahifat Allah*), a medium of divine communication oriented to radical social change. In this way, not only were modern media technologies and techniques, despite their non-Muslim invention, divinely permissible, they were also divinely prefigured in the Qur'an as God's "final message" to humanity. This rendered Islam, in comparison to other religions, a distinctively "mediatic religion," *din iʿlami*.[19]

I have written at length elsewhere about how Iqraa's formation as the world's first Islamic television was directly tied to this novel epistemology of the Qur'an as a "media text."[20] Indeed, by the time of my fieldwork at the channel a decade after it launched, the idea of Islam as a religion distinctively and exceptionally attuned to mediation had become a truism. This assumption was summed up in the pithy phrase *al-din iʿlam*, "religion is media," which surfaced during my research both in casual conversation and serious reflection. What remained to be shown was how Islamic media could be Islamic without only being *about* Islam, about how to pray or why to fast.

The Revolution Within unpacks how long-standing theological doctrines and precepts were elaborated in new ways to address ethical dilemmas centered on media and mediation, on the specific manipulations of communicative technologies and what these represent and afford for Muslim belief and practice in the present. I term these elaborations *theologies of mediation*.²¹ Such theologies scrutinize claims about the means and ends of media from a perspective oriented toward divine revelation, one in which media are inextricably tied to claims about what godliness demands. Indeed, my interlocutors in Islamic television production were as interested in going meta about media and mediation as I was, evincing a reflexivity about different mediums and about the relation between technology and cultural change. This reflection was fueled by an intense theological interest in harnessing the "power" of media for God even as it drew on their own educational backgrounds in media studies as a modern discipline.

Anthropological work at the intersection of religion and media has shown how religious subjects across different traditions often aspire to immediacy in their devotional practices, either by decrying semiotic forms marked as media as obstacles in their pursuit of unmediated contact or co-presence with God²² or through what Birgit Meyer has termed the "disappearing medium," that is, through not understanding some media as media at all and attributing to them instead the qualities of immediacy and transparency.²³ Media, in a word, has been felt to get in the way of the divine. Rather than try to break free, however, my interlocutors leaned into it, making the innovative mediation of divine revelation a key point of contrast between them and Salafi revivalists. If at Salafi channels television might as well be radio, at Iqraa the dazzling re-mediation of the Qur'anic message through the exploitation of television's affective affordances for intimate persuasion at a mass scale was a divine imperative demanding skill and craft. And the professional, media savvy, socially plugged-in television preacher—the "New Preacher"—was key to living up to this imperative and to Islam as a mediatic religion.

MAKING ISLAM "NEW" AGAIN

New Preaching followers coalesce around a set of pious sensibilities and discourses that are both widespread enough within Egypt to register as mainstream yet distinctive enough within the grassroots *da'wa* movement to be contentious. While "Salafi" is a term of self-description and was used by viewers of Salafi television channels, no one signaled their New Preaching preference through adopting comparable forms of self-identification. Still, there was no question *who* the New Preachers were for fans and critics alike during my fieldwork: they were Amr Khaled, Mustafa Hosny, and Moez Masoud.[24] On social media, fans collaged images of the three men framed by hearts, while critics replaced the hearts with red Xs. During my research at Iqraa, Hosny was without doubt the channel's "star" New Preacher, Khaled and Masoud having already left to start their own media production companies.

Hosny was passionate about being a television preacher. As he told it, one of his happiest moments came in 2004, when he saw himself for the first time on a video-editing monitor at Iqraa. He shed a few tears then, because he realized that his lifelong dream of trying to get as many people as possible to "taste the sweetness of faith" was being fulfilled. This had been Hosny's ambition from a young age. As a high school student, he would tape-record or take notes during mosque sermons and lessons, spend hours committing to memory what he had learned, and then eagerly preach it back to his friends as they passed the evening in the manner favored by most middle-class teenage boys: milling around their neighborhood kiosks sipping soft drinks, music blasting from dented parental cars. The lessons he learned performing for this irreverent, hard-to-please audience proved foundational to his later success on television. One lesson was that you cannot sternly scream love for God into most people; far more effective is gently and gradually creating this love by making religion attractive and relevant to them—fun even—and modeling the constant accessibility of godliness to even the most lax.

At first glance, the New Preachers—with their suits and jeans, glitz and glam—might seem to be unabashed modernists who celebrate Western culture and distance themselves from centuries of Islamic wisdom. This perception is promoted by the generally positive US media coverage of Islam's "up-to-date" preachers with their "moderate" and "upbeat religious message" catering to "upwardly mobile Muslims."[25] For their followers, however, the New Preachers were "new" in terms of their styles of media presentation, but the message itself, upbeat and moderate, was not novel but in keeping with long-standing Islamic insights. Indeed, the New Preachers did not want to revolutionize "Islam" in the sense of disrupting authoritative ideas and beliefs in favor of new ones. Instead, they aspired to revolutionize ordinary Muslims' understandings of what is "Islamic." This necessitated the recovery of core and unchanging revealed truths through their expression in new persuasive forms attuned to the aesthetic expectations and interactional sensibilities of contemporary, actually existing, Muslims.

The New Preachers agree with Salafis that the best generation of Muslims was the one closest in time to revelation. The age of the Prophet and his Companions, the time of *al-salaf al-salih* (the righteous ancestors) is thus the Islamic ideal that all Muslims should try to re-create in the present. However, while Salafi revivalists see this re-creation as one best accomplished through mimetic fidelity, the New Preachers see it as best achieved through resonant reconfiguration. "Continual transformation (*al-taghyir al-mustamir*) is one of God's traditions (*sunan*) for us," Hosny explained to his viewers in an episode on the pitfalls of fearing change. "The Prophet has warned us that Satan will make us afraid of change."[26] It is important to underline that the New Preachers do not hold a progressive view of Islamic history, in which each generation of Muslims is better than the one that preceded it. While they share an interest in resisting Salafi versions of Islam, the New Preachers' views on change are therefore distinct from those of self-identifying progressive Muslims whose quest for social transformation often "mandates a difficult, onerous, critical, uneasy engagement with the tradition."[27] For my interlocutors, tradition, and its daily embodiment in devotional piety, was the solution, not the problem.[28]

Still, the New Preaching stress on creativity, *ibda'*, in religious outreach was criticized by Salafi preachers as the gateway to *bid'a*, heresy. Salafi "sermon-givers see their task as allowing God's revealed words to be apprehended by listeners, not as skillfully conveying those words," as John Bowen explains in his overview of the literature: "Skill would be superfluous, perhaps morally presumptuous."[29] As I detail in chapter 2, Salafi preachers contended that the New Preachers' efforts to create a "dazzling *da'wa*" that appropriates the aesthetics and conventions of mainstream entertainment implied that the Qur'an was "not enough" on its own to move Muslims to greater piety. To be clear, like their Salafi rivals, New Preaching producers adhered to the orthodox doctrine of the miraculous nature of the Qur'an, its formal perfection and inimitability. Yet they believed that the Qur'anic message, to be properly apprehended, needs to be mediated in ways that are compelling for its contemporary receivers, ways that make full use of both the affective capacities of new media technologies and the globalized media cultures they enable. In postmillennial urban Egypt, that meant appropriating for *da'wa* the aesthetics of mass entertainment, from music videos to reality television to dramatic serials. This book shows how these contestations over what is entailed by divinely authorized practices of media-making reflect deep doctrinal differences that draw the boundaries of the religious and the secular in incommensurate ways, calling for more ethnographic attention to the social life of theology.[30]

THE SOCIAL LIFE OF THEOLOGY

Anthropologists of religion have generally been more concerned with critically excavating the latent, invariably Christian, theological presuppositions of our analytical categories than with ethnographically tracing the social life of theology in our fieldsites. This is especially true of the study of contemporary Islam. The dearth of ethnographic interest in Islamic theology reflects a broader conceptualization of Islam as a religion of praxis, not doxis, when compared to Christianity. The noted scholar of comparative religions W. C. Smith, for example, rejected the utility of the term "orthodoxy" by claiming that Muslims "have differed amongst themselves not on matters of theology so much as on questions of practice."[31] Similarly, Talal Asad has argued that in contrast to Christianity, Islam "relates more to how one lives than to what one believes."[32] The perception that theology *qua* theology is marginal to the practical questions Muslims grapple with underlies the conclusion of one recent book about revolutionary Egypt that arguments about Islam "are far less likely to focus on what to believe and far more likely to concern what is to be done."[33]

Questioning the transparency of this scholarly split between belief and practice, this book contributes to an emerging body of "theologically engaged anthropology" in its approach to theology as an ethnographically salient category inextricable from the more familiar disciplinary ones of ritual and ethics.[34] Theology does not merely exist in the abstractions of dogma, nor is it limited to learned commentaries on scriptural texts; it also has a rich social life: it is formed and transformed through believers' situated attempts to think through how they should apprehend and live in the world. Ignoring theology *qua* theology elides not only how it provides Muslims with ongoing resources to address new moral and practical problems about how to live as

Muslims, but also how Muslims seek to counteract, through theology, everyday problems they perceive as engendered by erroneous theological constructs in the first place.

To be sure, theology's embeddedness in social life is the background assumption of an Asadian anthropology of Islam concerned with interrogating the universality of secular liberal concepts through comparison with those of the Islamic tradition. In these accounts, however, the "Islamic tradition" remains theologically unmoored from specific doctrinal suppositions and their elaboration and interrogation by pious Muslims in their own arguments with each other. This has resulted in more of an invocation of internal disagreements than their actual exploration.[35] This tendency to overlook theological differences is evident in a recent debate over the "everyday" turn in the anthropology of Islam. Participants on either side appear to share a key premise: that what constitutes a "pious attachment"—or what represents a "secular liberal" one—is a matter of settled consensus among Muslims, who have only to decide which to aspire to. Muslims' internal diversity is glossed over as a "simple fact" with seemingly little analytical consequence.[36]

The Revolution Within shows how these attachments, and the relation between piety and everyday life, are differently elaborated and contested within the Islamic Revival itself, with important consequences for the production of both competing forms of Islamic media and competing notions of God and godliness. By debating analytically what religious adepts contest normatively, anthropologists neglect religiously grounded arguments about different forms of Islamic attachment in favor of religious-secular or pious-impious binaries, missing that these binaries are not stable but are configured differently through theological debate and its lived practice, through "God-talk" and its interactional embodiment in the everyday. What the debate frames as an anthropological divide turns out to be a theological one.

―――

The two main extant schools of Sunni theology are Ash'arism and Atharism. These schools hold differing ontological and epistemological assumptions that revolve around the nature of God, whether Qur'anic references to His attributes should be understood metaphorically or literally, and around the role of reason in relation to revelation and the changing social circumstances of its human recipients. While theologians of each orientation have debated esoteric questions of some remove from the daily life of the average Muslim—the superiority of angels versus prophets, for example[37]—their disagreements have also revolved around issues of lived importance, including the fundamental question of the relation between practice and belief. For example, Ash'arites have held that faith (*iman*) is above all an internally held conviction that naturally oscillates between doubt and certainty across a lifetime. By contrast, Atharis have held that *iman* grows and lessens in direct relation to the punctilious performance of ritual duties.[38] Such questions provoked schisms in the first centuries of Islam that by the medieval period coalesced into Ash'arism and Atharism as the most significant theological division within Sunni Islam.[39] Far from being relegated to musty medieval texts, the Ash'arism versus Atharism divide continues to preoccupy Muslims around the world as even a cursory Google search for "online '*aqida* [creedal] wars" reveals. This includes within Egypt's Islamic Revival, where it is reflected in the rivalry between the New Preachers and the Salafis.

The New Preachers adhere to the Ash'ari theological mainstream institutionalized by al-Azhar. Although established by Egypt's Shia Fatimid rulers in 970 CE, al-Azhar has been the premier center of Sunni Ash'ari orthodoxy for a thousand years.[40] Like in the past, al-Azhar in the present period recognizes all the four main schools of Sunni jurisprudence (the Hanafi, Maliki, Shafi'i, and Hanbali madhabs) as valid in their differing interpretations of the Qur'an and the Prophetic canon, the hadiths, the two most authoritative sources of Islam.[41] The proper acquisition of knowledge from and about these sources comes not from reading them independently, but from obtaining an *ijaza*, a "license" to disseminate the teaching of specific texts or subjects based on studying them with a qualified teacher in an embodied chain that links back through the centuries to the Prophet and his Companions.[42] Al-Azhar's emphasis on the embodied character of knowledge transmission—summed up in the dictum that "knowledge lies in hearts, not in writing" (*al-'ilm fil-sudur la bil-sutur*)—included the incorporation of the practice of pious companionship and other Sufi disciplines as legitimate modes of spiritual self-purification aimed at moral excellence through cultivating intimacy with the divine.[43]

For its adherents, Ash'arism is the moderate synthesis of two theological extremes: the rationalist (and now largely defunct) Mu'tazila and the literalist Atharis.⁴⁴ Eponymous founder Abu Hasan al-Ash'ari (d. 935) argued that relying exclusively on either reason (*al-'aql*) or revelation (*al-nass*) was dangerous and insufficient, with the properly Islamic approach being one that balanced between constraints of the inalterable texts of the Qur'an and the hadiths and the changing possibilities of their human understanding. As institutionalized at al-Azhar in the modern period, Ash'ari theology emphasizes that grasping the "higher aims" (*maqasid*) of revelation leads to a "realistic jurisprudence" (*fiqh al-waqi'i*). This, in turn, leads to an ethical valorization of interpretive pluralism and an abhorrence for declaring Muslims as heretics or even apostates for their differences. Such emphases are framed as a hallmark of al-Azhar's paradigmatically moderate, *wasati*, ethos.⁴⁵

The New Preachers saw their role as making this moderate ethos, and the Ash'ari theological conceptions underlying it, accessible and relevant to ordinary people through "innovative" and "dazzling" media programs. As we see in chapter 3, the notion of moderation promoted by Iqraa's television producers was radically different from secularist security-focused constructs of "moderate Muslims" as those who are lukewarm at best about following religious strictures, or advocate for religion as a matter of private conscience with no collective stakes. The New Preachers exhort their followers to lead lives marked by more pious engagement with social issues, not less, and they decry the ways in which secular Westernization has made that aspiration more challenging to meet. Far from rendering them moderate in the sense of secularizing, their elaboration of Islam as a religion dynamically responsive to current circumstances and hospitable to difference and pluralism marked them as moderate in the Ash'ari sense promoted by al-Azhar.⁴⁶

In contrast to Ash'arism, Atharism advocates a strict adherence to the "clear," literal meaning of the Qur'an and rejects the use of rational speculation to understand the nature of God. Its adherents stress that the religion revealed to the Prophet Muhammad and practiced by the first three generations of Muslims, *al-salaf al-salih*, was a simple one of submission to divine dictate. Its correct apprehension does not require complex theological elaborations, thus foreclosing the disagreements and divisions that inevitably attend these. As such, this theological approach denies that it is one at all—it is rather the purified creed of the Prophet, Islam in its original understanding, one free from the "outside" influences marking Ash'arism's interpretive scholasticism. A core Athari theme is the centrality of purifying Islam from heresies, from *bid'a*.

Bid'a—literally, "innovation"—is extensively thematized in Islamic theology, where the term refers to practices or beliefs without Prophetic precedence. Most Ash'ari theologians categorized *bid'a* in terms of the axiology of Islamic jurisprudence: obligatory, recommended, permissible, reprehensible, and forbidden. This scale allowed for praiseworthy and even compulsory transformations in Islamic practices.[47] A minority of premodern Islamic scholars like Atharis rejected this scale, arguing that *bid'a* admits of no moral or legal flexibility, being inherently a misguidance.[48] Importantly, Atharism considers Ash'arism's synthesis between reason and revelation to be itself the heretical result of Islamic scholars' engagement with ancient Greek metaphysics. Instead of looking to bridge revelation and reason through the interpretive pluralism underwriting the madhab system, Atharis look to hadith to elucidate the Qur'an, earning them the moniker *ahl al-hadith*, the hadith partisans. Rejecting the authenticity of the Prophetic saying "the diversity of my community is a blessing," Atharis follow Hanbali jurisprudence as the most faithful to the practice and understanding of the Prophet and his Companions and reject the legitimacy of the other madhabs.

Atharism was (and remains) a minority theology but gained renewed vitality through the efforts of the eighteenth-century reformer Muhammad Abd al-Wahhab, the eponymous founder of Salafi Wahhabism, who made the eradication of *bid'a* a central platform of his *da'wa*.[49] In modern-day Egypt, Ash'arism was the unchallenged theological mainstream until the 1970s, when the Salafi grassroots piety movement took off. Through mosque study circles and cassette sermons, Salafi doctrines and interactional norms became more widespread. By the time of my fieldwork Salafi preachers had their own satellite television channels and a significant online presence. The country's leading Salafi media preachers during this time were Muhammad Hassan, Abu Ishaq al-Huwayni, and Muhammad Ya'qub, who all claim to be "students" of the influential Salafi hadith specialist Nasir al-Din al-Albani (d. 1999).[50] While Salafi is an endonym, the preachers and groups who claim it do not always accept the claims of others to it. The Salafi movement—whether in Egypt or elsewhere—is a heterogeneous one with its own set of internal struggles and contestations over who belongs to the "saved sect," *al-firqa al-najiyya,* the single Muslim group that will be saved from the hellfire according to a Prophetic hadith, although all Salafis are theologically Athari.[51] For many Muslims, Salafi pietists are arguably most recognizable by a set of distinctive appearances emulating, as they see it, the Prophet Muhammad and his family, such as a chest-length beard and shaved mustache for men and an opaque face-covering and gloves for women. For Salafis, piety is figured as such mimetic fidelity to the Prophet's and the first Muslim community's practice of Islam, one ostensibly free of cultural and historical contingency and thus universally applicable without much modification. More broadly, in contrast to the New Preachers' emphasis on being realistically religious through approaching the Qur'an as a text whose interpretations can legitimately vary over time, Salafis contend that it is society that must change to stay true to the singular meaning of the Qur'an.[52] In the name of "higher objectives," al-Azhar and its followers have made the prohibited permissible, introducing into Islam ideas and practices that spread heresy and moral laxity.[53]

The ever-present moral peril of *bid'a* was a central theme of Salafi preaching during my fieldwork. Many Salafi preachers open their television programs with the Prophetic saying: "Beware of matters newly begun, for every matter newly begun is innovation [*bid'a*], and every innovation is misguidance, and every misguidance is in Hell." In this view, what is "Islamic" was fixed in the seventh century and to embrace alteration, to incorporate new elements, is to corrupt Islam. This extends from devotional novelties (prayer beads) to social ones (birthday celebrations) to political ones (democracy).[54] On their channels, Salafi preachers warn their viewers against the errors of *ahl al-bid'a*, "the people of innovation," that is, Muslims who claim to be following God's injunctions while in reality pursuing their own desires. In this way, the evaluation of practices or beliefs as *bid'a* is not just a technical legal matter but goes to the heart of the question animating all participants in the piety movement: What is pleasing to God? Accusations of *bid'a* pragmatically work as a moralizing commentary that impugns a Muslim's devotion to divine desire and its embodiment in prophetic praxis. Within Salafi spaces, the New Preachers are frequently scorned as *ahl al-bid'a*. The process of purifying Islam from their heresies necessitates cultivating an attitude of principled rejection toward them and their followers as outside of the "saved sect."[55]

The exclusivist claims of Salafi revivalism to salvific truth and moral rectitude rankled my interlocutors within New Preaching circles. From this perspective, Wahhabization is like Westernization, a form of imperialism although in a theological, not secular, register.[56] Both constitute a destabilizing rupture of Muslim life that unsettles the authority of past precedents and long-standing social customs in the name of a universalism that makes little room for difference. The predominance of Salafi conceptions of piety within the grassroots Islamic Revival makes it harder, not easier, for most Muslims to resist the attractions of secular lifestyles as they conflate the particularism of Salafism's "repellent" norms with Islamic piety writ large.

To be clear, Islamic television preachers rarely spend time in learned polemics over the respective merits of these theological schools. Instead, their programs are platforms aimed at helping their own regular viewers navigate the myriad challenges of living piously in a context where it is difficult to do so.[57] Their exhortations, however, reflect the broader doctrinal assumptions that give each of these theological orientations their distinctive character in relation to each other. To pay attention to these distinctions is to appreciate the ways in which the boundaries of the religious and the secular—and the sensibilities these boundaries authorize, the subjects and publics they sanction and aspire to—are drawn differently within the piety movement.

SECULAR-RELIGIOUS DIFFERENCE AND THE ANTHROPOLOGY OF ISLAM

Such theological differences and their lived stakes have not been meaningfully described in ethnographies of the Egyptian piety movement, nor have they informed anthropological thinking about the religious-secular binary. In his influential book *The Ethical Soundscape*, Charles Hirschkind suggests that participants in Islamic Revivalism, whatever their differences may be, geared their pious self-cultivation through media toward the realization of a "common moral project" defined by its distinction from a "secular" sensorium and public sphere.[58] In a later article published after the revolution, he claims that identifying the preachers whose sermons he writes about as specifically Salafi "has little analytical value" because Egyptian Muslims "appreciate a variety of preaching styles" and may listen to "preachers representing distinct, and even opposing, interpretive trends," from the Salafi preacher Muhammad Hassan to the New Preacher Amr Khaled.[59] There is therefore not much to be gained in exploring distinct preaching media styles in relation to their specific theological schools and associated ethical sensibilities.

Along these lines, some colleagues have suggested to me that these two *daʿwa* orientations simply hold divergent views about which aspects of modern life are compatible with a godly society. There is no deep or incommensurable fissure here, but merely "the narcissism of minor differences," a Freudian phrase capturing how the fiercest struggles take place among groups that in reality differ little. In addition, some might claim that centering theology to make analytical sense of Islam's internal diversity is inconsequential insofar as the "coherence" of a tradition renders variations within it less significant than differences between it and other traditions. While internal differences might be what matters most to a tradition's participants, anthropologists' own tradition of critical comparative inquiry makes them far more interested in seeing the proverbial forest than the trees.[60] Each chapter of this book shows the ways in which this is a mistaken understanding and how adopting it precludes a more complex understanding of how secular and religious distinctions take form in the first instance. Here, I focus briefly on how the theological differences *The Revolution Within* explores over what is secular and what is religious invite a reconsideration of the analytical limitations of Asad's influential concept of "Islam as a discursive tradition."

Aiming to account for the "considerable diversity in the beliefs and practices of Muslims," the idea of a discursive tradition has two main features.[61] The first is that tradition involves change as much as continuity. The key to coherence is apt reconfiguration of past ideas and practices to meet the demands of the present. "The idea that traditions are essentially homogenous has a powerful intellectual appeal, but it is mistaken," as variation is a fundamental aspect of tradition and does not undermine its unity.[62] This ties into the second main feature of the concept of discursive tradition: interpretive diversity. According to Asad, "argument and conflict over the form and significance of practices are therefore a natural part of any Islamic tradition."[63] This view distinguishes between the fixity of revelation and its changing interpretation, suggesting that "the ingenuities of human interpretation are endless" even though "divine texts may be unalterable."[64] The anthropological idea of Islam as discursive tradition thus challenges secular liberal assumptions that religious traditions, particularly the Islamic one, demand "unthinking conformity," that "real tradition" is "unchanging, repetitive, and non-rational."[65] Such suppositions are rooted in Orientalism and its essentialization of Muslim societies as static and monolithic.[66] As I noted in the preface, after 9/11, the importance of this analytical concept for interrogating Western assumptions about itself in relation to Islam became more urgent.[67]

But it is not just Western scholars harboring latent Orientalist tendencies or explicit secular liberal ones who see Islam as essentially fixed and the Qur'an as beyond interpretation. So do some Muslims. As I detailed, Ash'ari theology makes space for innovations in Islamic practices in the interest of maintaining their social relevance and resonance, while within Athari theology the Islamic tradition does not admit of change or reconfiguration but instead calls for punctilious repetition and imitation. In addition, while Ash'arism upholds interpretive pluralism as a divine mercy, Atharism condemns it as a human heresy that displaces God as the ultimate arbiter of His own words.

To understand the ethnographic stakes of such divergent appraisals of the Islamic tradition, we need to refocus our attention from how we as anthropologists should *analytically* make sense of Muslim difference to how Muslims themselves *theologically* make sense of their tradition's internal diversity. These are decidedly different orientations for an anthropology of Islam. Indeed, while the notion of an "invented tradition" might be, from an analytical perspective, "banal" and of "not much significance,"[68] most passionate accusations exchanged between rival Islamic revivalists hinged precisely on the claim that the opposing group was not merely incorrectly interpreting and practicing Islam but actually "inventing a new religion," *bi-yikhtar'u din gadid*.

This lack of attention to tradition as contested theological content is what makes the anthropological concept of Islam as discursive tradition inadequate—it leaves untroubled its own features, as if they were self-evident. But in accepting these features of change and contestations analytically, as anthropologists we are accepting one theological orientation's normative vision of what constitutes tradition to make sense of Islamic tradition writ large. The anthropological concept of Islam as a discursive tradition is thus not purely methodological or analytic, as its defenders insist, but also unwittingly substantive and normative.[69] It is an unacknowledged appeal to a particular theology of Islam to enable a particular kind of secular politics toward Muslims. In this book I approach "tradition" as my interlocutors do: not as analytical concept, but as theologically elaborated content that makes some concepts and forms of life possible and others less so.

To be clear, I am not arguing that our conceptual frameworks as scholars of Islam must be equivalent to those of Muslim interlocutors, that their theological view of Islam necessarily trumps our anthropological one. Our role as anthropologists is to make sense of connections and patterns that are often obscure to those who inhabit them, and analytical concepts are one way to do so. In my fieldwork, however, I quickly ran up against the ethnographic limitations of analytical indifference towards my interlocutors' own theological concepts of Islam. For example, on learning that I teach a course called "The Anthropology of Islam," one of my interlocutors informed me that this was a contradiction in terms. He suggested I rename the course to "Anthropology of Muslims" because, after all, anthropology was the study of humans, not God. It troubled him greatly that in presenting my course as about Islam but in practice teaching about how Muslims understand and live Islam, I might be inadvertently eliding for my students a crucial distinction between divine revelation and its human interpretation and practice.

This distinction had implications for how the "secular" was differently theologically elaborated and internally contested within the social world of Islamic television. My interlocutors at Iqraa defined secularism as the ideology that religion should have no bearing on governance. To be secular was both to subscribe to this ideology but more generally to live one's life in a manner unconcerned with the question of what God has revealed or what the Prophet has prescribed, and to do so deliberately, not just out of carelessness. In other words, secularity, from a pious perspective, is a lived condition of epistemological and ethical indifference to divine sovereignty. On the level of the state, this indifference could take the form of policies, laws, and institutions. This Egyptian revivalist understanding of secularism matches Egyptian secularists' own self-definition: as one such intellectual explains, "I am a thorough secularist, so I absolutely refuse to cite religion when I am dealing with a secular question. I reject the line of reasoning that 'Umar [the second caliph] said this, or such-and-such a verse of the Quran says that.'"[70] During my fieldwork, I did not meet a single revivalist from any theological orientation who advocated for secularism in this sense. The disagreements between the New Preachers and the Salafis hinged not on being for or against secularism, but rather on secularity's practical identification in terms of specific beliefs, sensibilities, and ways of acting in the world. This had implications for media production. As this book shows, Salafi pietists condemn as "secular" *daʿwa* media that resembles Western cultural forms. However, the New Preachers promote this same media as "religious," reserving the label secular for media unconcerned with divinely defined limits, even as those limits remain subject to dispute and varying interpretation.[71]

Put differently, although both the New Preachers and the Salafis rejected the secular, and cared deeply about determining the differences between the religious and the secular, their theologically substantive conceptions of these differences led them to adopt radically distinct Islamic media strategies. Assimilating the New Preachers and their Salafi counterparts as each simply representing a "current" in a shared project of self-cultivation aimed at "excellence at piety"[72] in contradistinction to a secular subjectivity or sensorium thus has descriptive and analytical purchase only if we assume that such currents not only recognize each other as "pious" but also recognize themselves as distinct from "the secular" *in the same way*.

In this book I consider how and why media content and aesthetic forms are evaluated as Islamic—or contested as secular—by those who make and consume them.[73] Certainly, as Jessica Winegar has argued, secular and religious discourses have "become so entangled that finding an origin for them, and/or separating them out and naming them 'secular' or 'religious,' occludes major complexities of social life."[74] Winegar makes this point in relation to the New Preachers, arguing that their ideas about the transformational power of art are indistinguishable from secularist discourses and need to be contextualized within Egypt's changing political economy. This book offers a way to do so by ethnographically tracing the ways in which New Preaching productions were deliberately tailored to appeal to Egypt's middle class, whose particular tastes and expectations were naturalized in a theological register. At the same time, chapter 2 unpacks how their appropriation of secular aesthetics and media forms to reimagine Islamic media was deliberate and posited as a theological imperative. In this way, while their aspiration to revolutionize Islamic media in practice transcended long-standing religious-secular dichotomies, this aspiration was not theologically indifferent to secular-religious distinctions. The revivalist identification of secular and religious worldviews as products of irreconcilable epistemologies differs from the theoretical understanding of the secular and the religious as relational, co-constituted categories.[75] In sum, the difficulty with analytically identifying some Islamic positions as "secular"—whatever the claims of those who advocate them—is that it elides Muslims' own contestations of what is secular and what is religious, obscuring the theological proccesses of their social formation.

The Revolution Within shows how the boundaries we have come to think of as "religious" versus "secular"—of conformity versus creativity, ambiguity versus certainty, exclusivism versus pluralism—are internal to the Islamic Revival, marking off the prescriptions of particular theological orientations from others. To pay attention to the social life of theology is to appreciate the ways in which the boundaries of the religious and the secular are drawn differently within the piety movement. The stakes of that difference increased dramatically with the 2011 uprising.

RELIGIOUSLY REVOLUTIONARY

Egypt's revolution was a hypermediated one.[76] It was so in the sense that it was covered intensively by all the major international news channels, with millions around the world tuning in to learn about the latest development set against the iconic aerial shot of Tahrir Square. It was also so in the sense that social media platforms played a key role in mobilizing people and circulating counternarratives to those of state media.[77] While academics argue about how and to what extent social media like Facebook and Twitter were in fact "digital Tahrir Squares," as one news outlet put it, ordinary Egyptians take for granted their positive role, with new parents even naming their babies "Facebook."[78] By contrast, the one thing most people seem to remember about the role of Islamic media and preachers in relation to the revolution is that they militated against it. Al-Azhar's highest-ranking officials did not endorse the uprising but warned against its potential for disorder.[79] Prominent Salafi preachers argued that mass protests lacked Prophetic precedent and urged their followers to stay home.[80] Even the leaders of the Muslim Brotherhood, the Mubarak regime's most organized opposition, did not have an unambiguously pro-uprising stance in the early days.[81]

If we rewind the revolutionary tape and look more closely, however, we will see that none of these positions went uncontested from within. Many of al-Azhar's students and scholars joined the protests in Tahrir, with the institution's official spokesperson resigning so he could take part.[82] The largest Salafi organization eventually sanctioned the participation of its members in protests.[83] The Muslim Brotherhood's youth wing demonstrated alongside others from the start.[84]

We can also glimpse the New Preachers and their supporters in the revolutionary timeline.[85] Amr Khaled flew back to Cairo the day after January 25 to be in the country, leading two academics to begrudgingly note that, among Islamic figures, "strangely it was the person everyone had thought to be the least inclined to get involved in politics, Amr Khaled, the cool young preacher and religious conscience of the Muslim middle classes, who supported the protest movement the most openly."[86] On January 27, I watched on YouTube a homemade video by Masoud and Hosny jointly urging protesters "to continue demanding your rights." A couple of nights later I watched another YouTube video showing Masoud on January 28, the "Friday of Rage," alongside other protesters in the streets leading to Tahrir Square, not far from where I had to take cover with others in a building stairwell to escape the tear gas and water cannons being deployed by security forces. On February 6, thirteen days after protesters succeeded in taking over Tahrir, I watched Khaled on BBC Arabic reject the claim of Saudi Arabia's chief mufti that the uprising was a "conspiracy against Islam" and insist that the "will of the Egyptian people" must be respected. On February 11, the night Mubarak finally resigned, I watched on the same channel a disheveled Khaled pause his celebration alongside thousands of others in Tahrir Square to share that this was the happiest day of his life.

Over the next year of Egypt's transitional period from military to civilian rule, the New Preachers continued to express an unambiguously pro-revolutionary stance in social media posts, interviews, in-person events, and their own television programs. Asked on February 23 what the revolution was for, Khaled answered, "just one word: freedom."[87] Three months later in a live Iqraa broadcast on May 20, Hosny told his viewers to not lose hope in face of counterrevolutionary machinations and that temporary instability was a small price to pay for a lifetime of freedom. The next year, in a public gathering on January 22 commemorating the first anniversary of the revolution, Masoud called for the security forces attacking protesters to be brought to justice and the ruling generals to step down.

For all their vocal support and active participation, the New Preachers were rarely counted among "the revolutionaries." This even though their stance fits secular activists' own definition of "the revolutionaries" as those who simultaneously opposed both the remnants of the Mubarak regime and organized Islamism.[88] While I hope that readers experientially familiar with the timeline of the revolution will get a different insight into it as I analyze it from the vantage point of my fieldwork with Islamic media producers, I realize that ultimately skepticism about the revolutionary relevance of the New Preachers is less about the stances they actually took and more about a priori "radical" horizons. Most revolutionary-minded Egyptians I knew doubted that religious revivalist idioms could facilitate their progressive demands for sweeping transformation; if anything, their invocation, and the authority it carried, was one of the very things that the revolution aimed to displace. And for many others outside the social world of Islamic television, piety, no matter how creatively mass mediated, was but a relic of the tired culture wars Egyptians hoped to transcend. If the New Preachers and their followers represented a revolution at all, it was ultimately a "conservative" one, and thus not truly, really, revolutionary.[89]

Such assessments are informed by a deeply entrenched sense of revolution as inherently oriented toward the new, the unprecedented, the alternative, and of religion as fundamentally oriented toward the old, the established, the authoritative. Even the most careful ethnographers of the revolution tend to delimit its boundary as, if not secular, then at the very least not religious. Samuli Schielke argues, for example, that the "path of religious commitment" is distinct from the "path of revolutionary critique," in that the latter is defined by a "celebration of debate and difference" that is presumably absent from the former.[90] As I discuss in chapters 3 and 5, however, my New Preaching interlocutors upheld difference and disagreement, and pluralism and coexistence, as intrinsic both to Islamic *and* revolutionary commitment. The revolution, they argued, offered hope for a return to a more ethical piety that was marginalized by both Salafi dogmatism and state authoritarianism. Islamic piety in the New Egypt would be an inclusive one tolerating disagreements, whether over religion or politics. This required recovering—not overcoming—Islamic theological precedents. Indeed, the idea that building a better future necessitates rejecting the past is a particularly modern Western one, superseding an older meaning of revolution as *return*, not overturn.[91] Instead of assuming a universal definition of revolution, an anthropology of revolution focuses on "how revolutions are defined by the people who are involved in them."[92]

The Revolution Within shows how pious practitioners brought the theological and the revolutionary into intimate relationship through their situationally shifting evaluations of phenomena even as they claimed to merely find this relationship in scripture. It shows how piety as ethical striving, just like the stakes of new forms of Islamic media, became freighted with revolutionary possibility.

THE ETHICS OF THE REVOLUTION

A common New Preaching lament is that, even after decades of Islamic Revivalism, there are many religious Egyptians (people who prayed, fasted and regularly preformed Islam's ritual obligations) with "no ethics," and ethical Egyptians (people who were fair, kind, and acted with integrity) with "no religion." As I show in chapter 3, the New Preachers' solution to this asymmetry was the mediation of a more other-oriented piety through a doctrinal elaboration of Islamic moderation, *wasatiyya*. Instead of the Salafi concept of piety as the quality of one's submission to God enacted through ritual fastidiousness, a balanced piety, one in which people both "had religion" and "had ethics," equally emphasized the quality of one's interactions with others. This other-oriented piety went beyond individual behavior in the everyday to include striving for social change.

The idea that piety included both ritual self-cultivation and social activism undergirded Iqraa's expansive notion of Islamic media. Islamic media didn't have to be about religion in the "narrow" sense of creed and ritual but could be about anything. Six months after its launch, the channel's inaugural director was already arguing for reducing *da'wa* programs in favor of more entertainment, social content, and participatory formats. This ambition was realized with Amr Khaled's debut program for the channel, *Sunnaʿ al-Hayah* (*Lifemakers*). It was everything Iqraa's producers wanted: innovative in its interactive format, eliciting viewer participation on- and off-screen, and innovative in its content, addressing important social issues from employment to education to drug addiction, while incorporating entertainment by "Islamic pop stars." The program was very successful. *Lifemakers* brought in more than 80 percent of the channel's advertising revenue during its 2004–2005 broadcast year and put Iqraa on the Arab world's media map. The preacher himself was put in charge of Cairo-based program development. Although Khaled's tenure at Iqraa was brief, over the next twenty years a succession of newer New Preachers joined the channel as it showed it could indeed deliver on its promise to create a compelling alternative to both secular and Salafi media.

In hindsight, my interlocutors would look back on Islamic media like *Lifemakers* as having planted the seeds of the 2011 revolution and anticipated the spirit of Tahrir Square. "The Salafis before the revolution would say we have to change ourselves and that we have to be patient with the ruler. That wasn't any good for changing society," one New Preaching fan and *Lifemakers* member, Samia, explained to me. "Then there were the secularists and the leftists, they saw themselves as Mr. Perfect and only saw that society is what needed to be changed. Moez Masoud, Mustafa Hosny, and Amr Khaled struck a balance between these two extremes." After the revolution, as Salafi preachers surprised everyone by becoming political—"not in a good way," she added—and as the secularists continued to paint all Islamic revivalists with the broad brush of extremism, Samia felt that the socially engaged, other-oriented piety of the New Preachers offered much-needed hope. The revolution within the self they advocated would instigate a revolution within the piety movement against dominant Salafi norms that would in turn connect a new generation of Islamic revivalists to the promise of the 2011 revolution, to the "ethics of the revolution" (*akhlaq al-thawra*).

But where pious viewers saw social solidarity, academic critics saw neoliberalism. While anthropologists have long critiqued exclusively political economic accounts of Egypt's Islamic Revival for their implication that "religious ideas and commitments have no independent cognitive force, no power and attraction aside from the socioeconomic correlates that predispose particular groups to adopt them,"[93] this caution falls aside when it comes to neoliberalism, a totalizing term that often becomes, as Julia Elyachar argues in relation to Egypt, "a shorthand for indicating all that is wrong with the present."[94] In many accounts, the New Preachers became a shorthand for "neoliberal Islam."[95] Their politics of ethical self-transformation comes at the expense of radical structural change, critics charged, thus entrenching the neoliberal status quo. Given neoliberalism's stealth "economization of everything"[96] the impulse to see it in everything makes intuitive sense—indeed, I made similar arguments myself in relation to the New Preachers as I was conducting my fieldwork.[97] But as I concluded my research amid the unraveling of the heady promise of Tahrir, I began to appreciate the importance of my interlocutors' aspiration to "make a difference" even in a world not of their own choosing, let alone their making.

To be sure, the sense that the revolutionary road was best traveled on Islamic television through social activism was in part a survival strategy in an unpredictably repressive context. When an American journalist asked Khaled about his "political agenda" in 2007, at the height of *Lifemakers'* popularity, the preacher gave a candid yet cautious response: "I don't know if you can understand the situations in our countries or not. I can't imagine if I started my program *Lifemakers* and talked to the youth about democracy. After the second episode . . . ." He leaves the sentence unfinished, and then continues: "The aim of the program, without saying democracy, is to give [youth] the chance to do something. And I started the philosophy of projects to not clash with the governments in the Middle East. This is the philosophy . . . . They need the chance without a clash because we cannot afford the clash." "I never talk about democracy," Khaled concluded. "But look what I am doing." What Khaled was doing was maneuvering within and around existing constraints and power structures in the hopes of eventually being free of them. In this view, revolutionary politics wasn't about immediate denunciation but long-term transformation.[98] Still, even for those progressives who might agree with the strategic value of remaining pragmatic, the revivalist focus on self-transformation dodges hard questions of entrenched power structures in its individual scale. The entwinement of self-cultivation and collective change is hardly unique to religious revivalism, however; it is widespread across a range of socioeconomic and political contexts.[99] And in 2011, Egypt's New Preachers were not alone in seeing dispositional transformation as inherent to the revolutionary project, as the almost immediate nostalgia for the "spirit of Tahrir"—*Its solidarity! Its parity! Its tolerance!*—among progressive activists illustrates.

Significantly, the New Preachers' stress on the ethical dimensions of the revolution allowed for the participation of far more ordinary people in creating the New Egypt than a focus on party politics or doctrinaire revolutionary purity. It is important to remember that even at the height of the eighteen-day uprising, only a minority of Egyptians went to Tahrir. This doesn't mean that few Egyptians supported regime change and were in favor of continuing authoritarianism. Such a clear-cut, either-or depiction doesn't do justice to the shifting positions of Egyptians from all walks of life toward the most extraordinary event of their lives. My mental shorthand for these Egyptians, which included many of my own family and friends, is the murky middle: murky because they didn't hew to the sharp political positions, refusing to fit neatly into predetermined categories, whether made up by analysts or by activists, and in the middle because they continually seesawed in their affective reactions to the revolution. They were at once defiant and afraid, hopeful and anxious, craving freedom but also desiring safety. They wanted change but were wary of uncertainty. These Egyptians often had no well-defined ideologies to fall back on as they struggled to make sense of unfolding events. Instead, they relied on their commonsense understandings for navigation, understandings that were often nested, tacitly or explicitly, within Islamic theological reason, thanks in no small part to the pervasive Islamization of public life and spaces since the 1970s, including by and within state institutions.[100]

Long after the encampment disbanded in Tahrir, the question of how do "we participate in the revolution" (*nishariq fi al-thawra*) remained an urgent one for my murky middle interlocutors within New Preaching circles. Their definition of a "more ethical" piety as one oriented around social impact as much as self-cultivation was grounded in the taken-for-granted assumption that Islam was a "comprehensive religion" (*din shamil*). While the construct of Islam's distinctive comprehensiveness is paradigmatically associated with the Muslim Brotherhood, it has become so pervasive within modern Islamic thought that it exceeds any exclusive association with state-oriented Islamism.[101] Nevertheless, assuming that, by default, Islamic television producers who saw their mission as promoting piety would be sympathetic to the Muslim Brotherhood's electoral ambitions, my progressive friends were surprised to learn that many of my interlocutors at Iqraa shared their skepticism about the Islamist group. Like secular critics, many Islamic media producers perceived the Brotherhood's rhetoric and behavior after Mubarak was toppled to be arrogant and incompetent, nepotistic and exclusionary. The fact that the Brotherhood claimed to be acting in the name of Islam while behaving badly jeopardized their own mission of disrupting secular stereotypes about how pious people think and act.[102] At the same time, the New Preachers had to contend with persistent rumors that they were secret Muslim Brothers, or at least indistinguishable from them.[103] After Khaled was banned from preaching by the Mubarak regime in 2002 and left the country in self-imposed exile, a prominent Egyptian liberal intellectual argued the preacher's "appearance is calculated to deceive" and that "he is just like the other Islamic theocrats [she specified the Muslim Brotherhood], but he says it with a smiling face."[104] Almost a decade later in September 2010, at the cusp of the uprising and a month after I formally started fieldwork, an interviewer asked Hosny what he would say to those who say that the New Preachers' discourse "resembles that of the Muslim Brotherhood." Hosny replied that the group doesn't have a monopoly on "making religion relevant to life" and that such an approach is part of the "collective inheritance [of Muslims] from the prophets."[105] This focus on lived "relevance" is more than anything the New Preaching calling card. Indeed, as I show in chapter 4, many of the people with whom I spent time were drawn to the New Preachers because they were interested in a piety that went beyond self-cultivation to promote social transformation. But they persistently refused to conflate this transformation with the ideological claims of a single organization. This double refusal made them distinct from conventional Islamists like the Muslim Brothers, with their focus on electoral wins, and from conventional pietists like the Salafis, with their focus on ritual perfection. It also marked them off from al-Azhar, whose theology they shared but whose scholars tended to eschew grassroots social activism.

In general, producers working at Iqraa saw themselves not just as *muttadayinin* (religious) but also as *islamiyin*. Since the 1970s, this term has been used by a wide variety of Islamically oriented movements and groups to describe themselves.[106] By the time of my fieldwork, however, the utility of *islamiyin* as a catchall term was waning due to the mainstreaming of Islamic ways of reasoning. Still, my interlocutors used this term in self-identification when engaging with people outside of what they called *al-sahwa al-islamiyya*, literally, "the Islamic Awakening," commonly called the "Islamic Revival" in academic writing.[107] After 2011, as Egyptians became more and more polarized politically, the New Preachers tried to remain above the partisan fray by eschewing all religious labels altogether. After all, their followers in the murky middle ran the gamut of electoral preferences and were impossible to categorize as champions of one ideological camp or another. In an August 31, 2012, post on his official Facebook page, a couple of months after the highly divisive presidential election, Hosny wrote:

> Some ask me: are you Sufi? Others say: You are Salafi, but trying to hide it; others swear that I am from the Brotherhood, while others describe me as from the New Preachers trend. To all these people I would like to say I am simply a Sunni Muslim. . . . I respect all the trends, the scholars and the preachers of the community.

While many comments praised Hosny for his ecumenism, others saw it as betrayal—if you are friends with everyone, you are loyal to no one. Preaching to the murky middle made you morally murky.

Still, the New Preachers' ethical, as opposed to ideological, approach to the intersection of religion and politics resonated for their dedicated viewers who were generally supportive of the 2011 uprising as a call for more social justice, freedom, and pluralism but who didn't have doctrinaire notions about how to achieve these aims. Again, they were neither conventional secularists who believed in a principled separation of religious norms from state governance nor were they conventional Islamists who believed that Islam requires the establishment of political parties to govern in its name. By insisting on a distinction between Islamic piety and partisan politics without segregating ethics from the political, Iqraa offered such viewers an expansive, yet relevant, Islamic media that put ordinary people—and their capacity to think, feel, and do otherwise—at the center of a New Egypt.

FIELDWORK AT HOME, DURING A REVOLUTION

I began the fieldwork informing this book the summer of 2008. Between 2010 and 2013, I did two and a half years of continuous fieldwork in Egypt, with regular return visits between 2014 and 2018. My longest research stay in Egypt centered on Iqraa, where I spent time with those among my interlocutors most committed to the vision of piety and polity promoted by the New Preachers. These were the producers who came up with and researched programs, who created content for Hosny's website and social media accounts, who ran the preacher's live gatherings. These were the viewers who tried not to miss a single gathering, who watched episodes not once but twice or thrice, who volunteered for Hosny's initiatives, and who, if they had a connection to someone at the channel, showed up to say a shy hello to the preacher and maybe have a selfie taken on set to post on social media later. This intense engagement with Islamic television preaching was not the norm even within revivalist circles. And like any workplace, no matter how lofty its mission, Iqraa brought together individuals with a variety of aspirations and concerns, not all having to do with promoting piety. While some had come from mainstream channels to Iqraa because they believed working for an Islamic channel was a duty with heavenly rewards, others were at the Islamic channel in the hope of getting experience so that they could move on to one of the better resourced entertainment channels. And many readers might be surprised to learn that not all of Iqraa's employees were Muslim: there were Coptic Egyptians as well as Jewish and Christian non-Egyptians working there during my fieldwork, mostly in the translation department. But focusing my fieldwork on those who made the New Preachers' conception of piety central to their work and life clarified for me both the foundational assumptions of this conception and its stakes for those who hold it.

In case it's not already clear, let me state explicitly that this book is not an ethnography of Salafi television preaching and I do not aim to explicate Salafi self-understandings apart from how they relate to the New Preachers. Rather, I am interested in what my interlocutors called *al-salafiyyin*, "the Salafis," to the extent that this category was their main foil. What did the New Preachers and their followers find so wanting about Salafi piety, whether ritually, socially, ethically, or politically? How did their sometimes polemical and caricatured evaluations of Salafism play out in the way they imagined and created their own alternative forms of Islamic media? While it is important not to uncritically reproduce such narratives of the opposing side at the analytical level, as Brian Larkin cautions,[108] ethnographically centering them does allow for a better understanding of how specific media—and sensibilities, dispositions, and practices—become "Islamic" for some Muslim adepts but not for others and what this reveals about the shifting theological boundaries of the religious and the secular within the social world of Islamic television. Such a focus necessitates restraining, to some degree, my own anthropological impulse to unmask such internal accounts as empirically inaccurate and instead to take them as ethnographic vantage points yielding insight into the anxieties and desires animating religious revivalists.

I won't pretend though that as an Egyptian and a Muslim I am personally neutral to these rival projects. So, let me be transparent: if I were ever forced to choose between New Preaching media or Salafi ones, I would choose the former. In fact, I made a choice akin to this when I pulled my child out of a weekend Islamic school in the US that, following Salafi strictures, forbade birthday celebrations and smiling at non-Muslims as "un-Islamic." Still, the reality is that I only watch preaching programs of *any kind* so I can ethnographically write about them. Neither the New Preachers nor Salafi ones speak to my own sensibilities, and the fact that my ethics and politics are generally indifferent to religious referents marks me as external to the Islamic Revival in an important sense. But just as this book is not an ethnography of Salafism, it is not an auto-ethnography. I try to keep my own beliefs and politics out of it as much as possible.

This wasn't easy. Egypt was not just my fieldsite—it is also my country. I felt fortunate to be there during the historic uprising of 2011, although it wasn't always clear to me how—or whether—to disentangle my own investments in the promise of the revolution from my anthropological commitment to understanding how my fieldwork interlocutors, fellow Egyptians, lived out their own political and ethical certitudes. Even before the revolution, this uncertainty surfaced at various times, and not just from my side. For while I was an outsider to the social world I was researching in some ways, I was an insider in others. My age, gender, class, education, level of religious knowledge, and leisure preferences were, I would find out, typical of how

Islamic media producers typically imagine their target audience. This facilitated my fieldwork greatly. On both the production and the viewing sides, most of my interlocutors were women I could easily have met at a friend's birthday party or a family wedding. I met them instead at brainstorming meetings, studio recordings, location scouting, and in-person events. My presence didn't attract much attention because what I was doing—mingling, asking questions, taking notes, helping—was like what half a dozen other people were also doing at any given time. Producers rely on volunteer, fan-based labor for several aspects of their work, such as running Hosny's website and online forums as well as organizing his seminars. At these, a dozen volunteers could be found buzzing around, wearing headscarves or T-shirts with the name of Hosny's most recent Ramadan series printed as they set up screens and seats. In addition, media production students would sometimes attend shoots to gain practical experience. These occasional visitors at various times mistook me for a fellow trainee, a journalist, and a fan. Due to the impression created by the limited currency of the Arabic term for anthropology—*'ilm al-insan*, literally, the science of the human—I was also mistaken to be a self-development coach.

At the same time, to regular employees it was clear my intention in working at Iqraa was not to promote piety through media, but to research and write about their own efforts to do that. Iqraa's Saudi director Sallam boasted that I was following in a "long line" of researchers who knew the historic significance of the Islamic channel. This doesn't mean that my interlocutors did not have reservations about me. They were aware that the average person in the United States, where I was completing my doctorate, insofar as Americans had an opinion on Islamic television, would most likely have a negative one. During the early days of my fieldwork, Randa, Iqraa's director of translation, at times worried about my "agenda" in researching the channel—she later "confessed" (the word choices are hers) that her fears were allayed only when she watched a documentary film I had made on observant Muslim American fashion designers. She judged the film an apt translation of Islamic norms of female modesty for a Western audience and came to trust that I harbored no adversarial or Islamophobic intentions. But she also judged me a religious novice who might inaccurately convey the "message of Islam" to a global readership.

Such concerns didn't wholly dissolve with time or familiarity. During one evening shoot toward the end of my fieldwork, Emad, the channel's Cairo manager, commented that "only God knows what you are writing in that," pointing to one of the small notebooks I always had with me. Since this was after many months of cordial conversations and interactions, my feelings were hurt. The next time I went to the channel, I made sure to give him photocopies of all my published articles and essays on Islamic television preaching, neatly arranged by year in a folder, including an article I had written in Arabic on Hosny for a prominent local newspaper.[109] "So you know what I am writing," I told him. Looking a little embarrassed, he told me he had only been joking.

"I actually like to meet people who are against us," he said, revealing a reservation about my intentions that he had been more polite (or savvy) than Randa to openly voice. "It's good for them to see how we actually are." He recounted that a few years ago a hostile journalist had only to spend a couple of hours at Iqraa to completely change his opinion for the better. "Anyone who gets to know us ends up loving us," he said with a chuckle. Still, he took the folder from me. Hosny's public image was carefully curated by Emad, who felt responsible for protecting it, not just as the preacher's direct boss but as his older, more experienced mentor. (Indeed, the one rule set for my access to the preacher's team was that no photographs I took at Iqraa could be published, hence their absence from these pages.)

Being human, and with anxious reservations of my own, I also secretly scrutinized my interlocutors for their unvoiced ambitions or failures, in my estimation, to live up to their own declared ideals. When one famous preacher kept me waiting for over an hour past our appointment while I could hear him in his office laughing on a personal call, I thought, *What a hypocrite. What happened to the Islamic virtue of keeping promises?* When a preacher gave me what he said was his main phone number, but it led to a paid hotline, I thought, *What a charlatan. He cares more about money than God.* Conversely, when Hosny was late to our first meeting and called me not once but twice to apologize that he was on his way, I thought, *Now, there goes a decent person who practices what he preaches.*

Most times, however, my concerns were less about any gaps between my interlocutors' declared ideals and their actual practices, and more about how my own sensibilities might conflict with theirs and derail fieldwork. I sent a panicked email to my advisor before my first visit to the channel asking if she thought I should wear a headscarf, for instance. As a Muslim woman, I worried I would be judged from the get-go as religiously lax. But I wasn't planning on wearing a headscarf all the time while living in Cairo and it felt wrong (hypocritical?) to put it on just when I was at my fieldsite. My advisor told me that I should do whatever made me, not others, most comfortable in this situation. As I came to know my interlocutors better, I realized that my expectations of their expectations reflected my own preconceived notions of what pietists are like. I am glad I learned this lesson on the earlier side because from then on I would try to refrain from assuming the answer to the question I was investigating: What does "piety" look like and entail for these specific Muslims at this specific time?

With the revolution, the stakes of off-site encounters with my fieldwork interlocutors going awry increased. I remember, for instance, talking on the phone with Randa, two nights after the first mass protests. I told her about my plan, which I was keeping from my parents, of joining marchers to Tahrir Square the following morning on January 28. Her response was that, from an "Islamic perspective," I should not be going to these potentially dangerous demonstrations as this was the singular duty of men. She also knew that, like her, I was a single mom. What would happen to your kid if something were to happen to you? she worried. Randa's views were by no means representative of the other women I worked with at Iqraa, some of whom I would later meet by coincidence in the Square. At the same time, I felt that overtly disagreeing with her might jeopardize my fieldwork relationship. In the days that followed, I went so far as to limit her access to my Facebook page, where I was posting updates from the protest site. As an anthropologist, I knew her reasoning was important to understand and situate within a broader narrative about the intersections of religion, gender, and politics. As another Egyptian Muslim woman, however, I found her position incompatible with my own sense of what was appropriate. Nevertheless, like most anthropologists aspiring to "take seriously" my interlocutors, I bracketed my own political and ethical judgments as much as possible. I didn't challenge Randa outright even as I tried to create space for myself to be part of the revolution that was separate from my fieldwork *about* the revolution's impact on Islamic television. For a time I even kept two separate journals, an observer in one, a witness in the other.

But precisely because I am not merely an anthropologist but an Egyptian living through a once-in-a-lifetime event, my interlocutors at Iqraa at times construed my hesitation to put on the table my own convictions not as a well-intentioned effort to avoid "imposing" my own political views on them but rather as indifference to our shared political fate. For example, a heated discussion arose once in Iqraa's break room about the difference between a "theocratic state," an "Islamic state," and a "secular state." This was a discussion dominating newspaper columns and talk shows nationwide just before the 2012 election. During the discussion, I remained silent. I had published an essay on the subject,[110] but I worried that interjecting with my own views would not only curtail a rich moment of ethnographic observation but also alienate those in the room who might feel differently. Eventually my silence became too loud and one person asked pointedly: "Why aren't you giving us your opinion? Do you not care?"

This producer's worried comment highlights how the intersections of friendly fieldwork relations and off-field commitments could make frank conversations around issues of common concern more difficult, not less. Anthropologists tend to dwell on such dilemmas as intrinsic to the ethnographic encounter, as I have just done, but of course the problem of ethical and political difference—and the possibility of friendship therein—transcends the encounter between researcher and research subject. It structures the everyday and not-so-everyday encounters within social worlds that exist and continue long after we have closed our notebooks and published our books. Again, while I was not an Islamic revivalist, however much time I spent with (and liked many of) those who were, I was an Egyptian living with other Egyptians in the most challenging of times. How to live together with difference was an enduring concern for my interlocutors, both on-screen and off, as this book shows.

To reiterate this book's main claims: All Islamic revivalists see themselves as passionately concerned with leading a life pleasing to God and with calling others to do the same. All unanimously reject secularism as political ideology. All see piety as requiring, above all, embodied discipline. But while Islamic revivalists profess their commitment to piety as the most significant aspiration of their lives as Muslims—and, indeed, in their view of any properly Islamic life—they do not share a singular moral orientation. Rather, there are deep differences among Islamic revivalists over the very definition of piety itself. This book shows how these differences are theologically informed and traces their social consequence for both religious media production and revolutionary politics.

The Revolution Within is divided into two parts that take readers from the emergence of the New Preachers in the decade leading up to the Tahrir Square uprising to the tumultuous two years of freedom and inventiveness—but also precarity and divisiveness—following the removal of the Mubarak regime. Each chapter centers on the social life of a theologically elaborated concept my interlocutors in Islamic television deemed crucial to the revolution they aspired to ignite within the piety movement and within the nation more broadly. The first part examines how Iqraa producers navigated the political economy of satellite television and marshaled new aesthetic and technical strategies to reconfigure what counts as "Islamic media"—and what piety substantively and interactionally entails—for a new generation of youthful participants within the Islamic Revival. This is the first sense of "the revolution within" that the book title references. The second part takes up how the "revolution within" Islamic media connected to the 2011 revolution for "bread, freedom, and social justice," as the famous protest chant went. It charts how my interlocutors in Islamic television aimed to cultivate within viewers as a pious imperative a revolutionary ethos oriented toward creating a "New Egypt" of social solidarity and coexistence that could overcome the country's "ethical crisis." In the epilogue, I examine how this crisis came to a head in 2013 as the security state reasserted itself, spelling for many the definitive demise of the promise of Tahrir. Far from being a simple secularist versus Islamist struggle for power, the events of that summer exposed deep rifts among ordinary people over the ethical, social, and theological shape of the New Egypt. For many of their fans, the New Preachers' silence during this period was a principled refusal of polarization; for some, it was a strategic tactic of long-term survival in a volatile context; for still others, it was a cowardly retreat from the engaged ethics these preachers claimed as their own.

In all cases, the everyday social life of theology continues and with that the always latent possibility of a New Egypt caught between memory and hope.

PART I

One
CALIBRATION

"CUT!" THE DIRECTOR ZAKY, A MIDDLE-AGED MAN WITH A TRIM beard, glances at his watch. "We are going to film that again."

A young actor costumed in torn jeans and a stained shirt picks up the shovel he had just thrown down and assumes a look of grim determination. He pushes his hair back and starts digging into the specially created mud pit in front of him. I am standing to the side taking notes, excited to be at one of my first fieldwork experiences. Still, I stifle a yawn and glance at my own watch.

It's past midnight but it will be a few hours yet before the shoot of the bromo—Arabic industry-speak for trailer or short promotional spot—for Resala's Ramadan season wraps up. It is the summer of 2008 and Iqraa has just marked its tenth anniversary, but the recently launched Resala is garnering more publicity as the even "more entertaining" Islamic satellite channel. The shoot is not far from Iqraa's studios in Haram. The central boulevards of the middle-class district near the Pyramids are flanked by high-rise buildings and crowded with cars, but the part we are in is a sprawl of sand.

Zaky, apparently satisfied with the scene, yells an instruction over his shoulder. A few seconds later a beam of light appears over the mud pit, emanating from a xenon-arc lamp mounted to a crane. A cameraman on a dolly-track keeps the actor in frame as he throws down the shovel, falls to his knees, and reaches out with open arms to the light, as if to embrace it. His chest visibly expands as he basks in its artificial glow, his expression transforming from grim to grateful. The production manager on the set later explained the concept: After the shot with the actor on his knees, the camera will pan upwards and zoom in on the light beam. In postproduction the beam will be transformed into a Ramadan crescent moon. In the crescent will be the names of the programs offered by the channel, and the phrase "enrich your fast" will flash on the screen. The idea the bromo aimed to convey is that watching Islamic television during the holy month is a form of spiritual development akin to the bodily one of fasting.

During a lull in the filming, the production manager introduces the director Zaky as a seasoned practitioner of "Islamic media" who can assist with my research, then hurries away to attend to a crisis involving cable wires.

"Actually," Zaky says to me once the production manager is out of earshot, "I prefer to see myself as someone who creates *fann hadif* (ethical entertainment). But this type of production usually ends up on Islamic channels because they are the only ones interested in that kind of thing."

I ask Zaky if Resala's profile as an Islamic channel owned by Saudi prince and media mogul Alwaleed Bin Talal translated into an above-average budget for the kind of ethical entertainment he aspired to create. Zaky shakes his head—Resala's budget was "very bad," he tells me. He continues with a sneer: "Clearly the Prince is spending the real money on his *other* channels." Alwaleed had founded one of the region's biggest media entertainment conglomerates, Rotana.

Would you prefer to be at these other channels? I ask. The director again shakes his head and gestures around him: "Everyone on this crew is happy for an opportunity to practice our profession without incurring more sins. That's rare in our industry. Working for an Islamic channel means less money, but we get more *agr* (rewards) with God."

Still, he goes on, as a freelance director he does not want his professional name associated with the low quality of the Islamic channels, and so he prefers to take jobs only from the more "professional" channels like Resala or Iqraa. For even with Resala's "very bad" budget, he still has enough to direct a bromo with trained actors, special effects, and set design.

Islamic media producers like Zaky and the ones I came to know during my fieldwork at Iqraa two years later were passionate about revolutionizing what counts as "Islamic media." From its founding in 1998, Iqraa set out to be a safe satellite harbor for an imagined "ordinary" Muslim viewer who wanted to enjoy television while not transgressing God's limits. To meet that need, Iqraa aspired to produce a wide range of content, from reality shows to dramatic serials to children's programs. This expansive ambit was key to the channel's self-definition as an Islamic—not merely religious—one. Sallam, Iqraa's Saudi managing director during my research, explained to me the difference this distinction makes as plainly as he could: "We don't call Iqraa a religious channel but an Islamic channel, and there is an important difference between the two. Religious channels present purely religious programs—Qur'an, prophetic sayings, fatwas, and so on—while Islamic channels present all types of programs as long as they are Islamically correct."

For Sallam, as for the Iqraa producers he managed, limiting Islamic media to what they termed "direct *daʿwa*"—*God-says, the-Prophet-said*—was a mark of the theological limitations of both Salafism and secularism. In insisting that entertainment and virtue were separate, that they belonged to distinct domains, Salafists and secularists alike limited piety to ritual worship while perpetuating stereotypes of Islamic media as devoid of pleasure. Iqraa producers, by contrast, argued that what made media Islamic was not necessarily that it was *about* Islam. They sought to recover piety's worldly dimension so as to chart a middle path between Salafi asceticism and secular dissipation. In turn, they revolutionized what counts as piety for a generation of middle-class Egyptian youth coming of age with satellite television.

This chapter explores the ways in which the political economy of privately funded satellite television both created opportunities and posed challenges for this revolution. It shows how directors like Zaky aspired to create Islamic media that was doubly unconventional: their Islamic media would go beyond the "conventional" religious programs of Salafi television in adopting mainstream media genres, from the music video to the cinematic film, while also disrupting the conventional amoralism of secular entertainment by carefully hewing to divine parameters. Through such distinctions, Islamic producers recuperated the media industry as a powerful terrain for cultivating piety. But these ethical aspirations were thwarted by a lack of sufficient resources. Despite being owned by billionaire businessmen, Islamic channels like Iqraa and Resala had to scrape by on a shoestring budget compared to the entertainment satellite channels launched by the same businessmen and against which Islamic producers wanted to compete. This called for savvy maneuvering within the Arab satellite industry's flows of capital, whether creative, financial, or political.

Put simply, Iqraa producers sought to discipline and shape media capitalism beyond economic motives to new moral ends: the exchange of advertising revenue for audience attention did not have to be about maximizing profit—it could be about maximizing piety. But this required more money than they usually had access to. The theological potential of television collided with the material reality of limited budgets. As they navigated this tension in their everyday production practices, my interlocutors made evaluative distinctions about their industry's political economy that hinged on the ways in which capital was *calibrated* within it.

What I gloss as calibration here is what in Arabic my interlocutors often termed *dabt*. *Dabt* connotes a competence and exactitude of practice that is beyond moral reproach because all is as it should be Islamically. An individual who has achieved *dabt* within themselves is one who has regulated their desires and actions to conform to Islamic standards. An institution characterized by *dabt* is one judiciously arranged—in this case, its media form and content are calibrated to enact godliness. My interlocutors desired to recalibrate the economic arrangements of what they called "conventional" (*'adi*) media so that they corresponded with theological doctrine, while ensuring that the results meet the aesthetic expectations of "professional" or "high-quality" productions. In this way, calibration—in analogy with its common meaning of adjusting an instrument so that its standardized units of measurement correspond to reality—involved reference to immutable divine standards, to God, as the really Real within the constantly changing techniques and genres of media production.

Calibration was not without risk. Iqraa producers had to contend with widespread moral panics about the entanglements of preaching and petrodollars. In *Folk Devils and Moral Panics,* Stanley Cohen coined the term "moral panic" to capture the ways in which disproportionate media attention to particular subcultures, or "folk devils," can provoke intense public opprobrium. Moral panics, he argued, are about social identities that are not only in and of themselves damaging, but also symptomatic of deeper, often abstract, ills.[1] Islamic television channels, and their high-profile preachers, were without question the folk devil of the new millennium in Egypt, speaking to a new unsettling of authoritative practices of pious endeavor by changing media economies and their enmeshment in broader circuits of capital, commodity, and celebrity. Iqraa and its "New Preachers" were turning religion "into a commodity to be bought and sold," many Egyptians felt. As another observer put it, *daʿwa* should not be for dollars.[2]

Such anxieties speak to deeply held notions of the religious and the economic as domains of incommensurable value. But to understand how, why, and with what effect my interlocutors embraced capital calibration as crucial to revolutionizing Islamic media, we need to go beyond the familiar lament that the commercial corrupts the sacred, which prevails even in the academic literature. Rather than treat, as most do, Iqraa and its New Preachers as simply reducible to the neoliberalization of the region's political economies, I approach Islamic television's political economy as a terrain of struggle for both material resources and ethical efficacy.

My interlocutors at Iqraa were not indifferent to the perils dollars potentially posed to *daʿwa*. As they saw it, the conventional political economy of Arab satellite television is troublingly centered on capital accumulation and profit maximization without concern for the divine accountability awaiting in the Hereafter. However, this required not the condemnation of capital but rather its judicious calibration, its *dabt*. Money, far from posing a moral threat to Islamic piety, was key to its sustainability on a mass scale. *Daʿwa* should definitely not be for dollars, but *dollars should be for daʿwa*. At the same time, the calibration of capital requires vigilance precisely because it is inherently dynamic and unstable. For producers, it was not always easy to know when a program, for instance, had hit the sweet spot of moral suasion within diversion, and even once calibrated they knew it would likely need to be recalibrated as time wore on and audience expectations evolved. This inevitably called for more dollars.

More broadly, by making the ends and means of media and its political economy of interest to divine self-disclosure, my interlocutors redefined piety as not just about disciplined habits of godly self-fashioning but about the godly calibration of resources, whether material or creative, within their chosen profession. In contrast to the widespread moral panic about the entanglements of preaching and petrodollars, from the perspective of Iqraa's producers it doesn't really matter *why* a rich Saudi businessman wants to start an Islamic channel—what matters is that this channel, once founded, could leverage capital resources to create alternative media institutions, imaginaries, and practices marked "Islamic" that would upend secular stereotypes while offering a compelling alternative to Salafi piety. To disrupt both Salafi and secular media conventions, the conventional binaries of power versus virtue, wealth versus rectitude, fame versus humility would have to be radically reconfigured, if not cast aside. Understanding this reveals the ways in which the struggles to define the "Islamic" are inextricable from struggle over capital's calibration.

THE SHAYKH

The emergence of privately owned television channels like Iqraa in the 1990s was a direct outcome of evolving media technologies and changing economies in the Arab world. Most Arab states retain exclusive access to terrestrial television, as Egypt does through the Egyptian Radio and Television Union (ERTU), established a decade after television's introduction in 1960. Satellite communication technologies emerged in the 1980s with the launch of Arabsat by the Arab League, led by Saudi Arabia. Egypt followed suit in 1998 by establishing its own satellite operator, Nilesat, through a joint public-private holding, with a majority share held by ERTU. However, it wasn't until the early 2000s that new legislation allowed for the establishment of private channels.[3] By 2010, a decade after private television legalization, millions of satellite dishes dotted urban rooftops, most of them offering free access after a one-time receiver purchase. Nilesat claimed that 95 percent of households in the Middle East and North Africa region tuned in to the 700 channels on its signal offering serialized dramas, political and social talk shows, foreign films, music videos, and reality-based entertainment.

In 1998, Iqraa made history as the first self-identified Islamic channel to launch on satellite and it remained the only one until 2006. Its public prominence owed much to the fame of its founder, Saleh Kamel (1940–2020), a highly influential mover and shaker within pan-Arab satellite television. His Arab Radio and Television (ART) channels were among the first to venture into the groundbreaking territory of providing round-the-clock entertainment, contributing significantly to the widespread adoption of satellite television in the Arab world.[4] At its debut, Iqraa operated under the umbrella of ART, itself a subsidiary of Kamel's Arab Media Corporation (AMC), one of the first Saudi media production companies. AMC was part of the Dallah al-Baraka conglomerate, which Kamel had founded in 1969.

Iqraa's employees referred to Kamel simply as "The Shaykh," the conventional honorific for either wizened religious scholars or Gulf royalty. Kamel was neither. Born in the Saudi mountain town of Taif, Kamel began his working life as a civil servant before starting what would become one of the biggest business enterprises in the region. Identifying as a "global Saudi company," Dallah al-Baraka, according to its website, has multibillion-dollar investments in over forty countries in sectors as diversified as real estate, finance and banking, transportation, and healthcare and employs 60,000 people across the Middle East and Southeast Asia.

Out of Dallah's thousands of employees, Iqraa's share amounted to 200 people, over half of whom were in Egypt, illustrating the importance of this country for the channel. Nevertheless, the only official mention I saw of Dallah during my fieldwork at the channel's Cairo branch was a large glass-encased poster in the lobby titled "The Employee Pledge of Dallah al-Baraka Group." In faded black type were twenty-three moral practices and dispositions that individuals working for the company should commit to. These ranged from "respecting work hours and being punctual" to "not being envious of co-workers" to "upholding the rulings of Shari'a in all dealings" to "being committed to creativity and innovation."

No one at Iqraa ever pointed the pledge out to me on our daily trips up and down the stairs. One afternoon as we passed the poster, I asked the group I was with about it; they stared at me blankly when I described it as "the employee pledge." One person accompanied me back down the stairs to take a closer look and chuckled while reading the lengthy directives. When I asked what the pledge meant to him, he shrugged his shoulders and said it was a good reminder to "be mindful of God in our work." Nevertheless, almost every single producer I met or interviewed, across gender and generation, told me that they felt working for an Islamic channel like Iqraa was a source of *baraka*, of blessings. The elevation of one's professional labor into an ethical intervention with salvific consequences was for many of my interlocutors a mark of Iqraa's distinctive calibration as a television channel at once professional and godly.

If Dallah existed for most of Iqraa's employees as a distantly moralizing authority to which one could remain largely indifferent on a day-to-day basis, The Shaykh had a more vivid existence. This wasn't because he made regular visits to the channel—he didn't come to the studios during my almost three years there, and none of the long-term employees I asked recalled him visiting. Instead, The Shaykh was a pixelated presence, hosting his own program on Iqraa from its Jeddah studios. Kamel was a roly-poly man with a trim white mustache. He usually wore black-rimmed eyeglasses and a Gulf-style ankle-length *thobe*. He exuded the air of a pedantic professor, apt for the role he played on his show as an expert exponent of Shari'a-compliant capitalism and ethical entrepreneurialism. Indeed, his corporation Dallah frames its operations in pious terms, declaring its intention to "develop" Muslim countries as a theological obligation.

In the mid-1990s Kamel was honored for his contributions to the development of Islamic finance and banking by a Saudi research institute. In his award acceptance speech, he noted that "gone are the days when people used to deny the existence of higher moral values governing economic activities." Nevertheless, many big businessmen still put profit over piety, Kamel lamented, imperiling not only their own salvation, but also the fate of the entire Muslim community, or *ummah*. Hewing to the Qur'an and the Prophetic example in economic life would enable Muslim countries around the world, from Africa to Asia, to "catch up with the glorious and prosperous past of this Ummah in both material and moral terms." He urged his audience to commit their institutions, corporations, and factories to upholding Islamic strictures in order to counteract the impoverishing dominance of Western capitalism.[5]

In incorporating the economic within the domain of religious reason, Kamel participates in a long history of Islamic theologians, intellectuals, and activists who underscored the necessity of capital for resistance against foreign domination. During the colonial period, they urged wealthy Muslims to "the pursuit of profit for Islam's sake." European colonialists held up these entwinements of the commercial and the sacred as evidence of an instrumental insincerity of Islam—and more specifically of Muhammad, a prophet who was first a merchant.[6] This disdain reflects broader Euro-American presumptions of a categorical separation between the affairs of "economy" and the affairs of "religion," between material fact and moral value, that many contemporary Muslims interrogate.[7] For example, in his ethnography of Malaysia's "Islamic finance" sector, Daromir Rudnyckyj shows how its expert proponents desired to achieve through Qur'anically derived principles an alternative form of capitalism that was more ethical and humane than the dominant debt and interest-based system.[8] The replacement of the Western system with a new Islamic one would lead to equity and prosperity for all. To be sure, commentators have long noted capitalism's ability for self-reinvention through crisis. Writing on the history of various Islamic intellectual and institutional challenges to capitalism, Charles Tripp notes the latter's "colonizing power has partly been due to its capacity to disembed practices from pre-existing moral and social constraints, isolating them and recombining them in ways more conducive to acceptance of global capitalist enterprise."[9]

The difficulty of creating real alternatives to the regnant capitalist order was not lost on Muslim advocates. Rudnyckyj's Malaysian interlocutors regularly debated the challenges of making "pious finance" tenable. And even as he was accepting the award for his contributions to developing Islamic banks, Kamel shared that "in all frankness, . . . if I were to start all over again, I would not choose the bank as a framework for the application of Islamic teachings in the field of economy and investment." The banks that call themselves "Islamic" still harbor "the flaws of the Western capitalist system," he argued.[10] As the next sections explore, the difficulty of correctly calibrating the Islamic was a feature of Kamel's alternative media ventures as well.

THE IDEA OF ISLAMIC MEDIA

Kamel's speech was published in 1998, the year Iqraa went live. At his death two decades later, the Shaykh was eulogized more as "the father of Islamic finance" and "a pioneer of Islamic banking" than as the founder of the world's first Islamic television channel. However, just as Kamel convened an annual gathering to develop and debate the idea of an economy that was specifically Islamic, each year he hosted a conference on how to make media Islamic. Called Iqraa, like the channel that came out of it, the conference brought together businessmen, media professionals, and scholars interested in Islamic media. One of them was Abdulkader Tash, who became Iqraa's debut director.

Tash was part of the first generation of Saudi media scholars trained in the US. He chaired the mass communication department at Muhammad ibn Saud University in Riyadh and served as the editor of several *da'wa*-oriented magazines and newspapers. A public intellectual, Tash's writing addressed questions of cultural change, media dependency, and asymmetries in knowledge production between Muslim countries and the West. In tackling these themes, Tash drew inspiration from a variety of sources: from influential Azhari-trained Egyptian theologians like Yusuf al-Qaradawi and Muhammad al-Ghazali; from the Islamization of knowledge movement that took off in the 1970s and '80s; and from the Third Worldist call for a "new information order" to counter a Euro-American cultural imperialism masquerading as globalization. Above all, however, Tash looked to the robust body of scholarship that had emerged around the idea of Islamic media and its dual aspiration to show how Islam, from the moment of its revelation, concerned itself with media and how the best of modern media insights and practices were anticipated by the Qur'an.

This was first suggested by Abd al-Latif Hamza, one of the Arab world's pioneering media scholars, in a 1965 textbook he published for the new mass communication courses at Cairo University.[11] The book, which claimed to be the first media studies book in Arabic, concluded with a short section on media in Islamic history. Here, Hamza planted the seeds of a whole new field of inquiry as he made the novel claim that Islam was above all a mediatic religion, *din i'lami*. By this he meant that Islam was distinctive in its theological concern with communication, with the medium of the Message. Hamza's definition of media was capacious. It was not limited to the modern inventions of the printing press, radio, television, or the cinema. It also included the communicative formations of not just sermon and poetry but even the bazaar and pilgrimage. Hamza reprised this claim of Islam as an exceptionally mediatic religion in more depth with his 1971 book *Media at the Dawn of Islam*. Most significantly, he reframed the Qur'an as "God's newspaper." Like the modern newspaper and other media with their assumed power to bring about social change, the Qur'an at its seventh-century revelation led to "revolutionary change" and "created a new society." Hamza saw his book as a challenge to "the conspiracy of silence" around Islam and media on the part of Western scholarship and a reclamation of "the dignity of the Arab scholar who shouldn't wait for European scholars to inaugurate this uncharted area of intellectual inquiry."[12] Hamza was not the first to turn to media this way, however. Looking to media for its transformative potential resonated with a longer history of Arab intellectual engagement with "communicability, or consciousness of the force of mass communication" that predated its disciplinary thematization.[13] Still, the professor confessed that he was nervous about his attempt to think through the Qur'an from a "media angle," for it required both deep knowledge of Islam and of modern mass communication.

In the book's afterword, Ibrahim Imam—one-time dean of Cairo University's media faculty and founder of al-Azhar's media studies department—praised his senior colleague Hamza for making media studies "relevant to the Islamic world." At the same time, Imam expected that the average reader would be skeptical about what "media has to do with Islam and what Islam has do with media." After all, he conceded, Islam predated modern mass media. Would not the concepts of this new field of study be "a hostile takeover" of Islam?[14] Indeed, the effort to make media a field of theological inquiry and theology a terrain of media theory was met with skepticism not only from Imam's secular leftist colleagues but also his religious ones. One of the first students of the media studies department Imam established at al-Azhar told me that they were often derided by others within the venerable institution for "studying something religiously useless."

Imam rebutted these sentiments, insisting that not only is Islam an intrinsically mediatizing religion but mass mediation also is a religious imperative, a *fard dini*, "made incumbent on Muslims by God and no less important than other ritual obligations such as fasting and alms-giving.... This [media] responsibility is what distinguishes the Muslim community from all others."[15] It follows that divine revelation is an apt epistemic terrain for mass communication studies, and across dozens of books and articles Imam elaborated on his mentor Hamza's claim that Islam was a mediatic religion, a *din i'lami*.

By the 1990s, just two decades after Haṃza's pioneering book, Islamic media had become an established subfield of mass communication, and mass communication a subfield of Islamic studies, in Egypt and in Saudi Arabia. Through their scholarship, teaching, and institution-building, media scholars like Imam and Tash seemed to have achieved a calibration of the Qur'anic logic (*al-mantiq al-Qur'ani*) of media with the media logic (*al-mantiq al-i'lami*) of the Qur'an. Still, much remained unsettled in practical terms. Could impious Muslims or even non-Muslims create media that was nevertheless Islamic? Or did Islamic media have to be created by "committed" Muslims beyond moral reproach? If so, what hands-on competencies in media work should such Muslims have mastered? The questions that provoked the most debate, however, centered on content: Is Islamic media synonymous with religious or *da'wa* media, with pious exhortation? Or can any media content—sports, entertainment, news programs—be Islamic, and, if so, what makes it so? The establishment of Iqraa as the world's first self-declared Islamic television did little to settle the question.

When Kamel established Iqraa in 1998, he recruited both Tash and Imam. The former was based at the channel's headquarters in Jeddah while the latter put together a Cairo-based team to figure out what Iqraa's Islamic media would be. As I have traced elsewhere, The Shaykh's determination to set up a dedicated Islamic satellite channel must have seemed like an answer to a prayer.[16] Kamel embodied an ideal of calibration of financial and moral capital. He was a serious media player who had also cultivated a pious reputation. Just as his company Dallah al-Baraka and his Islamic banks were self-consciously Islamic alternatives to not only business-as-usual in global finance but also unrealistic total withdrawal from this, so too would Iqraa be an Islamic alternative to the uncritical embrace of globalizing Western media as well to its fanatical rejection. Kamel's capital investment in the world's first Islamic television channel allowed for the creation of media content that, like his finance and banking ventures, acknowledged divine dominion. But this didn't mean that the channel would be limited to the "direct *da'wa*" of religious preaching, to being about Islam. Indeed, Iqraa wanted to compete with mainstream channels by offering viewers all kinds of media content: drama, sports, children's shows, even music. Reflecting this aspiration, the channel's first slogan, which popped up intermittently on television screens under its green calligraphic logo, was "the pleasure of ethical media," *mut'at al-i'lam al-hadif*. As the world's first

Islamic television channel, Iqraa would achieve an exemplary calibration of enjoyment and edification. The media it produced could be Islamic without a single Qur'anic verse quoted, Prophetic saying narrated, or ritual practice exhorted.

The programming reality, however, didn't match this expansive idea of Islamic media. Tash lamented the preponderance of "talking-head" religious programs just six months after Iqraa's launch, arguing to reduce such programming in favor of more entertainment and social content as well as more participatory formats. Three years later, after he had left Iqraa and was involved in discussions to establish other Islamic satellite channels, the media scholar was still frustrated at the sense that such channels should be limited to religious sermonizing. Again, he had to stress that Islamic media is much more expansive: "There is a fundamental difference between the concept of *da'wa* media and Islamic media." While the latter strives to conform to "Islamic conceptions of the universe, life and human beings," it is not, unlike the former, necessarily *about* those conceptions.[17] Again, Islamic media, just like liberal or leftist media, could be about anything. To this aspiration, however, The Shaykh's media empire was both palliative and poison, posing challenges to the calibrated efforts of Iqraa's producers to revolutionize conventional expectations of "Islamic media."

MORAL PANICS ABOUT ISLAMIC MEDIA

Challenges to the revolution within Islamic media also came from without, from critics who saw all religious media as equally troubling. Religious channels were always comparatively minor players in the transnational Arab satellite sector, even when they attracted such outsized attention. In 2010, when I started my research, there were only 18 religious channels broadcasting on Nilesat, Egypt's main satellite operator, out of over 500 channels, constituting a relatively small fraction of broadcast time. Islamic channels were not even that popular with viewers: Industry-generated audience assessments are hard to come by in the region, but a reputable 2009 survey puts viewership preference of religious channels at 10 percent in Egypt, far behind movies at 20 percent. In Saudi Arabia, the preferences for movies over religious programs was even more pronounced at 22 percent versus 7 percent.[18] Despite their relative dearth and comparative unpopularity, religious channels attracted disproportionate critical attention because they fit into broader concerns about Egypt's changing political economy and the implications of these changes for long-held understandings of the role media should play in a country's collective fate.

In 1962, a decade after toppling Egypt's monarchy to replace it with a "revolutionary socialist" state, Nasser created the Ministry of National Guidance (later to become the media ministry), effectively putting all media, whether newspapers, radio, or television, under state control. Nasser framed mass media as powerful instruments of collective consciousness. The revolutionary potential of media was predicated on its structural autonomy as a state-owned enterprise, free of "exploitative" commercial investment and the whims of advertising revenue. The "public ownership" of the "means of public guidance" is what gave media producers the freedom to create the "revolutionary" content that citizens should be consuming, irrespective of actual audience preferences. While mass media under a colonially complicit monarchy had become a mere business, *tijara*, in the new revolutionary order it would have a lofty vocation, *risala*.

The state control of media under Nasser marked the end of the lively and contentious press that flourished pre-1952. There was more room for alternative media narratives under Sadat and Mubarak, but state media remained overwhelmingly security-focused. Indeed, Safwat al-Sharif, Mubarak's longest-serving (and much maligned) information minister from 1982 to 2004, came from a military intelligence background. Under his leadership, the considerable resources of the ERTU were mobilized to meet goals deemed in the "national interest" including, starting in the 1990s, combating "religious extremism" as violent attacks carried out by Islamist militants took place around the country. Even television producers critical of the state embraced this goal. As Lila Abu-Lughod shows, during this period secular left-leaning television producers were committed to a national media that addressed the citizen rather than the consumer.[19] This commitment underwrote both their critique of the state for reneging on the developmentalist dream and their collaboration with it to raise awareness about the threat "Islamism" posed to the nation.

These "dramas of nationhood," as Abu-Lughod calls them, played out not just within media content, but within media structures. Egypt's media landscape again dramatically shifted with the introduction of the internet in 1993 and the legalization of privately funded—that is, non-state-owned—mass media for the first time since before the 1952 revolution. This included on satellite television. The growth of a private satellite sector was made possible by the Mubarak regime's 1990s privatization push as part of the International Monetary Fund–led structural adjustment programs that began in the 1970s with the Sadat presidency and increased in the 1990s and early 2000s under Mubarak. Dubbed *khaskhasa* in Arabic, privatization provided unprecedented openings for both local and foreign investors in previously state-monopolized sectors, from steel to shipping to strawberries. Privatization, along with the deregulation of corporations and the withdrawal of state-funded social services and subsidies, also constitutes the core of neoliberal economic policies. As Middle East scholars have shown, these policies have largely left the poor behind and entrenched structural inequities in the region.[20] Even earlier, in the 1960s, the Arab revolutionary rhetoric of uplifting "the peasants and the workers" through state-led economic redistribution was belied by the routine reality of a corrupt and politicized allocation of public resources to regime loyalists who then became richer under neoliberalism.[21] And even as Egypt's economy grew in real terms in the first decade of 2000, much of that wealth remained concentrated among a coterie of regime allies and insiders. The increasingly conspicuous corruption of "crony capitalism" was one of the main drivers of the protests that led to the downfall of the Mubarak regime.[22]

Satellite television's political economy more or less followed the trajectory of crony capitalism under *khaskhasa*, with the first private channel, *Dream*, founded by a prominent businessman with close ties to Mubarak's inner circle. Many began to worry that satellite channels would become mere mouthpieces for narrow corporate interests.[23] Editorial after editorial likened satellite channels to a tsunami engulfing hapless citizens with a surfeit of content, leading to familial dysfunction, moral crisis, national disunity, political paralysis, class warfare, and even depression and psychosis. Intellectuals who came of age during the revolutionary fervor of the early 1960s waxed nostalgic about a simpler time when citizens contentedly tuned in to a handful of carefully curated channels dedicated to the collective good. The emergence of self-described Islamic channels only provoked more anxiety about the socially corrosive effects of satellite media. Even among the local intellectuals who lauded the privatization of previously state-dominated domains of cultural production, including media, for enabling "cultural players to carve out new sites of resistance to state domination," there was no support for non-state Islamic channels like Iqraa.[24] Instead of being harbingers of freedom and inclusion, Iqraa and other Islamic channels perpetuated troubling societal trends toward religiously justified exclusion and intolerance, many worried. One prominent pundit suggested that Iqraa's true name was *Ikrah*, or "Hate" in the imperative tense.[25] These critics made no effort to distinguish one Islamic channel from another, painting the entire sector in broad strokes as propagating "extremism" and "commodifying religion."

This contrasted with Islamic channels' own internal distinctions. In an early interview about Iqraa, Shaykh Saleh Kamel framed the Islamic channel as a media alternative to both secular Westernization and Salafi rigidity. It was designed, he shared, to appeal to "someone like me, not completely to the left or the right—and there are millions [of Muslims and Arabs] like me. (I) wanted to present a more tolerant, middle of the road message to the Arab and other peoples of the world."[26] Just as Kamel had attempted to forge through his corporate and banking ventures an Islamic alternative to secular economies, his new television channel would rework the emerging satellite industry to broadcast content calibrated to both rebuff "sinfulness" and "fanaticism," thus saving the average Muslim Arab viewer from falling into either extreme.

Nevertheless, across the ideological spectrum critics charged that Kamel had not correctly calibrated his own media empire. His ART channels were at the time the most popular entertainment ones on satellite. While in Egypt these subscriber-based satellite channels had to compete with free state terrestrial channels offering similar content, for Gulf audiences ART marked a new exposure to cultural productions that would not have been allowed on their own government-owned channels, such as films, dramas, and music videos featuring women dancing, singing, and acting.[27] Indeed, Kamel's carefully cultivated public image of probity contrasted with the mediated glitz of his celebrity wife, the Egyptian cinema star and singer Safa' Abu al-Su'ud, whom he met when his company AMC produced some of her films. Safa' had her own show on ART. For an hour each week, she dazzled viewers with her coiffed locks, stylish evening dresses, and witty repartee with Arab celebrities she hosted on air. Despite Iqraa's Jeddah branch location in the same high-rise building as the channel broadcasting her show, strictly speaking, her show would not have been allowed on Iqraa as the Islamic channel had an on-screen hijab policy for program hosts.

Policies like these are taken by Iqraa's critics, whether liberal or conservative, as evidence for how the self-declared "middle-of-the-road" channel was but a Trojan horse for their opponents. For secularists, the channel was synonymous with a stifling conservatism and the hegemony of troubling religious sensibilities in Egypt and across the Arab region. One feminist writer stormed out of an Iqraa televised dialogue between liberals and Islamists in which she had been invited to participate, in protest of the hijab policy.[28] Meanwhile, Salafi preachers decried the channel for even showing women on screen at all, clear evidence that Iqraa was a medium of mass misguidance, not pious moderation.

For critics on the left, the seeming internal contradictions of Kamel's media empire highlighted a more fundamental structural problem: that religion had become a commodity subject to market forces of supply and demand. Whatever Kamel's declared ethical intentions, private Islamic channels like Iqraa showed that the inexorable neoliberal logics governing Egypt had extended into the realm of the sacred and transcendent. This made Iqraa no different from the mainstream satellite channels it presented itself as an Islamic alternative to. It, too, aimed above all to turn the lucrative attention of the Arab world into advertising dollars, commodifying religion in the guise of promoting piety.

It didn't help that the emergence of Islamic satellite channels and their media preachers tracked with the growing visibility of an explicitly Islamic consumer culture. By the late 1990s, it was not uncommon to see the adjective "Islamic" appended to goods and services from swimsuits and elevators to wedding entertainers and maid agencies. Cultural and intellectual elites blamed these changing public tastes on structural privatization and its ostensible "cheapening of moral sentiment" as even the Qur'an became a mere "commodity."[29] The idea of full-time "professional" preachers on privately owned television channels was thus bound to raise eyebrows, given the moral skepticism about the legitimacy of making a living just through *da'wa*. Even Egypt's first president had weighed in on this issue: "The Prophet used to work like everybody else," Nasser complained. "Islam was never a profession."[30]

Such moral panics also surface in the academic scholarship on Islamic television. "The motives behind the foundation of the very first influential religious channel, Iqra', in 1998 were almost exclusively commercial," writes one media scholar. Kamel is but a "proxy for the Saudi ruling elite" and his Islamic channel mere cover for his own financial interests, argues another.[31] Like their local versions, academic moral panics revolve around fears that the pernicious commodifying logics underwriting capitalist formations are expanding to encompass all aspects of social life, even the transcendent. Accordingly, scholars home in on the political economy of the Islamic satellite sector, as if that were the key to unmasking the hidden commercialized and politicized motives of its media producers.

These criticisms speak to deeper concerns over the reconstitution of "religion" under neoliberalism. Anthropologists working at the intersection of "markets and moralities" have urged an attention to how these are not incommensurable domains of value but constitute each other. Whether it is the development of a "structural adjustment Islam" in Mali, the sense that a "poor Muslim cannot be a good Muslim" in Sri Lanka, or the "Islamizing of economic practices and an economizing of Islamic pious practice" in Jordan, recent scholarship has tracked how new ways of thinking about and practicing religion emerge in tandem with changes in political economic structures.[32] Still, most of the academic writing on neoliberalism focuses on its colonizing extension of market logics, transforming at some fundamental level the fabric of society. As Naomi Haynes has pointed out, these transformations are inevitably cast as destructive, with the prosperity gospel of the Pentecostalist churches she studied in Zambia, for example, overwhelmingly framed as "a socially corrosive force, a handmaiden of neoliberalism."[33] A similar argument is often made in relation to the New Preachers, who are consistently cast as promoting a "pious neoliberalism" through a "neoliberal *da'wa*."[34]

However, the neoliberal tenet that individuals and institutions should be shaped above all by market principles of profit and loss was precisely what my interlocutors saw themselves as countering by centering divine dictate in their production strategies. This does not mean they ignored market principles entirely but rather that they aspired to reshape them for moral ends. Concerns about the entanglements of commercial transactions with the transmission of religious belief and practice stretch beyond contemporary capitalist formations into the premodern period, with theologians debating the permissibility of buying and selling Qur'anic manuscripts, for instance, or of charging money to teach its recitation.[35] Like these earlier Muslims, my interlocutors made granular and contextual distinctions over what counts as the commodification of religion, over which economic practices commodify and which do not.

For example, when I mentioned my frustration with the simplistic tenor of much of the pecuniary-based critiques of Islamic television in a conversation with one of the New Preachers a year into my research, his response caught me by surprise: "But it is true. Some people really are in it just for the money. A preacher will sign with one channel and give them his word, but then he gets a better offer from another channel and moves on to that one." Warming up to the subject, he had gone on:

> I make zero money from my programs. Zero. I cover my production costs through my own business and then I donate the programs to channels. For free. Now I have no problem with other preachers making a lot of money, as long as they are transparent about what they do with it. Who knows, maybe they are donating all of their profits to charity, but they should tell us if that is the case.

This preacher came from a wealthy background and was able to marshal income from a family business to underwrite the cost of his television programs, which were renowned (and envied) in the Islamic media world for their spare-no-expense aesthetic. He prided himself on only making programs when he felt "inspired," rather than adhering to the usual Ramadan seasonal schedule. He was initially reluctant to talk to me because he was displeased that I had referred to him in writing as an "Islamic televangelist" and was worried that I would continue to do so. This label was not of my own coinage and was used self-referentially by other New Preachers, I had pointed out. He countered that this is because such preachers do not understand the highly negative connotations of this American-centric label and its association with financial scandal and corruption. "Televangelists are, by definition, in it for the money," he opined. He could see no moral reason in asking viewers, most of them without much means, to donate their hard-earned money to fund megachurches, private jets, and lavish lifestyles. Unlike Christian televangelists in the US and elsewhere, Islamic television preachers do not solicit funds directly from their viewers or congregants. Instead, they rely on the institutional funding of the channels employing them, which, like other channels, rely primarily on advertising revenue for their operating budget. Which is why maximizing audience attention remained important even for channels that did not aspire to maximize profit but instead sought a new vision of piety subversive of both Salafism and secularism.

Again, this required calibrating capital, not condemning it. As Ahmed Abu Haiba, a prolific promoter of new kinds of Islamic media and Amr Khaled's debut producer, put it in a press interview at the launch of Resala, "If I lose money, that means I'm not appealing, that means I don't have my viewership, that means I'm not promoting my ideas."[36] For him and other producers, the commercial success of their programs—defined by increasing viewership rates across ever more diverse demographics and by the increased attractiveness of their programs to advertisers and corporate sponsors—was an indicator that their moral message was spreading, that they had successfully calibrated.[37] Indeed, in the end, many of Iqraa's own producers found their channel ethically wanting not because it entangled pious concerns with material ones but because it did not attune them as skillfully as it should, resulting in a comparative absence of money within Islamic television, as we see next.

MEDIA FUNDING AS CHARITABLE GIVING

For an outlet so often accused of peddling religion for profit, Iqraa's premises were decidedly unglamorous, a fact not lost on its employees, who complained about having to wipe down their keyboards with bleach to ward off cockroaches or rarely being able to find suitable parking. The channel was located on a dusty side street in Haram, a neighborhood reviled by Cairenes as a concrete eyesore even as tourists flocked to the area's Pyramids and Sphinx. I usually parked alongside the poultry seller across from the channel's entrance. Chickens, pigeons, and ducks clucked, cooed, and quacked away in their cages. The poultry store was next to the street's only snack vendor and Iqraa employees would press the tips of their headscarves against their noses to block out the stench when we went to buy soft drinks. Being bareheaded, I was always relieved when we returned to the olfactory neutrality of central air-conditioning. The channel's offices had an underfunded, public sector feel. Three clean-shaven men supervised by an older mustachioed one presided over the front desk in rumpled beige uniforms in the style of 1980s bureaucrats, penning visitor ID numbers in a thick ledger. Beyond the front foyer was an open-air courtyard flanked by two squat buildings, the one to the right housing the studio sets and broadcast rooms, and the one to the left the offices. The studios not in use by Iqraa were rented out to other television channels, providing a key source of revenue for the channel. The studio sets were colorful and up to date, changing with each program season, always smelling of upholstery shampoo and fresh paint. By contrast, Iqraa's administrative offices were small squares crammed with wooden desks. The fluorescent white of the overhead bulbs threw an unflattering glare on the tired gray of the walls. Nowhere to be found here were the marble shine and recessed lighting of the open-plan spaces of Egypt's private media companies. As a physical space, Iqraa in Cairo conformed to neither my nor its employees' aesthetic expectations of a channel belonging to Kamel, a man whose fortune numbered in the billions of dollars.

By the time of my fieldwork, Dallah had divested from most of the ART channels, including Iqraa, but Kamel remained financially responsible for the Islamic channel through a dedicated charitable endowment, a *waqf*. Waqfs are durable instruments of voluntary religious giving, or *sadaqa*. Like the mandatory almsgiving of *zakat*, the *sadaqa* contributes not only to the worldly welfare of the recipient but also to the otherworldly salvation of the giver. The institutionalization of charitable endowments through the waqf enables the giver to continue accruing divine recompense for their pious giving even after they die. Typically, wealthy Muslims in the Arab world endow institutions like schools, hospitals, and orphanages that cater expressly to the community's poor, whose welfare is enjoined in various authoritative religious texts. That there would be one dedicated to a television channel—and a glitzy one aimed at well-off middle-class viewers at that—was unusual. It was theologically predicated on the argument that media is a pillar of Islam and extending that to the *funding* of media as also a divine obligation, a legitimate way of "giving to God."[38] Islamic media theorists argued that the human founders and funders of television channels were but proxies for media's true owner, God. The premise that God ultimately "owned" Islamic media channels circumscribed their use to ends sanctioned by Him, irrespective of market demands or trends. This ownership philosophy is one of the ways in which Islamic media political economies were ethically and theologically distinguishable from secularist ones, whether capitalist or communist.

But Iqraa, like any other satellite channel, could not remain entirely removed from regnant political economic arrangements, including within the structure of the waqf. Iqraa's waqf replenishes itself through money made through real estate investments and the profit of a select number of Kamel's commercial projects. This follows broader patterns reconfiguring the waqf's institutional ordering across the modern Muslim world in ways different from its premodern iterations. As Nada Moumtaz shows, while the increase in waqfs over the past thirty years reflects Islamic revivalist attention to charitable giving as a pious obligation, it is also inextricable from the modern state's property regimes. Waqfs have changed from "God's property" to "an explicit legal personality, whereby it 'owned' assets, and the economic activity that allowed it to finance its purposes became external to the act of charity."[39]

But even if the financial reality couldn't stay true to the programmatic ideals of Islamic media as divinely owned, the waqf was crucial to Iqraa's continuing existence as the world's oldest Islamic satellite channel by acting as a capital buffer against capitalism. Forty percent of Iqraa's operating costs are covered by renting out its studios to other channels. Another 10 percent comes from advertising and content sales to other channels, both of which varied from year to year. The significant shortfall was covered by the waqf. This financial structure put Iqraa above the vagaries of advertising revenue, viewership trends, or increasing competition. It also enabled Iqraa to spend more money on broadcast and program production than most other Islamic channels. The channel paid $2.5 million annually to appear on twelve satellite platforms. Most other Islamic channels had to make do with just Arabsat, which set them back only $200,000 a year at the start of my fieldwork in 2010.

But the waqf didn't only insulate the channel from the quarterly revenue vagaries—it also was a safe harbor against capricious winds of political fortunes. And so the channel continued to broadcast even when Kamel, along with his one-time media partner and fellow Islamic television investor Alwaleed and other prominent Saudi business and political elites, were detained in 2017 by the new Saudi ruler Mohammad bin Salman. Even with Kamel accused of corruption and sequestered along with fellow billionaires in a five-star hotel suite turned prison, even with the future of his for-profit businesses so precarious, Iqraa's preaching programs continued to air and its employees continued to get their paychecks. When I spoke to a producer at Iqraa in Cairo by phone a few months into the detention, he was distressed at The Shaykh's political predicament, but not worried about his own livelihood as an employee of The Shaykh. And the channel continued even after Kamel died in 2020 just shy of his eightieth birthday.

Equally significantly, the waqf marked the moral seriousness of The Shaykh and thus the moral seriousness of Iqraa and its producers. While, as we will see, Islamic television insiders are at times as skeptical as their external critics about the motivations of the key players in their industry, everyone I spoke with, including those whose own Islamic media ventures were harmed by Iqraa's competition, felt that The Shaykh was sincere in his dedication to Islamic publicity, that he put piety over profit or politics. The waqf was an institutionalization of that individual commitment to God. The waqf structure worked so well that Iqraa's producers were frustrated that not *enough* wealthy Muslims saw financing media as a legitimate way of "giving to God," as an Islamically mandated charitable practice.

"They think, why should I spend a few hundred thousand dollars to finance a religious program when I can build a mosque, buy a dialysis unit for a needy hospital, or build an orphanage," a freelance director who frequently worked for Iqraa told me. "They think that is a more important way to spend their money, but what they don't realize is how much of the corruption (*al-fasad*) in our society is due to the media and how important it is to create alternatives." This director, like most of his colleagues, ascribed much power to his métier. In the wrong hands, media degrades minds and distorts hearts, leading impressionable audiences astray. In the right ones, media uplifts and reforms, changing the fates of individuals and nations alike. "They"—those who had accumulated enough capital to give it away—needed to theologically understand that harnessing the transformational capacity of media was an ethical obligation, a divine imperative.

The sense that creating alternatives through capital calibration was a theological duty informed the channel's first backers. In an essay titled "Do We Need an Islamic Satellite Channel?" published four years before Iqraa's founding, Tash argued that establishing an Islamic channel in this "satellite age" was important because Muslims are increasingly confused by the struggles among different groups in their countries. On the one hand, there are the secularists who promote Westernization and eschew Islam as a distinctive theological framework. On the other hand, there are those claiming to act in the name of Islam while being purveyors of religious extremism. An Islamic satellite channel would "protect" ordinary Muslims against both trends by "promoting the spirit of true religiosity that is built on moderation in belief and conduct," defined by a flexible responsiveness to, as opposed to fanatical rejection of, modern circumstances and culture.[40] While Tash was a trenchant critic of secularism and liberal Westernization, he was most concerned with the internal fissures of the region's Islamic Revival. In a prior essay titled "Virtuous Self-Cultivation or Creating Alternatives?" Tash sought a middle path between what he characterized as two contending camps of "Muslim preachers and reformers": those who urge a focus on pious discipline through ritual practice and those who focus on creating practical alternatives to the Western structures and institutions dominating Muslim countries. Tash argued that these are not mutually exclusive paths. In fact, pious self-cultivation and the creation of Islamic structures across all domains of contemporary life go hand in hand. To appreciate this relation, one has to understand the foundational nature of Islam as a "dynamic and fluid religion, not frozen in time or place." Indeed, if the Islamic Revival is to achieve its goal of undoing the "the years of ignorance and civilizational decay that Muslims have lived through," its proponents would need "an Islamically modern framework (*sighaya 'asriyya islamiyya*) characterized by both stable principles and creative application."[41]

And so there were no qualms about Iqraa's existence as an Islamic channel being enabled by the vast commercial and media enterprises that made its endower a wealthy man. The patronage of pious billionaires like Kamel was a way for Iqraa as an ethical media venture to recalibrate capitalist tools away from profit maximization to more godly ends. Through the political economy of the waqf, Kamel achieved his goal of creating a sustainable media institution for future generations and, producers were always quick to point out, his salvific goal of having a sustainable source of mercy for his otherworldly existence—to balance out, someone might mutter, the sins of his other channels. For even if The Shaykh himself was a man of personal probity and sincere piety, even as he himself saw his entertainment channels as a way to counter wantonness by presenting content better attuned to the moral sensibilities of the Arab viewer than the average Hollywood or MTV fare, he accrued sins every time one of his channels aired a risqué film or music video, which was, according to my interlocutors at Iqraa, unfortunately often.

Ultimately, however, Iqraa as a channel was *not* profitable—revenue rarely exceeded costs, according to one of the channel's Cairo accountants. The best one could aim for was financial sustainability. And this meant not that Iqraa brought in money, but that it simply *had* enough money to not care about having to *make* money no matter what. Where external critics saw an unseemly commodification of the sacred, industry insiders saw a moral opportunity: Kamel's calibration of capital challenged the supremacy of conventional capitalism that put the bottom line above all else, including God. *Daʿwa* absolutely should not be *for* dollars; but it certainly needed dollars to exist on a mass scale. The problem was that there were rarely enough.

CASH CRUNCH

In theory, Iqraa's political economic links to one of the region's richest businessmen presented pious media producers unparalleled resources for Islamic publicity. Some had even joined the channel on the assumption that they would finally have at their disposal all the resources they needed to make top-notch programs that would take Islamic media in new, exciting directions. After all, Iqraa was owned by the same man who had helped create no less than MBC, the region's most-viewed channel.

One senior producer, Hossam, for example, had been excited to be recruited to such a famous Islamic channel after working in a much smaller Salafi one that, he shared, stifled his creativity and offended his pious sensibilities. Iqraa, he felt, would support both his professional and ethical ambitions, and he had expected that his production budget at Iqraa would be much bigger. But it quickly became clear that compared to the leading entertainment channels Iqraa said it wanted to draw viewers away from, Hossam would have to create most programs on a shoestring budget. Like Zaky, the director I met at the Resala bromo shoot, Hossam worried that his professional reputation was being harmed because of Iqraa's smaller production budgets.

"If I was forced to, God forbid, film a bedroom scene," he shared, "I would still want to film it really, really well." He wouldn't compromise his media production standards even in a situation compromising to his pious standards.

"My colleagues [in mainstream channels] criticize Islamic satellite channels for doing things that are visually stereotypical and conventional," complained Hossam, "but what they don't realize is that we don't have the big budgets and resources that they have. They expect every program to be like Moez's *Al-Tariq al-Sah (The Right Path)* but that can only be the exception." This 2007 highly acclaimed Iqraa production was shot on location in four countries. Across thirty episodes, the New Preacher Moez Masoud walked the streets of London and Istanbul, rode a speedboat in the Red Sea, and visited famous museums and swanky art galleries. Iqraa hired a dozen people as editorial assistants for the series, more than half of the usual number of people on its Cairo branch payroll. This was not a financially sustainable model for every production, but it remained the ideal.

Iqraa required at least 7000 broadcasting hours per year. There was simply not enough money to create new productions to fill all those hours, and instead the channel relied on reruns and content acquired from other channels. One of these reruns was Mustafa Mahmud's series for Egyptian state television *Al-'Ilm wa-l-Iman, (Science and Faith)*. This highly popular program by a doubting turned devout doctor aimed to show how Islam and modern science were not in contradiction but complementary in their insights about the natural world. While innovative when it first aired in the 1980s, repurposing well-produced foreign documentaries about timely topics from astronomy to AIDS, by 2010 it was almost impossible to watch, so dated its aesthetic, so degraded the image. Yet Iqraa continued to air it year after year, lacking the resources to create an up-to-date new program on the same theme.

"It is like you constructed all these beautiful window frames in a nice house, but you look out the window, and there is nothing to see, there is no view," Fikry, Hossam's colleague at Iqraa, complained to me one afternoon in Iqraa's breakroom, idly playing with the remote control of the small television set perched on a dusty table in the corner. He zapped through a few channels before stopping at CBC, one of the newest and glitziest Egyptian satellite channels, which rented studio space from Kamel's Misc at the very building complex we were in. The contrast between the slick images playing and Fikry's frustration at being unable to create this content at Iqraa was poignant. The Shaykh had spent so much money on setting up the Islamic channel's "window frames"—renting and buying costly real estate, putting in place a complex and multitiered administrative structure—that these took up to 70 percent of the budget, leaving little money for creating new broadcast content, "the view." Producers like Hossam and Fikry were thus bitterly amused by the popular perception of Islamic channels as get-rich-quick schemes. Such accounts belie their experiences of having to rely on volunteer labor, make do with outdated technology, pay for office supplies out of their own pockets, or watch new entrants like CBC quickly rise to the top of viewers' watch-list, leaving them and their channel behind.

Iqraa Saudi's director Sallam blamed the situation on a wider media political economy that had entrenched biases against religious publicity and had yet to catch up with Iqraa's revolutionarily capacious sense of what counts as Islamic media. Most advertisers just avoid Iqraa because of their "conventional" notion of what it means to be an explicitly Islamic channel, he said, and corporations, especially multinational ones with big marketing budgets, want to avoid getting embroiled in any controversial areas—religion, like politics, was one of those areas from their perspective. This skittishness translates into much lower advertising revenue. The year he came on board the channel, in 2006, MBC grossed $68 million in advertising. Iqraa? Only $6 million.

Nevertheless, the cash crunch wasn't due only to external factors but also to factors internal to the very political economic arrangements that producers lauded as key to Iqraa's credibility as a channel that could afford to be exclusively attentive to divine command and indifferent to audience demand when it conflicted with the former. If capital is construed in the narrowest sense as available cash, then what the waqf as an Islamic calibration of capital allowed was more keeping the lights on from year to year and less funding for growth and expansion. The nonprofit model of the waqf enabled the channel to make production decisions based on its values as opposed to what would make money. This funding model protected the channel from the moral risks of capitalism but also foreclosed the material rewards of market competition. In this sense, the channel's calibration wasn't perfect, at least from the perspective of its producers. Setting up a television channel as a charity had led to stagnation over time because increasing expenditure did not translate into increased divine return. This was the danger of the media channel as charity model—a set and forget attitude that brought stability but little innovation.

For example, Fikry traveled to Saudi Arabia once to meet the owner of a transnational Islamic television channel broadcasting from Egypt. The owner asked him questions so basic about the channel that it became clear that he had never watched it. In fact, when the owner tried to find the channel on his office television at Fikry's request, it turned out that its frequency was not downloaded.

"Clearly, this man's mentality was, 'Okay, I am going to set up an Islamic channel and get divine recompense for this good deed,' but that's it, there is no follow-through," Fikry complained. "Even if something is not for profit, but is for God, it doesn't mean that it should be mediocre. It should still be excellent." Indeed, Fikry felt that channel endowers were missing out ultimately on even greater divine recompense by not working harder to make sure Islamic channels could truly compete with the hundreds of channels, whether they be secular or Salafi, vying for audience attention. This meant being at once edifying and entertaining. But essential to the production of high-quality entertainment was the one thing the Islamic television channels like Iqraa, or even Resala, widely perceived as more innovative on the strength of the programs it debuted in its first years, lacked enough of: money. Tareq el-Suwaidan, Resala's Kuwaiti inaugural director and a popular television preacher in his own right, gave me some comparative numbers so that I could better understand the scope of the problem: "The yearly operating budget for MBC is $350 million. LBC [a popular Lebanese channel] spends $20 million on producing *Star Academy* [a music reality show]. Our entire annual budget is just $5 million."

"Islam is a *nizam shamil*, a comprehensive system," he went on, echoing an oft-invoked trope among Islamic media producers.[42] "So we create channels that try to do everything, but then we do everything badly." Suwaidan didn't mention during our meeting in 2011 that his channel's budget had initially been $30 million, a respectable although not lavish number, and was drastically cut after just one year, leading to a noticeable decrease in quality. Instead, I had learned about this from Zaky.

"If The Prince doesn't spend, then who is going to spend?" Zaky had asked during the bromo shoot, pointing out that this operating budget was chump change for Alwaleed, whose fortune was put at a staggering $20 billion at the time. Because billionaire princes and shaykhs weren't spending, their employees had to get creative and figure out how to compete with conventional channels on a budget. From this financial pressure emerged a set of further distinctions, provoking even more scrutiny of the political economy of Islamic television.

PROFESSIONAL DISTINCTIONS

Iqraa and Resala were the only Islamic channels with production operations in Egypt until the late 2000s when a series of self-identified Salafi channels emerged. Preachers who had achieved great renown in the 1990s for their cassette sermons—notably Muhammad Hassan, Abu Ishaq al-Huwayni and Muhammad Ya'qub—featured prominently on these channels. Such channels were, from my interlocutors' perspective, a problem. They got in the way of their attempts to revolutionize Islamic media. As we have seen, Iqraa media producers believed that the political economy of Islamic television should be calibrated to enable the creation of media that was both professionally excellent and beyond moral reproach, thus radically reconfiguring viewers' expectations of "Islamic media." That the structural reality of limited budgets led them to fall short of this theological ideal was frustrating. So, too, was the rapid emergence of channels that called themselves Islamic while being, from my interlocutors' perspective, anything but. Their flaws were often attributed to a lack of "professionalism."

Professionalism went beyond a checklist of discrete competencies and skills specific to the media industry. It also included an aspiration to "innovation" and "excellence" that shaped dispositions toward one's work and was reflected more broadly in the political economic structures that enabled it. As media anthropologists have long noted, the very processes of media production—and not only of media content—often have high stakes for their participants, creating distinctions between "us versus them."[43] Individuals within a given field who embody a bundle of expected, if often tacit, norms and practices, are evaluated as professional; so, too, are institutions with particular infrastructures and technologies, workflows and policies, and, most importantly, an ethos of high production quality for broadcasts. For example, Tejaswini Ganti shows how value in the Bollywood Hindi film industry works through what she terms "sentiments of disdain and practices of distinction" that create boundaries between the self and the would-be competition—all those "unprofessional" amateurs responsible for "the primary financial, organizational, and aesthetic deficiencies of the film industry."[44] Similarly, from the vantage of Iqraa producers, the unprofessional novices giving a bad name to Islamic television were, without question, Salafi channels. In this way, "professionalism" not only shored up claims to religious authority[45] but delegitimized those of others.

Salafi television channels, my interlocutors lamented, were the equivalent of mom-and-pop shops: small, haphazardly run operations with no "five-year plans" or "strategic visions." The origin story of one of the most prominent Salafi channels was frequently brought up as evidence. I first heard the story from Zaky. He had worked first for the dedicated Egyptian Salafi channel, al-Nas, but quit after just a couple of months because he felt creatively hampered. He told me that al-Nas's managing director, an Egyptian, partnered with a Saudi investor to create a channel for the "simple people" (*li-l-nas al-basita*). The channel started out in 2006 interviewing people on the street about their problems, hosting dream interpreters, and airing private wedding videos sent in by viewers. During the first few months, the channel would occasionally televise guest lectures by Salafi preachers Hassan and Ya'qub. The audience response was positive, leading to these preachers receiving regular broadcast slots. As their shows commanded increasing viewership and media attention, the preachers stipulated that the channel had to cease airing entertainment content if they were to continue appearing on it. By the end of the year, the channel had morphed into a full-time religious one and its slogan changed from "A Screen for All People" to "A Screen Taking You to Heaven."

Despite its lofty promise, the channel continued to be run "like a small coffee shop or snack kiosk," the director complained. "All the people in charge at these channels—not just al-Nas, but also al-Rahma, al-Hikma, *all* of them—they have no media qualifications at all, just family connections. They don't possess a media mentality and it shows in how they run their channels and what they put out." He negatively contrasted these channels with the founding of Iqraa and Resala. Unlike what he deemed the opportunism of al-Nas's transition to an explicitly "Islamic" television channel, these channels' origin stories epitomized their media professionalism. They took years of careful consultation and planning. They involved teams of established media producers and scholars working across Egypt and Saudi Arabia in collaboration with the educated luminaries of the literary, academic, and business worlds, figuring out through brainstorming sessions, focus groups, surveys, and interviews each channel's mission and content.

On both the institutional and individual level, then, professionalism was evidenced through concerted reflection on what you were doing and where you were going. Professionalism meant having ambitious, long-term goals along with concrete plans and structures for realizing them. It meant a willingness to invest financially and ethically in reflection itself as a way toward industry distinction. One of the very first things Suwaidan shared with me was that Resala had spent $200,000 on top-notch media consultants to develop both a distinctive brand identity and a structure for attracting and retaining talented employees. When I asked to see a copy of this brief, he half-jokingly said that was too risky as it might fall into the hands of my colleagues at Iqraa. Iqraa and Resala saw each other as worthy rivals—as equally professional—whereas Salafi channels were deemed to be mere pretenders, unprofessional both in terms of their individual employees and their institutional identities. Still, "Salafi channels get more attention than they deserve," Suwaidan went on. "We have to work harder. Like I tell my team, let's not overthink this: if people tune in, we are successful; if they don't, we are not." By this measure, Salafi channels were the successful ones. However "unprofessional" their beginning, just a year after promising its viewers Paradise, al-Nas had become one of the most watched and talked about satellite channels in Egypt. Its success with viewers was such that over the next few years, the Salafi preachers who appeared on it founded entire new channels of their own. Muhammad Hassan, for example, put his new channel al-Rahma on air in 2007; he later teamed up with Ya'qub and al-Huwayni, the two other influential Salafi preachers who had appeared with him on al-Nas, to start al-Hekma.

The rapid ascent of Salafi television raised secularist alarm bells about "satellite religion" in general, an alarm in which the internal distinctions that mattered so much to my interlocutors dissolved: all Islamic channels, whether al-Nas and al-Hekma or Iqraa and Resala, were characterized as airing "fanatical" content as a part of a "foreign conspiracy" to "destroy the Egyptian mind."[46] Even while lamenting being lumped together with the Salafis by secular critics, my pious interlocutors were even more alarmed by the popularity of the Salafi channels. Just as their own political economy was a source of much external speculation hinging on uncovering their true intent, so did the financial arrangements of Salafi television become fodder for internal concern at Iqraa. While my interlocutors were quick to take offense at suggestions that their channel only aimed to "make money" or "play politics," they were also equally quick to attribute such motives to Salafi channels. Like Iqraa, the companies operating the channels were known and their owners regularly gave press interviews. Like Iqraa, their operating budgets were sourced from a mix of advertising revenue and charitable donations. But this was dismissed by my interlocutors as smoke screens hiding nefarious activity.

One New Preacher opined that Salafi channels were money-laundering fronts. (This accusation was similar to the one The Shaykh had to contend with following 9/11, when he, along with other prominent Saudi businessmen, was subject to a lawsuit alleging that Dallah corporation was financing al-Qaeda affiliates; he was eventually cleared.) Sallam, Iqraa's Saudi director, alleged that Salafi channels were funded by "powerful non-Muslim forces" desiring to "tarnish the image of Islam" by supporting the worst possible representation of it. Another producer characterized Salafi channels as a "Wahhabi invasion" (*ghazw Wahabi*) aimed at undermining, from within, Egyptians' "naturally moderate" religiosity.

"It is a type of intellectual warfare backed by a lot of money," he expanded. "Muhammad Hassan has his own channel. Which other preacher can afford to have his own channel?"

Many of my interlocutors were certain that Salafi channels, which before the 2011 revolution stayed clear of politics as a matter of doctrine, were being supported by Mubarak's security agencies. This theory was also popular with the Mubarak regime's own political opposition, whether secular or Islamist. Meanwhile, state-affiliated publications propagated the idea that Salafi channels were being funded by covert American money, which is how Salafi preachers themselves explained the forces behind the New Preachers.

The disparateness of these accusations reveals a great deal about how fragmented the field of Islamic television is, despite its pervasive scholarly and social depiction as monolithic. And the insider critiques speak to the multifaceted ambitions and aspirations of participants in the social world of Islamic television to harness, however incompletely, political and economic forces to their own ends. Embedded in questions about who is funding which channel and to what ends are deep-seated anxieties about who should be able to speak publicly for Islam—and with whose money. The competing claims of what is *really* going on that these questions provoke are connected with broader theological concerns about how Islamic publicity is being reconfigured and with what social and salvific effect.

Zaky and I kept in regular touch after we met during that midnight shoot in Haram. Following the 2011 revolution, I noticed that he developed a more positive outlook on the potential of channels like Iqraa and Resala for supporting the "ethical entertainment" he sought. From his perspective, the revolution had made more ordinary Egyptians realize that the type of entertainment they were offered under Mubarak was not true art but "empty" (*fadi*), designed to distract, not uplift. And the shortcomings of Salafi channels were becoming more apparent as their preachers fanned the flames of partisan polarization. Islamic channels like Iqraa and Resala, with their creative yet ethical media and their professional preachers, could serve as a bridge between these two extremes, he felt. Working with them he could produce media that was Islamic but expansive enough to overcome the attraction of both secularism and Salafism. That there were Muslims as wealthy as The

Shaykh and Prince Alwaleed who were ready to finance, if never with a lot of money, channels that made no money was a reprieve from the economistic focus on the bottom line that enabled sensationalistic and sinful content.

Like others I met, Zaky worked within the political economic configurations of broadcast television to meet what were often much more radical aims. To reduce the creative and pious ambitions of Islamic media producers like Zaky or Fikry to the "commodification" of religion by neoliberal privatization and Gulf petrodollars is to miss how the political economy of media comes to be a terrain of theological argument and ethical striving through the internal debates and critiques of those who labor within it. In his ethnography of Hollywood media workers, John Caldwell urges media studies scholars to take seriously "the industry's own self-representation, self-critique, and self-reflection" because the industry's cultures of production reveal a great deal about the production of culture writ large.[47] Media producers' critiques of the sensibilities and structures of their profession are essential to the kinds of media they create and how they make sense of it, he argues. Focusing on industry insiders' own critical evaluations of the structural arrangements of capital and creative labor that make up the political economy of Islamic media allows for a more nuanced analysis of media institutions as inhabited by actors with varied interests and diverse ambitions, both moral and mundane, pious and professional, that exceed the intentions of their funders.

I once asked Amina, a seasoned Islamic media producer, what was the aim of an Iqraa reality TV program she worked on. She chuckled: "You should be asking instead what my aim for the program was versus the preacher's aim versus the channel's versus the contestants'." Indeed, during fieldwork I remained surprised at the extent to which a preacher's control over "his" program ceased the moment he stopped recording, as the program entered a collective postproduction process with multiple and consequential authors, each with their own interests and views. Even programs by Mustafa Hosny—who as a "star preacher" had his own production team and budget and thus considerable scope in determining overall program ideas and episode content—were the result of contingent processes beyond both his direct editorial influence and the indirect shaping of allocated labor and funding. The on-screen content reflected who was at the brainstorming sessions and how much coffee they had, serendipitous leads in the field and who followed up on them, the resourcefulness and creativity of his team on any given day, as well as hard-to-predict factors of timing, opportunity, and access. Media ethnography, with its concern for these everyday contexts of production, is especially well suited to shed light on the troubles involved in any attempt to use media as a tool for social engineering or mass mobilization. This holds true in even more authoritarian media political economies than Egypt's during my fieldwork. For example, Narges Bajoghli's fieldwork with regime-allied media producers in Iran reveals how much they disagree with each other over the legacy of the 1979 Islamic revolution and what it means to aspire to an "Islamic republic." Their internal struggles play out in conflicting production strategies and practices within the same political economy of media.[48] Nevertheless, many Middle East scholars downplay the importance of everyday production practices for media content while holding up the power of "political economy" as self-evident.[49] It's as if the much-derided hypodermic needle approach to media reception—where audiences are passive receptacles injected with content—has now been applied to the production side: producers are passive recipients of cash infusions that determine the content they make. And so to understand a channel like Iqraa's "real" aim, the argument goes, we need to above all scrutinize billionaire businessmen's ties to governing elites. But effects and investments of ownership structures on media content are invariably negotiated, and sometimes subverted, by content producers, whose day-to-day work involves operationalizing allocated capital. Far from being the disembodied arrangements of predetermined structural logics, media economies are constituted by people with different levels of institutional access and power-making choices.

Taking seriously Islamic television producers' attempts to calibrate professional endeavor, pious aspiration, and structural conditions yields more insights into everyday workings of political economies of media than merely tracing who is funding which channel and why. More broadly, by tracking how Iqraa television producers interrogate their own political economy we can better understand how the "Islamic" is made and remade through the intersection of capital, connections, and creative ideas as well as through the differential positioning of media players and producers in relation to these intersections. This, in turn, reveals the ways in which abstractions like political economy, professionalism, and piety are calibrated at the intersections of structural conditions and opportunities, normative impulses and parameters, as well as shifting senses of what matters most to God and why.

That the material and ethical infrastructure of pious publicity, not only its content, matters deeply for the institutional calibration of the Islamic holds true for the idea of the "professional" Islamic preacher as well.

BECOMING THE "NEW PREACHER"

My commute to Iqraa offered a preview of the month's satellite television offerings, as the visages of actors, pundits, and preachers appeared on billboards, giving me something to look at during traffic jams. These billboards advertising TV programs became ubiquitous in the late 1990s and early 2000s as satellite channels proliferated. Each year, Iqraa rented many for Hosny's Ramadan programs, including on the Sixth of October bridge, one of Cairo's main throughways. While advertising for drama or news commentary rarely provoked outcry—after all, how else would anyone know what to watch?—many Cairenes I knew felt that for preaching programs such publicity was unseemly. As we saw, however, for Iqraa producers the efficacy of Islamic media was inextricable from its commercial promotion. Having billboards on the capital city's major bridge was not only a physical sign of success within a competitive mediascape; it was also a means of disrupting the average commuter's stereotypes about what she could expect to see on an Islamic channel and what an Islamic preacher looked like. Iqraa and its preachers, the billboard proclaimed, were as innovative and creative as the pop stars of the mainstream satellite channels being advertised on the next light pole. Far from being inappropriately commercial, the idea of the Islamic preacher as a trend-setting star was vital to the revolution within the piety movement my interlocutors hoped to instigate.

During my fieldwork, this idea had also become key to Iqraa producers' ethical recalibration of the often contradictory and rarely equal flows of capital, whether financial or creative, that constitute pan-Arab satellite media. Iqraa's founding ambition had been to present programs that were "Islamic but not about Islam," as the channel's Saudi director Sallam had put it. But it was too expensive to be so expansive. Instead of producing entertainment, the channel ended up producing a new kind of preacher, one who looked and talked like the middle-class youth he was addressing, one who was at once trendy and tender, dazzling and devout. Sallam explained to me that the channel was committed to "discovering and developing" talented "new preachers" through a five-year plan designed to catapult them to mainstream stardom. In speech and manner, taste and style, the television preacher, as the professional mediator of *da'wa* for a mass audience, would need to stand out. Cultivating preacherly celebrity allowed Iqraa to compete for the attention of middle-class viewers against much better funded secular channels while offering a grassroots alternative to Salafi preachers.

During my fieldwork Hosny was without doubt Iqraa's star. Born in 1978, as a college student Hosny pursued his passion for preaching in his free time by completing the two-year *da'wa* certification course at the Preachers Preparatory Institute. In 2004, he was a fresh graduate working in sales when he applied to a newspaper advertisement Iqraa placed for a "program presenter" based in Egypt. After multiple interviews and camera tests, he was offered his dream job. Most producers were graduates from Cairo University's prestigious Faculty of Media, a key feeder for the television industry. Their training taught them that media production was a domain that required expertise, a field that one could only participate in—be a professional of—once one had mastered the requisite knowledge and skills. At Iqraa, as I have described, professionalism—and producers invariably used the English word—was a form of institutional distinction from "amateur" Salafi channels. This was so on the individual level as well. While Hosny himself wasn't a media graduate—his bachelor's degree was in commerce—he was committed to the idea of media production as a professional standard, along with the idea of television preaching as also a profession.

Unlike a regular preacher, the professional television preacher—the New Preacher—didn't just have to master religious knowledge and be adept at figuring out the applicability of Qur'anic verses and Prophetic sayings to the new dilemmas and circumstances of contemporary life. As a career, not merely a vocation, television preaching demanded certain skills that, in turn, required institutional investment. Hosny, for example, had to learn extemporaneous and effective public speaking within the constraints of live broadcast. He had to know how to script a prerecorded episode. He had to be a resourceful team manager, delegating tasks when necessary, troubleshooting quickly, and assessing ideas and pitches tactfully. He had to know how to interview guests on his program and answer (or deflect) questions of viewers who called in. Most preachers on the channel were paid per episode or program, but Hosny had a monthly salary. Being on the payroll was designed to protect him from the exhaustion of the hustle and create time and space for him to create new, innovative content. The less a preacher had to worry about how to make ends meet, the more he would be able to create ethically efficacious programs, Sallam told me.

Hosny was prolific at Iqraa. He produced multiple programs for the channel while also publishing books, giving mosque sermons, leading in-person seminars, and regularly appearing on radio and television. He had to stay on top of a hectic production schedule while maintaining his own speaking schedule, especially as face-to-face interactions with fans were thought to be crucial for cementing a dedicated following. As more and more viewers watched his programs, the responsibilities and stakes only increased. *How can we make better content? How can we attract new viewers?* These questions kept Hosny and his media team up at night. In the early days of the channel, Iqraa's marketing budget allowed for buying ads in daily newspapers while ART's twenty other channels promoted Iqraa for free. As both Iqraa's production and marketing budgets shrank over the years, however, the channel had to find cost-effective ways to capture public attention and direct it toward its star preacher. Billboards were one way to do so.

I had started compiling an archive of Hosny's billboards, leaning out of my car window to snap photos. One afternoon, I brought in my camera to Iqraa to show Hossam and Fikry. Over sandwiches and tea in the break room, we took turns clicking through the photos on my camera. Hossam paused at one image of an ever so slightly air-brushed Hosny smiling beatifically, arms folded across his chest, this season's program title and channel logo above his head.

"We have a product—religiosity—and we advertise it using *daʿwa*," Hossam said. "What this means is that we have to create in people, first, desire for this product and, second, show them how to acquire it, how to become committed to it."

Iqraa producers like Hossam regularly characterized their work as "marketing ethics" or "selling piety." This wasn't intended as analogy or casual metaphor. *Daʿwa* was, for them, not *like* advertising—it *was* advertising, advertising for God's message. Hossam explained the importance of preachers maintaining an attractive image across different outreach platforms to do so. It wasn't only that their billboard had to look as good as the Egyptian A-list celebrities on the next pole. Their YouTube playlists had to be as well organized and their Facebook pages as well curated. Viewers had to feel like they "really knew" the preacher, that he was akin to a sympathetic friend, not a stern judge.

He tapped the camera's thumbnail image: "Now we are not going to accomplish this by bringing in an old man with a long beard, putting him in front of a camera, and then have him lecture viewers for hours on 'God says,' 'the Prophet says,' 'you must do this, you must do that.'" While saying this Hossam had adopted a gruff tone. "Such a preacher can't successfully market Islam."

One reason such an approach would be unsuccessful is because it is too direct, he elaborated. People resent being lectured to. Advertising and media work through more subtle association, through engendering not-quite-conscious feelings and subliminal desires in people. The effective preacher is thus someone who does not necessarily *tell* others what to do but *shows* them what they can have and who they can be, if they emulate him. The preacher himself was a "living advertisement for Islam." As such, he had to appear as "innovative," "relevant," and "accessible" as the religion he was calling people to.

Such motivations help contextualize the New Preacher Amr Khaled's headline-making statement that "I want to be rich so that people will look at me and say *'You see, rich and religious,'* and they'll love God through my wealth." Commenting on this declaration, two academic authors lament that it shows that the preacher "has become a media product."[50] For my interlocutors, that the preacher, and thus piety, was a "product" that required savvy selling was not a failing to be lamented but a professional challenge.

Fikry, who had been nodding in agreement as Hossam spoke, weighed in as he started clearing the sandwich wrappers: "It is really the ABCs of advertising." He gestured to my hair: "To convince you to buy a certain shampoo, for example, I am not going to make a long, boring speech listing the benefits of this shampoo and telling you how it will nourish your hair. Instead, I am going to project a 'before and after' image of a woman who washed her hair with it, and you will see for yourself how silky your hair will be."

The before-and-after image is an old advertising strategy. It invites consumers to connect and identify with the product as the medium of their desired transformation, their better future selves.

The before: *You are spiritually lost, your faith smothered by a sinful shell, boozing and dating without shame. You run after the latest fad or singer but are heedless of God and the Afterlife.*

Or: *You are diligent in your prayers, exacting in your fasts, the lengths of your beard and trousers Prophetic. But your piety is sullen not sweet, angry at everything and everyone, alienated from the zest of life.*

The after: *You can be close to God and His Prophet, while also enjoying the world and its delights—you don't have to choose. If I can do it, so can you.*

Let me show you how.

Two
INNOVATION

ONE EVENING IN NOVEMBER 2010, MUSTAFA HOSNY CONVENED A seminar titled "Technology and Godliness" at the Sawy Cultural Wheel. A popular community center in an upscale Cairo neighborhood, Sawy hosts many events, from jazz concerts to smoking cessation clinics to, for a brief time after the 2011 revolution, political debates. Hosny's events at the center were always well attended, and as the main hall reached capacity, people spilled into the garden. There, young men and women made themselves comfortable on the grass, sitting cross-legged or kneeling on coats and shawls, to watch the preacher on the outdoor screens. Dressed in jeans and a collarless shirt, Hosny spoke in a seemingly improvisational manner as he paced the stage, a spotlight following him. Everything about this seminar—from the venue to the mixed-gender seating to Hosny's stylish clothing—was calculated to subvert stereotypes about what participating in the Islamic *daʿwa* movement entailed.

So did the evening's surprise announcement: Hosny had collaborated with a famous pop singer and actor, Khalid Selim, on an album with the same title as the preacher's most recent series on Iqraa, *Madrasat al-Hubb* (*The School of Love*). The musical incarnation of the *daʿwa* program consisted of ten songs by Selim intercut with pious exhortations by Hosny on godliness, *rububiyya*. Selim, with his chiseled physique, chart-topping tunes, and heartthrob celebrity, made for an unlikely *da'wa* partner. And that was precisely what made him attractive for pious outreach. Working with him laid down yet another stone on the ambitious road New Preachers like Hosny were paving: radically reconfiguring what Islamic media looks and sounds like. Key to this ambition was the idea of *ibda'*, of creative innovation, as a theological imperative oriented toward this-worldly flourishing and otherworldly salvation.

The New Preachers adhered to the orthodox doctrine of Qur'anic inimitability. Yet they argued that the Qur'anic message needs to be continually re-presented through contemporary media forms to remain relevant to their target audience of middle-class urban youth. Doing so is in keeping with the Qur'an's own avowal of a single eternal message delivered via a variety of messengers and contingent forms across time. After all, God says: "We have not sent a messenger except in the language of his people to clarify the message for them" (Qur'an 14:4). Put differently, while God's truth is absolute, this truth is contingently conveyed. The Prophet Muhammad himself had used all the "media technologies" at his disposal in his own *da'wa*, tailoring it to his addressees. Indeed, every prophet conveyed God's message in not just the language of his people, but through their prized media. Moses performed magical feats for a society that valued that; Jesus healed the sick at a time when people were plagued by disease; Muhammad's miracle was the Qur'an itself, whose linguistic inimitability overwhelmed a society that esteemed poetic expression above all. And even then, the Prophet did not always rely on reciting the Qur'an; he sometimes told stories, as does God Himself in the Qur'an. *Da'wa* practitioners should thus stay true to this divine dynamism in their own efforts to propagate God's final revelation.

Hosny's media team at Iqraa interpreted the Prophetic hadith that "God will send every hundred years those who renew religion in the community" to mean that they had a theological obligation to produce new forms of Islamic media. But creative innovation in pious publicity is especially important precisely because of the Islamic Revival's high visibility and pervasiveness. From my interlocutors' perspective, the piety movement in Egypt had been so successful that people in a sense knew the Qur'an *too well*.[1] Familiarity had robbed them of the ability to be moved by the Qur'an, especially as their attention was captivated by an arresting array of new media designed to titillate and distract. They argued that to instill piety, the timeless didactic content of *daʿwa* needs to take new form. Song and sermon need not compete for the sensory attention of believers but can conjoin to amplify godliness.

At the Sawy seminar, Hosny cited the hadith about religious renewal in explaining why he made the musical *daʿwa* album. He told attendees about the time he rode a bus to work a decade earlier and the driver was playing a famous cassette sermon that prohibited watching television as *haram* and likened the medium to the anti-Christ. Today, he joked, this cassette preacher probably has his own television channel, but remains against the culture of television. Even with the spread of the Islamic Revival and the proliferation of religious channels on satellite, many ordinary people are repelled by the idea of piety, as "those who call themselves the pious have set up barriers between themselves and the rest of society," Hosny argued. This wasn't the Prophet's way, the preacher went on; the Prophet engaged with the culture and technology of his time and "didn't just recite the Qur'an all day." Like the Prophet, Islamic preachers must work "through the technology and language of our time to spread the values God loves, otherwise we are going to be a cabal of the pious (*maʿshir al-multizimin*) disconnected from the rest of the society." If we continue with conventional ways of doing *daʿwa*, Hosny concluded, that disconnect will only grow, leading to even more alienation among ordinary people.

This chapter delves into the New Preachers and their producers' strategies of innovation in Islamic television and how these mattered to revolutionizing piety, on-screen and off. *Ibdaʿ* derives from the Arabic root *b-d-ʿ*, to invent or to initiate something new. The Qur'an (2:117) refers to God as the "Originator (*badiʿ*) of the heavens and the earth." Created by God with the disposition to emulate some of His divine attributes, humans are enjoined to cultivate creativity as a virtue, my interlocutors argued. To be sure, human innovation will inevitably fall short of divine originality. As one producer told me, the airplane, while impressive, is but an imperfect approximation of the bird, just like the camera is of the eye. Despite the impossibility of coming close to divine creativity, *ibdaʿ*, the aspiration to do something that hasn't been done before, especially with the ethical intent of "benefiting people," was nevertheless for my interlocutors intrinsic to Islamic piety and media production alike.

Innovation for my interlocutors specifically turned on the ability to dazzle viewers through the aesthetic possibilities of television as an image-centered medium while cultivating a sense of intimacy across the screen that would sustain viewers' commitment to the path of piety. Innovation involved incorporating acting, music, and special effects; shooting on location as opposed to an indoor studio; and allowing ordinary people to share the screen with the preacher. To be sure, the producers I worked with at times overstated their innovation, neglecting both continuities with older revivalist aesthetics and, as described in chapter 1, the constraints posed by limited budgets. Still, the production practices I observed were motivated by the assumption that if you wanted to move middle-class Muslim youth, you had to find new and unexpected ways to mediate the Qur'an. Receptivity to the Qur'an as God's final "message" hinged on factors external to the message itself, namely its resonant re-mediation.

This theology of mediation is implicit in the religious publicity efforts of other Islamic television preachers. For example, the Indonesian Aa Gym understood his mission in terms of "rebranding" Islam to make it accessible to his middle-class audience.[2] It also is not limited to Islamic revivalism. British evangelicals, operating in a secularized milieu in which "God-is-difficult-and-dull," premised their innovative biblical outreach projects on the idea that "Christ spoke the language of the culture he was in."[3] For New Preachers like Hosny, the current language of the culture—and thus the necessary form of religious renewal—was entertainment. The challenge was advancing this *daʿwa* strategy within a revivalist context long shaped by a powerful counter argument, one that repudiated entertainment forms and the "dazzlement" they engender.[4]

Against a theology of *ibdaʿ*, Salafi preachers offered a theology of *bidʿa* that censured religious innovation as heretical. The New Preachers' experimentation with entertainment forms was condemned by their Salafi counterparts within the piety movement as irredeemably "Western." More specifically, Salafi preachers warned viewers against the New Preachers through criticizing them as *ahl al-bidʿa*, "the people of innovation," that is, Muslims who claim to be following God's injunctions but in reality pursue their own desires. In this view, efforts to create new ways of doing *daʿwa*—and, by extension, new visual and sonic expectations of pious publicity that resemble too closely that of "secular" culture—open the door to misguidance, as if the Qur'an were "not enough" to move humans to greater piety.

The New Preachers' acceptance of change as intrinsic to Islam as a tradition is shared by scholars working within the anthropological idea of Islam as a "discursive tradition" that is constantly changing and reconfiguring as it encounters other traditions and modern regimes. Work inspired by this analytic has offered a powerful critical rejoinder to Orientalist assumptions of Islam as a static and rigid religion that cannot adapt to modern circumstances. This was a secular stereotype that the New Preachers and Iqraa producers were invested in dismantling as well.[5] Nevertheless, the idea that orthodoxy requires conformism and precludes innovation is central to Salafism. For Salafism, the Islamic tradition does not admit of reconfiguration but only of the punctilious repetition of the "original Islam" of the Prophet Muhammad and the first generations of Muslims. In this way, for Salafi Muslims the Islamic tradition *is* unchanging and repetitive.

To be clear, the New Preachers agreed with Salafis that the best generation of Muslims was the one closest in time to revelation. The age of the Prophet and his Companions, the time of *al-salaf al-salih* (the righteous ancestors) was thus the Islamic ideal that all Muslims should try to re-create in the present. However, while Salafi revivalists saw this re-creation as one best accomplished through mimetic fidelity, the New Preachers saw it as best consummated through resonant reconfiguration. The New Preachers argued that the Salafi interpretation of *bidʿa* had created a damaging divide, or *fagwa*, between religion and daily life, enabling the spread of both fanaticism and secular dissolution. They argued that not all innovation was prohibited, with the Prophet supporting the adoption of new practices and customs so long as they were beneficial. Ironically, by labeling all innovation as misguidance, Salafis engaged in what they continually condemn others of doing: rupturing the Islamic tradition.

These internal revivalist struggles over the permissibility of appropriating secular media aesthetics and forms are located within wider doctrinally grounded debates that turn on different understandings of divinely created human nature and the role of human mediation in relation to revelation.

These struggles draw the boundaries of the "secular" and the "religious" differently to form competing theological conceptions of the Islamic tradition itself.

As Hosny put it in a conversation with me about his *daʿwa* album: "It is our tradition to change!" He went on:

> The Qur'an was revealed in the language of the people. God sent down prophets who speak their people's language. People now have a different language. So we have to translate the original language of the Qur'an into a language that people today can understand. If they don't understand the Qur'an, how can they love what it teaches?

The New Preaching evaluation of transformation as intrinsic to Islamic piety is grounded within the Ashʿari theological assumption of the evolving character of ethical aptness, or social "reasonableness," in which practices or norms could be, from an Islamic perspective, appropriate for one time and space, but not for another. Over the past century al-Azhar has institutionalized an ethic of *waqʿiya*, or reasonableness, as a middle ground between the "secular" marginalization of Islamic epistemologies and disciplines and the "fanatical" indifference to contemporary social realities.[6] Both extremes thwart the dynamic transformation on which the Islamic tradition depends.

INNOVATIVELY TRADITIONAL

"It is one of God's mercies that He made permissible many ways to preach, because there are many kinds of people," Hosny explains. We are sitting in Emad's office, which doubles as Hosny's own when needed.

"Someone may not find the way I look acceptable for an Islamic preacher," he goes on, "and will reject me as ignorant before I even say a word because to him I look like a young guy who is out to party, not preach about God (*ʿayiz yibarti, mish yidʿu al-nas ila Allah*)." He points to the muted television set in the corner, tuned to Iqraa, and showing one of the channel's Saudi-produced programs. On-screen is an older man with a long beard wearing a white gown and headdress. "But then another person will look at this preacher and think, *Oh, I definitely don't want to be like him, I don't even want to know what he is saying!*" Hosny continues. "Instead, this person might be thinking: 'I want to learn about God and my religion from someone who looks like me, who will understand me and talk about things relevant to my life.'" Having variety in preaching styles, content, and persons is important, Hosny concludes, because ultimately God's truth must be able to reach all.

It is commonplace to argue that the emergence of new media technologies has not only "commodified religion" but also led to a "fragmentation" of religious authority in Muslim societies. In its strongest formulation, this framework holds that satellite television and the internet have "democratized" and "individualized" Islam, displacing the institutional orthodoxy of theological centers like al-Azhar.[7] Adopting this framework, many scholars mistake the New Preachers' media savvy as a challenge to the authoritative traditions of al-Azhar.[8] But in paving a path of media professionalism for the Islamic preacher, my interlocutors at Iqraa aspired not to disrupt al-Azhar's authority but to bolster it through creatively remediating its teachings for an audience of "ordinary people" primed for distraction.[9]

This innovative remediation was necessary precisely because of what Dale Eickelman calls the "objectification of the religious imagination."[10] Mass education and mass media over the past fifty years have afforded Muslims around the world unprecedented opportunities for religious autodidacticism, so who needs to declare disciplined allegiance to a Sufi shaykh or enroll in years of dense study at an Islamic institution far from home when one can learn "about" Islam by reading a book, listening to a cassette, or watching a program? But, as Hosny explained in one Iqraa program, "Our religion is one of transmission from heart to heart, from shaykh to shaykh (*din al-talaqi min sadr li-sadr, min shaykh li-shaykh*). Even the Prophet, the greatest man, learned from the Angel Gabriel." Religious knowledge is best acquired through the embodied encounter with exemplary others. It is not just what one learns, but how and from whom one learns that matters.

Even though he is a "new preacher," Hosny's sensibilities are thus in keeping with a long history of knowledge acquisition through co-presence that mark traditional seminaries like al-Azhar. In contrast to modern mass education's depersonalized conception of knowledge in which every student has direct access to a text which needs no teacher,[11] Hosny insisted on the primacy of face-to-face learning for his formation as a preacher. Significantly, this insistence aimed to subvert not only secular modes of knowing, but also Salafi ones.

As he shared in a televised interview on the channel Dream with the talk show host Amr el-Leithy in June 2011, Hosny almost fell victim to Salafism, to "the cassette shaykhs," as a teenager. He was saved when he began to learn "at the feet of shaykhs." By this he meant he joined the revived study circles of al-Azhar, obtaining several *ijazas*. *Ijazas* are authorizations to teach in specific areas of religious knowledge. They indicate that one has studied a text with a qualified teacher, who himself had acquired this knowledge from qualified teachers, thus forming an unbroken chain of transmission. *Ijazas* are a hallmark of the companion-based pedagogy of al-Azhar in which students learn by watching and emulating their instructors. This methodology contrasts sharply with the Salafi text-based approach in which "habitus acquisition from living exemplars has no essential place."[12]

In speaking about being saved from "the cassette shaykhs"—that is, Salafi preachers—through learning "at the feet of shaykhs"—that is, Azhari shaykhs—New Preachers like Hosny aspire not to challenge al-Azhar but to embrace its "protective" edifice of centuries of institutionalized Islamic theology.[13] His role as a television preacher was to share traditional knowledge certified by his *ijazas* in innovative ways without laying claim to being an authoritative producer of such knowledge. Hosny's media team continually attempted to ensure that his viewers did not orient to him as a person with al-Azhar's fatwa-giving authority. This involved prescreening callers during live episodes and directing those who had a jurisprudential question to Dar al-Ifta', the country's official fatwa-issuing body. Zayna explained that such interventions were necessary because Hosny's youthful viewers often conflated the role of the *da'iya*, the preacher, with the role of the mufti, the fatwa-giver. Overhearing our conversation, another member of the team chimed in: "There is a difference between calling people to God and giving fatwas. Anyone can call people to God, not just shaykhs. Even I can be a *da'iya*; so long as I don't engage in fatwa-giving, nobody can say I am doing anything wrong."[14]

Importantly, however, the New Preachers' deferral to al-Azhar as the standard by which claims to Islamic knowledge should be judged went together with a criticism: that this venerable institution had failed in making its deep knowledge comprehensible to the average person. The inaccessibility of the Azharite tradition to "ordinary Muslims" created openings for the

Salafi "cassette shaykhs" to wield unprecedented influence over the grassroots *daʿwa* movement. During the 2011 eighteen-day uprising this failure acquired even higher stakes. In a television appearance on the Egyptian satellite channel al-Hayah, a week into the protests that began on January 25, Hosny appealed to al-Azhar's head, Ahmed el-Tayeb, to "use" him and other New Preachers—he mentioned Moez Masoud—because "we have a lot of loving fans" (*muhibbin*). He went on: "I have a talent for getting my voice heard. I am part of a generation that felt a barrier with al-Azhar, even though my own shaykhs are from al-Azhar. But the ordinary person can't relate to the turban and the gown."

I watched Hosny's television appearance with Mona, a viewer who had grown up with the New Preachers. Most of her friends, though, didn't share her identification with the Islamic Revival, although during those eighteen days that difference didn't seem to matter much: they were all supportive of the protesters in Tahrir Square, even as most of their parents prohibited them from joining. I had gone to the Square, however, and Mona had invited me over to give her a firsthand account. As we watched, Mona chalked up her friends' indifference to al-Azhar not merely to the inaccessibility of its knowledge, but also to the "negative image" Salafi preachers had given piety.

"Islam has been presented to most of my friends in a way that it makes them feel that it is not universal, that it cannot fit into any kind of society or age," she said as we lounged on her living room couch. "That is what the New Preachers are changing—"

"They are making Islam universal?" I interject.

"No," she shakes her head, "Islam *is* universal, it doesn't need to be made so. But they are presenting it in a way that brings that out."

She goes on: "Remember how Moez [Masoud] said that the problem is at bottom a spiritual one? Like, a lot of my friends are turning to new things like meditation or yoga to find spiritual support. The New Preachers are doing something really smart when they present supplications as a spiritual meditation. It is the same content as always, but in a new context, with a new frame."

Mona's comment identifies the allure of the New Preachers not with the disruption and "fragmentation" tradition but its novel remediation. They put it in a "new frame" that showcases Islam's universalism because to do otherwise—to insist on fidelity to inherited forms from a different time—would put that universalism into question. "Islam doesn't change," Hosny assured me in our conversation about the ideal attributes of a preacher, "but our realities constantly do. So preachers have to translate Islam into ways that make sense for us now." As we will see, this translational capacity was aimed at making Islamic media relevant and exciting to an imagined middle-class audience of "ordinary youth" primed to think otherwise, people like Mona's friends who by virtue of their lifestyles and class background were most in danger of succumbing to the secular lure of Westernization. As Mona discerned, addressing such Egyptians meant above all puncturing the conflation of piety with its "repellent" Salafi version.

DESPERATELY SEEKING "ORDINARY YOUTH"

During brainstorming sessions, Cairo manager Emad sometimes brought out a poster on which were pasted a collection of photos of young people milling around Cairo's malls. The collection was a visual concretization of the audience whose attention producers aimed to capture. One of the photos was of a woman in her twenties striding past glass storefronts, shopping bags swinging. *What is she worried about?* Emad would ask. *What does she care about? Where is she going next?*

Hosny's media team regularly discussed during such sessions their target viewers and the best strategies to solicit and retain their attention. Class was central to these discussions. As anthropologists have shown, class is above all a lived experience at the center of which are immaterial and affective things.[15] Hosny and his media team at Iqraa wanted to center piety within the lived experiences of upper- and middle-class Egyptian youth, what producers like Emad called "the Class A and Class B Plus." By this they meant young professionals and university students who were economically comfortable enough to afford discretionary spending and leisure time. More importantly, however, the Class and Class B Plus had a "cosmopolitan" sensibility, as Hossam explained to me during one of our afternoon conversations in the channel's breakroom. When I asked him what he meant by "cosmopolitan," he replied: "People like you. You travel abroad, speak English, watch Hollywood films, dress fashionably. You probably drive a nice car and eat regularly at chic restaurants. You are our target audience."

The New Preachers' inroads into cosmopolitan class segments that historically showed little interest in religious revivalism caused consternation within Egypt's media industry. "It's something like a mania, with fans and stars," one observer shared in an interview. "Just like it's good for some people to say they were at a party with Amr Diab, they want to go to a lecture with Amr Khaled."[16] For others, that the same people who appreciated a pop singer like Amr Diab now appreciated an Islamic preacher was not a trivial media trend but a troubling political one. For example, Wa'il Lutfi, a columnist for the steadfastly secularist magazine *Rose al-Youssef*, warns in his best-selling book on the New Preachers that they were stealthily drawing the country's powerful elite into the Muslim Brotherhood's orbit.[17] Indeed, the most widely circulating rumor when Khaled suddenly left Egypt in 2002 was that he had been forced into exile by the government because one of President Mubarak's family members had donned the hijab after watching his programs. New Preachers like Khaled, many felt, were but "radical Islamists in sheep's clothing."[18]

Western academic analysts, however, have tended to analyze the New Preachers not through the prism of politics but of commodification. In this scholarship, the New Preachers are lambasted for fostering an "air-conditioned Islam" conducive to neoliberalism.[19] A New Preacher like Amr Khaled was a "Shaykh Marina"—the name of a sprawling gated beach town on the Mediterranean coast with a reputation for exclusivity in the early 2000s—promoting a "piety of privilege."[20] This critique misses the ways in which a classed construction of piety was a deliberate one aimed at audience resonance. Within Egypt, certain social milieus—avant-garde artists, Marina beachgoers, foreign-affiliated researchers, for example—are assumed to be cosmopolitan by default, enjoying a perception of what Mark Allen Peterson calls "connectedness" to transnational popular culture. By contrast, Islamic revivalists are assumed to be parochial. It was this assumption that Hosny's media team wanted to upend through revolutionizing Islamic media. In doing so, they aspired to what James Hoesterey, writing about Aa Gym, Indonesia's equivalent of a New Preacher, calls a "prophetic cosmopolitanism," in which the connectivity of modern lifestyles is reclaimed as Islamic with the Prophet Muhammad setting the standard.[21] A "piety of privilege," a piety that appeals to the Class A and the Class B Plus, is the *whole point*, not a discreditable ambition to be ferreted out by critical scholars.

Islamic television viewers themselves were quick to pick up on this. A viewer I came to know well, Hania, wasn't remotely from the Class A and Class B Plus. She didn't have access to Marina, but she appreciated that the New Preachers could reach its vacationers. Where she lived, in the relatively poor quarter of Shubra, the conservative environment created its own moral pressures for modest dress. In a place like Marina, she felt, the environment exerts the opposite pressure. "It's easy to go from a *galabiyya* [loose-fitting garment associated with rural and lower-class women] to a headscarf. But how do you go from bikini to hijab?" Hania explained. "They really need Amr Khaled over there. They are drowning and he is offering them a life raft."

The life raft the New Preachers were offering was tailor-made for the specific moral challenges posed by cosmopolitan lifestyles. In her influential book *Desperately Seeking the Audience,* Ien Ang argues that within the TV industry the construct of "the audience" is disconnected from "getting to know what real people think and feel and do in their everyday dealings with television."[22] This is not what I observed at Iqraa, where producers urgently wanted to connect with real people in order to help them, to give them a life raft to the Afterlife. To determine their audience preferences and needs, my interlocutors drew on their conversations with actual viewers within their circles. This was not too different from how I as an anthropologist often scrutinized everyday interactions for what light they might shed on broader phenomena, as my interlocutors were quick to pick up on. Not infrequently Zayna asked me how the viewers I knew were reacting to the theme of a series or to a particular episode segment. She made sense of my ethnographic commitment to understanding the everyday reception and evaluation of Islamic television by comparing it to her own quest as a media maker for "real connection" to her audience through a better understanding of their lives.

This comparison inspired me to borrow from Iqraa's production toolkit and try out the creation of an ideal viewer avatar. A marketing research strategy, the ideal avatar is a conjuring, grounded in study and experience, of a hypothetical person who is both most excited for and most in need of a product, service or, in this case, a particular kind of Islamic media. I named my avatar Noha. She is not based on an actual person but a composite that reflects a pattern in lifestyle and demographic background I observed in my fieldwork.

Noha is a twenty-two-year-old woman about to finish her bachelor's degree at Cairo University in English literature. Bubbly and talkative, she wears jeans and sneakers paired with Zara sweaters matched to a colorful headscarf wrapped in the "Spanish" turban style. She lives with her parents and younger brother in a nice-ish if small-ish apartment in the middle-class neighborhood of Mohandiseen. Noha is single and wants to stay that way until she graduates and starts her dream job working for the local office of a multinational company. Still, she has been nurturing a quiet crush on a university classmate she sometimes has coffee with (never alone, always in a group!). In the meantime, Noha's volunteer work with charities gives her a sense of moral purpose. The rest of her free time is spent reading: her degree in English has not killed her love for Jane Austen novels and she has a growing collection of the Arabic translations of contemporary American self-help books. When she does go out, she likes to go to the cinema with her friends or her brother, usually to see the new Hollywood blockbuster and rarely to see Egyptian films with their "cheap romance."

Noha is active on social media. On Pinterest, she creates inspirational boards of scenic travel destinations and evening hijab looks. On Facebook, she follows the accounts of all the New Preachers and on YouTube she subscribes to their channels. She appreciates how Amr Khaled, Moez Masoud, and Mustafa Hosny make religion "easy," *sahl*—that is, comprehensible, do-able, and relevant. Most of all, she values the New Preachers for practically modeling how one can grow closer to God, be pious, while also continuing to live a normal life, an ordinary life—her life.

At the same time, Noha would like to better understand the "deeper" meaning of the Qur'anic verses she recites during her daily prayers. She feels like she is still missing, not quite grasping, the "Big Picture" of Islam, and how her own commonsense notions of right and wrong fit into that picture. Can it be, for example, that a girl who wears a headscarf but spends all day maliciously backbiting is superior from God's point of view to a girl who doesn't cover her hair yet is always careful with her words and their impact on others? Didn't the Prophet teach that religion is ethics? So why do some of the most visibly pious people, the ones with the bushy beards or black-veiled faces, sometimes behave so badly? Noha is sure that this picture will come into focus the more programs by the New Preachers she watches and that she will, through them, reach that sweet spot of pleasing God while also pleasing herself, of living her best life mindful of the Afterlife.

My avatar Noha would be an example of what Iqraa producers called "ordinary youth," *al-shabab al-'adi,* although her class background was far from average given Egypt's socioeconomic inequalities. To be an ordinary youth was not only to not know much about religion, but also to be uninterested in learning more from the usual sources—parents and schools, mosque shaykhs and lessons. Importantly, to be ordinary was to partake in the mainstream leisure available to middle-class youth—going to the cinema, hanging out with friends at the sports club, lazing on the beach in summer, and perhaps traveling to Beirut or Istanbul or, for some, to Paris or London. These activities were taken for granted as the sorts of "cosmopolitan" things the Class A and Class B Plus did or wanted to do. What was not taken for granted—and what producers wanted their viewers to know—was that these were things *pious* youth could also enjoy. Hosny's media team felt that he and other New Preachers were the only ones producing *da'wa* that could appeal to "ordinary youth" like the ethnographically informed avatar I created.

Commenting on his target viewers as the head of production at Iqraa, Emad characterized them as "flexibly religious, they are religious one day, and not so religious another day." They are still forming their everyday habits, he told me. And to affect them, you have to start by disrupting expectations of Islamic media—and of the Islamic preacher. The proliferation of Salafi television channels with their "rigid" theological content and "unimaginative" program formats had, my interlocutors believed, only exacerbated the indifference of the Class A and Class B Plus, turning this segment off the whole notion of piety.

This assumption was shared even by Iqraa producers who weren't on Hosny's media team. Early in my fieldwork, Madame Nawal, a subtitler in Iqraa's translation department, explained that in her opinion, "Amr Khaled and other [New Preachers] like him succeeded in making religion something chic, something wow, you know—before, people thought being religious was something *baladi* (vulgar), something for the poor." Madame Nawal didn't hide the fact that she didn't really think much of Amr Khaled and his *da'wa*. Like many others, she found his high-pitched voice and heightened emotionalism off-putting. She also didn't think he had anything to teach her of value. Being a middle-aged woman already well versed in religious knowledge, adept at its ritual practice and with mature ideas about what it means to live as a Muslim, Madame Nawal was no Noha. But she conceded that the Nohas of Egypt really needed the Amr Khaleds of Islamic television. "Amr Khaled was the first preacher to speak directly to the internet youth," she said. "That is what those [within the piety movement] who attack him and Moez Masoud and Mustafa Hosny don't realize: there is no one else talking to these youth." She agreed that it was a theological imperative to make Islamic media that appealed to Egypt's economically well-off because they were so spiritually bereft. And because the Class A and Class B Plus have "seen it all," preachers had to constantly innovate. In a diverse mediascape, after all, the next channel is always a push of a button away.

PIETY BEYOND THE COUNTERPUBLIC

Back at the Sawy center, Hosny prepared to introduce his album with Selim. His collaboration with the pop star had been sparked by the popularity of the opening sequences, or *titres*, that Iqraa had commissioned for each of Hosny's programs since 2007. The channel had pioneered these preacher-singer collaborations with Amr Khaled's series *Lifemakers*. The catchy titres were one of the ways producers tried to overcome the tedium they imagine direct *daʿwa* elicits in viewers. While Iqraa's Egypt producers abjured direct *daʿwa* as "too conventional," limited production budgets dictated that they had to frequently adopt this format. There were simply not enough funds to shoot every program on location in spectacular sites or to rent costly cinema-quality cameras. At most, Hosny's team aimed to do this just once a year, usually for their Ramadan lineup. The rest of his programs were shot primarily in Iqraa's indoor studios. The challenge for producers was how to create "dazzlement" within these direct *daʿwa* programs. Catchy titres were one solution. The channel's research showed that the titres, which were uploaded onto YouTube as stand-alone videos, generated high interest. Selim had done the titre for Hosny's last Ramadan series, and within a few months it became the most watched video on the preacher's YouTube channel.

Hosny and his producers, like other New Preachers, took an approach to Islamic media that was "promiscuous." Questioning the assumption that "different publics each have their own circulatory modes, their own discursive forms, so that one can neatly be separated from the other," anthropologist Brian Larkin uses promiscuity as an analytical trope to think about instances "when one public takes the discursive forms used to constitute another public."[23] Such promiscuity has a long history within *daʿwa* movements, with historians showing how the now taken-for-granted spaces and techniques of Islamic pious propagation across diverse Muslim societies often took direct inspiration from the colonial-era projects of Christian missionaries, including in Egypt where Islamist organizations like the Muslim Brotherhood were determined to "fight [missionaries] with their own weapons."[24] Within the revivalist circles I researched, promiscuous appropriation goes beyond skilled instrumentality and, indeed, beyond a desire to convert or confound the conversion attempts of others. Borrowing was reasoned to be a moral good grounded in the Qur'anic ideal of *taʿarruf*, of mutuality and engagement. In chapter 5, I discuss the ways *taʿarruf* as an Islamic ethic informed my interlocutors' revolutionary aspirations for coexistence across difference. Here, I focus on how this theologically grounded ethos of engagement grounded their media innovation.

As he stood on the Sawy stage, Hosny played to his audience a few songs from his album with Selim. The music reverberated over the blue-black waves of the Nile. At the end of each song, most of the listeners applauded. But mixed in with the enthusiasm was a dash of skepticism. It expressed itself that evening in the form of a question scribbled on one of the small pieces of paper that uniformed volunteers passed up in batches to Hosny. Instead of working with a pop star, why had Hosny not collaborated with an Islamic devotional performer (*munshid Islami*)? Looking up from the paper, Hosny walked over to the edge of the stage.

"We can't be here," he said, pointing to his feet, "and the rest of society over there." He gestured to the opposite edge of the stage. "If we had used an Islamic *munshid*, only the pious would have bought the CD and these people are tired of religion themselves," Hosny had replied. "They want to hear some music! When a pious guy . . . hears the latest song by [pop star] Amr Diab, he makes a big show of being morally offended, but he is tapping his foot to the beat. But the balanced person (*al-insan al-sawi*) who attends religious lessons but also has fun, he doesn't have this hunger, so when he . . . hears this type of music, he is unaffected because he already has alternatives to listen to. And that is our goal with this album, to create an alternative."

Subverting the idea of piety as categorically antagonistic to mainstream culture was thus one of Hosny's aims in working with Selim, an entertainer with wide appeal and no previous links to the Islamic Revival. Adopting the largely Westernized aesthetics of Egyptian popular culture made manifest the mutuality of *ta'arruf* as both an important aim for new forms of Islamic media in a deeply polarized society and an intrinsic quality of the life such media promoted as godly. "The godly person is nonconfrontational (*ghayr sidami*)," Hosny told attendees. "He lives with the people, with the good and the bad among them, and he doesn't see the bad as just bad. We are all the same, just some of us have knowledge of things that the other person still doesn't. So [the godly person] embraces all [people], he works within their culture and technology.... If this embrace (*ihtidan*) is not there, we will end up with the two extremes of the lax (*sayyibin*) and the fanatical (*mutashaddidin*)."

In this way, the theological feasibility of *ta'arruf* as an everyday ethic depended on the existence of entertainment options responsive to divine dictate. To distinguish this kind of cultural production from the secular Westernized one indifferent to religious convictions, as discussed in the previous chapter, the producers I worked with used the shorthand *al-fann al-hadif*, literally, "purposeful art," better glossed in English as "ethical entertainment." A similar emphasis on making and consuming morally correct and/or socially impactful leisure activities has become prevalent over the past decade within Islamic activist circles in both Muslim-majority societies and the West.[25] Within Egypt, the New Preachers have advocated for the religious permissibility of these kinds of artistic productions and contributed the most to their growing currency among urban middle-class participants in the Islamic Revival.

The promiscuity of New Preaching publicity, its appropriation of entertainment forms for *da'wa*, provoked criticism from Salafi participants in the piety movement. Egypt's leading Salafi preachers have long criticized popular culture as incompatible with religious virtue. As Charles Hirschkind shows, the disciplined audition of their cassette sermons in the 1990s enacted an Islamic counterpublic that distinguished itself from a secular sphere indexed most prominently by the entertainment industry.[26] Definitionally oppositional, counterpublics organize around discourses and performative modes that are distinct from those of the dominant public sphere. In this way, counterpublics are simultaneously enclaves of withdrawal from mainstream norms and sensibilities and terrains of action geared at forging alternatives to them.[27] The Salafi counterpublic of cassette sermon audition was a response to the troubling "Westernized" sensibilities ostensibly attending media like films, music, or television drama, media that threaten to overwhelm Muslims. From the Salafi perspective, the New Preachers' appropriation of mass entertainment forms for preaching and their public support for performing artists constituted an insidious colonization of the piety movement's Islamic counterpublic by the secular sensorium of Egypt's dominant public sphere.

The Salafi counterpublic's rejection of mainstream cultural forms is similar to other conservative religious groups concerned with maintaining their distinctiveness. This is often done not just through social abstention from mainstream culture but also through doctrinally calling attention to the hazards posed by "external" media. For example, Ayala Fader shows how ultra-Orthodox rabbis in New York City evaluated the internet as a bigger threat to Jewish moral life than the Holocaust.[28] Likewise, Salafi sermonizers argued that to cultivate piety, Muslims must avoid entertainment media and disavow those who produce and consume it. Indeed, Salafi television preachers devote much airtime to disparaging the New Preachers as *shuyukh al-fannanat*, "women artists" being in this Salafi theological imaginary the only group who could possibly take their religious claims seriously. In doing so, the New Preachers exposed themselves as *ahl al-bid'a*, as heretical innovators.

Crucial to this evaluation is the specific interpretation of *bid'a* within Salafi theology as that which lacks Prophetic precedent in both the ritual and social realms. The Salafi antithesis of *ahl al-bid'a* is *al-firqa al-najiya*, the saved sect. According to a Prophetic tradition, the Muslim community will be divided into seventy-three sects, only one of which will enter Paradise. The saved sect comprises Muslims who hew to the Prophet and his Companions' understanding and practice of religion, an understanding not bound by time and space but essential for all time and every space by its own temporal-spatial proximity to the moment of revelation. In an important sense, the saved sect is not a sect at all—it is Islam itself, the original Islam of the *salaf*, the first Muslim community, before the advent of interpretive disputes and foreign influences. Most modern Salafis, including Egyptian Salafis,[29] understand themselves as the only present-day adherents to the correct religious creed and praxis—as the saved sect—and maintaining a distinctive visibility is key to that self-determination. Indeed, central to Salafi piety is the idea that correct belief includes mimetic fidelity to the Prophet's sartorial appearance and social practice. As Aaron Rock-Singer shows, far from being "superficial" markers of religiosity, as critics charge, within Egyptian Salafism wearing hemmed pants, growing a long beard, and maintaining strict gender segregation are of great importance in terms of visually signifying orthodoxy.[30]

Belonging to the saved sect also necessitates a particular ethical response toward the nonsaved, that of repudiation, as well as the cultivation of feelings of hatred (*bughd*) and enmity (*'adawa*) toward them. This sociability is thematized through the doctrine of *al-wala' wa-l-bara'*, or loyalty and disavowal, a standard topic of Salafi sermons in which it figures as a foundational aspect in the struggle against *bid'a*. Salafi Wahhabi scholars recuperated the doctrine in the modern period to govern interaction and sociability not just between Muslims and non-Muslims but also among Muslims themselves.[31] Thus, the doctrine became directed at Muslims engaging in "un-Islamic" practices, including their own non-disavowal of "non-Muslim ways," evinced, for example, in their names, dress, gestures, comportment, or media choices. Within the Egyptian piety movement after the new millennium, this doctrine was important for the Salafi rejection of media that adopts the sonic and visual aesthetics of mainstream entertainment even while claiming a religious mission. In one representative criticism, the outspoken Salafi preacher Wagdy Ghoneim wonders how the New Preachers could even consider themselves Islamic preachers when they neither look Islamic—being unbearded or insufficiently bearded—nor draw exclusively on the Qur'an and the Sunnah in their homiletics, marshaling instead references from popular culture to philosophy to poetry. "If [preachers] don't limit themselves to God-says/the-Prophet-said, you should know then that they are quacks," Ghoneim argued in a television program excerpted on YouTube. As we saw, this is precisely the *da'wa* form that Iqraa producers on Hosny's team abjure as boring and conventional. But for Ghoneim, *for da'wa to be da'wa*—for preaching to be truly Islamic—it must exclusively adhere to this putatively "pure" discursive form.

My interlocutors at Iqraa were troubled by the sense of moral superiority attending this Salafi counterpublic. At its most controversial, this sense of superiority fueled the separatist militancy of groups such as Al-Takfir wal Hijra in the 1970s, whose leaders argued that true believers must repudiate an immoral wider society by withdrawing and creating enclaves of virtuous resistance, in this way making a *hijra*, or migration, akin to that of the Prophet from idolatrous Mecca to faithful Medina. My interlocutors saw a version of this holier-than-thou separatism within even Egypt's peaceful and nonmilitant mainstream Salafi movement and saw their "innovative" media as a critical response to it. Hosny invariably defended his frequent collaborations with some of Egypt's biggest pop singers in theological terms, arguing that a person committing sins could still be a person who loves God and God commands us to respect all human beings, even if they sometimes err. "Who are we exactly to refuse to collaborate with a person who has sins—are we ourselves without sins?" he wrote in a 2013 Facebook post responding to criticisms that yet another pop star had done the titre for his program that Ramadan. "We all have sins, myself included." If an entertainer wants to collaborate on a work of ethical benefit, the last thing "the pious" should do is to deny them the opportunity.

Significantly, the New Preachers' theological investment in ethical entertainment made secular-minded Egyptians as anxious as Salafi-identifying ones, but for the opposite reason. Rather than worrying that religion would cease to be properly religious through illegitimate innovation, these observers fret that art would no longer be truly artistic once governed by theological criteria. An Egyptian diplomat who overheard me speaking about my research at a social gathering in 2012 was quick to interject that it was hard for him to wrap his head around something like an Islamic music video: "What is the point of taking something that is not Islamic and pretending it is? What does religion have to do with entertainment or creativity?" For him, as for Egyptian film stars and directors concerned about the overly chaste aesthetics of "clean films,"[32] an important aim of art is to question norms and transgress tradition, not hew to them.

Seeking a middle ground between the secular jettisoning of tradition as inimical to innovation and the Salafi notion of tradition as repetition untainted by novelty, the New Preachers aspired to an Islamic media that would bridge Egypt's divides. What made their *da'wa* a revolution within Islamic media was that it was expansive enough in both content and form to potentially dissolve the exclusionary distinctions on which all counterpublics are based. To be sure, the New Preachers share with their Salafi counterparts the assessment that the sensuous effects of entertainment are powerful and potentially morally perilous. In an episode in his 2012 Ramadan series *Worldly Enchantments*, Hosny proposed that modern entertainment is beguiling: it entrances us, potentially corrupting our *fitra*, our divinely given natural disposition. Many Muslims, including the devout, watch without batting an eyelid the passionate kisses and embraces of cinema stars. This indifference to religiously impermissible visual depictions—evidenced by not, say, jumping up and switching the channel—is a troubling sign that *fitra* has become corrupted. People nowadays are no longer in control as entertainment media has reshaped their lifestyles. This wasn't always so—previous generations would be embarrassed at such scenes, visibly flustered, covering the eyes of their children in shame before averting their own eyes. That such strong reactions are now uncommon is a troubling testament to the power of entertainment.[33]

But it is precisely entertainment's power to affect us thus that makes its skilled exploitation theologically incumbent on Islamic preachers as professional promoters of piety. As one producer who worked on the series told me: "We don't want the eye to get tired. Dazzlement in regular media is a half-naked Lebanese woman singing. How do we get dazzlement in religious media? Through the capacity of the camera." And so Iqraa allocated a bigger than usual budget to *Worldly Enchantments* while shooting the series on location in "dazzling" cities like Dubai and Istanbul. A critique of the world's enchantments had itself to be enchanting to be effective. There are no qualms here about Muslims consuming *da'wa* media as entertainment[34]— that is precisely what Iqraa producers deemed to be their revolutionary goal.

DAZZLING *DAʿWA*

Emad was fond of reminding the producers he managed that "television is not radio." This refrain was almost a mantra at Iqraa. It was a reminder that television called for content that was qualitatively different from exclusively auditory media. And it was also a critique of "others" within the social world of Islamic television—that is, Salafi channels—who seemingly did not grasp this distinction and treated television as if it *were* radio.

"I could give my back to the television screen or close my eyes, and my experience of the program wouldn't change," Emad elaborated. "Their notion of *daʿwa* is very conventional (*taqlidi*): basically, a preacher just sitting in front of the camera and speaking."

Hosny's producers used the negative label *conventional* as a shorthand for programs adhering too closely to the genre of direct *daʿwa*, *daʿwa mubashira*, further glossed as "God-says/the-Prophet-said." Programs in this mold featured a preacher in a studio setting narrating Qur'anic stories or events from the Prophet's and his Companions' lives, or else the program pivoted around moral exhortation that exclusively cited Qur'anic verses and Prophetic sayings. For Iqraa's professionally trained directors, cinematographers, and editors, this style did not present opportunities for *ibdaʿ*, for creative innovation.

By contrast, Emad and the rest of Hosny's team at Iqraa wanted "to create religious media that is close to viewers' lives, not far from life like the Salafis," he said. "We can do this by using nonreligious tools such as songs or acting within the *daʿwa* program, but also by talking about things that matter to them, like dating, leisure, or studying." From this perspective, the narrowness of Salafi piety—its doom-and-gloom (*ghamm wa-hamm*) tenor and disconnect from everyday life—was reflected in the narrowness of its televised *daʿwa* forms. Indeed, the problem with Salafi television preaching was not just its seemingly irrelevant message but its indifference to the medium as the message. Instead of what they derided as *daʿwa mubashira*, direct *daʿwa*, my interlocutors at Iqraa sought to produce *daʿwa mubhira*, dazzling *daʿwa*.

Dazzlement, *ibhar*, is intimately linked to the visual—its root is *bahara*, which means to "glitter, to shine, to dazzle, to overwhelm the eyes."[35] Dazzlement encompasses being sensuously moved. Its Arabic etymology suggests a telltale sign of its achievement: *bahara*, to dazzle, is closely related to the verb *buhira*, to be out of breath. To dazzle is to be breathtaking. Iqraa producers presumed that their Class A and Class B Plus viewers have "seen it all," so to dazzle them—the thinking went—an Islamic preaching program had to be as visually sophisticated as the entertainment media they regularly consumed. The more that a preaching program broke with the conventional mold of a person speaking directly to the camera, the better chance it had of competing for the attention of "ordinary youth" against the trivial dramas airing on mainstream channels.

Iqraa producers' stress on visual dazzlement was part of a broader set of industry assumptions about how to capture audience attention. Chihab El Khachab shows how Egyptian filmmakers desired to participate in what they identified as a "global trend toward increasing bedazzlement (*ibhar*) in motion pictures entertainment."[36] Dazzlement is an effect of production skill evidenced by audience reaction: *How did they do that?* was the question that should be ideally provoked by the captivating, "magical" effect of skillful camerawork and editing in tandem with artful storytelling. The filmmakers he worked with ascribed dazzlement to the cinematic big screen, with Hollywood blockbusters setting the standard. While lacking the big budgets and technical resources of cinema, my interlocutors in Islamic television also aspired to what they called "cinema quality" within their small-screen productions. Within this ambition was the premise, both tacit and explicit, that the visual had tremendous ethical potential.

When I asked what made television so different from radio for preaching, many of my interlocutors answered by ranking different media technologies based on the level of sensory engagement they felt each demanded. Iqraa's director Sallam explained that reading was more passive than listening, which itself was more passive than watching. You don't have to be really engaged when you are listening to the radio; you can easily multitask—you can be driving, for example, or doing housework. But with television you must keep your eyes trained on the screen if you want to understand what is happening. When it comes to *da'wa*, he went on, "radio is stronger than print and television is stronger than radio. But one-way television [programs that are monologic] is less powerful than interactive television [programs that elicit viewer participation]."

Sallam's sensory rankings have a long history within communication studies. The famed midcentury media theorist Marshall McLuhan characterized television as a "very involving medium" that creates in viewers an inward sense of collective participation in broadcast events, making television "addictive."[37] Similarly, one of the first Egyptian books on television contends that television, unlike radio, had a unique capacity to provoke a sense of synchronous participation within viewers by "monopolizing" the senses.[38] The authors published this book after the country's first television broadcast to explain the sensory effects of the new medium to Egyptians from "the peasant to the professor." Anticipating McLuhan, they argued that television's "magic" lies in its capacity for sensory responsiveness as viewers become immersed in the on-screen world as if they were experiencing it directly. Television's immersive tunneling of attention, the training of both sight and audition onto a small square, "beguiles," causing many to spend more time mesmerized by the flickering screen in their living room than they would listening to radio sets or reading newspapers.

Fifty years later, my interlocutors continued to reflect on what made television "magical" or "addictive" and on how to harness this quality to mass mediate Islam in innovative and creative ways. To remain indifferent to the affordances of television, to treat it as if were merely radio with a screen, amounted to a shirking of the ethical duties incumbent on being a professional promoter of piety. Islamic television didn't have to be dull and difficult. It could be dazzling. From this perspective, then, not only is television *not* radio, but television is also *better* than radio for the cultivation of a pious sensorium.

As the next two sections show, for my interlocutors in Islamic media the power of television as a dazzling technology of piety lies in two aspects. One is its ability to provoke a vivid sense of a place or event, its capacity to make you feel like you are there, including in the miraculous time of divine revelation, the time of the Qur'an. A second power of television is its capacity to forge a sense of intimate connection between the preacher and his viewers across the barrier of the screen.

VISUAL PIETY

In Egypt, as in other Muslim-majority countries, the Qur'an is above all aurally encountered, with Qur'anic recitation the soundtrack of much of daily life.[39] So much so, my interlocutors argued, that most Egyptians have become "bored by the Qur'an."⁴⁰ This troubling development calls for new ways of reexperiencing divine revelation. The Qur'an's "electric effect" on its immediate recipients had been dulled by familiarity and needed innovative media strategies to be experienced anew as dazzling. Dazzlement thus aimed to induce in contemporary viewers the original response of the Qur'an's original audience, and the strategies for its production were visually oriented.

My interlocutors' stress on the visual as a space of pious possibility disrupts the conventional notion that, of the Abrahamic religions, Christianity is the "most visual" and that Islam, by contrast, is centered more around "technologies of the voice." Indeed, there is a stress on audition in analyses of Muslim piety, with anthropologists examining in detail *daʿwa* formations in which listening is "privileged as the sensory activity most essential to moral conduct."⁴¹ This emphasis has led to rich anthropological theorizations of what it means to "sound Islam."⁴² There is much less comparable attention to the role of images and visual technologies in creating the experiential conditions of Muslim piety. A notable exception is Jacquelene Brinton's astute study of Shaykh Shaʿrawi (1911–1998), one of the first preachers to appear on television and whose Friday sermons on state television were watched by millions of people. Brinton calls attention to how the recurrent visual encounter with Shaʿrawi through decades of watching led many people to see him as saintly and to bestow on prints of his image the capacity to bless, to be a source of *baraka*. Images, whether still or moving, thus enabled positive assessments of the preacher's own piety and the ability of his dedicated followers to hone their own, giving rise to new forms of visual piety in Egypt.⁴³ Theorizing the visual through the Islamic was also important to my own early research on the New Preachers.⁴⁴ Still, there remains a widespread scholarly perception that Islam is a peculiarly aniconic, if not iconoclastic, religion.⁴⁵

To be sure, there is a long-standing theological thematization of prohibitions on making images of ensouled creatures, of humans and animals. Salafi preachers in their programs regularly invoked the religious dangers of dolls in playrooms and portraits in living rooms, for example, or even of gazing too long at oneself in the bathroom mirror—or, perhaps, of owning a photograph of Shaʿrawi. Such objects and practices open the door to being entranced by something other than God, a step in a slippery slope to idolatry, to *shirk*, the ultimate sin. To recuperate the few salvific benefits of the televisual and avoid its many harms, Salafi preachers advise their viewers to watch only their own *shirk*-free, deliberately undazzling channels. Visual technologies, whether photography or television, were to be approached at best with caution, not embraced, precisely because of their enchanting effects.[46]

For my interlocutors, however, Islam's "sensational forms," what Birgit Meyer defines as the "modes for invoking and organizing access to the transcendental,"[47] went beyond the aural to include the visual. Iqraa producers' investment in dazzlement as above all a visual experience was informed not only by media industry standards and discourses but also by theologically grounded evaluations of the nature of divine revelation itself. The Qur'an itself anticipates the sensorially immersive quality of television. The "directness" of Salafi *da'wa* modes does not do justice to God's own vivid rendition of stories, moments, and events in such a way that they seem immediate, unfolding in an imaginative three-dimensional space that—much like television—seamlessly incorporates the audience. The Qur'an had "dazzled" the Arabs at the time of its revelation, the New Preacher Amr Khaled argued.[48] However, the dazzling effect of its original revelation has not been stable across time and space but has instead required ongoing strategies of mediation attuned to changing contexts of reception.

The New Preaching emphasis on the way in which God's final message is replete with "dazzling" images is not new. The visuality of the Qur'an had been influentially explored by the mid-century Egyptian literary critic turned Islamist intellectual Sayyid Qutb. Arguing that classical Qur'anic commentaries had overlooked the aesthetic dimensions of the divine text, Qutb focused on what he called the Qur'an's *taswir fanni*, its imaging modes, to convey to his contemporary readers the experiential intensity of the first encounter with the divine text. As Issa Boullata explains, Qutb felt that "when a person reads the Qur'anic text or listens to it, he is transported, through its words, to another level of reality in which he forgets that he is being exposed to words; he imagines he sees actual scenes as they unfold, watches real events as they happen, and witnesses existing persons as they act."[49] Qutb's interpretation of Qur'anic verses as "scenes" evinced a cinematic imagination that informed the "word as camera style" of popular Salafi cassette sermonizers in the 1980s and '90s.[50]

Like their Salafi rivals, the New Preachers' *da'wa* style is characterized by *taswir*. From the start of his career at Iqraa, Hosny employed highly visual language in his preaching, asking his audiences, for example, to imagine themselves approaching the gates of Paradise or to see in their mind's eye the Prophet smiling as he greets them.[51] But unlike Salafi preachers, the New Preachers aspired to go beyond the "word as camera" style to produce a dazzling *da'wa* centered on the immersive affordances of physical, not metaphorical, cameras.

One important strategy of dazzling *da'wa* was the elaborate visualization of Qur'anic stories and events from the life of Prophet Muhammad and his Companions. For example, in an episode of his Iqraa series *'Ala Khuta al-Habib (On the Path of the Beloved)*, Khaled, dressed in a striped polo and sneakers, retraces with his camera crew the Prophet's ascent up Mount Thawr in Saudi Arabia.[52] There the Messenger of God hid with his Companion Abu Bakr for three days, on his way to sanctuary in Medina after leaving his beloved birthplace of Mecca. Khaled framed finding the cave at the top of mountain as the climax of the Prophet's hijra, a dramatic journey that millions of pilgrims re-create each year.

"Why did we choose to film this?" Khaled asks his audience at the beginning of the hike up. "Because we want to feel like we are there with the Prophet living this moment of the birth of Islam, the birth of the glorious history of Islam." A hiking hour later, Khaled is on a ledge further up the mountainside. "Those of us filming this are all really tired and thirsty," he shares. As it is Ramadan, he and the film crew are fasting. "But we are all feeling the effort the Prophet exerted for the sake of the Message."

In the next scene the sweat beads up on Khaled's brow. He is visibly out of breath. He is finally at the entrance of the cave, where during the Prophet's time a spider had miraculously woven a web to mislead the disbelieving tribe members meaning to harm the Beloved.

"As we are climbing and filming, we are all feeling a strange nearness to the Prophet. We started at 6 a.m. and it is now"—Khaled glances at his watch—"9:15 a.m. Three hours! We did this climb with the sole intention of showing you the effort the Prophet expended. We could have filmed in the air-conditioned studio. We could have filmed when we were not fasting. But this sweat [he points to his brow], this sweat reminds us of the Prophet."

Khaled calls viewers' attention to the spatial-temporal compression afforded by television. Through the capacity of the camera to capture the preacher's physically belabored journey to this sanctified site, we at home watching can ourselves remember, feel, and even appreciate the Prophet in a new way. This on-camera reflection on the affordances of the camera was a signature of Khaled's programs. In his two-season series *Qissas min al-Qur'an* (*Stories from the Qur'an*), broadcast first on Resala, we see him knee-deep with rolled-up sleeves in a sunlit river, a straw basket bobbing gently. He imagines out loud what Moses's mother must have felt at this difficult moment of separation. The pathos of the instrumental music backgrounds Khaled's passionate rehearsal of God's promise: "We will certainly return him to you, and make him one of the messengers" (Qur'an 28:7). Toward the end of the series, Khaled gives viewers the ultimate gift: the ability to "see for themselves" one of God's miracles. At one of the twelve sites where Moses pounded his magic staff to let water gush up from dusty rock, Khaled preaches: "Thank you O God for bringing us all here to see. We [as Muslims] of course believe in the Unseen (*al-ghayb*). But still God left a miracle for us to see with our own eyes."

He looks directly to the camera: "Do you want to prostrate to God right now? Do it. Submit to His Power and Majesty. I am speaking to you all from my heart because I am seeing with my own eyes this divine miracle." Khaled gestures to the water cascading behind him: "Look at this scene! . . . Have you ever seen this before? . . . I don't think anyone has ever filmed this before."

When this series aired in 2007, Khaled was the most watched television preacher in the Arab world. By the time of my fieldwork just three years later, we had seen it before and many had filmed it already. The Islamic television producers I worked with no longer evaluated Khaled's preaching style and content as dazzling, but rather as over-the-top, contrived, and awkwardly sentimental. These shifting appraisals point to the ways in which images are not inherently powerful—"dazzling," in the phrasing of my interlocutors—but become so through shared seeing and historically formed ocular expectations.[53] It is the skill of production to shape, recognize, and even anticipate those expectations, which could change dramatically from one blockbuster film or viral TV series to the next, for, as one Iqraa producer put it to me, "If you are bored with the image, you won't even hear what is being said"—even if what is being said is the word of God. This concern underwrote dazzling *daʿwa*'s second main strategy: the cultivation of a new kind of intimacy with the preacher that would engender deeper intimacy with the divine.

INTIMATE INNOVATIONS

"I want to make media that creates a real relationship (*ʿilaqa haqiqiyya*) between people and God," Ahmed Abu Haiba shares as he passes me a plate of cookies across his desk. "But the competition and everyday problems of this industry makes it easy to forget that intention, until God sends a kind person like you to ask me what the point of all of this is."

An affable middle-aged man with an impish grin and a trim goatee, Abu Haiba is a legend within Islamic television. Dubbed "the maestro of Islamic media" by the *New York Times*, his CV is a chronology of the industry's most significant milestones. We first met in 2010 in his swanky office at 4Shbab, a channel he was promoting as the "Islamic answer" to MTV, the famous US music video channel.[54] Before that he served as the inaugural program director of Resala, branding the channel as the edgier, more entertaining successor to Iqraa and the ethical, more edifying alternative to MBC, the biggest pan-Arab entertainment channel. Abu Haiba is also a playwright and novelist but his biggest claim to fame is that he produced his friend Amr Khaled's first television program in 1998.

At the time, Khaled was informally preaching in sports clubs and private homes. Abu Haiba decided to take his heartfelt style on-screen. He rented a studio and filmed several episodes with a live audience of a show he titled *Kalam min al-Qalb* (*Words from the Heart*). No channel wanted the program initially. Abu Haiba was forced to release it on videotape and peddlers sold copies on the sidewalk amid used clothing and cheap kitchenware. It became enough of a street sensation for Egypt's first private television channel, Dream, to acquire it and for Iqraa's founder Kamel to take notice. The Islamic channel was struggling to find ways to broadcast Islamic media that was fresh and exciting while remaining economically viable. Khaled's preaching fit both criteria. When The Shaykh came calling, Khaled didn't have to do much to convince Abu Haiba to annul his exclusivity agreement. The two friends agreed that they were in it "for God." Egyptian creativity calibrated with Saudi capital, they felt, would be an unstoppable force that would revolutionize Islamic media.

Indeed, across all his different media ventures, Abu Haiba's ambition was clear: to take Islamic media in innovative directions so that it could compete with the glitz and glam of secular entertainment while offering a compelling alternative to Salafism.[55] Intimacy was as important as dazzlement to this aim. Abu Haiba felt that the prevalence of Salafi media had led to the perception that the appropriate relationship to God was a fearful one. Salafi preachers came off as stern judges on the constant lookout for how people were falling short of divine commands. An important aspect of innovation in Islamic media thus centered on promoting an alternative relation to the divine, one grounded in intimacy, not fear. "I want people to be able to talk about God like they are talking about a friend," he shared during our interview. "With a sense of affection that comes from really knowing God." The Arabic word I am translating as "intimacy" is *hamimiya*, the root of which is *hamim*, which means "close" or "dear." *Hamim* can refer to a particular quality of friendship; in the Qur'anic lexicon it connotes a devoted friend. Through intimacy with the preacher, one cultivates a close relationship to God. In other words, to "really know God," as Abu Haiba put it, you have to feel like you really know the preacher.

To do so, Abu Haiba, like other Islamic media producers, believed that it was imperative to move away from a "conventional presentation of religion." Among Abu Haiba's inspirations for *Words from the Heart* was the melodramatic testimonials of Christian televangelism. The idea of moving beyond stories from the Qur'an and Islamic history, and to include instead the real-life stories of ordinary people "speaking from the heart" about religion, was a novel one. "I believed that if we did this with Islam," Abu Haiba told an interviewer, "it would be a new experience for Islam."[56] The series was participatory and interactive, with Khaled inviting spontaneous reflections from the studio audience. Unlike the highly specialized and circumscribed jurisprudential domain of fatwa talk—which as we have seen the New Preachers steered clear of—heart talk was an inclusive genre of public comment. Dazzlement was crucial to getting people's attention, but intimacy was key to sustaining piety.

Over the next twenty years, *Words from the Heart* became closely associated with a succession of newer New Preachers. When the series first aired, however, its resemblance to Christian televangelism was negatively noted. The secularist magazine *Rose al-Youssef* ran a cover-story "exposé" in 2006 juxtaposing a photo of Amr Khaled with that of the Egyptian Protestant preacher Maurice Sameh. It gave credence to the widely circulating rumor that the Islamic preacher had attended Sameh's Sunday services, sitting in the back to take notes. The New Preacher's emphasis on developing a loving "relationship" to God was seen as an unseemly imitation, if not "theft," of the popular Protestant preacher's style.[57]

During our interview, Abu Haiba dismissed these concerns about appropriation as missing the point. He explained that what he called "televangelism" was above all a "media technique, a style," open to adoption by religious television producers from any tradition, whether Muslim or Hindu. He also stressed that the idea of loving intimacy with God has always been essential to Islam, and that critics only perceived it as novel because of the dominance of Salafism within the *da'wa* movement. In adopting the style of Christian televangelism he was merely giving a timeless religious truth a new, contemporary form—much like Christian preachers themselves. Still, by televising heart talk, by centering ordinary people's "personal feelings," Abu Haiba created a new ideal for Islamic media. The preaching program would be a mass-mediated *fadfada*, a colloquialism for conversational exchange that is intimate and from the heart, the kind of conversation you would have with your best friend over tea and cookies or late into the night on the phone. That a few tears would be shed during such talk is only natural, and so Khaled's guests and studio audience often cried. Abu Haiba augmented the affective power of such tearful moments through dexterous editing and well-chosen sonic accompaniment.[58]

Importantly, *fadfada* as media innovation hinged not only on audience self-disclosure, but also the preacher's. Iqraa's producers imagined that part of instilling love in ordinary youth for Quranic and Prophetic imperatives was having the preacher himself, not just "ordinary people," speak about his attempts and failures—his ups-and-downs—to get closer to God and embody the Prophet's praxis in a way that was moving and memorable, frank and heartfelt. Practitioners commonly gloss this type of performance as belonging to *al-raqa'iq*, a genre aiming to "soften the heart" to make it more receptive to divine dictate. Producers hoped that sharing the preacher's struggles would cultivate a sense of closeness with viewers and motivate them to reform themselves.

One of Iqraa's most widely watched programs, *Tariq al-Sah* (*The Right Path*), exemplifies this strategy. Airing in Ramadan of 2007, it was the New Preacher Moez Masoud's first Arabic-language program for the channel and it led to him becoming much better known among Egyptian audiences. Its major theme was the stock New Preaching one that piety, far from being an onerous renunciation of worldly delights, was a condition easily attained within an aspirational middle-class life of movie watching, music listening, and museum visiting. Producers during my fieldwork wistfully remembered the program, which was shot in scenic locations such as London streets and Red Sea waters, as setting the standard for a dazzling *daʿwa* that their limited budgets could only rarely attain. But what also made *The Right Path* so innovative was how much it centered on the preacher's own journey from laxity to piety. Masoud came from an affluent background marked by a liberal lifestyle of partying. After three of his close friends died in quick succession, one in a drunk-driving accident, Masoud experienced an existential crisis that led him to "search for God."

Masoud's pious transformation was narrated in a deeply personal way. In an early interview Masoud said that he did not aim to persuade people through "preaching," but simply through "telling the story" of his own and others' paths to pious persuasion.[59] This required reflecting on past sins. In one episode, for example, he is standing in the main square of Covent Garden in London, a popular leisure destination with many bars. He says that this is a familiar scene for him but he is looking at it through a new lens—not one of desire, but of pity. "I used to love traveling abroad so I could come to places like this and get away from all those constraints we have [in Egypt]. I lived this life before, I know it very well."

My interlocutors at Iqraa took the series as a highly successful example of how to connect with the travails and temptations confronting middle-class youth. Masoud's capacity to explore his past mistakes was what made him such a compelling moral exemplar. Still, Salafi preachers criticized this narration of past sins as itself sinful. They argued that the Prophet cautioned Muslims to keep their sins private because their mass mediation could lead to their social normalization. I broached this point with Zayna and Nashwa, two producers on Hosny's Iqraa team, during a joint interview.

"Well, the religious scholars disagree about this issue," Nashwa replied. "One opinion is that a person shouldn't talk about past sins, that this is between him and God. Another opinion, and this is the one I agree with, says that many youths want to change but feel like there is no hope, that because they have done this or that, God won't accept their repentance. So, if they have as a role model a preacher who says, look, I used to not pray too, but now I pray regularly and on time, then that will give them hope that God will guide them too."

Televising the preacher's story of personal transformation from vice to virtue was more powerful than simply talking about it in the abstract, she felt.

Zayna agreed: "What I like about Moez is what I like about the other New Preachers too: they started out just like us, just ordinary people. They weren't born super pious. So I feel like they are really close to us (*'uraybin minna awi*). They are people who struggle like us, who make mistakes just like us." Talking about past sins was an efficacious strategy of cultivating piety in others so long as the right intention is in place. There is a difference, she went on, between a person who drinks alcohol at night and boasts about it the next morning to his friends and a person who regretfully talks about his previous history of drinking so that others who are still struggling with this vice can feel that their own repentance is within reach.

"We tend to put pious people up on a pedestal, especially if they are famous," Nashwa said, shaking her head. "This gets in the way of making us feel close to them, of making us understand that they are just regular people like us, who commit sins and can feel regret and turn back to God." Nashwa pointed out that in the Qur'an the idea of repentance, *tawba*, is almost always coupled with the idea of reform or making right, *islah*. Repentance wasn't reducible to feelings of contrition but involves redress. For her, the New Preachers were part of that active process of reform and their credibility revolved not around their pious distinction, but on their own struggles to (imperfectly) lead a pious life. "They are just like us," New Preaching fans would invariably say—just a little bit further along the pious path. By contrast, Salafi preachers were "very far" (*bu'ad awi*). The spatial metaphors of nearness and distance capture an emotional sense of intimate connection that was freighted with positive theological significance.

However, the deliberate cultivation of intimate familiarity at times led to morally fraught encounters between the preacher and his fans hinging on their ambivalent texture. Specifically, Islamic media producers were troubled at the idea that some of the interest shown by viewers toward Hosny might be romantic in nature, or perceived as such. Slim and trim with wavy hair and deep brown eyes set in a tanned visage, by any measure he was handsome. This was a quality that the mostly female producers on his media team carefully avoided remarking on, but which his mostly female viewers waxed eloquent about to me and to each other, even as they acknowledged that he was married with two kids. Producers' strategies for creating intimacy at a distance were so successful that some viewers recast their relationship to Hosny as one that could easily extend beyond all screens to more private encounters. Many emailed and called the channel asking for Hosny's personal telephone number. The policy was to refuse these requests. Most people accepted this, but others continued to email or call. Not infrequently a person would cry on the phone, explaining that they were experiencing a "catastrophe" (*musiba*) that only Hosny could solve. In such cases, a member of the media team would try to help, serving as a sort of proxy preacher even though they were as young and inexperienced as the viewers who sought counsel.

The intensity of these interactions left a toll. Halfway through my research, I came upon Zayna sitting in the stairwell of Iqraa's studio building, head between her knees, mobile clutched tightly. She had just hung up with a crying viewer in crisis and was now herself in tears.

"I wish I had a magic lamp to help them," she said as I sat down on the steps next her. "They think because I work for an Islamic channel that I will have all the answers or give the best advice. But I don't know what to say most times! And on top of that I have my own problems to deal with, too."

Another time Zayna was so distressed by a caller's heart-wrenching sobs that she begged Hosny to contact her back. Hosny relented but, in the end, what seemed to the caller to be a problem of grave harm was, from the perspective of Zayna and the preacher, comparatively trivial: her husband was a workaholic who spent all day at the office, and she felt lonely. Hosny wasn't sure what he could do for her and indeed judged it inappropriate that the wife felt that he *could* do something.

Intimacy, like dazzlement, was thus a double-edged sword: while crucial to the realization of a theology of innovation in Islamic media production it was also potentially detrimental to the very piety such innovation aimed to promote.

THE PERILS OF INNOVATION VERSUS THE IMPORTANCE OF STAYING NEW

In the view of the New Preaching producers I worked with, Salafi television's shunning of entertainment media forms discredited it as "conventional." For Salafi-identifying Egyptians, however, this avoidance is precisely what made their channels morally authoritative. This argument was brought home to me early in my fieldwork during a conversation with Zaynab, a family acquaintance who equates television with the Salafi channels and *da'wa* with the Salafi preaching triumvirate of Muhammad Hassan, Abu Ishaq al-Huwayni, and Muhammad Ya'qub. Zaynab enjoyed watching these preachers and felt they offered her practical guidelines for how to live virtuously in what she saw as a largely immoral society. She did not, however, value such preachers for offering "innovative" or "creative" programs; such criteria did not positively enter her viewing calculus the way they did for fans of the New Preachers. To the contrary: Zaynab knew that much of my interest in doing fieldwork at Iqraa stemmed from a curiosity about new forms of Islamic *da'wa*. From her perspective, however, the types of media Iqraa broadcast disqualified it from being an Islamic channel and indicated instead that the New Preachers were new and inventive in the pejorative sense of "inventing a new religion" (*biyikhtu'ru din gadid*).

A few days after our conversation about my research, Zaynab sent me an email with the subject line "the shaykhs' refutation of the New Preachers" with links to YouTube videos presenting Salafi rebuttals of the New Preachers. One was an excerpt from a sermon by al-Huwayni, in which he criticizes the New Preacher Amr Khaled for encouraging newly veiled actresses and singers—the so-called repentant artists[60]—to continue working in the entertainment industry and not abandon it altogether. Al-Huwayni laments that Islamic television channels like Iqraa have given preachers like Khaled a platform to disseminate their erroneous ideas. "It is impossible for a man who has opened up even a single book of religious knowledge to say such words," protested al-Huwayni, claiming that all the Prophetic traditions Khaled uses as evidence for the permissibility of entertainment of whatever kind are fabricated.

"Millions follow [Amr Khaled] and consider him to be illuminating the way [to piety]. But what way is he illuminating? This is a catastrophe." Al-Huwawyni goes on to chastise religious spokespersons like Amr Khaled for being complicit in propagating things that come from the unbelievers (*al-kuffar*):

> We live in a society that is dominated by things contrary to God's religion, and part of the problem is that the people of religion don't want to provoke or be against the masses (*al-'awamm*). For [Amr Khaled] we are not just rigid in our beliefs, we deserve to be silenced because we have made life too hard ... but the Qur'anic verse is clear and self-evident: "If you love God, then follow [the Prophet]." So love means emulation and those who emulate [the Prophet] love God, and those who don't emulate don't love God, even if they swear to God that they do.

Al-Huwayni depicts New Preachers like Amr Khaled as catering to the whims of the masses by giving them a religious license to follow their own base desires. This is an example of *tamyiʿ al-din*, a corruption of religion aimed at making the path of piety more accommodating to attract more viewers and followers for personal gain and ambition. Such corruption is even more egregious in its promiscuous attitude toward dominant secular forms. Al-Huwayni implies that such preachers don't truly love God since they, in his estimation, are not following the Prophetic example. Far from celebrating the aesthetics of televised popular culture and their dazzling capacities for sensory engagement or affective immersion, Salafi preachers enjoin judicious restraint, if not outright censure toward such media. For them, being against such media is what defines an Islamic community.

One Salafi preacher likened new forms of Islamic media to the act of "presenting halal meat in a pig's skin ... this is presenting religion in an impure [*najis*] form." The impurity derives partly from such media frequently having music and singing and showing women on-screen, all prohibited in Salafi orthodoxy. In addition, such content too closely resembled Western entertainment media, rendering Muslims liable to what Salafi preachers deem the sin of imitating nonbelievers. Fearing that I would be led further astray through my fieldwork with the New Preachers, Zaynab urged me to instead research Salafi television channels because they "would never allow the sorts of programs Iqraa broadcasts. How can religion be combined with drama or music? Entertainment is the opposite of religion [*al-fann 'aks al-din*]." For Zaynab, "religion" here was synonymous with the truly Islamic—and thus with God's will, whether in matters of this world or the next—and her evaluation of what made entertainment antithetical to religion turned on the fact that she drew the boundaries between the religious and the secular differently than my Iqraa interlocutors. These boundaries, as we have seen, were doctrinally elaborated.

Over the following several years, Zaynab would continue to send me links to Salafi critiques of the New Preachers, and I began systematically looking for episodes about the New Preachers broadcast on Salafi channels. There were many. For example, in 2010, the Salafi al-Nas channel devoted several episodes to the New Preachers, in which preachers such as Mazin Sirsawi and Khalid Abdullah charged the New Preachers with being "secret Sufis"—Sufis being the epitome of heretical innovation in the Salafi creed—bent on creating what they called a "fake American Islam" that promoted secular norms. Polemics aside, what piqued my interest was the careful attention Salafi preachers devoted to the *form* of New Preaching programs as evidence of their moral turpitude. In one television episode after another, Salafi preachers argued that it was egregious to claim that entertainment forms could be either pleasing to God and the Prophet, or vehicles for praising God and the Prophet.

This is not to say that Salafis' own investment in the changing communicative infrastructure of pious propagation is negligible. In an important way, the history of the Salafi Wahhabi mission—and the enviable authority that the norms propagated by its adherents have come to enjoy within revivalist circles throughout the Muslim world—can be told through the changing technologies of mass publicity that Salafi revivalists have adopted with alacrity over the past two centuries, from the printing press to radio to television to digital media. More to the point, the rhetorical forms of Salafi sermons, notwithstanding their condemnatory substance, draw on disparate traditions, from political speeches to cinematic techniques to Sufism.[61] In censuring the New Preachers as un-Islamic, Salafi preachers are neither self-deluded nor duplicitous about their own *daʿwa* forms; rather, in common with other practitioners across religious traditions, they have come to see some religious media (e.g., a sermon recorded on cassette or on camera) as not in fact mediated in any significant sense, as im-mediate.

Birgit Meyer has aptly characterized this as the problem of "disappearing the medium." Media technologies once subject to intense scrutiny and debate can become routinely accepted as transparently communicative—until their use by new social categories resurfaces their status as transformative human artifacts. In the nineteenth century, for example, printing the Qur'an, hereto handwritten, was seen as problematic; in the twenty-first century, it was the digitization of the printed Qur'an that presented new conundrums about what constitutes the authoritative and authentic mediation of the divine scripture. The same goes for auditory media. At the turn of the twentieth century, new technologies of Qur'anic recitation such as the gramophone, and later the cassette, technologies about which there is little theological debate today—at least, when they are used by men as opposed to women—provoked passionate declamations from Islamic preachers and scholars. Even the microphone incited concern upon its introduction in the 1940s, with Salafi Wahhabi scholars objecting to its use in mosques as lacking Prophetic precedent; today, the mediality of the microphone has vanished for most Muslims. As Meyer argues, mediums can "disappear" or "appear," and that has less to do with their material properties and more to do with the social processes authorizing or contesting their use.[62]

Crucially, the New Preachers' own disparagement of the Salafis for conflating *daʿwa* with "direct" moral exhortation in the mode of God-says/the-Prophet-said also hinged on an assumption that some television performances are more or less mediated than others. Recall Emad's lament that Salafi preachers approach television as if it were radio, exhibiting what he saw as a negligent indifference to the technical-aesthetic affordances of a medium that is at once auditory and visual. Unlike Emad, Salafi television preachers (and Salafi-identifying viewers like Zaynab) lauded their programs as further evidence of their channels' promotion of "true Islam" through genuinely Islamic means, means untainted by religious innovation, especially innovation in the direction of secular cultural forms. The point is that even if Salafi activists may in their own way be as "promiscuous" as their New Preaching counterparts, only the latter explicitly promoted medial innovation through aesthetic appropriation as a theologically justified—and, indeed, enjoined—form of persuasive religious outreach.

"Let's be honest," Nashwa said during the conversation with Zayna, "religion is boring! It is much harder to watch a religious program than to watch a film." Echoing Emad, she argued that a preacher who "appears on television as if he was on the radio" could never compete with the titillating content just a click of the remote away. How to effectively capture attention, how to "get people to actually sit down and watch an entire episode" of a *da'wa* program, was a professional challenge with theological stakes. My interlocutors linked this challenge to innovation, *ibda'*, as a godly attribute. They cited the time the Prophet asked that a building missing a stone be rebuilt, saying to his Companions, "God loves those who undertake their tasks with excellence." This was especially so for those whose work was centrally concerned with promoting piety, Nashwa explained.

"You have to always be keeping up—with the news, with social trends, with what is happening in general," she went on. "We have to constantly think of new things or ideas to discuss or discuss old issues in a new away, so that no one will watch our programs and think *oh, we have seen this a million times*. So you have to stay new, especially as God has put you in a position to help create something beautiful, something that will influence people in a beneficial way."

Nodding in agreement, Zayna added it was a "sin" for Islamic television producers if music video producers were constantly innovating, and they weren't. "The world [of media] is always moving, and we can't just stand still, otherwise the film or serial will always win."

The New Preachers and their producers at Iqraa theologically wove innovation into the very concept of tradition. As they saw it, every generation faces the task of interpreting and adapting foundational texts to remain true to their original spirit while also addressing contemporary needs and possibilities. For members of Hosny's media team, devotion to the Prophetic tradition required constantly changing and adapting Islamic media; otherwise religion risks becoming obsolete, disconnected from the everyday lives of ordinary people. Fidelity to the past required innovation, not imitation. My New Preaching interlocutors' theological construal of innovation as integral to Islam resonates with the common scholarly understanding of Islam as a "discursive tradition" that is "constantly changing" and continually "incorporating newer elements into itself." This framework stresses that Islam is a dynamic, continually transforming, tradition.[63]

Salafi revivalists disagree. Far from being integral to Islamic tradition, innovation threatens tradition insofar as it entails a deviation from the historical forms of Islam as practiced by the Prophet Muhammad and the first pious generations of Muslims. The Salafi critique of the New Preachers orients to divine revelation as possessing a moral efficacy autonomous of mediating human artifacts. Expounding on the Salafi theological construal of Qur'anic language, Hirschkind notes how his interlocutors hold that "when humans fail to be convinced by this [revealed] message, the fault lies not in the words but in the organ of reception, the human heart. The message itself has been articulated in the most perfect of possible forms, the Qur'an."[64] From this Salafi perspective, the New Preachers continually calling attention to the medium as mattering, as something that needs deliberate and creative exploiting in order for a message—including a divine one—to be compelling or resonant to its addressees, is as egregious as their appropriation of Western aesthetics. The Qur'an as God's message to humankind does not need to be packaged, strategized, brainstormed, focus-grouped, or, indeed, inventively mediated. It dazzles on its own.

As we see next, these theological contestations over the means of Islamic propagation are inextricable from internal disagreements over its substantive ends, over what makes a practice virtuous, a public pious, a way of life godly.

Three
MODERATION

I EMPLOYED A RESEARCH ASSISTANT TO CLIP DAILY NEWS ARTICLES related to Islamic television during my fieldwork. While going through a 2010 issue of *al-Masry al-Youm*, an opposition newspaper with liberal leanings, she was struck by a full-page ad Iqraa had placed. Arrayed in a column were the images of four preachers with current programs on the channel: the New Preacher Mustafa Hosny, the Salafi preacher Mahmoud al-Masry; the Muslim Brotherhood–leaning Azhari scholar Yusuf al-Qaradawi, and the state-leaning Azhari scholar Ali Gomaa.

"This is the only place you will ever find these men together," she chuckled. I could understand my assistant's surprise. Salafi preachers were outspoken in their criticism of both the New Preachers and al-Azhar's scholars for promoting in pseudo-pious garb what they deemed secular Westernization. In turn, the latter two groups charged Salafism of contributing to secularization by making Islam repellent to ordinary people. Between the two Azhari preachers was also considerable animus, as the government-appointed chief mufti Gomaa supported the state and had no time for the independently minded Qaradawi, who had since the 1960s been calling out from his exile in Qatar both Salafi intransigence and Azhari acquiescence. Judging by my assistant's response, the ad was successful in conveying a key aspect of Iqraa's brand as a "moderate" channel: here was the Islamic channel you tuned in to when you wanted the diverse gamut of Sunni Islam.

This definition of what made Iqraa "moderate," *wasati*, was reiterated to me by producers at all levels. It was also officially enshrined in the channel's mission statement, which cited the Qur'anic description of Muslims as an exemplary "community of the middle way," *ummatan wasatan* (Qur'an 2:143). Growing up in Egypt in the 1990s, I most often heard this verse cited in the context of a comparison to the other "revealed religions." Islam, someone would casually explain, was balanced between the ascetic spiritualism of Christianity and the pedantic legalism of Judaism. At Iqraa, however, "moderation" as an essential theological attribute of Islam functioned as an internal critique of Muslims. By broadcasting programs and preachers adhering to mutually antagonistic orientations—whether those of Sufism or Salafism, Azharism or Islamism—Iqraa institutionalized moderation by avoiding what the mission statement termed obduracy, *tazammut*, and by facilitating tolerance, *tasammuh*.

An ethos of moderation defined Iqraa's mission from the start. In making the case for why an Islamic satellite channel was necessary, the channel's inaugural director Abdulkader Tash argued that Muslims were caught between two "extremes": secular Westernization and religious fanaticism, *ghuluw*. The paradigmatic example of *ghuluw* are the Kharijites, a group of seventh-century Muslims infamous for judging everyone else as apostates. In the contemporary period, their name has become a shorthand for "an overly pious zealot whose actions and ideas lie beyond the pale of normative Islam."[1] The Prophet had warned that there would be Muslims like the Kharijites, whose outward performance of devotion makes the piety of others look halfhearted, yet "the Qur'an does not go beyond their throats." There are many Muslims like that today, Tash lamented. Their *ghuluw* has contributed to secularization by making Islamic piety seem unattractive and unreachable to the average person. What ordinary Muslims needed was an Islamic channel that would promote "the spirit of true religiosity that is built on moderation in belief and conduct."[2]

Tash's approach was informed by the mainstream Ash'ari theological thematization of orthodoxy as the doctrine of the middle way, of "attaining equilibrium between undue difficulty (*'usr*) and extreme ease (*yusr*)."[3]

Crucially, accepting differences, and the disagreements they provoked, was key to this equilibrium. Tash complained that an intolerance of difference was rife among contemporary Islamic revivalist groups. This was worrying because interpretive pluralism is what enables Islam's universalism, its responsiveness to differences of time and place, and ensures piety's relevance for practitioners. This was the meaning of the famous Prophetic saying that "the differences of my community are a mercy" (*ikhtilaf ummati rahma*). Rejecting this hadith is a sure sign of *ghuluw*, Tash concluded.[4]

In this chapter, I examine the ways in which moderation was doctrinally elaborated, interactionally instantiated, and given institutional form within the social world of the New Preachers, their media producers, and followers. I do so by approaching moderation as a theological concept whose lived significance is dynamically responsive to the shifting social contexts of its invocation. While the limitations of moderation as an analytical concept are self-evident, more ethnographic attention needs to be paid to its social life as a theological concept with everyday stakes. A theology of *wasatiyya*, "moderation," touched on a range of foundational matters of enduring concern to my pious interlocutors, from the connection between the nature of God and human nature, between human interpretation and divine revelation, and between ethics and ritual. At the heart of their interest in moderation was the desire to revolutionize the very concept of "piety" within the Islamic Revival.

As we saw, the New Preachers aspired to reconfigure conventional—that is, Salafi—notions of what piety entailed through creating new forms of Islamic media that showed the path to piety was one of pleasure, not pain. This did not mean, as Hosny warned in one episode of his 2012 series *Worldly Enchantments* dedicated to elucidating "true" versus "fake" moderation, that anything goes, that personal whims trump divine parameters.[5] Moderation was the judicious avoidance of the extremes of *ghuluw*, a righteous excessiveness that leads to fanatical rigidity, and *ghafla*, a heedlessness toward divine parameters that leads to moral degeneracy. These extremes only caused pain, whether in this world or the next, while moderation facilitated both the transient pleasures of ordinary life and the eternal ones of the Afterlife. In terms of Iqraa producers' media interventions, moderation destabilized the conventional markers of piety within the Islamic Revival by appropriating and repurposing for godly ends the conventional signs of "secular" culture, from enterainment preferences to gender norms to interpersonal interactions. These New Preaching elaborations—and their contestation by Salafi preachers, who also claim moderation as their own distinctive virtue[6]—once again reveal the theological instabilities of what counts as "secular" versus "religious" within the Islamic Revival.

Scholarship about moderation in relation to Islamic media has erased these internal instabilities from two directions: either by insisting that self-described moderate Islamic television channels like Iqraa are in reality "extremist"[7] or by analyzing Iqraa and its New Preachers as symptomatic of official efforts to produce an "ecumenical Islam" that is "consonant with the ideas of tolerance and civility propagated by US policy makers."[8] To be sure, it is not just Islamic revivalists who are deeply invested in promoting moderation. After the attacks of 9/11, the propagation of a "moderate Islam" became an important facet of US foreign policy in the Muslim world. For the US and other Western proponents, to be a "moderate Muslim" means to be only lukewarmly attached to living as a Muslim, to hewing to Islamic parameters, and to be more invested in adapting to the "secular" lifestyles dominant in Western liberal societies. This is not how my interlocutors understood moderation. Unlike for Western policymakers, moderation did not entail making Islamic norms less central to everyday life through adopting a notion of piety that works "to refashion Islam along the lines of the Protestant Reformation," rendering religion a matter of individual, private belief.[9] Rather, moderation demanded a renewed attachment to the authority of centuries of "balanced" Islamic theological thought and its practice. These were under threat by both secularism and Salafism.

In making the case for why an Islamic television channel was needed, Tash pointed out that while "for Westerners, extremism is when Muslims try to apply Islam to every facet of life," for Muslims extremism isn't about the desire to hew to God's commands in everything they do, but is rather about trying to exceed them. This religious excess, he explained, was actually and ironically fueled by secularism. "We have secular extremist thought in the Arab world that calls for removing religion from the life of people and society and keeping it only in the mosque," Tash wrote. This instigates a backlash, leading to a religious extremism defined by an intolerance of difference and a sense of moral superiority. Writing in the 1990s at the height of violent attacks in Egypt and other Arab countries carried out by Islamist insurgents, Tash pinpointed the authoritarianism and repression of secular states as their root cause: "Extremism spreads in prisons and through torture." Just as there can be *ghuluw* in piety, there can be *ghuluw* in secularism and Westernization.[10]

Unlike Western policymakers, then, the media producers I worked with understood moderation not in terms of jettisoning pious norms and lifestyles in favor of liberal ones, but rather as a return to an Islamic theological imagination before its secularist disfiguration. Still, for some scholars the very idea of moderation remains an inherently "liberal prophylactic" that is "intimately connected to a larger secular politics of critique that seeks to domesticate and purify religion so as to make it more appetizing for liberal secular governance."[11] In this view, moderation can only reflect Western norms and interests, even if deployed by Muslims in Muslim-majority contexts. Such a privileging of Euro-American security-focused notions of "moderate Islam" not only overlooks the long-standing theological thematization of moderation as a paradigmatic Islamic virtue, but also the local political dynamics and contexts that make this thematization newly salient.[12]

This includes the 2011 revolution. While moderation may seem an inherently conservative stance antithetical to the disruption of the status quo, it was harnessed within the Islamic Revival to articulate a vision of a New Egypt that would transcend the country's entrenched secular versus religious polarization through a theological register. Appearing on the satellite channel al-Hayah during the eighteen days of the uprising, Hosny told the hosts of the program that "we need coexistence and accepting the other not only between Muslims and non-Muslims, but among Muslims." He shared that he had direct experience with all the different Islamic trends in Egypt, and while he appreciated "the good in each," his own authoritative reference was the *wasatiyya* of al-Azhar. During the politically tumultuous period between 2011 and 2013 that followed, the New Preachers would continue to stress the possibilities of moderation for radical yet sustainable collective change. Promoting an ethos of moderation on Islamic television would cultivate a revolutionary piety marked by love, not judgment, by pluralism, not exclusion, and by a concern for others' well-being, not just ritual self-cultivation. Moderation would be the radical basis of the New Egypt.

NATURALLY MODERATE

"We don't have to tie ourselves into psychological knots to be religious. Piety is the most natural thing in the world!" I was at an Asian restaurant in my neighborhood having dinner with Engy, a New Preaching fan I first met at an academic conference in Cairo focused on women, religion, and media. In her early thirties, Engy was a blogger who wrote scathing critiques of cultural attitudes toward women, from the stigma around asking for a divorce to the opprobrium encountered by middle-class mothers who work. As a single, middle-class mother with career ambitions, I appreciated Engy's hard-hitting jibes at patriarchy. From meeting her at the conference, I knew that Engy's critiques extended to what she deemed Salafism's disfiguration of Islamic piety, and this is what we had agreed would be the subject of our interview. As we waited for our appetizers, I turned on my audio recorder and asked Engy what she meant by "psychological knots."

"It is the idea that the more uncomfortable you are feeling, the more pious you are becoming," she elaborated. "This sums up Salafism: religion for them is a burden (*hamm*), and I can tell just by the way their preachers speak about it." She gave me Muhammad Ya'qub as an example. With his flowing snow-white beard and piercing blue eyes, Ya'qub was one of Egypt's most recognizable television preachers. "I can tell from his whole demeanor and from how he speaks that for him religion is this extremely difficult thing. This attitude really impacts my willingness to listen to what he has to say."

She went on: "You know that life here is already stressful, even for those with comfortable means (*al-nas al-mirtaha*). Just to accomplish a simple errand in Cairo is a burden: the pollution is awful, the traffic is terrible, everywhere you turn there is corruption. Yeah, we are here having this nice meal under air conditioning, but I wake up each morning already tired. So when I am learning about my religion, I am looking for someone who will calm me down, not stress me out."

For this reason, Engy preferred the New Preachers even though she had initially found Amr Khaled's distinctively high-pitched voice "really annoying" and had been critical of much of what he had to say. Then she went through a phase "where whatever Amr Khaled said, I took as gospel." By the time of our conversation in 2011, she had developed a more balanced approach: "I am at the point where he may say things I don't agree with, but it is okay. He is not a god, he is not infallible. He is a person and an opinion is just an opinion. He has a right to have an opinion and I have a right not to like it." Still, she regularly watched his new programs because she perceived him, like Moez Masoud and Mustafa Hosny, as expounding a natural religiosity, *taddayun fitri*.

Fitra is a Qur'anic concept referring to human beings' primordial, God-given nature (Qur'an 30:30). It names a positive disposition naturally inclined toward virtue. The stress on Islam as a natural religion, *din al-fitra*, is a hallmark of contemporary Islamic theological discourses. According to the interpretations offered to me, Islam is such in the sense that all humans are created with a disposition to be Muslim, a disposition that may be corrupted by upbringing or environment. But Islam is a natural religion in another sense: its ethical injunctions are in harmony with human nature. Islam does not ask anything of us that we are not already inclined to perform and value. In this theology, divine strictures facilitate the actualization, not repression, of our natural disposition.

This was a key New Preaching theme. In the first episode of his series *Ahla Hayah (The Best Life)*, Hosny explains that God created human beings not only *out* of love but also *to* love the world.[13] He didn't prohibit ordinary pleasures so long as they didn't lead one to commit sins. Many, however, either indulge in worldly delights without consideration for divine parameters or, at the other extreme, renounce the world as inherently corrupting and restrict permissible activities. This goes against the ethos of Islam as a moderate religion attuned to human nature. As we saw earlier, the New Preachers' capacious sense of what counts as Islamic media reflected a broader theological understanding of innovative transformation as intrinsic to Islam. Grounding the New Preaching advocacy for innovative *da'wa* forms was also a particular theological ontology of human nature, one that judged Salafi norms to be as "unnatural" as secular ones. A few days after Hosny launched his *"da'wa* album" with a pop star at the Sawy center, I met up with him for an interview. I asked him to elaborate on entertainment and leisure in relation to Islamic piety. "One of the characteristics of human nature is boredom," he replied.

We don't like to just do one thing all the time. So if religiosity just means I have to pray all day, I will get bored [*ha-azha'*]. If being religious means I have to recite the Qur'an all day long, I will be bored. But naturally Islam is comprehensive of all aspects of life. To have fun is to be godly, otherwise I would have to draw far away from God, have fun, and then come back to Him, which doesn't make sense.

In this theology of attention, being bored or remaining unmoved by religious speech—whether by preachers talking about the Qur'an or by listening to the Qur'an itself—is not due, as some sermonizers would have it, to an inadequate religious formation[14] but to the nature of human beings, to the way God created us. Even the most pious can't pay attention for more than a few hours without becoming distracted and restless. Instead of judging these bored pietists as failures, cater to them, Hosny insisted. Give them a way to be religious *in* the world, not in struggle *with* the world. Give them, in other words, a way to be human as God Himself intended. What should be promoted, then, was a natural piety, sustainable and above all realistic, a piety that fit into the everyday life of Iqraa's Class A and Class B Plus target audiences, the lives of middle-class professionals like Engy.

For my interlocutors, the norms propagated by Salafi revivalists are un-Islamic because they are unnatural: they suppress our God-given desires. Music is an example. "Even babies sway their bodies when they hear music," my colleagues on Hosny's team argued. That small children with an uncorrupted *fitra* would spontaneously move with the music gave evidence that this was a divinely sanctioned human inclination. While certainly the secular bracketing of entertainment as a domain that cannot be governed by religious norms stems from an unbalanced understanding of human nature, as it allows an animalistic drive toward unbridled gratification, the Salafi prohibition of entertainment was no better. It similarly foreclosed as a moral possibility a quality essential to human nature—enjoying life's ordinary pleasures.

To be sure, Salafis also subscribe to the idea of Islam as a natural religion; for them, however, the desire for entertainment is a corrupted one informed by a secular sensibility of what a "normal life" entails. Even athletic pastimes that may seem theologically uncontroversial compared to music and film are doors to impiety. Salafi preachers argue that there is a limited set of leisure activities authorized by the Prophet: taking a walk between prayer times, riding horses, archery, spending time with family, and learning to swim.[15] Anything else—including watching sports on television—distracts from the remembrance of God. For my interlocutors this was another example of how Salafi theology missed what Engy during our interview called "the bigger picture." That the Prophet practiced the usual sports of his time indicated that sports, as such, were permissible for Muslims, not that those were the only ones allowed.

To illustrate how New Preachers grasped "the bigger picture," Engy brought up the Salafi insistence that Muslim men should shorten their pants to emulate the Prophet Muhammad. In the Mecca of the Prophet's time, she explained, some wore clothes that dragged in the dust to show off their wealth. Rejecting the arrogance of this display, the Prophet and his Companions wore shorter clothes. Today, however, the social significance of long versus short garments no longer holds. The way she saw it, in their insistence that wearing short pants was an expression of emulative love for the Prophet, Salafis were ostentatiously displaying their 'superior piety as opposed to making piety practical for the average person. Because shortened pants didn't carry the same ethical significance in twenty-first-century Cairo that they did in seventh-century Mecca, to insist that Muslims must wear them was to impose an unnecessary hardship. Moreover, such mimetic fidelity to the Prophet frequently got in the way of communicating the message he was sent to reveal anew, "the bigger picture." Far from being "lax," *sayyibin*, as their Salafi critics charged they were for not wearing shortened pants, the New Preachers were "realistic," *waqiʿiyyin*.

This theological contestation of what it means to be realistically religious has been lost in the debate within the anthropology of Islam over how to understand the relationship between piety and everyday life. Arguing that "Muslims do not simply want to be good Muslims," Samuli Schielke calls for more ethnographic attention to the "ambivalent commitments" running through ordinary life.[16] In response, Nadia Fadil and Mayanthi Fernando contend that this focus on the "everyday Muslim" betrays a "tacit attachment to a set of secular-liberal sensibilities" that evaluates Salafism as "an impossible and unnatural way of being."[17] This was indeed the view of my interlocutors. For them this did not mean, however, that they were subscribing to secular liberal norms. Indeed, one of the most troubling consequences of Salafism's predominance in grassroots revivalist circles, in their view, was that it made secular lifestyles *more* attractive by promoting a piety that was unrealistic and unnatural.

In our conversation following the album launch, Hosny argued that many pious practitioners had also lost sight of the fact that Islam doesn't separate the world (*al-dunya*) from religion (*al-din*). "A person who makes a distinction between *din* and *dunya* has anxiety in his life," he said.

> This anxiety is caused by his desire to get closer to God and enter Paradise and get away from certain worldly things. But then this person begins not to go to work on time so that he can pray in the mosque, or starts not to go out to visit his relatives or to socialize with his friends so that he can stay at home to read the Qur'an. This creates a fissure in his life, a lack. He should realize that your ordinary self has rights over you (*inna li-nafsik 'alayka haqq*). So one needs to sleep, eat, go out, have fun. And this is all part of *din*.

Hosny's response reminded me of the religious studies scholar W. C. Smith's early observation that "the Islamic is not about being religious, but about being human," for "it is a fallacy growing out of the particularities of the modern West to think of religion as one of the factors in human life, among others."[18] Hosny was trying to recuperate a more comprehensive notion of *din*, of piety, that was the norm before the ruptures of secularism and Salafism alike. If secular Westernization "reduce[s] Islam to folklore, as if Islam is just a collection of ceremonies and customs, such as hanging lanterns from doorways or baking cookies during Ramadan,"[19] Salafism reduces Islam to ritual excellence, as if piety were just about praying and fasting. In this way, Salafis were not promoting piety, but *ghuluw*. And ultimately, this fanaticism stemmed from their unbalanced concept of God Himself.

GOD'S LOVE

An emphasis on divine love was a key aspect of the moderation my interlocutors aimed to propagate within the Islamic Revival. In one recorded lesson from the early 2000s, the New Preacher Amr Khaled lamented that "while hundreds of books and cassettes speak about the love of worshippers for God, very few speak about the love of God for worshippers." This imbalance, he went on, has led to a "relationship with God that is routinized (*rutini*), based only on a sense of obligation."[20] Scholars have noted that love is rarely associated with Islam by Western observers, even though it is a common theme in Islamic theology, especially within the Sufi corpus.[21] While not explicitly identifying with Sufism, the New Preachers drew extensively on the common Sufi theme that God's creation of the universe was motivated by love and that the cultivation of a sense of "friendship with God" was an important aspect of piety.[22] In a more recent book, for example, Khaled explains that God created human beings by blowing His own spirit into us out of love. The human-divine connection "isn't a relationship of Hell and Paradise, it is not a relationship of obligation and restriction, nor of social pressure, but it is a relationship of love that is unparalleled."[23] Indeed, my interlocutors on Hosny's team would regularly remind me that God "is closer to us than our jugular vein" (Qur'an 50:16) and "truly near" (Qur'an 2:186), and "with you wherever you are" (Qur'an 57:4). Such "nearness" (*qurb*), they argued, indicated a divine relationship to human beings characterized above all by leniency and affection. One of God's most beautiful names is al-Wadud, the Most Loving. Of all the divine attributes, al-Wadud was the simplest to grasp, as most people experience love daily for their family and friends. The human yearning for loving intimacy was part of our *fitra*, our innate disposition, and extended to the divine. But Salafi piety has led to an unbalanced sense of God for the average person, a God who is punitive and difficult to please.

For many viewers, the New Preachers' stress on God's loving intimacy to even the most struggling of sinners was a welcome relief from the Salafi emphasis on divine punishment. Engy told me that after watching Amr Khaled's 2006 series for Iqraa focused on explicating the ninety-nine most beautiful names of God, "I loved God. I *looved* God. I loved God because of the way Amr Khaled spoke about Him. You know when you are talking to someone dear to you and call him *ya habibi* (my love)—I wanted to call God *habibi*. Watching this program, I felt that God is so *hilw* (nice)." This sense of intimate affection contrasted with the hopelessness Salafi sermons provoked in her.

"Before Amr Khaled, you had to prepare yourself psychologically to listen to what the Salafis were saying on the cassettes," she said. "My parents would give me these cassettes and I would throw them away. After five minutes of listening, I knew that [according to them] I was going to Hell. So fine, since I am going to Hell just by living my regular life, to hell with everything, I will just do whatever. This really wasn't the way to reach someone like me." The extreme of Salafi *ghuluw* had almost led her to the extreme of secular *ghafla*.

Engy's experience highlights the ways in which the cultivation of pious moderation was theologically inextricable from the development of a "balanced" relationship to God characterized by love. Importantly, such love wasn't merely a felt interiority or an intellectual belief. As for Salafi revivalists, the performance of one's love for God included the habitual performance of ritual obligations. But loving God also had social—that is, other-oriented and interpersonal—dimensions that my interlocutors felt were routinely overlooked by Salafi preachers. For the producers of Hosny's 2011 Ramadan series *Uhibbika Rabbi* (*I Love You My Lord*), a key goal was to show the various ways that ordinary people can express their love for God by loving one another. For example, in one episode Hosny elaborated on what he called the "heart worship" of respecting and showing due consideration (*taqdir*) toward all human beings "no matter their ethnicity, color, religion, physical attributes, culture, [levels of] wealth or poverty."[24] All human beings, he explained, were created with the divine breath. To show regard for them is to show one's regard for God. In practical terms, this heart worship (*'ibada qalbiyya*) involves first and foremost refraining from harming others. He reminded viewers of the hadith about a man who entered Paradise simply for removing from the road a branch with thorns.

Heart worship also entails refraining from judging others as inferior. This ranges from the wealthy disdaining the poor to the pious disdaining those they see as sinful, for appearances can be deceiving, Hosny explained. "I am a preacher on television, but perhaps I have many sins that are hidden. So I cannot feel arrogant toward those whose sins are not hidden." He cited the time the Prophet told his Companions to stop cursing a drunkard, telling them that this was a person who despite his outward sins still had much love for God and His Prophet in his heart.

This stress on God's love and on loving others as an aspect of piety was for many regular viewers of Islamic television a revolutionary respite from the Salafi stress on God's punishment and judging others. One viewer, Hania, told me that switching from watching Salafi programs to New Preaching ones had a positive impact on her interactions with others.

"When I was following the Salafi preachers, I felt like God was a man holding a stick over my head," she shared. "I saw Him as angry with us all the time. That was my emotional image of God. It made me very judgmental toward others. Things were very black or white." The New Preachers allowed her to "see," or rather feel, God differently, more as a "loving mother."

"If you ran into the house with dirty shoes," she explained, "your mom will be angry with you, but you know she won't throw you out of the house." Moreover, Hania learned from the New Preachers that "God loves us regardless of anything. From the Salafis you get the sense that God loves us only when we are good and hates us when we are not good. But God loves us, full stop."

Later, in chapter 5, we see how for Hania after the 2011 uprising this emphasis on love acquired new political significance as it nurtured an aspiration for a New Egypt characterized by living peacefully together across Muslim-Christian difference. Indeed, in the immediate lead-up to the revolution Hosny had addressed the relationship of Muslims to non-Muslims in his 2010 *School of Love* series, arguing for love as its foundation. The importance of stressing God's love for my interlocutors was to revolutionize the conventional concept (*mahfum*) of piety, to shift its focus from ritual worship, *'ibadat*, to social ethics, *mu'umalat*. For to truly know God's love is to treat others with His ethics.

A MORE ETHICAL PIETY

"Why do we have so many religious people with no ethics and ethical people with no religion?" Reem lamented. "Why can't we have both religion (*din*) and ethics (*akhlaq*)?" In her late twenties, Reem had come of age at the height of Islamic Revivalism. The grassroots piety movement in which she considered herself an active participant had led to a growing awareness of religious strictures and of an increasing practice of devotional worship—of regular prayer, for example, or of veiling. Yet the everyday conduct of even the most visibly pious left much to be desired.

Consider, she asked me, the government bureaucrat who casually opens his desk drawer to receive a bribe even as his beard is still wet from ablutions and his prayer mat on the floor. This man, she mused, considers himself religious because he prays on time even while at work. He might even justify his bribe-taking on the grounds that the state agency employing him is itself corrupt. "But he forgets that religion is ethics (*al-din akhlaq*)," Reem said with the sad shake of her head. She was alluding to the Prophet's famous hadith that he was sent by God to help people perfect their ethics. The gist of this hadith was summed up in the colloquial phrase *al-din muʿumala* (religion is ethical interaction); it is commonly invoked as a form of rebuke for a person who adopts the conventional markers of piety (a headscarf or a beard, for example) but behaves badly with others.

The "imbalance" in Egyptian society that troubled Reem was a recurrent New Preaching complaint.[25] In his 2010 Ramadan series, *School of Love*, Hosny argued that the "Islamic Awakening" and the growth of religious satellite channels over the past decade had spread knowledge of divine strictures while failing to spur more ethical conduct.[26] Egyptians had split into two lamentable categories: Muslims who were devoted ritual practitioners but had dreadful ethics and Muslims who neither prayed nor fasted but had beautiful ethics.

The relationship between ritual discipline and ethical self-cultivation in Egypt's Islamic Revival has been influentially diagrammed by Saba Mahmood. She shows how a key goal of the Salafi piety movement she studied was to engender a pious subjectivity aligned with divinely dictated norms through the regular performance of ritual worship. For the New Preachers and their followers, however, while the piety movement had successfully instilled in many Egyptians the desire and willingness to perform ritual obligations, such performances were not creating pious subjects. The outward bodily practices were not leading to the correct inward dispositions that would then be expressed in ethical conduct. In this way, Reem's concern was opposite that of Mona, one of Mahmood's interlocutors. For Mona, unethical daily conduct stems from being in a constant state of *ghafla*, of heedlessness of God, that in turn leads to the inability to follow through on ritual obligations like prayer.[27] By contrast, Reem was concerned that so many had cultivated a constant state of God consciousness and a habit of prayer, yet continued to act unethically. This failure was so persistent and pervasive that it could not be explained away as individual, as a marker of what Mahmood calls "an inadequately formed self."[28] Rather, this failure is due to Salafism's theological corruption of what piety substantively and interactionally entails. By making ritual fastidiousness a stand-in for piety, Salafi revivalism had disfigured piety into affectation. The problem was not *ghafla*, but *ghuluw*—that is, the root problem was the "unbalanced" sensibilities (*nufus*) doctrinally deemed "pious" in the first place.

In one of our first conversations, I asked Hosny what he thought of the label *multazim*, "committed," commonly used as a term of self-description by participants in the piety movement. He pointed out that this word is not a Qur'anic one but "was invented by those who say 'we the committed' versus everyone else." He then launched into an impromptu lecture:

> This word should be erased from our dictionary because it has become too focused on appearance. What is the real difference between a woman who wears the headscarf and a woman who doesn't? The woman who doesn't is failing to perform a religious obligation, but the woman who wears it might also have numerous religious obligations she regularly fails to meet, like being honest with others or avoiding gossip about others. But if we call the head-scarfed woman 'committed,' and the uncovered one 'not committed,' we are wrongly limiting piety to outward appearances and external forms of worship and ignoring ethics, when piety is both.

Instead of "committed," Hosny preferred the term *rubbubiyya*, godliness, and a key aspiration of his programs during my fieldwork was to move viewers to "be a godly worshipper" (*kun 'abid rabbani*). This phrase is so emblematic of his preaching that when I asked producer Zayna for advice on what to gift Hosny at the end of my fieldwork, she immediately suggested a calligraphic rendition of it. A godly worshipper strives in her dealings with others to embody divine attributes such as fairness, generosity, and lovingness, to embody the most beautiful names of God (*asma' Allah al-husna*). In Ash'ari theology, these attributes are understood as faculties enfolded into human nature, the actualization of which is the ultimate objective of Islam's prescribed ritual forms. The influential twelfth-century theologian al-Ghazali devoted considerable attention to what he referred to as *al-takhalluq bi-akhlaq Allah*, "assuming the character traits of God as one's own character, an expression that Tim Winter points out "was already well known in the literature and was sometimes attributed to the Prophet.[29] Al-Ghazali was deeply concerned with how Muslims could purify their innermost selves to the point where they could embody "God's ethics."[30] His pedagogical process of virtuous self-cultivation "emphasizes the need to constantly cultivate attitudes that imbue inner meaning to each and every facet of outward ethical conduct"[31] and became a distinctive aspect of the broader Sufi stress on "meaning over form."[32] While not explicitly identifying with Sufism during my fieldwork, Hosny took up its language of *rubbubiyya* in his preaching. In an episode of *School of Love*, Hosny blamed the prevalent treatment of piety as ritual exactitude for "creating Muslims who cling to the performance of rituals solely as a means of avoiding hellfire. They do not taste the pleasures of divine beauty, pleasures which humans are naturally disposed to." Piety is achieved not merely through ritual worship, but also through striving to embody God's attributes—God's ethics—in social interaction.[33]

Far from enabling the acquisition of God's ethics, Salafi revivalists were propagating what my interlocutors called an "image piety" (*taddayun sura*) or a "numerical piety" (*taddayun raqami*). Their notion of piety fixated on visibility and quantity—piety as evidenced by the length of one's beard, the looseness of one's hijab, the number of Prophetic sayings memorized, or supernumerary prayers performed. My interlocutors had many anecdotal examples of this kind of piety. Here is one:

> A woman is an active participant in the piety movement, spending most of her free time attending mosque lessons, watching religious preaching on television, or memorizing the Qur'an. She is anxious to arrive at the mosque in time for the start of, say, the special evening prayers during Ramadan. She drives over to the mosque in a hurry, cutting off other cars and narrowly missing pedestrians; she double-parks in front of the mosque because she doesn't want to spend time looking for an empty spot; she elbows other women out of the way as she pushes herself into the mosque and only relaxes once she unfurls her prayer mat. This prayer mat she refuses to move an inch even as the space becomes increasingly crowded with other worshippers, and she snaps at anyone who tries to suggest that she budge.

From the perspective of my interlocutors, this woman's zeal to pray led her to behave unethically; this is because she did not understand that being a godly person means giving people their due before giving God His due.

At first glance, my interlocutors' critique of Salafi ritualism might seem to partake in what Talal Asad identifies as a secular understanding of rituals as acts laden with symbolic meanings as opposed to prescribed scripts to be performed.[34] As Gregory Starrett has shown, this understanding is indeed widespread in Egypt, with children across public schools being taught to approach "ritual behavior as a code that should be read rather than merely a habit that should be cultivated."[35] Like their Salafi counterparts, however, my New Preaching interlocutors understood ritual practice as an ineluctable component of creating the desire and capacity for virtue. They considered the common secular refrain that "religion is in the heart" (al-din fil-qalb)—a matter of interiorized feelings or inherited identity—to be incorrect, a misapprehension of the embodied discipline piety demands. What was being questioned then was not Salafi revivalists' emphasis on ritual practice but their ostensible failure to grasp what the virtues cultivated by such practice substantively entailed in terms of ethical interaction.[36]

To be sure, Salafism's well-known stress on technical excellence in ritual worship itself has doctrinal substance. For Salafi scholars, membership in the saved sect, al firqa al-najiya, is constituted both through belief in the pure creed ('aqida) of the Prophet and first generations of Muslims, and through exacting adherence to their ritual forms. Putting effort into mastering what to many might seem like ritual minutiae—whether or not to wiggle one's finger during the last cycle of prayer prostration, for example, or which foot to enter versus exit a bathroom with—is a distinguishing characteristic of the saved sect. From the Salafi perspective, most Muslims were not performing their ritual obligations as the Prophet did and were thus "in grave danger because God does not hear their prayers."[37] On their programs, Salafi preachers argued that the New Preachers' privileging of ethical interaction, of "religion as ethics," over creedal purity and ritual fidelity was yet more evidence of their stealth secularity.

Despite these claims, the scriptural basis of ethics mattered deeply to the New Preachers and their supporters and was in fact an axis of distinction vis-à-vis secular liberal sensibilities. Abu Haiba, Khaled's debut producer, shared in one of our conversations that a British journalist covering the launch of his Islamic music video channel irritably asked him why he characterized virtues like trustworthiness as "Islamic" when it was equally valued by non-Muslims like herself. He explained to her that ethics grounded in creed have a permanency that secular ones lack, holding people accountable to a transcendent power as opposed to shifting social standards. Still, Abu Haiba was most troubled not by the ethical failings of secular-identifying people but of religious-identifying ones. As we have seen, these run the gamut of severity, from the relatively minor double-parking Ramadan worshipper to the more serious bribe-taking bearded bureaucrat. Once again, from the New Preaching perspective, the Salafi stress on devotional rituals over interactional ethics results in a religious immoderation that contributes to secularization by giving piety a bad ethical reputation.

MODERATION AS MANY TRUTHS

In 2009, Iqraa broadcast a series by Hosny called *Khada'ukka fa-Qalu* (*They Tricked You and Said*). Broadcast live with recorded commentary from "ordinary people" on Cairo's streets, the series was one of the channel's most widely watched, continuing for four seasons. Each episode challenged a common misconception related to religion. Toward the end of the first season, Hosny tackled the incorrect assumption that disagreement, *ikhtilaf*, necessarily led to discord, *khilaf*.[38] He began by establishing human diversity (*tanawwu'*) as incontrovertibly providential. Because God created us to be different, He gave us a revelation that is expansive, relevant to all circumstances at any time. This expansiveness, while essential to the divine text, is actualized through its human interpretation. Because human beings bring different competencies and customs to their reading of the text, they will come to different conclusions about it.

The first Muslim community welcomed disagreement for the pragmatic flexibility it provided. Hosny reminded viewers that Umar, the second of the rightly guided caliphs, is reported to have said: "I would not be happy if the Companions did not disagree because if they didn't disagree, we wouldn't have facilitation (*rukhsa*)." By this he meant that having a multiplicity of legitimate views facilitated flexibility in the face of changing contexts. If only one interpretation were possible, there could come a time when circumstances make its application impossibly or unreasonably burdensome. For my interlocutors, this was also the meaning of the famous Prophetic saying that "the differences of my community are a mercy."

During the episode, Hosny cited examples of interpretive differences from the community of first Muslims led by the Prophet. Once, the Prophet said, "We won't pray *'asr* [the afternoon prayer] except in this town." One group of his followers took that statement literally and didn't pray until they had reached the town, another group took it metaphorically as a call to hurry up and reach the town before *'asr*, and thus prayed at the regular time. The Prophet did not denounce one group or the other as incorrect, showing that both interpretations were valid and could coexist. The members of each group did not accuse the other of being in the wrong.

Of course, Hosny continued, there are some fundamental issues about which no disagreement is possible: for example, that God is One, that the prayers are five, that Ramadan is a month of fasting. But these clear-cut matters are few—for most issues there are different, even conflicting, interpretations of divine intent. In addition, he wanted his viewers to know that this wasn't an interpretive free-for-all. As we saw earlier, Hosny was always careful to note on air that scriptural interpretation, *tafsir*, like *ifta'* (jurisprudential judgment), was a specialized activity not open to all Muslims but rather limited to the learned few, the ulama of al-Azhar. What Hosny was aiming to promote among his viewers was less a direct engagement with the authoritative texts of Islam, the Qur'an and the Sunnah, and more an appreciation for the multiplicity of viewpoints of those recognized as qualified to have actionable viewpoints, as well as the proper comportment toward those who follow scholars with different views.

The Prophetic precedents Hosny laid out for his viewers modeled the everyday interactional ethics of disagreement (*adab al-ikhtilaf*) that pious practitioners needed. If there are two conflicting opinions on a matter—for example, on whether using a string of beads for supplication is permissible or not—a Muslim can choose to follow either one. The person following the opinion proscribing the prayer beads can't accuse the one following the opinion permitting it of committing a *bid'a*, a heretical innovation. In fact, Hosny went on, "The *bid'a* is that we have rejected disagreement. In the past, scholars didn't say, 'This is *bid'a*' but said, 'This is an opinion.' Refusing disagreement is the real *bid'a* here." Importantly, this is not only because different people will read different things into the Qur'anic text but because the text itself, barring a few decisive utterances, carries more than one meaning.

If God had wanted there to be only one opinion, His revelation would have foreclosed the possibility of multiple interpretations.

Hosny's celebration of disagreement is grounded in what one scholar characterizes as the "remarkable" Ash'ari theological "willingness to tolerate equally authoritative alternative versions of religious truth."[39] A hallmark of this theology is its simultaneous commitment to the reliability of reason and the authority of scripture over reason. This stance understands revelation as ambiguous in its meaning and hence open to multiple interpretations, even as it upholds revelation's status as the definitive source of moral knowledge. These two seemingly opposing claims—that revelation is a source of certain knowledge and that human interpretations of revelation are necessarily uncertain—underlay the development of a complex ethical thematization of interpretive pluralism and disagreement within Ash'arism from the tenth century onwards.[40] Ventriloquizing his Salafi critics, Hosny rhetorically asked: "But what is the *haq*, the truth? The truth is *ikhtilaf*! But whom do we follow, what is the evidence (*al-dalil*)? The evidence is that we are disagreeing." Through such on-air interventions, Hosny like other New Preachers theologically expanded the ambit of *ikhtilaf* from a technical term describing differences across jurisprudential schools or within them to an ethos of interaction.

Hosny's episode on *ikhtilaf* elicited critical responses from Egypt's most prominent Salafi preachers on their channels. The most systematic critique came from al-Nas's Mazin Sirsawi, who the following year hosted a program pointedly called *It Is You Who Has Been Tricked*. More immediately, however, he dedicated four consecutive episodes to rebutting Hosny. Refuting Hosny's claim that disagreement was integral to Islam, Sirsawi put it like this: "The truth is one. There are no two truths. If the ignorant person would just be quiet, the disagreement would end."

Sirsawi's negative evaluation of disagreement was informed by the literal textualism of Athari theology. Atharism contends that the Qur'an is transparent in its meaning. The Qur'an does not need humans to interpret it; its clear directives just need to be applied, for "if God did not mean what he said," as Robert Gleave puts it in his discussion of Islamic literalism, "why did he say it like he did?"[41] Positing the possibility of multiple interpretations of the Qur'an displaces God as the ultimate arbiter of His own words, making divine revelation subservient to human reasoning. The aim of revelation is to guide humans by conveying the divine truth, which is by definition singular. Interpretive differences are a function of a textual ambiguity that does not obtain with regard to divine revelation.

To expound on these points, Sirsawi invited to his program the popular Salafi preacher al-Huwayni. Al-Huwayni informed viewers that the hadith about differences being a mercy was a fabricated one. Al-Huwayni was following the categorization of the influential Salafi hadith scholar al-Albani, who had famously lambasted al-Azhar's commitment to theological-legal pluralism as institutionalized in the madhab system as a heretical innovation that subverts the singular authority of the Qur'an and privileges uncertain human reasoning. From the Salafi perspective their own distinguishing trait as the saved sect is that they, unlike "the majority of Muslims," do not "blindly follow the opinion of others." As al-Albani famously put it, "Salafis follow scripture, not scholars."[42]

The dictum that the Qur'an is easy to understand, a "clear text" according to its own self-avowal and thus in no need of a specialized class of interpreters, underlies what many have glossed as an egalitarian, anti-elitist impulse within Salafism.[43] But while the text is open to all, it is not open to interpretation. In common with literalists from other religious traditions,[44] Salafi revivalists like Sirsawi and al-Huwayni do not see themselves as interpreting the Qur'an at all but merely as reporting its declarations. Disagreement between two scholars therefore indicated that one was ignorant or wrong. The very fact that scholars disagree was indeed further evidence that Muslims should hew to the plain meaning of the text. In this way, the different interpretations that Hosny's series parsed for his audience were irrelevant because such opinions could not trump clear Qur'anic or Prophetic texts. God will hold Muslims accountable not for their adherence to scholarly opinions, however learned, but for their adherence to the Qur'an and the Sunnah.

Indeed, the problem with Hosny's presentation of different scholarly opinions, al-Huwayni went on, is that he left it at that, with no final pronouncement about which was the "truth." The whole point of *da'wa* was to show people the truth—not to show people that there is disagreement over what is true, and as a consequence sow discord and moral laxity. Far from being a mercy, differences in opinion and judgment lead to confusion with catastrophic results in both this world and the next, al-Huwayni concluded. This Salafi theology of difference closes off multiplicity and ambiguity as an act of care and responsibility geared toward saving Muslims.[45] As Noah Salomon points out, Salafism's denial of the legitimacy of interpretive pluralism asserts Muslim "unity not in spite of difference, but rather one which is only possible through the destruction of difference."[46]

The Salafi erasure of Muslims' internal diversity worried my interlocutors at Iqraa. While they also bemoaned how divided the Muslim community had become, the response to this "fragmentation" (*tafakkuk*) was to reframe differences as complementary rather than antagonistic. As one producer put it, promoting Muslim unity (*wahda*) was distinct from promoting a unitary Muslim discourse (*khitab uhudi*), for the rejection of pluralism is ultimately what enables polarization and corrodes social bonds. As the first Islamic channel in the Arab world, Iqraa aspired to model pluralism in its own institutional practices. As we saw, Iqraa's branding of itself as a moderate channel hinged on its inclusive broadcast policy: preachers and scholars adhering to the different orientations of the Islamic Revival were, in theory, welcome.

Still, inclusion came with a caveat: Iqraa would give diverse preachers a broadcast platform so long as they were moderate within their own respective orientation. That caveat was designed to exclude those whom Iqraa decision-makers deemed too exclusivist within their own orientations. While Iqraa's Saudi management had the final call, producers in the Cairo branch had significant latitude to make their own evaluations, and relied a great deal on their direct interactions with different preachers. For example, Emad invited the Salafi preacher Mahmud al-Misri to create a program for Iqraa because he perceived him as "very open-minded" within the range of possibilities of Egyptian Salafism. He even convinced him to film inside a boxing ring to visually dramatize the program's subject, people's everyday struggles against Satan. That al-Misri agreed to this new form spoke to his relative centrism within Salafism.[47]

Such programming decisions were framed by my interlocutors as reflective of Asha'rism's historic "moderate synthesis" of two theological extremes: the rationalist Mu'tazila, who gave human reason too much latitude in discerning truth, versus the literalist Ahl al-Hadith, or Atharis, who gave reason none at all. For their part, Salafi channels did not allow the broadcast of programs by non-Salafi preachers, putting Salafi channels, as a category, outside of the normative bounds of moderation as defined at Iqraa. The Islamic television sector's contrasting broadcast policies thus instantiate broader competing theologies of disagreement—a divine "mercy" for the New Preachers, a human "heresy" for the Salafis. While the assumption that argument and disagreement are a "natural part of any Islamic tradition" has become integral to the anthropological idea of Islam as a "discursive tradition,"[48] as we have seen, these attributes are themselves the subject of intense theological contestations that draw the boundaries of "the secular" and "the religious" in incommensurable ways. At Iqraa, unlike at Salafi channels, ambiguity and pluralism were Islamic, not secular. Such theological evaluations were not only the fodder of on-air polemics, but had practical consequences for Muslims' personal and collective aspirations, as the next sections explore.

MODERATION AND WOMEN'S INCLUSION

It is November 2010 and Iqraa's Cairo manager Emad is brainstorming ideas with Zayna and Nashwa for the sequel of the *School of Love* series. In his mid-thirties, Emad wasn't much older than Hosny and the two men's relationship was characterized by brotherly banter. Emad's interactions with the mostly female team he managed were more restrained, but many of its members looked up to him as a mentor as well. Nashwa had started working with Emad as a volunteer on Hosny's team before transitioning into a salaried position. Volunteers were often recruited from the preacher's fan base and Hosny relied on their efforts to maintain his website, manage his social media, and organize his in-person events. Zayna was a graduate of Cairo University's prestigious Faculty of Media, where she had specialized in broadcast television, and was a relatively recent addition to Hosny's media team.

As I take notes at the door of the small room, Emad expounds a favorite strategy: the importance of "telling a story" in creating content.

"A viewer can watch a two-hour program, but the only thing they are going to retain and remember is the story," he explains. "The story condenses all the information and makes the moral lesson clearer. The story enters the mind (*bi-tidkhul al-'aql*) right away because we all love stories."

Nashwa nods in agreement. "It is not enough to just say the Prophet loved God, we have to find stories that show that," she tells Zayna. "And then also think of stories from life, of the things parents do for their children or spouses do for each other, to compare it to."

Everyone is quiet for a moment. Zayna hesitates: "Well, I think that these are two different types of love, the love one has for people, for our parents or for our friends for example, and the love we have for God." As she speaks, Nashwa types notes.

"But they are connected, we shouldn't think of them as separate," Zayna continues. "There is a hadith that says God makes His servants love those who love Him. So maybe we could search for stories that show this connection."

"Yes," says Emad, "that's great. I am going to tell Mustafa to use that."

During my fieldwork, Hosny was the only preacher at the Cairo branch with a dedicated "above the line" team, industry-speak for those involved in the creative development of a program. Hosny prepared the theological content himself in consultation with his trusted shaykhs, graduates of al-Azhar. The media team oversaw the rest of the content—researching statistics, finding experts, picking quotes, scouting locations, connecting with possible interviewees. This team was predominantly composed of women. Most people I knew outside the world of Islamic television were surprised to learn that Iqraa even had women on its payroll. Hiring team members representative of the New Preacher's audience—educated, young, and female—was a production strategy of forging connection and ensuring resonance. It was also a way of disrupting both Salafi gender norms and secular stereotypes about pious norms by practicing what one preached about women's work being both Islamically permissible and socially laudable. The inclusion of women at the world's first Islamic television channel, whether off-screen or on, was thus an important facet of Iqraa's moderation. Indeed, in its mission statement during my fieldwork, Iqraa listed "taking seriously women's intellectual contributions and supporting their role in society" as one of its strategic goals as a *wasati* Islamic channel.

Iqraa was the first satellite channel to broadcast programs by women preachers from across the Arab world. Some of them, such as Suad Saleh and Abla al-Kahlway, were Islamic scholars who had acceded to the highest ranks at al-Azhar and were already well known in Egypt for addressing "women's issues" like divorce, inheritance laws, and dress prescriptions.[49] Others, like Nadia Emara and Du'aa Amer, were not credentialed by al-Azhar and were more like the male New Preachers: young, glamorous, and with a knack for making piety accessible and relevant to "ordinary people." Beyond Egypt, Iqraa produced programs for the well-known Syrian Sufi-oriented scholar Rufaida al-Habash and her daughter, the preacher Sirin Hamsho.[50] Sallam, Iqraa's Saudi head manager, spoke proudly of the channel's track record with regard to women. He characterized the average Arab Muslim viewer as "caught between two extremes—between those channels where women appear as a commodity (sil'a) for men's pleasure and those channels that prohibit women from appearing at all, as if women weren't half of society or should only be at its margins (al-hamish)."

These two extremes were historically represented by privately funded Salafi and state-funded secular channels respectively. State television had a policy that barred veiled presenters (lifted only after 2011), and when it launched in 1998, Iqraa as the world's first Islamic channel set an important counterexample. "Look at Iqraa's announcers: They're so pretty, chic and smart. Hijab doesn't veil their thinking," one journalist who stopped getting invitations to appear on talk shows after she donned the hijab told an interviewer in 2003. "They're more presentable than some TV announcers with artificial hair colors and tons of make-up that make them look like aliens."[51] Nevertheless, if this journalist was barred from Egyptian state media for wearing hijab, a colleague who didn't would have found it difficult to appear on Iqraa, which had a tacit on-screen hijab policy. While most of the producers, like Zayna and Nashwa, wore hijab, I met a couple who didn't. Wearing hijab wasn't necessary for being hired in an off-screen role, but generally the only women who appeared on-screen were ones who wore hijab. One (male) producer told me that they were also careful when filming on location to blur shots of women who were dressed "inappropriately."

While Iqraa producers saw the on-screen versus off-screen distinction when it came to women's dress as an example of the "balanced" approach of Islamic moderation, critics across the secular-religious divide saw it as evidence for how the self-declared "middle of the road" channel was but a Trojan horse. For secularists, the channel was just another source of a stifling religious conservatism. One feminist writer stormed out of an Iqraa televised dialogue between liberals and Islamists that she had been invited to participate in, in protest of the hijab policy.[52] Meanwhile, Salafi critics decried the channel for showing women on-screen at all, arguing that this was prohibited even if the women wore hijab and even if they were preaching.[53] They also objected to Iqraa's employment of women producers, contending that Islam mandates the domestic seclusion of women whenever possible. Muhammad Hassan even advocated banning women from driving, as Saudi Arabia did until 2018, as a way of foreclosing the possible harms of women's mobility outside the home.[54] These gendered restrictions are outside of the mainstream in Egypt, making them an important aspect of Salafism's moral distinction vis-à-vis other Islamic orientations.[55] While not necessarily followed in practice, Salafi interactional ideals around gender set the normative bar for many Egyptians aspiring to lead more pious lives. For my interlocutors, however, these norms—much like their secular liberal parallels—were deviations from Islam's moderation.

For my interlocutors this moderation was epitomized by al-Azhar, which has been admitting women into its ranks as students and teachers since its state restructuring in the 1960s as a modern university with specialized colleges covering everything from medicine to media. Still, unlike other public universities in Egypt, al-Azhar's colleges are segregated by gender, and when it comes to the colleges of Islamic theology and jurisprudence, there is a widespread (male) sense that those enrolling women are less exacting. As Zareena Grewal shows, such gendered evaluations and exclusions are often critiqued by young pious Muslim Americans who travel to Egypt to study at al-Azhar in pursuit of an authoritatively "authentic" Islamic tradition.[56] Similarly, while Iqraa's female employees dismissed out of hand Salafi strictures and secular stereotypes alike as contrary to the Islamically correct moderation of al-Azhar, they felt that even the most moderate, Azhari-adjacent Muslims still had one problematic assumption: that women producers, like women preachers, best made content for other women as opposed to for everyone. They argued that the widespread participation of women in the 2011 uprising showed the limitations of this understanding. Women had gone to the streets alongside men and risked their lives for "all Egyptians," not just for other women.

During one interview in March 2012 at a coffee shop near Tahrir Square, Zayna told me that her position as the head of the editorial research team is challenging because it "requires a constant awareness—you have to retain all sorts of information, you can't assume that anything is irrelevant." She had joined Soha, who had directed several of Hosny's programs, and me at the cafe after prepping interviewees who had been in Tahrir Square during the eighteen days. I asked if they noticed any differences between what the men and women on the team felt was relevant.

"Well, the content we are preparing for Mister Mustafa is for everyone," Zayna quickly pointed out. I knew that Zayna had initially been recruited to be on the team of one of Iqraa's female preachers, but had chosen to switch to Hosny's team when the opportunity arose. She knew that even at Iqraa the programs by women preachers concentrated on "women's issues," whereas the New Preachers' shows covered a wide range of topics, even if most of the viewers were women. Working with the more high-profile Hosny was the better professional opportunity for an ambitious television producer.

"When I am preparing a script or researching a story, I am not thinking *I am a woman* while I am doing this. But at the same time, because I am a woman, that is naturally going to influence what I might notice or find interesting."

Soha jumps in: "Even Mister Mustafa doesn't have the final say about the content. He can give his own ideas, but we are all in conversation with each other. I feel like my opinion is respected and that the effort I am putting in matters."

Like most of the production team, Soha was a twenty-something graduate of Cairo University's Faculty of Media. She had a ready smile for everyone, but in the control room she was serious about business, exercising an air of authority that belied her under-five-foot frame. As the director, she oversaw the crew in the control room: the assistant director, the editorial assistant, the monteur whose job is to toggle between cameras, and the production assistant in charge of graphics. With the exception of the assistant director, these were all older and male.

Zayna adds, "Yeah, when I read comments online from viewers like 'oh, we watched this or that, and we changed because we watched this' and I think, *wow, God has put me in a team, in a place, that is having this impact, what a blessing.*"

"So you and Soha don't encounter any obstacles working in media that men do not have to deal with?" I ask.

"We do, but they come more from our life outside of work, to be honest," Soha explains.

> Like my dad was upset one time when I came home after work in a car with tinted windows. It was the channel's car but my dad made a big fuss about it. And I don't think whomever I marry will easily accept me staying late at work. But I don't plan to leave my work. I mean, maybe I will meet someone who deserves this compromise, but I want to feel first that I have accomplished everything I wanted to. So if an average guy tells me, "I don't want you to work," I will say, "Who are you to tell me that! I graduated first in my class!"

As we wait for our check, I ask the two women what they hope the future will bring in terms of work. "I talk to Mister Emad about this a lot," Zayna confides. "I told him I definitely want to become a better editor, but at the same time I feel like I can do something bigger. I want to be a person who inspires. He asked me if I want to be a preacher myself. I am not sure that I do, but I like that he asked me that. And if I do, I would want to be a preacher like Mister Mustafa, a preacher for everyone."

MODERATION AND POLITICS

It is late April in 2011 and I am meeting Iqraa's Saudi managing director Sallam face-to-face for the first time after speaking several times by phone. He had flown in from Jeddah for meetings with Emad, Hosny, and others at the Cairo station about the upcoming production season. The channel had polled viewers on its website about the revolution's impact on their television viewing habits and preferences. Seventy-six percent of the respondents shared that watching Islamic programs had taken a backseat to watching news coverage and political talk shows in the two months since Mubarak's toppling. My satellite installer also noted this change, telling me that while he used to automatically put all the religious channels first when installing a new dish—"to get blessings when people turn on their TV"—after the revolution people asked him to put channels focused on politics and news first. Iqraa, as a matter of long-standing policy, didn't do either. I wondered if that would now change.

Sallam is excited to be in Egypt at this heady time of promise, sharing with me photos he had taken of protesters still gathering in Tahrir Square, which was just over the bridge from the hotel lobby we are meeting in. "Egyptians are leading the way again! They are showing us once more what is possible," he enthuses as we sip our orange juice. But when I ask Sallam what he felt Iqraa's role should be at this historic time, he is emphatic that the channel must continue to "stay out of politics." This is the best way as an Islamic channel to uphold both the spirit of Tahrir Square and of moderation, he explains.

Before the revolution, Iqraa's abstention from political commentary and partisan endorsement was yet another distinguishing mark of its media "professionalism" and an aspect of its pious credibility with audiences. Part of the no-politics policy was pragmatic: Iqraa had neither the resources nor the expertise to cover fast-changing news cycles in the quality way of an al-Jazeera or a CNN. If preaching was a matter of not only knowledge but professional competence, then so was politics and it was best left to the professional politicians and the news channels. Plus, in this way you could more easily avoid crossing government "red lines" and being shut down. But there was also an important ethical dimension to why an Islamic channel, and Islamic media preachers specifically, should refrain from politics: the risk was too great that viewers would take their political pronouncements as theologically normative, conflating specific partisan stances with the stance of "Islam" writ large.

For this reason, several of my interlocutors argued, the Prophet himself upheld the distinction between religious decrees and political ones. For example, during the battle of Badr, an important event for the first Muslim community, a soldier questioned the Prophet regarding the latter's planned position on the battlefield. He asked the Prophet if this position was revelation (by God) or strategy (by him). When the Prophet Muhammad replied that it was strategy, the soldier advised God's Messenger that it was an ill-conceived one and that it would be better to position the troops elsewhere. The Prophet followed the soldier's suggestion. This story held a lesson with important revolutionary significance: even the opinion of God's final messenger was just that—an opinion responsive to revision upon further information or deliberation. Islam, then, should not be conflated with one particular group, party, or political position, and so it would be irresponsible of a preacher to make political proclamations in its name. Indeed, taking a particular position on political events would undermine Iqraa's identity as a moderate channel inclusive of a diversity of Islamic orientations.

After 2011, Iqraa's institutional investment in distinguishing itself as a moderate Islamic channel through abstaining from broadcasting politics became even more important for producers as Salafi channels and preachers attracted much public criticism for endorsing particular policies, politicians, and parties as "Islamic" and maligning those they opposed as "against Islam." The Salafi conflation of support for specific platforms with support of Islam started with the March referendum the month after Mubarak resigned. Because the outcome of the vote would be the first in Egyptian history that was unpredictable, not fixed as usual, the referendum felt like a dress rehearsal for a democratic New Egypt and dominated everyday conversation in the month after Mubarak's toppling. The referendum asked Egyptians to vote either "yes" or "no" on a set of constitutional amendments. Voting yes would pave the way for early elections, and this was the choice supported by the Muslim Brotherhood and "remnants" (*fulul*) of the Mubarak regime, the two most electorally organized groups in the country. Liberals, leftists, and many Coptic Christians supported the no vote, maintaining that they needed more time to organize. These differing preferences took on a sectarian tenor when Egypt's most influential Salafi preachers mobilized around the "yes vote" as the "Islamic consensus," arguing that passing the amendments would protect Egypt's "Islamic identity" by leaving intact the constitutional reference to Islamic law as the country's main legislative basis.

At Iqraa, some producers shared they were planning on voting yes, others on voting no, and those who felt most passionately about the issue tried to convince each other to change their mind. But no one I spoke with during that period framed these choices in "Islamic" terms. In fact, many of my interlocutors agreed with secular critics that the Salafi casting of the yes option as a "vote for Islam" was a deplorable "exploitation of religion" (*istighlal al-din*) for partisan gain that had no place in the New Egypt. They pointed out the

New Preachers who had come out publicly for voting no hadn't framed this as "God's choice," but merely *their* choice. By contrast, when the yes camp won with over 70 percent of the votes, the Salafi television preacher Mohammad Ya'qub dubbed it an "Islamic conquest of the ballot box," and advised Egyptians who weren't happy with the outcome to leave the country.

Linking political contest with the defense or promotion of Islam continued to be a feature of Salafi sermonizing over the next two years: During the 2011 parliamentary elections, the 2012 presidential elections, and the 2012 constitutional referendum, Salafi television preachers framed voting for the candidates, parties, and platforms they endorsed as "following Islam" and criticized these who felt otherwise as "against Islam." They understood such partisan commentary as an intrinsic part of their *da'wa* obligation to "enjoin good, forbid evil" because, as the director of one of these channels explained, "politics and Islam are intertwined and inseparable, unlike other religions."[57]

During our meeting, Sallam deemed this Salafi editorial policy an example of *ghuluw* and a discrediting of the entire Islamic television sector, which the average Egyptian was already primed to view negatively. For him, the best way for an Islamic channel to promote piety and the revolutionary ethos of Tahrir alike was to stay out of the cyclical vagaries of partisanship while remaining attuned to the "bigger picture" of the political. Iqraa's mission during this time wouldn't be to keep viewers up to date on current events or offer editorial commentary on them, but rather to help its imagined audience of "ordinary people" make their own ethical sense of these events. This is what Islamic moderation called for.

To be clear, my interlocutors at Iqraa did not object to Salafi channels' partisanship because they believed in a normative separation of religion from governance. While many liberal Egyptians rejected on principle any religious purview over the political and legal sphere, arguing that religion should be a matter of private conscience, not public order,[58] the people I worked with at Iqraa were as emphatic as the Salafis that secularism was antithetical, in an essential rather than historical way, to Islam. For them, secularism could not be justified or reasoned from within an Islamic frame. In the run-up to the 2012 presidential election, one producer, Hossam, told me that Muslims who call themselves secularists "don't really understand secularism. Muslims can be democrats or liberals, but they can't be secularists." This is because Islam guides and makes normative claims on every aspect of human life, including political life, while secularism as a matter of foundational principle compartmentalizes religious claims as distinct and irrelevant. That religion should be entangled with politics was unremarkable in a country like Egypt where most people identified as religious in one way or another and expected that "religion covers everything" (*al-din biyishmal kul haga*), in the words of one viewer. The political was governed and regulated by the religious in the sense that God's self-disclosure had something to say about all aspects of created life. But that did not mean that any group, including religious preachers and scholars, could claim to politically speak in God's name, could claim that their political view was uncontestably *the* Islamic one. The question that mattered at Iqraa, then, was not the secular one of where the line between the religious and political is,[59] but rather how religious preachers should engage with the political and to what ends.

As Sallam intimated in our face-to-face meeting back in April 2011, practicing moderation within Islamic television preaching involved approaching the political writ large through its everyday ethical dimensions while disavowing party politics as a specialized domain. Over the next year, Hosny's standard response, as well as the response of his social media team, to the frequent request by interviewers to share his "position" (*mawkif*) on a particular policy or party was to forswear politics as beyond his ethical ambit as a preacher.

"I am not a politician and won't be party to a political struggle," Hosny wrote on his official Facebook page in 2012. "I will strive to bring people together and not be divisive." That doesn't mean that Hosny or his team were uninterested or indifferent to party politics during this period. The uprising and its aftermath dominated hallway conversations and brainstorming sessions at Iqraa. As individuals they participated in protests, voted in referendums, and campaigned for candidates. But my interlocutors were adamant that partisan politics should not intrude into the content they were making, no matter how strongly they felt, because this would compromise their core mission of promoting Islamic piety and make them no different than the Salafi channels whose vision of piety they aimed to disrupt. As one producer told me, "If you say I am a politician and the ends justify the means, that's fine, that's what you are. But if you are claiming to speak in the name of

Islam or to serve Islam, you can't do that. You can't play politics while labeling yourself an Islamic channel. That just gives Islam a bad name."

Fikry, another producer, told me that Iqraa's eschewal of partisan commentary in favor of ethical exhortation was appropriate for an Islamic channel since "ethics is a space of agreement (*al-akhlaq masahat ittifaq*), ethics is for everyone. At the same time, ethics is the foundation of religion, so you get two birds with one stone when you make it the focus." In characterizing ethics as religion's "foundation" and in insisting on their universality, Fikry was referencing the oft-quoted hadith that the Prophet was sent to "perfect people's ethics" and the doctrine of *al-fitra*, which holds that God created all human beings with a natural disposition to act ethically. In this way, the theological idea of Islam as a moderate religion wasn't an obstacle to different people coming together but created space to act in common across difference.

Fikry's remark articulates an ethos of "shared space" that is responsive to a long history of Islamic media being seen as exclusionary and hostile to difference. It was also sensitive to the ways in which Egypt's media landscape had become more polarized as it had become freer with the fall of Mubarak. As Marc Lynch shows, during this period Egyptian "media outlets typically sought out a distinctive political niche and catered to that constituency to the exclusion of others. Islamists watched one set of television stations and Twitter feeds, while anti-Islamists watched an entirely different set. Those that attempted to remain even-handed often struggled to find an audience." This clustering, Lynch argues, "drove politics towards the extremes, undermined the common ground of politics, and intensified and accelerated conflicts and divisions."[60] My interlocutors worried constantly about this polarization and felt that their Islamic media could be an antidote. Because partisan politics was so polarizing, their preaching programs would address the political by mass mediating the ethical principles that should govern it.

As an example of this, in the run-up to the 2012 presidential election, Hosny turned to history—to Umar's seventh-century tenure as the second caliph of the Muslim community. He elaborated on-air about what Umar could teach contemporary Egyptians about what to look for in a potential president. In the episode airing on February 28, for instance, Hosny explained that Umar had advised his representatives not to look at how often people prayed and fasted as an indicator of their piety, but rather at how they interacted with other people. Ritual worship is an act of obedience out of love for God, but if it doesn't lead to worshippers loving other people and treating them well, then it becomes mere affectation that can repel people from piety. Egyptians should follow Umar's wise example and refrain from making quick judgments about who is pious and who isn't based merely on their adherence to ritual practice. Instead, they should prioritize a piety of ethical interaction. For regular New Preaching viewers like Reem who tuned in to the series every week, this was an example of how a preacher could remain above the partisan fray as a preacher while still engaging with the revolutionary possibility of a New Egypt.

So it was that many of my interlocutors were dismayed when Khaled didn't categorically rule out running for president when asked. On his website in April 2011, the preacher had even polled visitors on the issue, asking, "Do you support Amr Khaled entering political life?" Followers were divided: 40 percent answered, "No, that is not his role;" 13 percent said, "Yes, but not right now," while 48 percent voted that he should. Despite these mixed results, Amina, who had been on Khaled's media team when he was at Iqraa, spent hours on the phone trying to dissuade the preacher from taking this step.

"Politics is a dirty game," she told me. "We don't want our preachers to get dirty too."[61] While she like many I knew within New Preaching circles was alarmed that Salafis had abandoned their usual doctrinal position of staying clear of politics and had begun organizing political parties, she still felt that the best course of action for the New Preachers was to "stay above" electoral politics and remain focused on ethical exhortation. Unlike politics, ethics had the potential to unite Egyptians across their differences and to enable an ethos of moderation, of a piety theologically and socially attuned to "the bigger picture," as Engy and Sallam had put it.

THE MANY LIVES OF MODERATION

As a theologically elaborated concept with a lively social life, my interlocutors at Iqraa looked to moderation to steer a course between what they saw as the extremes of both Salafism and secularism across a variety of questions and domains, from what God is like to what human nature is like, from the role of women in the workplace to that of preachers in politics. It is clear that moderation within Islamic media was not about furthering Euro-American security ambitions through reforming Islamic theology along liberal lines. It has been hard for scholars in the Western academy to appreciate this, given the widespread trope of "moderate" Islam that formed after the attacks of September 11, 2001.

With 9/11, the trope of moderate Islam became central to the proliferation of surveillance and counter-terrorism targeting Muslim communities from New York City to Antwerp. This government instrumentalization of the concept of moderation through a security lens created distinctions between "Good Muslims" and "Bad Muslims" that elided the complicity of Western states in creating the structural conditions that gave rise to terrorism as a modern form of political violence. Here moderation invariably asked Muslims to prove that they were moderate by adopting a secularized religiosity that did not threaten the (neo)liberal status quo. Even before 9/11, this demand was anticipated by the "good Islam" promoted by the Egyptian state in its own media efforts to combat the legitimacy of religiously justified violence against it.[62]

Given this security lens, most critical analyses of the idea of "moderate Islam" focus on it as a technology of Western neo-imperial governance on a global scale, implicating Muslim-majority states from Pakistan to Egypt to Saudi Arabia in a project of secular liberal hegemony. These analyses assume that the forms of Muslim piety seen in the West as compatible with secular liberalism (Sufism, in most accounts) and those deemed threatening (Salafism) have remained stable across time. This assumption dehistoricizes the changing configurations of secular liberalism, empire, and specific Islamic formations, seeing normative continuities where there are in fact significant ruptures. Western attempts at promoting various forms of Islam have less to do with shoring up the particular sensibilities that attend them and more to do with maintaining strategic power within shifting geopolitical terrains. The Western life of moderation is neither doctrinally stable nor politically predictable, and it is important to remember this if we are to appreciate the social life of moderation as a contested theological concept for Muslims themselves.

The shifting status of Salafism within the Western imaginary is illustrative. Post 9/11, Salafi Muslims became the abject Other in Western media and policy discourses on Islam, which all too often dissected Salafi doctrines as gateways to violent ideologies and terrorist activities. Before 9/11, however, Salafism had been lauded by many Western observers and powerbrokers as precisely the kind of enlightened religion promoted by the Protestant Reformation. This comparison to Protestantism would recur, from the time of Salafism's emergence in the Arabian Peninsula in the eighteenth century well into twentieth century. In *The Wahhabis Seen through European Eyes (1772–1830)*, Giovanni Bonacina shows how the noted Swiss Orientalist chronicler Frederick Burckhardt, who would become the main Western authority on the Salafi Wahhabi movement for the next hundred years, favorably compared the movement to Protestantism. Against the widespread theological condemnation of Abd al-Wahhab and his followers by Muslim religious authorities from Casablanca to Cairo, the strict Calvinist lauded the religious reformer's zeal to "purify" Islam from dubious accretions and saw this as paving the way for a more direct individual engagement with scripture and a "return to the simple letter of the Koran." He commended Abd al-Wahhab's "puritanical" (the adjective was meant as a compliment that resonated with its Christian counterpart) rejection of "music, singing, dancing, and games of every kind" and his movement's principled antagonism to the "superstitious character of the cult of the saints [that is, to Sufism], similar to the Catholic cult." Enlightenment-era philosophers also praised Wahhabi Salafism, with one French Deist extolling the movement as one of fellow "free thinkers" bent on igniting a "revolution" in Muslim lands against religious "despotism" by preaching "an elementary, rational faith."[63] Into the 1900s, Western colonial officials continued to welcome Wahhabi Salafism as the enlightened antidote to "superstitious" and "backwards" Sufi traditions. Whether in Morocco or Sudan, European colonialists cast charismatic Sufism as particularly dangerous and, in alignment with Salafi critiques, favored a more text-based, scriptural religion.[64]

Western powers' promotion of Salafism continued into the postcolonial period. Successive US administrations looked to Saudi Arabia's official Wahhabi Salafi creed both as a bulwark against the worrying "radicalism" of Egypt's secular pan-Arabism under Nasser and as a "moderating" force against Black Muslim American militancy at home.[65] Cold War–era media depictions tracked with government rhetoric, with Saudi Arabia "consistently presented as embodying the right kind of 'Islam'" in liberal, leftist, and conservative newspapers alike.[66] This was during a period in which Salafi clerics were unrivalled in the power of their religious governance within Saudi Arabia. It was only after 9/11—which was masterminded by the Saudi billionaire businessman turned jihadi leader bin Ladin and carried out by Saudi and Egyptian members of al-Qaeda, a terrorist organization claiming a "Salafi" referent—that Western policy preferences swung the opposite way: Salafism was now framed as the very antithesis of the Protestant Reformation, and Sufism was no longer deemed extremist or backwards but instead held up as the epitome of "moderate Islam."

In this brief overview of the Western life of "moderate Islam" across time, we can see how mainline Salafi doctrines and interpretive practices do not change, nor do Western polities' declared investments in secular liberalism. What does change are Western political interests. Put differently, which specific Islamic orientations are positively mapped onto the Protestant Reformation and its attendant "moderation" by Western powers tracks more with contingent geopolitical imperatives and less with a transhistorical secularity.

Nevertheless, Saba Mahmood argues that the invocation of "moderate Islam" is symptomatic of a "normative secularity" that aims to create Muslims who are open to a "Western vision of civilization, political order, and society."[67] The idea of "moderate Islam" thus represents "a convergence of US imperial interests and the secular liberal Muslim agenda" in which both sides seek to create "a particular kind of religious subject who is compatible with the rationality and exercise of liberal political rule."[68] They do this through advocating for "new" practices of scriptural interpretation that are nonliteral and that approach Qur'anic meaning as historically variable. According to this analysis, the foil for this Western vision is Salafi "traditionalism."

From the perspective of many Muslims themselves, however, it is Salafi literalism that ruptures Islamic tradition and serves Western interests by conforming to the most insidious Orientalist stereotypes about Islam. As Thomas Bauer shows, premodern scholars generally took for granted that "the Quranic message harbors a plurality of meanings—that God speaks ambiguously."[69] This assumption that the Qur'an is a divine text with multiple meanings led to an appreciation of its divergent interpretations as enriching—not as disruptive. The recognition of the legitimacy of conflicting interpretations is the normative linchpin of al-Azhar's teaching of the four madhabs of Sunni jurisprudence as well the Ja'fari Shia one. In contrast to shifting Western attitudes toward Salafism, mainstream Islamic theological critiques of Salafism for its "fanatic excess" remain remarkably stable.

There is an extensive body of literature calling attention to itself as a "refutation" of Salafi Wahhabism that dates to the mid-1700s. These internal theological contestations—involving scholars from the Arabian Peninsula as well as the eastern and western parts of the Arab world, from Iraq to Egypt to Morocco—were concerned with countering precisely what the New Preaching television producers I worked with found so problematic about the Salafi theological imaginary: its insistence "on rebuking and accusing Muslims . . . of being infidels," in the words of one tract written during the lifetime of the movement's eponymous founder, Abd al-Wahhab.[70] These discursive battles between advocates and critics of Wahhabism continued even after the establishment of the modern Saudi state. What this means is that, as Madawi al-Rasheed has pointed out, after 9/11 the US and other Western powers became participants in a long-running internal debate *among* Muslims.[71]

Given this history, it is not hard to grasp why my interlocutors would take Salafism—like secularism—to constitute a rupture within the Islamic tradition. Both are understood to undermine moderation, leading to the extremes of either *ghafla* or *ghuluw*. Overcoming these extremes would lead to a revolution within the Islamic Revival and Egypt more broadly on multiple fronts.

MODERATION AS REVOLUTIONARY ETHOS

"The moderate natural thought is like an ember under the coal," Fikry mused during one of our breakroom lunches in the weeks immediately after Mubarak was forced to resign from the presidency. "It never really dies away, but it needs a breath of fresh air to light up again." He went on: "Mubarak's rule was not only corrupt, it was also stupid. It made us all corrupt and stupid. It's like we are all finally waking up from a drug-induced slumber, so it's still hard to figure out what we should do. But we will eventually revert to our natural state of moderation." The revolutionary possibilities of moderation continued to inspire Islamic media producers like Fikry months later. Indeed, the sense of moderation as the most radical solution became increasingly compelling as the country became more polarized.

Looking to moderation as a radical political solution has a long history in Egypt. Bettina Graf argues that the term *wasatiyya* was first coined by the independent-minded Azhari scholar Yusuf al-Qaradawi (1926–2022). One of the most influential Sunni theologians in the modern periods, Qaradawi's writings have been loosely associated with the reformist wing of the Muslim Brotherhood. He popularized the idea of *wasatiyya* in the 1980s to critique both state repression in Egypt and the armed Islamist insurgency against the state. More broadly, for the millions of Muslims who read his books and tuned in to his TV program *Shari'a and Life* on al-Jazeera, Qaradawi showed how to balance between the "rigidity" of Salafism and the "laxity" of liberalism.[72] Nevertheless, during his lifetime Qaradawi was often categorized on the one hand as an Islamic extremist by Western pundits and Egyptian secularists and, on the other, as a Westernizing secularist by Salafis.[73]

A more explicitly political genealogy of *wasatiyya* can also be traced in relation to the "New Islamists" in Egypt in the 1990s. The New Islamists—comprising intellectuals, journalists, and lawyers, many of them household names like Fahmi Huwaidi, Abdelwahab Elmessiri, Kamal Abul-Magd, Salim Al-Awa, and Tarek el-Bishry—positioned their religious discourse as a radical alternative to both the state Islam of al-Azhar, the ideologically exclusive Islam of the Muslim Brotherhood, and the violent Islam of Salafi-jihadis. They argued that their vision of an "Islam of the middle way," which stressed the equal rights of women and religious minorities, constitutional democracy, social justice, and the value of pluralism, was the most powerful way to resist Western imperialism, whether military, economic, or cultural. Their Islam would be, as Raymond Baker put it in the title of his book on the movement, "without fear."[74] The New Islamists played a key role in setting the intellectual parameters of a new political party called "The Middle," al-Wasat. Founded in 1996, it brought together a breakaway group of former Muslim Brotherhood members with liberals and leftists, including Coptic Christians. The party aspired to a "'middle' position between the rigid defense of the Islamic tradition and the wholesale adoption of values and institutions imported from 'the West.'" Its platform stressed pluralism as "the most important civilizational principle" while confirming the normative centrality of divine revelation for legislation.[75] A decade later, al-Wasat and New Islamist intellectuals became formative members of the Egyptian Movement for Social Change, or Kefaya (Enough). Kefaya gained international attention in the early 2000s for its bold street protests against the Mubarak regime. For many observers, however, Kefaya's most important contribution to change was that it brought together leftists, liberals, and Islamists to forge a new kind of politics explicitly built on "conciliation among the different ideological trends [which] thus opens the way toward creating a new mainstream."[76]

Talal Asad has characterized this openness as stemming not from the religious beliefs of Kefaya's members but rather from their political solidarity. At the same time, he calls attention to "the religiosity of individual Muslims involved in this movement" as one that "seeks the cultivation of feelings attuned to mutual care within the community, and in that sense it can lay claim to a democratic ethos."[77] This religiosity, however, is not theologically adiaphorous nor merely individual. Kefaya's sensibility—like those of the New Preachers and their followers that I have been tracing—resonated with a broader theology of moderation with deep roots within particular segments of Egypt's Islamic Revival. *Wasatiyya* theologically orients to religious plurality, whether between Muslims and other religious communities or among Muslims themselves, as divinely mandated, as a godly good. This theology is doctrinally disputed by Salafi revivalists, for whom pluralism is antithetical to the exclusive truth that Islamic commitment demands. For Salafis, Iqraa's institutionalization of an ethos of moderation, its posture of being a channel in theory open to all Islamic orientations, was a symptom of secularity, not piety. Like the theological elaborations of moderation this chapter has surveyed, the efforts of the New Islamists, al-Wasat, and Kefaya to institutionalize moderation on a political level were also dismissed by many secularists as a Muslim Brotherhood attempt to make political Islamism more palatable. The Muslim Brotherhood, for its part, dismissed this independent institutionalization as a secular attempt to subvert political Islam from within. The middle may have been a natural state, as Fikry put it, but it was also a lonely one.

Nevertheless, the idea of moderation as a radical political alternative, an alternative with revolutionary potential, continued to burn in the embers, touching on some of the most fundamental ethical, epistemological, and political questions of heated theological debate within the Islamic Revival. The next chapters show how the ethos of moderation was taken up by my interlocutors at Iqraa to mandate a piety attuned to social injustice and a piety attuned to coexistence across difference. Cultivating such a piety on a mass scale through Islamic media would instigate a revolution on multiple scales—within the self, within the piety movement, and within Egypt.

PART II

Four
IMPACT

I AM WITH SAMIA, AN AVID NEW PREACHING VIEWER, IN ONE OF Cairo's athletic-cum-social clubs, a mainstay of middle-class leisure. We are here to rehearse a skit she and some friends had created to promote, in her words, "the ethics of the Square" which were also, she reminds us, "the ethics of Islam." All university-educated professionals in their late twenties and early thirties, the close-knit group of men and women had gone together to Tahrir during the eighteen-day uprising. It is now September, nine months after, but when we speak about Tahrir, we do so in reverential tones, recalling neither the tear gas nor the fear, but the small acts of care. *Do you remember the chic madams sweeping the street? Do you remember how one sandwich fed a dozen? Do you remember the guy who put out his cigarette as soon as he noticed the smoke was choking the person next to him? Do you remember how he even promised he would try to quit smoking altogether? Do you remember?* For this group of pious friends such revolutionary memories recalled what it meant to "truly live up to Islam."

"We were beautiful," Samia sighs, and Amr, stubbled accountant, aspiring playwright, sticks out his arm: "Look—goosebumps." Listening again to my audio recording, I also get goosebumps.

Our goal for the afternoon is to turn our skit into a video for a campaign to persuade people to donate money they would have spent dining out to a charity dedicated to feeding the poor. Samia casts me in the lead role when I share my experience participating in an al-Jazeera documentary about Tahrir. As a few curious kids stop their game of chase to watch, I rehearse walking up to the club canteen counter, studying the menu, taking out my wallet, but then, just as the cashier is about to take my order, I shake my head and stride away, presumably to donate my lunch money. I am a little nervous and my expression becomes dourer with each rehearsal. The fourth time I approach the counter, the cashier jokes that at this point she is going to make a lunch donation herself—to me, so I can finally relax.

Despite my nonexistent acting skills, Samia is adamant that I continue because she wants to juxtapose the skit we are filming with footage from that al-Jazeera documentary showing my family—among many other people—bringing food supplies to the sit-in. In speaking with the film crew, I had connected not showing up empty-handed to the Square to a revolutionary obligation to use my individual resources, however small, to help further a cause I believed to be just. This, I felt, was also the socially engaged ethic that both Samia's campaign and my fieldwork interlocutors back at Iqraa were promoting. In the months following Tahrir, Hosny and his media team would tether this widely shared sense of the importance of mobilizing individual capacity for positive social impact, what they colloquially referred to as leaving "a mark (*basma*)," to the theological notion of *i'mar*.

I'mar is a Qur'anic concept that my interlocutors understood as mandating a relation of affective, ethical, and material care toward "the world," principally the world of other humans. Such a relation is incumbent on human beings as God's *khalifas*, or caliphs in English. Readers will likely be familiar with the term "caliph" in relation to political governance; following the death of the Prophet Muhammad in the seventh century until the early twentieth century, caliph was the customary title of the leader of the global Muslim polity. More broadly, however, the term means successor, the one who fills another's place. Within New Preaching circles, the term *khalifa* captioned the theological ontology of both the moment and purpose of human creation: "Remember," God tells the angels, "I am going to place a successive human authority on earth" (Qur'an 2:30). The status of human beings as God's collective caliphs comes with a responsibility unique to them: of *i'mar*, of having a positive impact on the world they have been entrusted with (Qur'an 35:37).

Taken together, these verses, my interlocutors explained, address the most fundamental theological question of why God created us. They are evidence that God, contrary to what many pietists believe, created human beings to worship Him not only through ritual practice and virtuous self-cultivation but also through actively striving to make the world a better place for others. Within the New Preaching theological imagination, living up to the divine obligation for *i'mar* is part of our innate disposition as humans and has consequences for one's own fate in the Afterlife when God will hold all souls to account for their earthly deeds. Zayna on Hosny's media team put it like this: "Your *fitra* is to help ameliorate the pain of others. That's how God created us, to feel pain when we see people suffering, and when we meet God, He will ask us what we did to help the poor and the downtrodden (*al-muzlumin*)." For her and other producers, social solidarity is an ineluctable aspect of piety, *i'mar* a cultivated attunement to injustice.

A theology of impact also shaped producers' ambition to revolutionize conventional expectations of what counts as Islamic media. From its inception Iqraa aspired to be an Islamic channel that would not just be "about Islam" in the sense of being about ritual practice and, as discussed in previous chapters, programs by the New Preachers emerged as a financially feasible way of living up to this expansive vision. In 2004, Amr Khaled's program *Sunna' al-Hayah* (*Lifemakers*) put Iqraa on the mainstream media map as it introduced to a generation of middle-class Muslim youth unaffiliated with any organized social movements the idea that community service and civic initiatives could be a form of worship, what he termed *'ibadit al-i'mar*. For its young middle-class viewers, *Lifemakers*' significance lay in its insistence that, acting together, they could accomplish the extraordinary despite the limitations of their resources and the constraints of their circumstances. The series spurred young people across the Arab world and beyond to create hundreds of grassroots groups, many adopting the name Lifemakers after the series. Whether it was building rooftop gardens, raising awareness about the health hazards of smoking, or organizing school supply drives for low-income students, Iqraa viewers took seriously Khaled's refrain that small efforts could add up to big change and that they had a religious obligation to at least try to make their communities better places, to try to help themselves.[1]

The New Preachers' turn to self-help is often interpreted, and dismissed, as a neoliberalization of religion. Mona Atia contends, for instance, that Amr Khaled's emphasis on self-transformation is part of a "pious neoliberalism" that leads "to the inescapable conclusion that failure to succeed in the neoliberal world is a result of individual shortcomings."[2] In this reading, the revivalist focus on cultivating personal dispositions comes at the expense of changing the neoliberal policies leading to poverty, ill health, or violence. This is a common critique leveled against self-help culture in general, that its "neoliberal" focus on improving the self precludes structural change and enables the continuation of an inequitable and unjust status quo, whether in Egypt or in the Western countries to which its origins are commonly traced.[3] On Islamic television, however, self-help was linked to *i'mar* as above all an other-oriented ethic. It was reinterpreted as an obligation to work for social change and took the form not of seeking self-fulfilling activities that bring one individual happiness, but of volunteering one's labor, time, and resources to help others. Put simply, self-help mandated not an inward turn but an outward one, whether to others or to God.

In the context of the 2011 uprising, the intersection of *i'mar* and self-help became even more important to Iqraa's desire to remain relevant as an Islamic channel while not wading directly into partisan politics. Promoting a broader understanding of the doctrine of *i'mar* became for my interlocutors a way to Islamically mass mediate a revolutionary disposition of "leaving a mark," of impact. At the beginning of the revolution, in those first few days back at Iqraa after Mubarak was toppled, we would congratulate each other by way of greeting, as if someone had just gotten married or had a baby; there was even a tray of celebratory foil-wrapped chocolates making the rounds from desk to desk. Like so many other Egyptians during this time, Iqraa producers framed Tahrir during the eighteen-day uprising as an "ethical model." Within its hard-won 500,000 square feet of autonomous rule, away from the self-serving machinations of the unjust state, Egyptians were peaceful and productive, creative and caring, democratic and dignified. The utopia they briefly created was free of the social ills that had come to define the country under Mubarak's thirty-year rule. Here there was neither corruption nor crime, neither acquiescence nor apathy. Tahrir prefigured nothing less than the New Egypt and its New

Egyptians, and it was clear that my interlocutors deemed that their most urgent role as Islamic television producers was to create media that did so as well.

But by the time I was working on the skit with Samia in September, nine months after those glorious eighteen days and their chocolate celebration, it was hard to imagine the spirit of Tahrir returning, let alone prevailing. Instead, the "old Egypt" of violence and repression had returned with a vengeance. On October 11, just two weeks after our rehearsal, security forces fired on a group of predominantly Coptic Christians protesting state inaction after the destruction of a church by Salafi vigilantes. This horrific event became known as the Maspero Massacre, in reference to the state television building where the protesters had converged, and was for my interlocutors, as for many others, a national nadir. The odds—whether those were figured as the repressive security apparatus, the collapsing economy, or the recriminatory party politics—seemed stacked against revolutionary success.

Despite this, Hosny's production team remained optimistic about Egypt's future and hopeful about the positive role Islamic channels like Iqraa could play by revolutionizing ordinary Muslims' expectations about what counted as piety and why. Their first new television series after the uprising was called *Ommar al-Ard*, which the channel translated into English as *Developers of the World*. Season 1 aired from January to May 2012 and each episode aimed to help ordinary youth cultivate the attachments, sensibilities, and skills necessary for sustaining the ethos of individual effort motivated by a sense of social responsibility undergirding a revolutionary "New Egypt." As his mentor Khaled did on *Lifemakers*, Hosny emphasized on-air that this was no mere television program but rather a transformative project. The preacher and his team saw *Ommar* as mainstreaming revolutionary consciousness, moving their middle-class viewers from misinformed subjects (*mughayibbun*) to informed spectators (*mushahidun*) to activists (*fa'ilun*). A key refrain over the next two years was "we want people to act, not just watch."

The challenge for the media team was how to mass mediate the connection between the revolution and piety in ways that would last beyond Tahrir and that would be relevant, accessible, and above all "not boring" for ordinary viewers. A significant solution came in the form of a theological adaptation of self-help literature, an inspiration that predated the revolution but became more important after it. Once its Islamic dimensions were properly revealed, my interlocutors believed, self-help could spark the inner transformation needed to make the revolution into an enduring ethic, a way of life, even as the promise of Tahrir seemed to grow more remote. Referencing famous Western self-help writers and globally acclaimed individuals, including non-Muslims, who had "left a mark" across a variety of domains became a way to inspire ordinary viewers and to expand the content of each episode beyond the "conventional" one of Islamic history, Qur'anic parables, and the Prophet's biography.

As this chapter shows, the reconfiguration of self-help through Islamic theology was key both to the political awakening of New Preaching viewers like Samia in the decade before the revolution and to their participation in Tahrir and beyond during it. While Anglo-American self-help promoters typically do not call out social structures as the cause of individual unhappiness, my interlocutors looked to self-help as a way of figuring out how to mobilize people to put in the effort necessary to fulfill the worship of changing conditions, of *'ibadit al-i'mar*. As Western self-help became tethered to this theological concept in a terrain of contested piety, its focus shifted from being true to oneself to being true to God, from believing in the power of the self to believing in the power of God. From the perspective of Islamic producers, this had always been the core insight of self-help but it had become clouded through materialism and secularization.

In his rich account of how one of Indonesia's most popular preachers similarly drew on self-help to make Islamic teachings more relevant and accessible for his middle-class audience, James Hoesterey cautions against "imposing the category of neoliberalism as a tidy, universal explanation" to make sense of this desire to "rebrand Islam."[4] Such caution is vital in analyzing media production particularly within authoritarian contexts. The adaptation of self-help for promoting *i'mar* was helpful in more ambiguously maneuvering within and around constraints and avoiding the not insignificant risks of direct political commentary and contestation. For middle-class viewers like Samia and others, the connection of self-transformation to social impact allowed them to feel that they, too, could participate in creating the New Egypt prefigured in Tahrir within their regular routines and with relative safety. For producers, the genre of self-help offered a way to create Islamic media that was at once revolutionary, responsive, practical to act on, and dazzling. Zayna put it bluntly: "At this point, religion has so much bad baggage in Egypt that your average young person will just shut down if you start with *God says, the Prophet says.*" Iqraa producers abjured this as direct *da'wa* that was boring to watch and difficult to internalize. "It is smarter to start with something they already find appealing and think has nothing to do with being religious and then show how it is actually religious." Their Ommar program would renew the theological ethics of self-help through the revealed truth of human beings as God's *khalifas* tasked with having a beneficial impact on the world while at the same time exploiting self-help's global popularity to create more innovative Islamic media.

Simply put, by presenting the desire to "leave a mark," to have an impact, in a theological register, Hosny and his media team rendered Islamic television a salient space for acting on the new sociopolitical feelings and desires instigated by the revolution, transforming in the process an extraordinary, once-in-a-lifetime event like a revolution into an everyday ethic.

POSITIVELY PIOUS, *APRIL 2011*

Amr Khaled strides across the stage of the American University in Cairo's auditorium to applause and whistles and takes a seat in front of a low glass table with a microphone. I glance to my right at Tante Susu, her smile just visible in the dimmed light as she clicks through her string of prayer beads. Tante Susu's daughter Mona was a freshman at AUC and had gotten us tickets to attend Khaled's talk through the Help Club, a student group she had joined her first term. Taking place less than four months after the 2011 uprising, Khaled's talk was part of the club's revolutionary awareness campaign focused on endemic social problems. Founded in the mid-1990s, the Help Club is one of the university's oldest charity-oriented groups. On campus, its members stood out for their visible piety: almost all the girls wore hijab and the boys took turns leading prayers in between classes, Mona told me. Tante Susu, a long-standing *da'wa* practitioner, was relieved that her daughter had found like-minded friends at a university with a reputation for partying, not piety. A firm supporter of the revolution, she was also delighted that the Help Club wanted its members to participate in building the New Egypt.

"We saw that Egyptians conducted themselves differently during the revolution and we wanted to make that change permanent," the club's president explained as he introduced Khaled. "The revolution is above all an ethical transformation."

"That's right," Tante Susu beamed.

Revolutionary ethics was the theme of Khaled's talk that evening. Like other New Preachers, Khaled characterized Egypt's difficult transitional period as an "ethical crisis," suggesting that the new national mantra should be "the people demand the ethics of the Square," a play on the famous revolutionary chant "the people demand the fall of the regime." For while structurally much had changed—competitive elections on the horizon, trials of police officers underway, media outlets airing more diverse views—Egyptians still behaved as if the old political dispensation were in place: taking bribes, ignoring laws, refusing to listen to those they disagreed with, and so on and so on. Ethics were the infrastructure of the revolution—like plumbing, invisible yet foundational.

"The ceiling for dreaming was so low before January 25th," Khaled went on. "People were afraid to dream. But now, if the students at this university won't dream, then who will? You don't have any excuse: you have money and you have the best education. God will ask you how you used your resources on Judgment Day. You are responsible for the unimaginable injustices (*zulm*) that we see in the country. Because to dream is really to sacrifice for others."

After reminiscing about the power of people coming together in Tahrir Square, Khaled noted that most of the people who were cleaning up Tahrir after the revolution weren't there during the eighteen days. "They felt jealous and wanted to participate. *It is not just the revolutionaries' country*, they said, *it is ours too*." Tante Susu and her family fell into this category. They had cheered the protesters on every day from the living room couch in front of the TV, too cautious—"too cowardly," Mona corrected—to physically join them. Once Mubarak stepped down, they joined the other families descending on Tahrir in celebration and committed themselves to the New Egypt in whatever small ways they could. This was one reason that Mona had been as keen as her mom about the Help Club.

"The revolution is not the renaissance (*nahda*) though," Khaled continued. "The revolution merely removed the obstacles to having a *nahda*."

"Yes, this is just the beginning," Tante Susu murmured, as she clicked through another bead.

Tante Susu and my mother had known each other since high school, coming of age in downtown disco parties. In the early 1990s, however, they drifted apart as their lifestyles diverged. After a serious health scare, Tante Susu swapped the form-hugging dresses and sleeveless tops my mom favored for loose-fitting gowns and headscarves and, eventually, a face veil. She quit her job making theater puppets, devoting herself to her growing family and to perfecting her ritual worship. When I interviewed her, Tante Susu remembered this time as her "Salafi period" and its nadir as her refusal to allow her eldest daughter to attend university and instead marrying her off shortly after her seventeenth birthday. This was highly unusual within Tante Susu's family background but not so unusual among the Salafi circles she was then spending most of her time with. But five years later, her daughter divorced with two kids and living back at home, Tante Susu made another dramatic change: She took off the niqab, bought colorful headscarves, and started avidly watching Amr Khaled. Remorseful about curtailing her daughter's education in the name of pious propriety ("I believed that it would have been sinful to send her to a place where boys and girls would mix"), she paid for a nanny so that her daughter could have time to take courses in whatever interested her. When the time came, she sent her younger daughter Mona to AUC so that she would acquire the sort of education that would help her "stand on her own two feet, no matter what."

Tante Susu tells me that she felt she was finally practicing what she called a *tadayyun fitri*, a piety that is natural, in sync with divinely given dispositions.

"Our religion is a moderate one, a balanced one," she explains. "The Prophet would always choose the easier of two permissible options. So why was I making my life so hard?" During her "Salafi period" she would count the pasta on her plate to make sure it was odd-numbered, because the Prophet loved performing odd-numbered (*witr*) prayers. "I was that zealous," she shakes her head. We were sitting in a small devotional space, a *zawiya* she called it, that she had created within her spacious two-story house. Qur'anic calligraphy adorned the walls and the air was fragrant with frankincense. Mona comes in for the afternoon prayers. Her mom tells her that it is her turn to be interviewed before we have lunch and leave for Khaled's talk at the university.

"There is a very big difference between piety (*tadayyun*) and fanaticism (*tashaddud*)," Mona says as she arranges three prayer mats side by side. How do you define fanaticism? I ask. "Making everything difficult and complicated and scary. Like of course praying on time is fundamental, but if you miss a prayer someone shouldn't harass you and call you an infidel! God is more merciful than that."

"And piety isn't just about avoiding sins," Tante Susu interrupts, "we have to actively do good, we have to be positive (*igabi*) in our piety. Especially now! Egypt is being born again after forty years of ethical and political corruption. But it's a messy birth, full of pain. We are seeing both the very best and the very worst of what we are capable of." While Tante Susu and Mona spoke about Tahrir in reverential tones, they were worried that the "new" Egyptians who made the revolution possible had reverted to their old ways. As these women saw it, the sustainability of revolutionary transformation depended on increasing the influence and attraction of pious moderation promoted by Khaled and other New Preachers: a piety that was balanced, positive, and other-oriented in its social activism. This piety lived up to the Prophet's exhortation to "work for this world as if you will live forever and for the next as if you will die tomorrow." By contrast, the Salafi focus on ritual perfection encouraged social apathy.

It would seem, then, that the surprising Salafi turn to politics after the revolution would be positively interpreted by my interlocutors. But as the next sections discuss, New Preaching fans like Tante Susu, Mona, and others did not see the Salafi preachers' backing of specific parties and politicians as a praiseworthy example of positive piety, but rather as partisan piety. While politics made ordinary people turn against each other, positive piety offered people an opportunity to help each other, to cultivate the right kind of dreams.

EVERYDAY CALIPHS, *JANUARY 2012*

Hosny stands at a chrome podium, facing camera one, with a bookcase and glass coffee table in the background, to his right a wall of photographic portraits. It's an eclectic collection that includes US figures such as civil rights activist Malcolm X and tech inventor Steve Jobs alongside Nelson Mandela, the leader of South Africa's anti-apartheid movement, and Shaykh Yassin, the assassinated spiritual leader of the Palestinian violent resistance movement Hamas, as well as Egyptians such as NASA space geologist Farouk al-Baz and heart transplant pioneer Magdy Yacoub. What unites them is the media team's belief that they are all, irrespective of their religious tradition, political orientation, or national origin, 'ummar al-ard, impactful individuals, making them fitting subjects for discussion on Hosny's program of the same name.

During the initial brainstorming sessions for the *Ommar* series, the primary focus was on highlighting successful community organizations and their potential role in the New Egypt. However, as Hosny's media team delved deeper into this concept, they began to feel that the average viewer might struggle to relate to institutions. Far more vivid and concrete would be to focus on the accomplished individuals behind organizations. Summing up the team's discussions in a November meeting the year before, Zayna emphasized the importance of showing "our viewers how they can become the kinds of people who are able to create these kinds of institutions in the first place." This task of hopeful inspiration seemed particularly urgent that month: protesters were once again being killed by security forces in Tahrir and ordinary people were increasingly anxious and afraid of what the future might bring. She took this team consensus to Hosny, who prayed *istikhara*, the Islamic guidance prayer, and he reported back that his heart felt at ease with the new direction.

The next step involved compiling enough success stories for an entire season. The team initially brainstormed a list of 200 candidates, which was later narrowed down to 50. This shortlist was then presented to Hosny, who, in consultation with Emad, made the final selection of 16 individuals. During this selection process, several criteria came into play, sometimes in competition with each other. One key criterion was that the individual's "success story" had to be dramatic. The obstacles they overcame hadn't been superficial or easily surmountable; rather, they had required resourcefulness and creative effort. Egypt wasn't the sort of country where success came easily except for the very elite or the very corrupt. The team owed viewers stories that realistically reflected the effort necessary to make a difference, to turn dreams into reality.

Given that over half of each forty-five-minute episode would focus on a single story, the shortlist also favored people who were already globally famous with personal details about them publicly available. However, the team was also eager to include ordinary Egyptians, relying on their personal networks to identify them. While these individuals might not have had the dramatic life story of a global political icon like Mandela, they brought interpersonal drama to the program by interacting with the preacher and his viewers on-air. For example, one featured Egyptian had developed an affordable type of paint. Featuring such examples as "success stories" helped convey that *i'mar* did not necessarily consist of extraordinary, world-altering achievements, but could be small in scale, within the realm of ordinary possibility.

It was essential to emphasize this point because the desire to "leave a mark," as articulated by Hosny and his team, was an integral aspect of human beings' theological ontology. Human beings are distinct from the rest of creation, possessing a divinely granted supremacy over the earth and other beings. However, this supremacy is not one of possessive ownership but of stewardship, of *khilafa*. Andrew March shows how the doctrine of *khilafa* influenced utopian theories of democracy and popular sovereignty among Islamically oriented political theorists from Tunisia to Egypt.[5] He argues that in the decades leading up to the 2011 uprisings the mainstream Islamist reinterpretation of Qur'anic verses on God's appointment of a vice-regent constituted a revolution in Islamic thought that made theologically persuasive the democratic premise that "the people" have legitimate—that is, divinely given—authority over their own governance. For my own interlocutors, however, the theological thematization of ordinary people as God's caliphs was salient not to necessarily revolutionizing party politics, but more fundamentally to revolutionizing conventional notions of piety within the Islamic Revival.[6]

Like his mentor Amr Khaled, Hosny linked the doctrine of *khilafa* to *i'mar* as a form of worship. As caliphs, human beings are tasked with acting toward each other and the natural and animal world within the parameters revealed by God, who is the true owner of the world. This dominion does not lead to domination, as it does in secular philosophies, but to a sense of caring responsibility. In entrusting human beings to be His "successors" on earth, God was mandating that they work toward its flourishing and betterment.

This was an innovative interpretation that widened the classical commentary of *i'mar* from agricultural cultivation to the ethical and material thriving of communities and countries through social activism. Again, the New Preachers connected this social obligation to the ontology of humanity. According to the Qur'an, God breathed His spirit into human beings He created from the earth's clay. Hosny explained on-air that just as God ordained that children come from their mother's womb to grow and to honor her, He created human beings from the earth's clay so that they may care for it in various ways. Humans are the only one of God's creations to be honored with the responsibility of *i'mar* because they are the only one made with the divine spirit—that is, with the potential to embody, however imperfectly, divine attributes such as wisdom, justice, or mercy.[7] This is why "God does not change the condition of a people until they change themselves" (Qur'an 13:11).[8]

This verse was an oft-quoted one at Iqraa, inspiring the title of Amr Khaled's widely watched 2004 program for the channel. My interlocutors generally took it to mean that the collective fate of societies and nations is closely linked to the moral character of their individual members, that the divine deliverance of a community is contingent on individuals working on their inner selves. This interpretation has deep historical roots, with the renowned nineteenth-century Islamic reformer Muhammad Abduh invoking the same verse to advocate for gradual social and political change as part of his anti-colonial strategy.[9] In the postcolonial era, both the Muslim Brotherhood and more militant Islamist thinkers, such as Sayyid Qutb, also drew upon this verse to underscore the importance of the establishment of an Islamic society as a step toward the formation of an Islamic state.[10] However, for my interlocutors, this verse's central interest lay not in the quest for state power but in cultivating a sense of social impact, of leaving a mark, as an essential aspect of Islamic devotional practice. The key takeaway of *Ommar* was that the power that God bestowed on human beings as His caliphs creates an obligation to worship Him through practicing *i'mar* in everyday life. Hosny's mission as an Islamic television preacher was to cultivate in his viewers of "ordinary people" a sense of empowerment to make good on their status as *khalifas*, as God's caliphs.

Hosny's team spent weeks brainstorming talking points to this effect, which were neatly bullet pointed on the preacher's podium for the broadcasts.

"Religion is about the world, not just about the relationship between a person and his Lord," Hosny explained to viewers tuning into the first episode. "I want to change the concept of piety (*mafhum al-tadayyun*) to include how people can benefit each other and this earth."[11]

He went on: "Self-cultivation (*tahdib al-nafs*) through ritual worship is the foundation of *i'mar*. But rituals (*al-manasik*) are ultimately about what is due from me to God. *I'mar* is about what is due between us as human beings. Islam is about both those things." Just as ritual worship fulfills God's rightful claim over us, *i'mar* secures the well-being of His creation. *I'mar* is not a matter of choice, Hosny continued, but is as obligatory for Muslims as the five daily prayers and the Ramadan fast. Like these pillars, *i'mar* is a means of cultivating godliness. In this theology of impact, piety goes beyond prescribed ritual self-cultivation to the cultivation of an ethos of care for others.

The sense that Islamic piety requires a social attentiveness to community needs is not specific to Egypt's New Preachers. For example, Kimberly Hart shows how villagers in rural Turkey "worked for God" in the sense of understanding their "good deeds" as at once interventions that change the world and spiritually prepare for the next world. Similarly, Jeanette Jouili explains that for many European Muslim women piety was simultaneously geared toward virtuous self-discipline and performing acts of citizenly care. Her interlocutors, who were also inspired by Egypt's New Preachers and their "Islam of the Middle Way," were in part motivated by a desire to positively represent Islam in face of its widespread secularist denigration in France.[12] In my own fieldwork, however, the stress on piety as *i'mar* was intended less to counter secular stereotypes and more to theologically debunk Salafism's overwhelming focus on ritual assiduity as the key to Prophetic emulation.

Hosny explained that "any person who loves the Prophet and wants to be like him should aim to have a beneficial impact (*yisib basma nafi'a*). If he is not trying to be useful to others, he must revise his notion of piety, because it is fundamentally wrong."

This emphasis on piety beyond conventional worship does not mean that the New Preachers took ritual any less seriously than their Salafi rivals. Hosny, like other New Preachers, was questioning neither the efficacy of ritual practice for forming durable virtuous dispositions over time nor the salvific consequences of rituals correctly performed. Rather he sought to move his viewers from a self-centered notion of piety (*my soul, my salvation*) to an other-centered piety (*my community, my relationships*) in order to connect them to new possibilities for radical change opened up by the 2011 revolution. *I'mar* was an everyday practice his ordinary viewers—young people who supported the revolution even if just from their living rooms—could adopt. Above all, then, through its premise of "we will build our country as we build ourselves," *Ommar* aspired to inspire its imagined audience of middle-class youth to connect their own pious potential to the promise of a New Egypt.

"START WITH YOURSELF"

"The most important thing we discovered in Tahrir is that we love Egypt," Hosny told his viewers in the first episode of *Ommar*. "We realized that this is *our* country, that we are now in control of our country (*al-balad baladna*). But we still don't know what to do with this responsibility. My new program will show you how to leave a mark (*basma*) on life."

The sense that "the country is now ours" was pervasive in the weeks following Mubarak's toppling in February 2011. Listening to the radio on my commute on February 22, I heard a psychologist explain that Egyptians under Mubarak had fallen victim to "depression and a feeling that this country doesn't belong to them, that they are just precarious renters. Now they feel finally like homeowners and so they are working to be better and to make the country better." He gave the example of friends who used to litter but now sweep their street on the weekend. This was happening in my neighborhood, where bands of volunteers took turns picking up road trash or repainting faded curbs, as many others did across the city.[13] For my interlocutors, such small acts of ownership were signs of the New Egypt.

As they were preparing for *Ommar*, the media team uploaded on Hosny's website a widely circulating pamphlet titled "The Ethics of the Square: Start with Yourself." I first saw it plastered on a light post downtown the month after Mubarak resigned. It began: "The 25th of January revolution isn't just a chance for political change in Egypt, but a chance for every person to prove to himself and to others that he's a real citizen and a real Egyptian. *This country is now ours.* [Make a promise]: I will not litter again . . . I will not give a bribe again . . . I will obey all traffic signals . . . I won't cheat on exams . . . I won't harass women."

Start with yourself is the quintessential self-help mantra and what critics often have in mind when they lambast the genre as neoliberal. Indeed, the most common critique of the self-help literature in the US is that its focus on individual behavior and attitudes does not acknowledge the power of structural factors in shaping life opportunities and trajectories. By asking people to focus on "fixing" themselves, self-help shores up the status quo because real change is about fixing policies, laws, and institutions. Similarly, observers of Egypt criticize the focus on "starting with the self" as a depoliticizing indication of neoliberal logics that occlude the real causes of misery and injustices: failing structures, not failing selves.

This critique is simplistic, overlooking the ways in which the structural *context* of self-help matters to its social efficacy in several ways. For one, if self-help invites criticism of depoliticization, this is partly by design. Self-help is a prefigurative politics especially well suited for making change under authoritarian rule. Prefiguration is the enactment of desired futures in the present of one's own life and interactions. Anthropologists have theorized the concept mostly in relation to radical leftist groups in Western democracies, showing how this activism in many cases revolves around bodily and affective experiences.[14] Prefiguration, however, might be even more significant for social change in authoritarian countries. Unlike in liberal democracies where activists can organize to change laws and policies through elections and mass mobilizations, in authoritarian states the costs of doing so are very high. Grassroots initiatives become one of the few ways available to ordinary people to try to make change. State-oriented Islamists like the Muslim Brotherhood have long realized this, of course, and their members built an extensive parallel network of social welfare institutions throughout the 1980s and '90s as an alternative to failing ones of the state. As Carrie Wickham shows in her classic study of the group during this period, its members "challenged dominant patterns of political alienation and abstention by promoting a new ethic of civic obligation that mandated participation in the public sphere, regardless of its benefits and costs."[15] In comparison, the prefigurative politics of the New Preachers' self-help is even smaller in scale and not organized by party politics, making it similar to the individual focus of Salafi piety. Yet, unlike Salafism's emphasis on a politics of ritual self-cultivation, it redirects attention toward the individual outward, to the individual's social impact on others as a theological imperative. In other words, start with yourself does not necessarily mean end with yourself. What is more, many of the "new" ways of thinking that scholars have argued became possible after the revolution—such as seeing "the political in the daily and the quotidian" or "a discernable DIY spirit [in which] people feel they can look after themselves"—have long been part of New Preaching discourses.[16] This why Islamic television producers look back on a program like *Lifemakers*, with its can-do ethos of social solidarity, as planting the seeds of the 2011 revolution.[17]

When I mention this to my progressive colleagues in the Western academy, they usually raise a skeptical eyebrow. As one representative critic laments, "By emphasizing individual strategies for success, prophets of the empowered self downplay the real structures of power and inequality in our society."[18] This dismissal of the power of the empowered self misses the ways in which regular Islamic television viewers like Samia and her friends felt compelled to join the mobilization in Tahrir, "go down to the Square," precisely because their consciousnesses of state failures—and sense that their efforts to rectify them could matter—had been raised through watching *Lifemakers*. From my interlocutors' perspective, then, Samia was *their* "success story" as Islamic media producers. She exemplified the kind of pious revolutionary practitioner Hosny and his team hoped to create through their innovative amalgam of self-help and piety—she was profoundly other-oriented and connected this orientation to her divinely mandated capacity for *i'mar*. She had the right dream—a dream for Egypt—and she took concrete steps to make it a reality.

This again calls for foregrounding the conditions of possibility that made the mantra "start with yourself" ethically exemplary of Tahrir and prefigurative of the New Egypt. Before the revolution, Hosny explained to me, starting with the self felt less possible because Egyptians felt they had no control over their ethical choices: "Why study hard for an exam when teachers actively encourage cheating? Why do things by the book when paying a bribe get things done faster? Why work hard when stealing is easier? Under Mubarak, ethics didn't get you very far," he argued. Egyptians had felt disconnected from the state of their own street, let alone the state that governed them. They felt like strangers in their own land, that Egypt was most definitely not theirs but, rather, the fiefdom of a corrupt autocrat and his billionaire cronies. But then in Tahrir Square, in a space where they were in charge, Egyptians caught a glimpse of how Egypt—how they—could be otherwise. They saw how a change in structural context enabled them to individually change from conformist to creative, from unfocused to determined, from cowardly to courageous, from divided to unified. My interlocutors at Iqraa believed that programs like *Ommar* could theologically contribute to changing Egypt's collective condition by helping viewers recapture that sense of agency over their own fates that they had experienced in Tahrir. The Revolution needed a revolution not only within the piety movement, but within the self.

RETURNING SELF-HELP TO ISLAM

Ommar aired alongside other New Preaching programs explicitly addressing the revolutionary moment, such as Moez Masoud's *Thawra 'ala al-Nafs* (*The Revolution Within*) and Amr Khaled's *Bukra Ahla* (*Tomorrow Will Be Better*). These series also focused on ethical transformation as part of a revolutionary praxis. Hosny's team at Iqraa nevertheless felt that their own program would stand out through its emphasis on the practical strategies that ordinary people could marshal in their everyday lives to cultivate the "the spirit of Tahrir." These strategies were based on what is commonly referred to in the US as self-help but in Egypt is called *al-tanmiya al-dhatiya*, or "self-development." To navigate this extensive literature, Hosny and his team relied heavily on the expert input of Ahmed El Aawar a prominent self-help popularizer and life coach.

"My goal is to teach people to realize their own power for change and to understand that as part of our religion as Muslims," Ahmed told me over coffee near his home office in Heliopolis. "That's also Mustafa's goal with his preaching. Working together can have an even bigger impact." Ahmed's trajectory from corporate executive to Islamic media consultant sheds light on the contextual intersections of religious revivalism and self-help both before and after the revolution.

Ahmed became Egypt's first "certified life coach" after his disenchantment with a lucrative career in corporate management. By his early thirties the bespectacled, curly-haired executive was being headhunted by the region's top multinational companies and making more money than he could spend. Nevertheless, he felt depressed, bereft of a life purpose. During this period, he read for the first time Stephen Covey's self-help classic *The 7 Habits of Highly Effective People*. It changed his life. Covey's book is typically understood by critics (most of whom appear not to have read it) as the epitome of neoliberal rationality, as an example of how even the self has become a site of economic management. But Covey's declared aim in writing it was to proffer an alternative to the corporate rhetoric of "productivity" and "efficiency" ascendant in 1980s America. He critiques the economistic logic of accumulation for accumulation's sake as ethically bankrupt and psychologically harmful and hopes to cultivate within readers a sense of concern and obligation beyond "me and mine."[19] Covey wanted Americans to stopping asking that quintessentially selfish question, *What's in it for me*, and realize that "true greatness" lies in "work[ing] selflessly—*with* mutual respect, *for* mutual benefit."[20] This ethical exhortation to look beyond the bottom line resonated with Ahmed. The companies he worked for were globally successful but hadn't done enough to translate their profits into social benefits, and he felt he was on the same track. He was wealthy enough at one point to own a boat, but how did that help anyone, really, including him?

"I started giving lectures about Covey's book in my sister's living room to some of her friends," he continued. "And I quickly started adding an explicit Islamic perspective to it." He had memorized the entire Qur'an at a young age and grew up in a family he described as "very religious." Throughout our conversation that afternoon he punctuated his exposition of the ins and outs of the training he received at Columbia University and coaching institutes in Switzerland with Qur'anic verses. Still, he felt that the "Qur'an on its own wasn't enough to get me, and the people I knew, out of this crisis, this crisis of the *me-first* mentality. I needed an on-the-ground application."

Covey's teachings gave him an up-to-date language and innovative frame for putting into practice what Ahmed believed to be fundamentally Islamic imperatives. After all, Covey's core insight about the power of habitual action to transform inner dispositions and thus to eventually change external circumstances was what the Prophet Muhammad taught. Covey's book allowed him to see how to connect his modern angst about careerism and keeping up with the Hasans with the "deeper meanings" of Qur'anic and

Prophetic injunctions he knew so well, and he wanted others to benefit from these connections too. He was, he told me, what the essayist Malcolm Gladwell in *The Tipping Point* calls a "maven," or "people we rely upon to connect us with new information."[21] Ahmed explains this as a God-given gift. "The Prophet teaches us that every creation has a purpose (*kull muyassar lima khuliqa lahu*). I had found finally what I was created for."

By 1999, Ahmed was renting hotel conference halls for his seminars and a few years later left his corporate career to devote himself full-time to life coaching. The New Preacher Amr Khaled attended Ahmed's seminars around this time and consulted with him. They would spend hours together at Khaled's house bandying ideas. Khaled's 2004 series for Iqraa *Until They Change Themselves*, in reference to the oft-quoted Qur'anic verse, came out of these brainstorming sessions. The series called on viewers to refuse to be "passive victims of failed states" and instead work together to effect needed social change. As Hosny would do later with *Ommar*, Khaled stressed that this was "not just a television program" but a collaborative project to reclaim power and reimagine futures on a national, even regional, scale.

Ahmed's working relationship with Khaled didn't last ("Nothing personal, the chemistry just wasn't there"), but his links to Islamic television continued when Iqraa hired him as a coach for Hosny and his media team. During my fieldwork, the team would gather every month in Hosny's home for sessions with Ahmed. Zayna told me that these meetings helped her understand the Prophetic biography through a "self-development eye" and this influenced her content creation as an editor. She would, for example, put effort into creating actionable points from Qur'anic stories of the prophets' lives, or in figuring out what would be the most memorable detail from an event involving the Prophet and his Companions. She understood the popularity of self-help in Egypt as lying in its practical accessibility and intimate register, already aspects of what producers considered "innovative" Islamic media.

Zayna was also surprised at how closely Covey's insights echoed Prophetic exhortations. Perhaps, she asked me, this "American Christian" (Covey was Mormon) had read up on the Prophetic biography and wasn't letting on? This was possible, I told her, but I wasn't sure. I did some research when I was back at my university library and found out that before writing his bestseller *The 7 Habits*, Covey had penned a missionary booklet titled *The Divine Center*. He argued that any group in the world could be successfully taught "many gospel principles if we are careful in selecting words which carry our meaning but come from their experience and frame of mind."[22] This evangelical strategy was itself similar to the New Preaching one. Indeed, Zayna might have found self-help rhetorical forms easy to adopt for *da'wa* because the genre itself, never mind its programmatic assumption of the power of self-discipline, re-mediates that of the traditional sermon.[23] The first line in the Scottish reformer Samuel Smiles's 1856 book, *Self-Help*, "Heaven helps those who help themselves," recalls the Qur'anic verse "God does not change the condition of a people until they change themselves." When I shared this with Zayna, she concluded that self-help spoke so readily to her as a pious Muslim because in the end, all human beings—she, her viewers, and Covey—have an ingrained human nature, *fitra*, that speaks loudly to us across time and space so long as we are willing to listen in new ways. In this way, Zayna saw Covey as more Islamic in his creative gospel reframings and other-oriented "positive piety" than the "unimaginative" Salafi preachers so focused on ritual perfection.

In mining self-help for its *da'wa* affordances, Hosny and his team were on well-trod terrain. One of Indonesia's most popular preachers, Aa Gym, with an audience of middle-class Muslims anxious about a rapidly changing Indonesia, aimed to "rebrand Islam" through combining contemporary self-help bestsellers like Tony Robbins's *Awaken the Giant Within* with Sufi teachings. Like the New Preachers, Aa Gym aimed his "cutting-edge Islam" at nothing less than a moral transformation of an entire nation.[24] The turn to Anglo-American self-help by Islamic figures goes beyond the contemporary period as well. Histories of modern self-help take Smiles's 1856 *Self-Help* as the first example of this genre. The book partook both in a broader Victorian sensibility about good character and in a progressive investment in the upward mobility of the historically downtrodden.[25] The book was translated into Arabic a couple of years later under the title *Sirr al-Najah* (The secret of success). By 1886 it had inspired Egypt's first Self-Help Society, focused on ethics and moral discipline (*akhlaq wa-tarbiya*). Timothy Mitchell traces how both British colonialists and their Egyptian nationalist opponents considered the uptake of self-help sensibilities useful to their aims. One prominent anti-colonial leader, Mustafa Kamil (1874–1908), had quotes from Smiles's book stenciled onto the walls of a school he founded. At a time when access to education was limited, he declared the school "to be his own practical application of the doctrine of self-help."[26] Self-help in this colonial context meant, above all, using one's own resources to help fellow Egyptians out of a cultivated sense of social responsibility grounded in a correctly formed ethical disposition.

Anglophone self-help continued to find a receptive audience in the postcolonial period, including within Islamic circles. The influential Egyptian theologian Muhammad al-Ghazali (d. 1996) published in 1956 an Arabic commentary on the American self-help classic of his time, Dale Carnegie's *How to Stop Worrying and Start Living.* He was so inspired by the book he felt it necessary to "return the book to its Islamic foundations." Al-Ghazali dubbed Carnegie and other American self-help advocates "American Sufis," arguing that they were (unwittingly) participating in a venerable Islamic tradition of self-cultivation as the key to collective empowerment.[27] Like Kamel in the 1890s and al-Ghazali in the 1950s, Ahmed, Zayna, and others at Iqraa believed that a self-help ethos "returned to Islam" could scale up to a New Egypt by making it possible to inhabit Islamic piety in what they deemed an innovative and revolutionary register. It would do so by cultivating hopeful, helpful, people.

SELF-HELP AS OTHER HELP, *SEPTEMBER 2011*

The afternoon following the filming of the skit with Samia, I meet her for an interview at the private Islamic school where she teaches science. She is wiping the blackboard as her students file out to hop onto the buses idling outside, her floor-skimming skirt and hijab splotchy white with chalk dust. She asks that we do the interview in English so she can practice the new vocabulary specific to *da'wa* that she learned from a course she recently completed on "how to explain Islam to non-Muslims." This course, she tells me, is part of her self-development regimen, inspired by all the New Preaching programs she had been watching over the past decade. She connects these programs to her road to Tahrir Square in our interview.

After getting divorced, Samia found herself with more free time and more freedom to use it as she wished. She started to volunteer in one of Cairo's Lifemakers groups—grassroots, youth-led organizations inspired by the New Preacher Amr Khaled's eponymous Iqraa series—to tutor needy schoolchildren. She went on from there to volunteer at the cancer hospital, then at the central food bank, then Resala, one of Egypt's biggest charities. It was in these spaces, interacting and developing relationships with people who were too poor, too downtrodden, too precarious, to ever be part of her everyday social world, that she began to develop what she called "political awareness," *wa'y siyasi*.

"I wasn't political at all—I couldn't name a government minister or a party or anything like that," she says. "But seeing all these people living in such difficult, difficult conditions and seeing how the government wasn't helping them, but making their lives even more miserable, I started paying more attention to politics. They [Mubarak's government] took away people's social security and their health benefits. How can they afford medicine or medical care?"

Samia switches to Arabic: "Most people's salaries are shit—still, they must pay taxes and they get nothing in return. Our country is full of resources and foreigners come here and get rich and leave, but the poor stay poor. Look at most of our schools—do you think they are like this?" She gestures to the computer on her desk, the hardbound books on her shelves. "No, the government schools are so awful, they have no resources, no chairs for students to sit on and no money to pay their teachers properly. But despite this everyone was quiet. Why were we all so quiet?"

So when protests erupted, she thought, *Finally! Things are going to change.* When she saw people acting out and speaking up, including her friends from yesterday's skit, she knew she had to join them.

She goes on, her voice rising with emotion: "You have to understand, I didn't go down to Tahrir Square for myself. I am comfortable. I went to a good school, a British one. Now I work in a good school. My father is a successful businessman. We live in a nice area in a nice building. We are not needy. But so many, so many Egyptians are. So I went to Tahrir for them."

As we get ready to leave the school, she tells me that after what she experienced in Tahrir, her dream became to one day be strong enough in faith and resolve to walk away from her tuition-based private school job and teach in one of the city's free public schools. Most students who attend Egypt's derelict government-run schools are the ones from families so poor they have no other option. "I know my switching jobs won't help fix this shit system (*al-nizam al-khara dah*), but at least it will help one school or even just one classroom," she says. "Isn't that better than nothing? And at least I will be able to stand before God on Judgment Day and say that I tried my best." For Samia as for so many others I met during my fieldwork on Islamic television, having an impact, trying her best, was laden with eschatological expectation: the effort to alleviate another's condition in this life was a simultaneous investment in alleviating her own condition in the Afterlife. But to be able to devote herself to this other-oriented dream, Samia had to become a particular kind of person: a person who didn't waste time watching TV dramas or gossiping on the phone or shopping at the mall but who instead concentrated on how to "leave a mark" on the world that makes it better for others. In this way, the reconfiguration of self-help through an Islamic theology of impact, like her volunteering, was key to Samia's dreams for the New Egypt prefigured in Tahrir.

The target audience for Hosny's consciousness-raising preaching was not the "subaltern" typically targeted by leftists, but rather the middle class. The goal was to make "Class A and Class B Plus" viewers like Samia more aware of the country's widespread social and economic inequalities and to engender within them feelings of obligation toward the more vulnerable and precarious Egyptians who suffered them. As Emad put it in one of the planning sessions for *Ommar*, "Part of what's wrong in Egypt is that some people feel like nothing *is* wrong. Our first step is to get people to open their eyes to the problems and the second is to get them to participate in fixing them."

Hosny's producers felt that a powerful way of accomplishing these aims was to introduce their viewers to Egyptians who had succeeded in mobilizing others toward social activism. One of the first such individuals featured on *Ommar* was Dr. Sherif Shehata, an engineering professor who helped found one of the country's most well-known charities, Resala. Amira Mittermaier conducted ethnographic fieldwork at one of Resala's branches and notes that many of the charity's volunteers looked up to New Preachers like Hosny, with one joining Resala after learning about Dr. Sherif on Iqraa.[28] Resala's projects run the gamut from providing clothes for low-income university students, to giving out food in impoverished neighborhoods, to running a free hospital and an elementary school. In the decade leading up to the revolution, Resala had grown into the largest volunteer-led organization in the Arab world, with over sixty branches across Egypt.[29] For my interlocutors, Dr. Sherif's success story was without question exemplary of *i'mar*, of positive impact.

In November 2012, Hosny announced that he had formed a voluntary association of his own, called Ommar al-Ard, like the TV program. In a video recording released on his Facebook page, Hosny explicitly noted that the development (*tanmiya*) aims of his NGO—its commitment to projects that allow the poor "to live with dignity"—"should be the role of the government but we are not going to wait for the government."[30] While other media figures were responding to the revolution by turning to politics, he went on, his initiative would enable viewers-turned-volunteers to have "a real impact," to "leave a positive mark," while remaining independent from parties and "organized ideologies." This strategy of partisan agnosticism is favored by civic activists across the Global South as a way of surviving in volatile political contexts.[31] And because in Egypt the voluntary associations started by pious middle-class professionals have been long perceived as a recruitment tactic to mobilize the poor to join (or at least sympathize with) the Muslim Brotherhood and against the secular state in the Mubarak period,[32] it was especially important for Hosny to stress the apolitical nature of his NGO. As we have seen, part of his distinction as a professional preacher was a principled commitment to remaining "above" the partisan fray.

Funded through donations, Ommar the NGO was managed by volunteers who were Hosny's friends, most of whom had day jobs working for multinational corporations. I spoke with the person in charge of the organization's first campaign, which connected houses in a rural Delta village to safe drinking water. She was an upper-level executive in one of the country's biggest telecommunications companies; she barely had enough time to help her kids with their homework, let alone help a whole village. But it was outrageous to her that so many Egyptians lacked reliable access to this necessity, that water fit for drinking and washing was for many poor people, even in Cairo, something to struggle for and worry about on a daily basis.[33] While the 2011 revolution promised to change this situation, in the meantime Egyptians like her with comparatively more resources—with privilege, to use an Americanism—should not wait for corrupt and incompetent state agencies to act, but must do their part because ultimately they would be held accountable on Judgment Day for all their deeds, big and small. She approvingly cited Amr Khaled's recent initiative in his Lifemakers NGO bringing together revolutionary icons like Wael Ghonim and beloved film stars like Mohamed Sobhy to raise $1 billion from corporations to build roads and sewage systems, even schools and hospitals, in Cairo's marginalized "informal" quarters, or slums. The telecom executive saw this initiative, like Hosny's, as an example of a solidarity grounded in divine accountability, of people acting on their responsibility to ameliorate injustices as God's caliphs.

Nevertheless, for many left-leaning academics such middle-class activism and its institutionalization in civil society groups, unlike working-class action, was of little consequence to the revolutionary mobilization of Tahrir.[34] Instead of indicating a revolutionary piety, volunteerism as a pious practice subject to divine rewards illustrated the takeover of religion by the calculating logic of neoliberal capitalism, of which the New Preachers are a prime example.[35] In Egypt as elsewhere across the Global South, scholars have noted the simultaneous decline of state-provided services and rise of the voluntary sector under neoliberalism. Many argue that the nongovernmental organizations of this sector have a depoliticizing effect, turning political questions of justice, inequality, and oppression into technical issues of policy reform. As one academic critic puts it in relation to Egypt, there is "too much civil society, too little politics."[36] However, other scholars caution against ascribing so much power to neoliberalism. On the basis of her fieldwork at Resala, Mittermaier argues for the coexistence of calculative logics alongside other economic theologies within Egypt's Islamic charities that "unsettle claims about an all-pervasive neoliberalization of everyday life."[37] I agree. As I have suggested, the histories of self-help, whether in Egypt or the US, cannot be simply reduced to neoliberalism. And even if self-help and volunteerism *are* irredeemably neoliberal, can they nevertheless offer resources that help individuals counter neoliberalism's social and economic harms? Can neoliberal tools build a New Egypt that even the critics of neoliberalism would recognize as more equitable and just?[38] The next sections take up these questions.

FEELING THE REVOLUTION, *FEBRUARY 2012*

On the director's screen in Iqraa's control room a small American boy with a big grin toddles on fiberglass legs. Both of Cody's legs had been amputated just after his first birthday, but the local children's hospital provided him with prosthetic limbs so sophisticated they allowed him not only to walk, but eventually to swim, run, and cycle. Cody wants to one day represent his country, the United States, in the Paralympics, and his smile fills the screen as he comes up for air in a bright blue pool while the upbeat soundtrack tells us, "When you dream, dream big."

Cody's clip was a brief but memorable part of *Ommar*'s episode on courage. Over ninety minutes, Hosny parsed for his viewers three different modalities of what he characterized as an important attribute of the Prophet Muhammad: the imaginative courage of "thinking outside the box," the bodily courage of "overcoming physical fears," and the ethical courage of "critical self-reflection." Cody's clip was an example of bodily courage. Editorial assistant Zayna had come upon it through keyword searches for "success story" and "inspirational story" on YouTube. She was so moved by Cody that she continued scouring the video-sharing platform until she found an upload that was at high enough resolution to broadcast. These videos were a cost-effective way to add an element of dazzlement to an episode, introducing what producers called a "visual break" within broadcast content that consisted mostly of Hosny speaking in the studio. The other break was each episode's "report from the field," or location interviews with "ordinary youth" who exemplified the episode's focus. Before Cody's clip, viewers had heard from three individuals who each exemplified one of the three types of courage: the imaginative artist who created T-shirts with Arabic calligraphy as an "authentic alternative" to Western logos, the brave doctor who risked his life treating protesters in Tahrir Square's makeshift first-aid stations, and the self-critical smoker who owned up to his nicotine addiction and found a way to quit.

The bulk of the episode, however, was dedicated to recounting the life of the iconic Islamist activist Zaynab al-Ghazali (1917–2005). In her best-selling memoir from the 1970s, Ghazali vividly described details of the torture she experienced following her arrest by the Nasser regime on charges of conspiring with the Muslim Brotherhood to assassinate the president. Her memoir was part of a broader set of autobiographical narratives by Islamists centered on their "exemplary suffering" as political prisoners.[39] Hosny's editorial team of twenty-something Egyptians were unfamiliar with Ghazali's story, however. In their discussions of what they would highlight from it, they didn't home in on the details of her memoir that typically interest historians, such as Ghazali's volatile relationship with feminist pioneers like Huda Sha'rawi or with the male leaders of the Muslim Brotherhood. Instead, they read Ghazali's story as that of a person with a preternatural self-confidence bolstered by a pious steadfastness that gave her courage to transcend the roles typically expected of women of her generation and become an impactful activist. Hers was an "inspirational story" of universal appeal in much the same way Cody's was, a story of courage that many viewers could connect to on an emotional and visceral level irrespective of politics. "I got goosebumps reading about what she went through," Hosny shared during the live broadcast. "Yes," Soha, the director, murmured in the control room, "her courage is dazzling (*mubhir*)."

As we learned, dazzlement as affect, ethic, and aesthetic was key to the power of the televisual to revolutionize what counts as Islamic media, reshaping pious subjects and publics. After the 2011 uprising, dazzlement also became a site of inspirational investment in a New Egypt. The inspirational is that which catalyzes a sense of possibility, altering our perception of our own abilities. The inspirational makes us feel that our circumstances, however challenging, are changeable, that things could be otherwise. The visceral responses of viewers hearing about a woman praying in a prison cell as attack dogs snarled or seeing a child climb a mountain despite not having legs is what affectively connects Zaynab al-Ghazali to Cody despite the radically different contexts of their courage.

To be sure, my interlocutors at times harbored skepticism about the contextual aptness of their own content. When I watched Cody's clip together with some of Hosny's staff in Iqraa's control room, many of us in the room wiped away tears. A few moments later, Soha, the director, turned to Emad, and expressed some reservations about the appropriateness of airing this clip. Cody could never have succeeded had he been born in Egypt, a country where the vast majority of people lack access to the health and technology resources he was able to draw on, she said. Was Cody, a citizen of one of the richest countries in the world, a suitable inspiration for Egyptians? Or would "this video just give our viewers false expectations?"

Emad's response was quick. "No, we are not giving false expectations," he said, "because now is the time of inspiration and dazzlement. If we were back in the era of Mubarak, I would agree with you. But we are in a new era. We can dream now. This video shows how one child overcame his disability and said yes to life."

He leaned forward and gestured toward the screens on the control panel. "I want to make viewers ashamed of their own petty worries," he continued. "The problem in Egypt is that we always had to have low expectations. After the revolution, we have now a chance to set new benchmarks. And this is important now because people no longer remember the spirit of Tahrir. People are very depressed!"

Emad could have seen this depression not as a problem to redress but as a radical political affect.[40] Indeed, many on the left critique self-help for its optimism, which they argue promotes a "depoliticized notion of the self" in contrast to what they deem the more political feelings of anger and despair.[41] But as a pious Muslim, Emad considered despair a quality of disbelief, negating divine sovereignty more fully than mere disobedience as it questions the certainty of God's mercy and justice. He reminded us that Satan's name Iblis derived from the root verb "to lose hope." Hopeful striving no matter one's hardship was the correct orientation of the believer, a way of "thinking well" (*husn al-zann*) of God. If you want to see hope, just look at how people acted toward each other in Tahrir, Samia and her friends had reminded me during our skit. To sustain hopefulness as a disposition is to incite new possibilities for revolutionary action and pious self-transformation alike, forming the moral and affective infrastructure of the New Egypt.

This is not to say that Emad himself was uncritically optimistic: "Ninety percent we won't be able to achieve our goals, but what is important is that 10 percent feeling that we might be able to," he concluded. "So showing these videos is very important because they give us that feeling."

For Emad then, the point is not that viewers should be like Cody. Differences in structural and cultural circumstances prevent that. But, according to Emad, for Egyptians after the revolution to have low expectations of their own capabilities as individuals and of the capabilities of Egypt as a polity was neither more accurate—nor more helpful—than to have high ones. Emad wanted to extend the sense of radical possibility made possible by the radical outcome of Tahrir—namely, the removal of a corrupt and unjust leader from power through peaceful protest—as affective reserves to meet continuing challenges. He saw broadcasting Cody's story not as giving false expectations but, rather, as creating new ones. Egyptians had retreated once again into their gripes and mediocre goals; they had to be reminded that they could "dream big," as they once did in the Square.

Still, not all viewers were convinced that Cody's courage was for them. Once Cody's clip was uploaded on Hosny's YouTube channel, a subscriber commented that "this stuff makes sense only if you live in a country that actually values human life." A member of Hosny's web team replied: "It is enough that God values humanity and that we value ourselves. The drive for success has to come from within and shouldn't be hampered by external obstacles, no matter how difficult."

When I read this comment, I cringed a little. It seemed insensitive to the challenges any ordinary Egyptian, let alone a disabled one, has to deal with in trying to accomplish mundane tasks like commuting to work on overcrowded and unreliable public transport, and let alone achieving big goals like getting a job in a failing economy. It didn't seem fair to ask overburdened people to assume the additional burden of cultivating optimism about their ability to deal with it all. When I shared my concerns with Zayna, she answered that it is precisely in a country like Egypt with entrenched structures and policies that militate against the average citizen's ordinary comfort, not to mention success, that people had to muster more internal resources to survive and not despair. For her, watching inspirational videos or learning about success stories could help with this. Cultivating a sense of responsibility for changing collective circumstances as a pious obligation, no matter the systemic hardships, was the task Hosny and members of his team like Zayna set for themselves. She reminded me that the Prophet urged us to persevere no matter the odds, saying, "If the Day of Resurrection comes upon any one of you while he has a seedling in his hand, let him plant it." For Hosny's team, this Prophetic saying encapsulated a sentiment they wanted their first program after the revolution to convey: striving in the face of severe obstacles—or even certain failure—was at once godly and revolutionary. After all, planting a sapling at the literal end of the world is not about future potential, but about intentional action as a divine imperative irrespective of actual results.

Sometimes this emphasis worked, with real viewers reporting experiencing more empowering feelings about adversity through the program. For example, Hania credited *Ommar* for helping her emotionally deal with her ongoing problem of not being able to find a job. Hania's predicament was shared by millions of other middle-class university graduates, who have the highest rate of unemployment in the country at almost 40 percent, with women being most unlikely to find a job after finishing their degrees, a situation that worsened after the revolution.[42]

"I used to feel so, so depressed about this," Hania told me. "I was like in this big dark hole where I just felt it was so unfair, that I studied so hard in university and that I just didn't deserve this." *Ommar*'s broadcast of the challenges others faced inspired her to adopt a different attitude, one she characterized as both more hopeful and more reliant on God. She realized the power of her own thoughts over her own actions. Thinking *Why is this happening to me, I don't deserve this* made her feel resentful and lethargic, leading her to mope around the house in her pajamas all day. Thinking *God hasn't willed it yet, and what can I do in the meantime?* made her feel optimistic and energized, leading her to take skill-based courses in her field to give herself an edge over other applicants. Watching Hosny's program wasn't going to get her a job, but it gave her the wherewithal to deal with her own negative feelings about not having a job. She scaled this up politically: "Right now we as Egyptians have to believe in ourselves, in our own power. That's what Egypt needs right now."

An hour later as we prepared to leave the control room, I asked Emad to tell me more about how videos like Cody's figured into the new series' aims. He again brought it back to the relation between dazzlement, *ibhar*, and impact, *i'mar*.

"The idea of inspirational videos was developed first in America by experts in psychology and self-development, and they work! We were all crying as we watched it, right? We were all dazzled (*inbaharna*) by the video.... No one is going to remember the whole script of what Mustafa said over ninety minutes, but they will remember . . . *how they felt* when they saw Cody." In this perspective, the feelings that viewers were imagined as having as they watched the life stories of different exemplary individuals created the sense of possibility on which revolutionary transformation depended. And, in a virtuous circle, the dramatic changes of the revolution opened up more space for having that Cody-feeling in the first place.

For Emad and others at Iqraa, the most egregious sin of the Mubarak regime was how it created a generation of Egyptians indifferent to the dream of a different Egypt. Their Islamic media could combat political depression by broadcasting dreams, however ambitious or far-fetched—just as the toppling of a thirty-year dictatorship through peaceful protest seemed impossible before January 25. The revolution was not merely an event but also a feeling: a feeling of limitless possibility powered by individual hope and grounded in collective action. That "Cody-feeling" of believing that one could still flourish despite obstacles beyond one's direct control is what Iqraa's viewers needed.

Of course it would not always be easy to spark inspiration and spur effort this way. Not all viewers could be so quickly moved to focus their dreams outwards rather than inwards, leading to frustration among Iqraa producers that their programs were not having enough of an impact.

DREAMING FOR EGYPT, *MARCH 2012*

The air was getting stale in the crowded control room, the breeze from the small window no match for four people at work under the stress of a live broadcast. I fanned myself with my notebook while moving closer to the open door. A few feet ahead, Zayna sat next to Soha in front of a series of box-shaped screens showing different angles of Hosny on-air. Zayna cradled the plastic arm of a push-button phone between her ear and shoulder while jotting notes on a legal pad. A viewer had called the station number flashing on the bottom of their television screen and Zayna was responsible for screening calls during this episode and deciding which would be broadcast. For the third consecutive time this evening, however, she hung up without patching the caller through to go on the air. Soha shook her head in frustration.

"You can't keep doing that," she said. "We need a caller on air soon. Mister Mustafa has been talking for too long. People are getting bored. We need to change it up a bit." She turned to the assistant director on her right and told her to go to camera two, a wide shot of the studio.

Zayna pulled forward the edge of her red satin hijab to cover her hairline, before wiping her sweaty brow with the back of her hand.

"None of them had questions that are relevant to the program theme," she said. The first rejected caller had been concerned about her daughter's recent strange behavior and wanted to ascertain how to find out if she was possessed by a djinn, invisible beings that are mentioned in the Qur'an. The second, a teenaged boy, had wanted to know if it would be all right by God to tell his classmate that he was in love with her. These were not in and of themselves bad questions to put to the preacher. But, in Zayna's estimation, these topics were irrelevant to the episode's theme of sharing dreams of revolutionary significance—that is, dreams that could lead to *i'mar al-ard*, to positive social impact.

An important way in which Hosny, like other New Preachers, sought to distinguish his programs within the Islamic television sector was through a heightened attention to viewer interaction across the divide of the screen. To facilitate and encourage such participation, his producers would regularly post a question on social media midway through a live episode, asking viewers to respond via a Facebook post or by calling in. For the *Ommar* series, Hosny wanted to focus on viewers' hopes and aspirations, on their dreams: what they were and how they had succeeded in accomplishing them or planned to. Hosny encouraged viewers to share this with the channel via email or social media. "We will put all the dreams you send us in a video and show it on television because maybe you don't have a dream, but when you see other people's dreams, God will inspire you to acquire a dream of your own."

During the series' broadcast, however, Hosny's team felt frustrated viewers were not engaging with this interactive project, despite the effort they had put into conceiving and workshopping the theme in focus groups and through feedback questionnaires in the months leading up to the program premiere. With weeks of irritation thus building, Zayna, usually calm and soft-spoken, now raised her voice. "What do you want me to do?" she asked Soha, who as the director was in charge of the broadcast.

"Just tell them what to say," Soha grumbled back.

This was not an unusual proposal. Producers would often coach viewers calling in on how to reframe a question so that it fit the episode's theme. This strategy sometimes backfired, however. A viewer would agree to go along with the proposed question, only to revert to their original "irrelevant" question once they were on the air talking to Hosny. The preacher himself would then try to pivot to the episode theme in his response, but the awkward situation would invariably embarrass the producer who had let the caller on-air. Zayna, as sensitive as she was conscientious, was trying to avoid being in this position.

But after a few more minutes of rejecting potential callers and ignoring the increasingly exasperated look on Soha's face, Zayna consented to patch a call through on the condition that the viewer explicitly relate her question to the episode theme. She gave her a suggestion: "Yes, you can tell Mr. Mustafa about your fear that you will never get married, but also ask him about what you can do to learn to think positively about it so that this dream, God willing, becomes true."

The sound technician, the third person sitting in front of the control panel, usually had little editorial input but now he muttered loud enough for us to hear: "Maybe people are tired of dreams. Maybe they just want to live their lives for real."

―――

Over coffee a couple of weeks later, I asked Zayna why so many viewers seemed uninterested in engaging with the program's aims.

"Mister Mustafa is talking to millions of people at once, but each person feels he is talking to them individually," Zayna explained as we waited for our lattes. "Mister Mustafa has spoken hundreds of times on his programs about marriage, covering all sorts of common problems. Hundreds! But a viewer still wants to ask him in-person about her own marital problems because she wants to feel that the response is specifically about her and her own life. People are strange like that."

As described in chapter 2, viewers take great pleasure and comfort in "confiding" their personal problems to a preacher like Hosny who is "just like them." After the revolution, the success of New Preaching programs in cultivating these feelings of intimacy seemed to be more liability than asset, or least Hosny's producers complained more about the demands for personal attention. The expectation they had so carefully crafted that their media would be a space of *fadfada*, of heartfelt confiding, became an obstacle to their mediated efforts to create a revolutionary disposition oriented toward a sense of responsibility for the "bigger" problems of the nation, toward "building Egypt." This disposition should ideally manifest in viewerly engagement with the space of shared public reflection created by Hosny's program. The resistance or indifference of viewers to such exhortation indexed the continuing elusiveness of the New Egypt. The spirit of revolutionary Tahrir remained trapped in the time-space of those original eighteen days, a distant dream far removed from the everyday ones of ordinary Egyptians struggling with love or loss, ambition or anxiety.

Of course, Iqraa producers were as liable as their viewers to succumb to the lure of personal "trivial" goals over lofty, other-oriented dreams. In preparing for *Ommar*, producers did the dream exercises themselves, which involved making concrete what success felt and looked like. For Zayna, success was feeling she was having a beneficial impact on others, especially those in need. But, she shared shyly during the meeting, she also really wanted to lose weight: "That would make me feel very successful."

The point for producers then was not to abjure small goals like weight loss but rather to remain contextually sensitive to how they were inapt examples for public mass mediation aimed at world flourishing—again, the point of self-help within Islamic media was not to be happy but to be helpful. As Zayna saw it, their target audience of middle-class, educated youth had the most potential to be agents of revolutionary transformation because they had the means to do so. Most Egyptians did not get to have a dream but had to struggle to survive. Those who could have a dream needed to wake up to their own unfulfilled potential to make the world a better place, and Hosny's *Ommar* series aimed to show them how. But they remained too self-involved, too caught up in "their own petty worries," as Emad put it during the Cody broadcast.

"Egyptians have lived through a revolution but haven't revolutionized their lives," Zayna concluded as we waited for the check in the coffeeshop. What do you mean? I asked. "I mean they don't feel for Egypt (*mish hasin bi-Masr*)." While yes, Hosny's history of inviting heartfelt confiding was now having unintended consequences, viewers also had to take responsibility for their own failure to live up to the promises of Tahrir, at least within their own sense of what mattered. "Egypt right now needs us. We have to become better, become better for Egypt," Zayna said. "And they shouldn't need a preacher to tell them that after all we have been through."

MAINSTREAMING MEDIA IMPACT? *JULY 2013*

Just a few weeks after the mass protests in 2013 that led to the ouster of the Muslim Brotherhood president, I visited Iqraa for the last time. The mood was somber and subdued even among those at the channel who had joined the protests that summer. Still, producer Fikry insisted on giving me a tour of the recently renovated offices. Gone were the wooden desks and fluorescent lights. The space was now chrome with recessed lights and sleek furniture in green, the color of Iqraa's calligraphic logo, which was etched on the glass doors separating offices. The facelift was welcome but still Fikry was frustrated, complaining that his creative ideas for new content were routinely dismissed as too costly. By this time, Hosny himself had left his full-time position at Iqraa to join al-Nahar, a new satellite channel. As part of the deal with Nahar, Hosny allowed for the concurrent broadcast of his Ramadan program for his new channel on Iqraa as well. He took with him to the new channel Iqraa's Cairo manager, Emad, and most of his media team, including Zayna. Everyone was confident that appearing on a more mainstream channel like al-Nahar would scale up Hosny's audience in unprecedented ways. The wider exposure to viewers beyond the niche of Islamic television was already translating into more subscribers and engagement on the preacher's social media platforms.

As he gave me the tour, Fikry hinted several times that al-Nahar, whose name translates to "Daylight," should have poached him too, even as he criticized its editorial coverage of the events of that summer as obfuscating disinformation: "They should change its name to al-Layl (Nighttime)," he grimly joked. As upset as he was about being left behind, though, he felt that Hosny made the right move from both a professional and an ethical perspective, and that he should have left Iqraa even earlier. Hosny had previously rebuffed several offers from conventional channels because he feared that his moral message would be distorted by appearing in between programs that might directly contradict the godly parameters he was calling for. Now, however, he and his media team believed that appearing on a mainstream television channel like al-Nahar was crucial to the project of cultivating godly youth on a mass scale, a mission more hampered than helped by its association with Islamic channels, even a "professional" one like Iqraa.

Fikry agreed. "If you want to reach people and have real impact, you have to go beyond the religious channels," he said. "If you are watching a religious channel, chances are you are already religious. What is really great [for *daʿwa*] is to have a religious program in between all the dramatic serials and music videos."

I was surprised at Fikry's support for the move because he himself had left the world of mainstream entertainment television production behind to work for Islamic channels. Many Iqraa producers had experience with mainstream satellite ones. Even though they had enjoyed more resources, they remembered their work for such channels as a source of great anxiety in that they frequently had to work on productions they considered sinful. They constantly worried that their profession was paying the bills on earth but ultimately costing them their place in Paradise. One of the things that many of my interlocutors most appreciated about working for a channel like Iqraa was that they didn't have to make moral concessions to do their job. They could pursue their profession and make a decent living for themselves and their families while also enjoying a sense of ethical ease.

In an earlier conversation, Fikry had described how as an assistant director working on music and beach tourism programs he found himself having "an ethical crisis," *azma akhlaqiyya*. He had grown up in a pious household, memorizing the entire Qur'an by middle school with the encouragement of his father, who was a graduate of al-Azhar. He credits those formative years for instilling a kernel of conscience that was never quite snuffed out by the lax, anything-goes environment of the film and music industry. He would find himself doubly embarrassed when he took time to pray on a shoot—embarrassed in front of his colleagues, who poked fun at "Shaykh Fikry" and embarrassed "in front of God" that he was participating in this environment in the first place. While he wasn't the one dancing or sunbathing in front of the camera, he worried that in merely filming such images he was rendering his own earnings *haram*, religiously forbidden, as well. An image started invading his tired thoughts at the end of a long night of shooting, he tells me. He is directing a model in a bikini on a beach and he suddenly drops dead right there and then. Would his Lord be pleased to see him? Would *he* like what God probably had in store for him? At the same time, as a junior employee with a young family to support, he felt he didn't have much of a choice. He owed his wife and children some measure of financial stability. He discussed these concerns with a pious mentor whose opinion he held in very high regard.

"This man really changed my life," Fikry told me. "It was just a couple of words, but they made a big difference for me. He said: 'If I told you, don't work in this field because the money is *haram*, then what I am actually saying is that all those who work in these types of media are not good people and that good people like you should leave it and God will take care of you. But then media production would be emptied of people who have these seeds of good (*badhrat khayr*) within them, people who can gain the experience they need to do good through the media later. So you are only responsible when you have a choice. When you have a choice, what will you do? Continue in these types of programs? Or make beneficial programs?'"

Fikry's mentor reframed media production as not simply a job whose value lies in its material ability to sustain an individual's livelihood but as a broader enterprise that could, correctly done, be a source of positive impact and ethical benefit to millions of people. Media could contribute to *i'mar al-ard*. His advice motivated Fikry to pursue advanced credentials that would put him in a better position to choose. He enrolled in a European video production program centered on documentary storytelling and made a short film that won several awards in local and international film festivals. As he gained more experience and confidence, he began stipulating the programs he was willing to work on at his channel. And, just like his wise man predicted, an opportunity to join Iqraa presented itself, and he jumped at the chance.

Fikry's professional path to Iqraa reflects in its aspiration for ethical impact that ethos of *i'mar*. Given the right individual intention and the right structural conditions, everyday work routines could be a source of other-worldly salvation and creative benefit. As the world's first Islamic channel, but as a channel that was not merely "about" Islam, Iqraa could revolutionize the entire satellite media sector. As discussed in chapter 1, in theory, Iqraa modeled for other satellite channels, whether secular or Salafi, media that was excellent from both a technical production quality perspective and an ethical one. That the reality fell well short of this ideal made it morally incumbent on Iqraa's star preachers to seek better media platforms to disseminate their message, Fikry felt. This explained Fikry's support for Hosny's move, even though Iqraa's own reputation suffered through its inability to retain its "star" preacher. That "conventional"—that is, non-Islamic—channels would compete over preachers as they more commonly did over pop stars was a sign that producers like him were truly having an impact.

Were the New Preachers chasing more impact, though, or more celebrity? Sallam, Iqraa's Saudi head, was less convinced than Fikry of the former when I spoke to him on the phone in Jeddah some months later. The fact that every single one of the New Preachers left the channel was not lost on him: Amr Khaled and Moez Masoud were both on Iqraa's payroll for only a short time before leaving to start their own media production companies. Sallam explained these departures in terms of individual moral failure. "What can I say," he sighed, "money changes people's ambitions."

From a different perspective, Sallam seemed to be lamenting the very incentives and structures of stardom the channel he helmed created, for the ambition was always to draw on the political economy of mass media for mass ethical impact while not getting corrupted in the process. Perhaps the channel couldn't retain its New Preachers because it could not keep pace with the increasing individual ambitions to have a "positive impact" that it had helped fuel with its own institutional stress on the importance of impacting the mainstream of "ordinary people" through reimagining what counts as Islamic media. It had been the first channel to take seriously the idea of Islam as a mediatic religion and, in so doing, it became a casualty of its own revolutionary success: in redefining the ambit of the Islamic so expansively, it made the idea of an "Islamic channel" redundant. In this way, the revolution within Islamic media might be complete.

CODA, *NOVEMBER 2015*

A couple of years after my fieldwork ended, a US-based scholar published an academic article denouncing the rise of Islamic self-help literature in Egypt. Jeffrey Kenney argues that this literature "conflicts with notions of the self found in the Qur'an" in promoting a "personal belief system where individual loyalty to one's own self comes first." Its appropriation by the New Preachers "demonstrates the extent of which religion has been commodified," with piety becoming akin to "laundry detergent, cars, and cell phones." Self-help, he warns, is "without a sense of higher moralities" and only leads to "unengaged and uncaring citizens."[43]

As soon as I read it, I emailed a pdf of the article to Zayna. One of the self-help figures the author had criticized was Ibrahim Elfiky, a frequent guest on Hosny's programs whose sudden death in an apartment fire in February 2012 was mourned on *Ommar*. Kenney had also critiqued a published collection of "success stories" that Zayna had used as a reference in preparing for the program, so I figured she would be personally interested in reading the article. Zayna called me the next day and got straight to the point.

"This man clearly doesn't understand how individual change is related to social justice," she said, and not in her usually soft-spoken tone. "Self-development isn't about being selfish at all! It is about becoming a better person who can help make the lives of others better." She paused for a breath. "I have never read a single self-development book that made me think of only myself. On the contrary—everything I read to prepare for *Ommar* and after made me want to learn about how I can help others, about how I can change our world." For her, the goal of self-help was not self-centered happiness, but other-oriented helpfulness.

But is it really your responsibility to make other people's lives better? I asked. I explained that much of the scholarly critiques of self-help are about the ways in which its discourses center individual responsibility and inner change while having little to stay about institutional accountability and external change. Could Zayna be doing this as well?

She let out a sigh of exasperation. "You remember the Nahr El Khair project we did in Ommar [the NGO]? Well, obviously it was the government's responsibility to be piping clean water into these villages. But it wasn't doing this and people still have to drink water to survive. So we had to do something ourselves."

"Anyway, if changing people's ideas and beliefs doesn't really make a difference," she went on, "then why did this person bother writing an article?"

Zayna perhaps misconstrued the point of scholarly critique, which is rarely concrete recommendation or applied change. But academic critics also misconstrue the point of exhortations to self-help on Islamic television programs. For my interlocutors at Iqraa, the onus is to try and make Egypt a little better, not merely to bemoan it. Because, after all, they are the ones who have to live with the effects of their country's structural problems, lacking the capacity of "radical" scholars to write about them from afar. Some within the academy recognize this. Feminist scholar Sara Ahmed, for example, has argued that "to assume people's ordinary ways of coping with injustices implies some sort of failure on their part—or even an identification with the system—is another injustice they have to cope with."[44] Giving up hope, or forgoing optimism, however cruel,[45] may be a privilege only a few can afford. It is easy to be cynical from the academic armchair and to laud this cynicism as a radical critique of the neoliberal structures that the armchair is literally enabled by. As Ahmed points out, "The more resources you have the easier it is to make such a critique of those whose response to injustice is to become more resourceful."[46]

Ultimately, for my pious interlocutors God was the ultimate resource. And it is clear that He asks us to change our individual selves so that He changes our collective condition. Self-help for many was an affective, intangible resource that helped them make that change. While it is certainly true that self-help techniques and discourses can be antithetical to social solidarity and structural change in focusing so much of one's mental and practical energy on improving the self, this focus can also sustain hope through turbulent times by making even the most ordinary of actions—making a to-do list, speaking up during a meeting, not littering—*feel* momentous. The political potential of that feeling of mastery in daily life, and its ability to sustain and fortify resolve, shouldn't be dismissed so easily.[47] Indeed, as I lived with my interlocutors through the dramatic, often violent, upheavals of the so-called transitional period after Mubarak's toppling in 2011 and then Morsi's in 2013, I began to appreciate that an important step toward social impact is to cultivate the courage to believe in one's own capacity for self-transformation. The creative re-mediation of self-help on Islamic television helped middle-class Egyptians like Samia, Hania, and others I met feel that they *could* contribute to the success of the revolution in some way, however small, that ordinary people like them could be God's caliphs. These feelings are themselves revolutionary as they constitute alternative ways of imagining and being that prefigure the New Egypt. In this way, the refraction of self-help through a theology of impact, of *i'mar*, recognizes in ways more nuanced than its critique the lived contexts in which possibility and catastrophe coexist, whether in this world or the next.

Five
COEXISTENCE

"I SAW GOD IN TAHRIR," THE NEW PREACHER AMR KHALED SHARED in his debut appearance on state television a week after Mubarak was toppled on February 11, 2011. "Anyone entering Tahrir Square immediately noticed a different spirit (*ruh mukhtalifa*). It was as if God were with the people there—Muslim and Christian, young and old, men and women, the people and the army."[1] While some Egyptians found proof of the revolution's righteousness in miraculous sightings of supernatural beings who did battle on behalf of protesters,[2] for Khaled the proof of divine presence was simple: human co-presence of different Egyptians in the square.

In testifying about Tahrir's "different spirit," the Islamic preacher joined many others who found the mass mobilization inspiring because it showed that "other ways of 'living together,' notably between Christians and Muslims, are possible."[3] Some of the most memorable images from those eighteen days are of Christians forming a protective circle around Muslims while they prostrated in prayer, of shaykhs and priests chanting together, of women in headscarves protesting alongside women without. Because calls "for living together" have long been attached to radical politics in Egypt, these images of solidarity across various kinds of difference became iconic of the revolution itself, illustrating the deep desire for a New Egypt that would transcend the sectarianism of the authoritarian past with a commitment to a pluralistic future.

For many local observers, however, the sensibilities associated with Islamic revivalists like Khaled were antithetical to that future. In this reading, the mobilization in Tahrir was self-consciously secular, its inclusive ideals negating the pervasive religionization of life during the Mubarak period, whether by state-adjacent institutions like al-Azhar and the Coptic Church, by oppositional organizations like the Muslim Brotherhood, or by grassroots revivalists like the New Preachers.[4] Outside Egypt, some commentators echoed this evaluation, with the famous "radical" philosopher Slavoj Zizek arguing that what made it "immediately possible for all of us around the world to identify with [the Tahrir uprising]" was that its "frame is clearly that of a universal secular call for freedom and justice."[5]

Khaled's testimony of sensing the divine as he protested offers an alternative account of what made the uprising extraordinary. It locates what Zizek calls Tahrir's "sublime moment" of Muslim-Christian solidarity squarely within a theological frame. As a godly space Tahrir was not just about the disruption of unjust power, nor only about the reversal of a corrupt economic order. More fundamentally, it was about the birth of a new arrangement of sociability and interaction across Egypt's divisions, whether between Muslims and Christians, or between Muslims themselves, grounded in the assumption that human difference was by divine design. Tahrir was a godly space because within it competing truth claims and styles of living, especially religious ones, coexisted without devolving into discord or strife.

During the forty-five-minute interview, Khaled returned to the theme of Tahrir's "different spirit" several times. He told the program host that Tahrir taught him a "lesson in love." It was the protesters' love for one another that facilitated the return of "Egypt's spirit of participatory inclusion (*ruh al-Masriyya al-musharaka*)." In this sense, the New Egypt wasn't novel at all. It was rather the true Egypt that had been there all along but couldn't express itself due to decades of state misrule. This framing was a common one. Many people during this time spoke of the revolution as allowing the "true Egypt" to emerge, as discovering that who they wanted to be—brave and peaceful, just and inclusive—was who they really were all along. Khaled explained that an urgent task facing the country was crafting a "new religious discourse" worthy of the true Egypt of Tahrir. While under Mubarak preaching had mirrored politics in being monolithic (*uhudi*), the revolution called for a pluralistic notion of Islamic piety grounded in a theology of *ta'ayush*, of coexistence.

My interlocutors at Iqraa agreed. As described in chapter 4, Hosny and his team at the Islamic channel imagined their programs as facilitating a revolution within viewers by making an other-oriented ethos of social justice and solidarity intrinsic to pious self-cultivation. Similarly, to help sustain the political miracle of Tahrir, Hosny and his team looked to spark another revolution within—this time within the piety movement's dominant orientation toward difference itself.

This chapter focuses on how the creative elaboration of a theology of coexistence through Islamic television was central to this mission. Moving across key moments in the revolutionary timeline from the Mubarak toppling in 2011 to the protests against Muslim Brotherhood rule in 2013, I show how the New Preachers and their producers aspired within this turbulent time to create a New Egypt that was peaceful and pluralistic, a country characterized by what they termed an "acceptance of the other," *qubul al-akhir*. The Islamic media they created drew inspiration from the Qur'an and Islamic history to revive a pious culture of coexistence rooted in a doctrinal understanding of human diversity as not merely inevitable, but necessary and valuable—as an aspect of divinity. Importantly, their theology of coexistence also addressed Egyptians' intense political polarization in the wake of Tahrir. The New Preachers' Islamic media would contribute to creating a much-needed "culture of accepting the other" through theologically reframing an ethos of interpretive pluralism and amity across difference—whether between Muslims or between Muslims and non-Muslims—as an intrinsic component of piety.

Ta'ayush, coexistence, is not a Qur'anic word. Nevertheless, my interlocutors argued that it was the social outcome of the Qur'an's invocation of *ta'arruf*, following this verse: "We made you into peoples and tribes so that you may get to know one another (*li-ta'arrafu*)" (Qur'an 49:13). *Ta'arruf* points to an active process of mutual engagement across various kinds of human difference. These differences are indicative of divinity, for did God not say that "one of His signs is the creation of the heavens and the earth, and the diversity of your languages and colors" (Qur'an 30:22)? As my interlocutors understood it, the evident pluralism of human cultures was not coincidental but a manifestation of divine intent, for "had God willed, He could have easily made you one community" (Qur'an 16:93). Because human diversity is divinely created, they argued, Muslims must orient toward with it with a positive attitude of mutual knowing and engagement, or *ta'arruf* in the language of the Qur'an. This made coexistence an active process of knowing the other as opposed to a mere passive toleration of their difference. Indeed, *ta'ayush* as a theological virtue has an affective dimension, that of *ulfa*, or affection and friendship. These qualities not only constituted Tahrir's "different spirit" but the pious sensibility toward difference the New Preachers theologically promoted.

This aim disrupted both long-standing secularist and Salafi imaginaries of religious difference. Unlike for liberal and leftist activists, the solution to problems of religious difference lay not in secularizing religion—that is, rendering it a question of privatized belief distinct from collective life—but in theologically promoting the positive affirmation of difference within the piety movement. And in contrast to these secular activists, for my interlocutors, the possibility of a New Egypt hinged not only on changing laws and institutions but also on habits and sensibilities. An exclusive focus on the structural determinants of inter- and intra-religious conflicts, commonly called "sectarianism" by Middle East scholars, fails to address how they are exacerbated by everyday interactions and embodied sentiments. Their Islamic media would foster revolutionary transformation through revolutionizing, on-screen and off, what dispositions toward difference were cultivated as "Islamic" within the piety movement.

The New Preachers' theology of coexistence also functioned as a critical rebuttal of Salafism for other Muslims in which theological investments in affective attachments to Christian Egyptians become terrains for working out the Islamic Revival's own struggles over who gets to define what pious sociality entails, and what determines what is pleasing to God and why. Salafi revivalists judged the New Preachers' invocations of coexistence and pluralism to be an incitement to secular liberalism dressed in misleading religious garb. Refuting Khaled's declaration of having seen God in the Square—itself, they noted, a heretical statement since only the Prophet was able to see God in this world—Salafi preachers argued that Tahrir had been a profoundly un-Islamic space, a space "outside of religion," *kharaj al-din*, precisely because it had brought together men and women, Christians and Muslims. Against a theology of coexistence, they offered a theology of refusal, of *bara'*. Salafi television preachers dedicate much airtime to the doctrine of *al-wala' wa-l-bara'*, loyalty and disavowal, which enjoins Muslims to show loyalty to their coreligionists and disavow non-Muslims. Modern Salafi Wahhabi theologians extended the doctrine from proscribing interactions between Muslims and non-Muslims to also proscribing interactions with Muslims who engage in "un-Islamic practices." This includes failing to declare their enmity to non-Muslim ways, as evidenced not just by whom they befriend but also by their dress and comportment.[6] As a theological injunction, *bara'* had political implications. Salafism prohibits the bracketing of religious difference in pursuit of a greater good; the divine command to enjoin religious truth cannot be suspended to achieve practical political ends, however laudatory.[7] Indeed, what the New Preachers saw as evidence of God in Tahrir—the coexistence of multiple attachments and forms of life in pursuit of a common aim—their Salafi counterparts saw as evidence for moral turpitude and doctrinal error.

Even Salafi-identifying Egyptians who had supported the revolution drew on these theological construals of the perils of co-presence in their criticism of the specific form the Tahrir Square protests took. For instance, my family acquaintance Zaynab had asked her mosque teacher whether it was permissible to go to Tahrir. Yes, her teacher said, so long as Zaynab's husband accompanied her and their intention in going was to support the creation of a country where the Shari'a, God's revealed law, would be finally applied. However, Zaynab witnessed many practices and voiced sentiments in Tahrir that were antithetical to her sense of piety, whether it was men and women camping together or protesters chanting, "Don't say I am Muslim, or I am Christian; just say I am Egyptian." Clearly her own intention in being there was not shared by many others and her teacher advised not to go again, since to do so would be to lend support for un-Islamic causes. Far from being pleasing to God, co-presence across difference was perilous, and Zaynab left the Square feeling not inspired and uplifted, but alienated and disturbed. For her, God had most definitely not been in Tahrir.

Such differing evaluations of Tahrir by the New Preachers versus their Salafi counterparts is yet another illustration of the theological instability of the religious-secular distinction within the piety movement and the limits of this distinction's analytical definition. Critiquing the prevalent characterization of the Tahrir Square uprising as a secular one, Hussein Agrama argues for analyzing it instead as "asecular," that is, as unconcerned with secularism's foundational "question of where to draw the line between religion and politics."[8] Similarly, Charles Hirschkind contends that Tahrir "drew sustenance from a unique political sensibility, one disencumbered of the oppositional secular versus religious logic and its concomitant forms of political rationality" that emerged from the cross-ideological solidarity of the Kefaya movement.[9] But like the categorization of Tahrir as a "secular" space, the counternarrative of Tahrir as "asecular" misses the ways in which the Square's status as "secular" or "religious," and how that mattered for the intersection of religion and politics, was theologically adjudicated and contested—including by those affiliated with Kefaya.

More broadly, anthropologists of religion have traced normative pluralism's "openness and acceptance of others' religious views" to a specifically secular liberal Protestant genealogy "gone global."[10] As a cognate concept, coexistence would appear to partake in this secular history. Raja Abillama contends, for example, that the idea of Muslim-Christian coexistence is foundational to Lebanese secularism, endowing the state with a distinctive moral-legal identity that requires "a constant disciplining of the religious sentiment" as a private, individual matter.[11] As this chapter shows, however, coexistence in a theological register involves not the bracketing of religious sentiment but its recentering in ways that make Islamic piety, not secularism, the normative guarantor of inter-religious amity. This was accomplished through a doctrinal elaboration of affirming sensibilities and interactional norms related to religious difference, sensibilities and norms that were, indeed, theologically dismissed by Salafi participants in the Islamic Revival as inherently "secular." In this way, the long-standing divisions of Egypt's Islamic Revival over the very definition of piety refracted through rival preachers' contestations of the theological status of Tahrir.

Ethnographically tracing the social life of coexistence as a theological imperative in relation to the 2011 uprising thus provincializes the liberal conceit of pluralism and toleration as modern achievements exclusive to Western cultures and alien to Islamic ones while showing how their invocation in an explicitly religious register mattered to provincializing similar Salafi claims.[12] Once again, the revolution within the Islamic Revival over the very definition of piety was inextricable from the revolutionary struggle for a New Egypt.

"SIDE BY SIDE," JUNE 2011

I am at Sami Yusuf's music concert, sitting on a plastic folding chair in front of an outdoor stage along with a few hundred people. Dubbed by *Time* magazine "Islam's biggest rockstar," the British-Azeri singer became famous in Egyptian revivalist circles after performing on Amr Khaled's *Lifemakers* series on Iqraa back in 2004. As an artist mindful of divine parameters, Yusuf's music exemplified the creatively capacious sense of "Islamic media" the New Preachers promoted. Some of his catchiest songs revolved around expressions of love for God and the Prophet Muhammad, while others addressed social issues like war and poverty.[13] Yusuf's sensibility as a self-identified pious Muslim was also radically inclusive. In a television interview, Yusuf shared that while "music is part of my worship as a Muslim, I sing for everyone." He told the program host that one of his most memorable moments in Egypt was when an elderly Coptic Christian woman embraced him. "I felt her love. Although she is not Muslim, the spiritual yearnings of my music reached her," he said. "We can't monopolize God. We are different and we will never all be the same, but we could be closer to each other, we could celebrate our brotherhood."[14]

I had found out about the concert from Amina, a former Iqraa producer. While she no longer worked in Islamic television, she retained close links to several of the New Preachers and was a guest of honor at the concert along with Resala's director, the Kuwaiti New Preacher Tareq el-Suwaidan. Amina had been asked to give a few introductory remarks and she focused on the imperative of connection across difference. I wasn't surprised. The past two months had been hard. In March, a church was set ablaze during a clash between Muslims and Christians on the outskirts of Cairo, just a couple of metro stops from my neighborhood, and the next week a dozen people were killed protesting this arson. In

May, Salafi-identified vigilantes had converged around a church in the working-class neighborhood of Imbaba following rumors that a Coptic convert to Islam was being held captive. Many Christians and Muslims lost their lives in the armed clashes that ensued, and two churches were burned down.[15]

On stage, Amina cited the Qur'anic *li-ta'arafu* verse as validating both the sense that "we don't all have to be same" and that we must "build bridges and get to know each other beyond binary oppositions." Yusuf's music, Amina told the audience, exemplifies this Islamic ethos, one that was now needed more than ever to actualize the revolutionary promise of a "New Egypt." As the young people and families around me whistle and applaud, Yusuf finally takes the stage. He shares that he was in Tahrir Square during the revolution and that he felt in that space that he, too, was a "part of Egypt."

"Tonight," he goes on, "is not about politics or suspicion. Tonight is about unity, solidarity, and building the New Egypt."

―――

The next time I see Amina, it is August. As I turn on my audio recorder for the interview, we reminisce about the concert, which had been the first one by an international artist since Mubarak was toppled. The months since the concert had been even tenser than the ones before, and not only in terms of Muslim-Christian relations: just two weeks after the concert, security forces had attacked protesters in Tahrir with rubber bullets and tear gas, injuring a thousand people and killing dozens. Most troubling was how many people we knew justified this violent crackdown as necessary. Amina tells me that this shows how much Egyptians needed "a culture of coexistence," *thaqafit al-ta'ayush*. When I ask her to tell me more of what this phrase means to her, she asks if I had seen Amr Khaled's series *Da'wa li-l-Ta'ayush* from 2007. The series, whose title can be translated either as "A Call for Coexistence" or "Preaching Coexistence," focused on *ta'ayush* as a "religious obligation" (*farida*) that is as incumbent on Muslims as the five daily prayers. I had seen some of the series when it first aired, but after my interview with Amina I rewatch its thirty episodes on YouTube.

Each episode recalled stories and situations from the Prophet's biography as well as from Islamic history that were characterized by a principled "acceptance" (*qubul*) of difference. Khaled's central point was that coexistence, harmoniously "living with others," wasn't alien to Islam but "rooted in our own history and values, in the Qur'an." It is not bad for us to be different, the preacher pleaded on air. "Many Muslims can't imagine this. But difference is a cosmological reality." If God had willed, He could have created humans who were all the same; since He didn't, it follows that diversity indicates divinity and must be respected. Muslims in the past understood this better than Muslims today, Khaled argued. For example, the founders of the four schools of Islamic jurisprudence respected each other's opinions, viewing their disagreements as beneficial and helpful to their aim of addressing Muslims' differing ritual and social needs across space and time. And while today Sunnis and Shias are fighting each other in Iraq, Khaled added, in the past Sunni and Shia scholars "took knowledge from each other." "We have to have an imagination of our lives together," Khaled told the millions of viewers across the Arab world who tuned in. "There can be no renaissance without us learning how to live together."

This including not just coexisting with other Muslims but also with non-Muslims. Khaled devoted an episode to the Pact of Medina, a formal agreement drafted by the Prophet Muhammad after his emigration to the city from his hometown of Mecca in 622 CE. With the pact uniting the various tribes and religious groups, including the Jewish ones, under a single political entity, each group within Medina had the freedom to practice its religion and was responsible for its internal affairs, while agreeing to defend the city from external threats. For Khaled, the Pact of Medina offered an important precedent for contemporary Muslims in how the Prophet dealt with non-Muslims: not as a minority to begrudgingly tolerate but as an integral part of society.[16] This could only happen through an Islamic sensibility that positively embraced difference as an aspect of divinity. Addressing secularist worries that the Islamic Revival was exacerbating inter-religious conflict, Khaled put it like this: "To those who say that piety will lead to extremism, [I say] our religion is full of coexistence, we don't have to fear it."

In preaching coexistence, the series offered a theological alternative to the Salafi doctrine of *bara'*, refusal. *Bara'* hinged on a repudiation of the legitimacy of religious difference. Socially, this doctrinal disavowal called for minimal interactions with non-Muslims and "misguided" Muslims and the cultivation of an affect of animosity toward both as an aspect of piety. In a televised commentary on the *da'wa* content broadcast by Iqraa and Resala, the Salafi preacher Wagdy Ghoneim lambasted the New Preachers' call for coexistence as a euphemism for religious laxity (*tamyi' al-din*) aimed at imitating the West. He saw as evidence for this the New Preachers' use of the semantically neutral "the other," *al-akhir*, in reference to non-Muslims, as opposed to the substantively evaluative term "the disbelievers," *al-kuffar*. *Kuffar* in Arabic has the same connotations that "infidel" does in English and is considered a derogatory term by many Egyptians, not least Christian ones. But Salafi preachers insisted that this was the only Islamic term possible for non-Muslims, arguing that the Qur'an is unequivocal about who is a *mu'min* (believer) and who is a *kafir* (disbeliever).[17]

"An Islamic preacher creates programs called 'You and the Other,' 'The Acceptance of the Other,' 'Coexistence with the Other'—who is this 'other'? They are disbelievers!" Ghoneim argued. "May God destroy these criminal preachers! Religion has become wishy-washy, there are no more distinctions such as 'Muslim' or 'disbeliever.' No, it has become 'you and the other.' Who is this other? What does 'the other' mean? Is [the other] a disbeliever or a Muslim? Let's be clear." Like other Salafi preachers, Ghoneim excoriated these programs as yet more evidence that the New Preachers were stealth secularizers bent on destroying Islam from the inside out by "Americanizing" it.[18]

But the New Preachers' invocations of coexistence were as much against secular absorption as they were against Salafi disassociation. Addressing "the West," Khaled made clear on-air that "coexistence isn't about giving up our land or our culture and religion and adapting to your own." That would be cultural imperialism, not coexistence.[19] Indeed, coexistence wasn't inevitably about assimilating differences but helping to maintain them, as I learned from Amina. Watching Khaled's program as a high schooler had helped fortify, not dilute, her pious resolve within her overwhelmingly secular social environment.

"When I was younger," she shared, "I went through a period when I felt that in order to show people the right image of Islam, I had to show them that I was like them. I would go out of my way to mention that I enjoyed the music they liked, or that I watched the same movies—even when I had my reservations." This desire to "fit in" was forged through her challenging experiences as the sole hijab-wearing student in one of Cairo's most elite schools—a place populated by "expats, mostly British and Canadian," or "very, very Westernized Egyptians." The school's social scene, marked by dance parties and the expectation to bring "a date," sharply contradicted her conservative upbringing: "My dad wouldn't even let me go to the mall alone, let alone a dance." She recalled this period as a lonely one. Upon enrolling at the American University in Cairo, she found herself in a more diverse group of peers, encountering "more balanced people." Yet she still struggled to fit in as one of the few students on the liberal campus who identified with the Islamic Revival. During this time, she began to follow New Preachers like Amr Khaled and Moez Masoud, whose teachings empowered her to say: "Well, I am actually not just like you, I am different. And my difference is okay. They [liberal friends] should accept my difference, just like I accept theirs."

For Amina, the culture of coexistence she learned from the New Preachers was about striking a balance between "losing" one's religion through assimilation versus isolating oneself from the rest of society in the name of "preserving" one's religion. This balance also made Islamic coexistence distinct from secular liberal tolerance. "Tolerance is hierarchical, like someone is on top and someone on the bottom and if you are on the bottom, the minority, you don't have the power to fight back," Amina explained. "Coexistence is more side by side, not top and down." Coexistence was not about "putting up" with minority groups one dislikes, but rather about living together with *ulfa*, amity, and *ihtiram*, respect.

Still, at first glance, the ethos of coexistence promoted by the New Preachers does appear to be akin to liberal tolerance. Both orient toward human difference as inevitable; both emphasize noncoercion of the minority by the majority. But there is a fundamental difference between the pious notion of coexistence and the secular ideal of tolerance. Liberal concepts of tolerance center the individual as an autonomous rights-bearing subject entitled to a life free from external constraints, especially the normative ones of religious traditions. By contrast, the grounds for *ta'ayush* were not individual rights but divine dictates. Coexistence looks to God's revelation, not human preferences, for the ethical parameters of social interaction across difference. This theological grounding also rendered the affective ambit of coexistence distinct from secular tolerance. Political theorist Wendy Brown argues that in

Western liberal democracies invocations of tolerance often serve to merely "regulate aversion" to the perceived differences of minoritized groups as opposed to positively affirming them. "Dislike" and "disapproval" are foundational, not antithetical, to tolerance as a liberal norm, a norm that after the 9/11 attacks was weaponized to distinguish a "civilized West" from a "barbaric Islam" as the US and its allies invaded Afghanistan and Iraq.[20] By contrast, the Islamic construal of coexistence positively affirmed differences as divine design. This called not for the begrudging bracketing of religious difference as a matter of private belief but an engagement with it in a constructive, mutually enriching register, or as Amina put it, "side by side." With the 2011 revolution, the stakes of coexistence, of Muslims side by side with non-Muslims, became for her, as for others I knew within New Preaching circles, closely linked to the ethical shape of a New Egypt beyond religious sectarianism and political polarization.

"THE FRIENDSHIP OF THE SQUARE," *JANUARY 2012*
The line for an event on "The Revolution: Past, Present and Future" at the Sawy Cultural Wheel in Zamalek stretches down the sidewalk and around the corner. I wrap my scarf tighter against the chill as I join the queue, the conversational din around me overlaid by the whoosh of traffic. I am supposed to be attending the event with Hania. We had met the year before, a month before the uprising, at a New Preaching seminar at the center. Sitting next to each other jotting notes, me for research, she for personal edification, we had struck up a conversation and exchanged numbers. Over the next year we stayed in touch by phone and attended other New Preaching gatherings togethers. Today she was running late and had texted me to go in without her.

As the queue inches closer to the entrance, the woman in front of me unfolds the newspaper advertisement publicizing tonight's speakers. These include newly elected parliamentarians, professors, revolutionary activists, journalists, poets, musicians, and two preachers: the Protestant preacher Maurice Sameh and the New Preacher Moez Masoud.[21] In contrast to the disappointing realities of violence and polarization after the uprising, Sawy's revolutionary commemoration recalled Tahrir Square's utopian promise of Egyptians peacefully engaged across their differences.

Still, attendees had their favorites. "I came just to see Moez [Masoud]," the woman tells her companion, who leans over to peer at the newssheet. "I hope he speaks first."

Masoud ends up being one of the last speakers, but audience members still enthusiastically whistle as the stubbled preacher takes his place alongside Pastor Maurice, whose church abutting Tahrir Square is the largest evangelical congregation in the Middle East.[22]

"I love the revolution," Masoud begins. "I am thankful for this revolution, but I want to thank God foremost because He made it possible. He inspired us to stand for justice."

In impassioned tones, Masoud speaks about the need for a speedy transfer to civilian rule. He calls out as unacceptable the efforts by state media to tarnish the reputation of revolutionaries like the Azhari shaykh Emad Effat, who was killed earlier that month at a sit-in, or to explain away November's caught-on-camera assault of a female protester.[23] But the topic Masoud speaks most about is how Muslims should feel and act toward Christians. More unites Muslims and Christians than divides them, he says. To be sure, each religion has a distinctive creed, yet "those differences don't stop us from uniting in this world for freedom, for justice, for bread, for human dignity." Masoud reminds the audience that the Qur'anic word *mawadda*, which connotes feelings of friendship, co-occurs with *mahabba*, or love. Loving friendship was both a revolutionary ethic and an Islamic one. Its presence in Tahrir Square prefigured a New Egypt that was truly godly. Those Muslims who argue otherwise, "those who say that these differences in 'aqida (creed) make it impossible for [Muslims] to live side by side as humans with Christian Egyptians," Masoud goes on, "are lying about God's religion."

Creedal differences between Muslims and Christians matter only in the Afterlife, not in this world: "They don't matter to our interactions with each other, to us loving each other, respecting each other, eating with each other."[24] Masoud tells the audience that this first anniversary of revolution is an occasion to "revive the revolution within ourselves" (*i'adit ihya' al-thawra guwwana*). What we need to bring back, the preacher argued, is "the friendship of the Square." To live up to the promise of their extraordinary political revolution, Egyptians must actualize in their ordinary life the ethical aspirations of coexistence and engagement across difference, including religious difference, that now feels so elusive.

Masoud ends with a chant: "Say it whichever way you want: 'Down, down, with the generals' rule!'"[25] The audience immediately picks up the refrain, lifting it with one voice into the night air. My mobile pings with a text from Hania, who has finally made it to the center: "He is so amazing!:)"

Masoud's preaching about love across religious difference at a commemoration of the Tahrir Square uprising rendered solidarity and friendship with non-Muslims unequivocal theological imperatives. This offered Hania and other New Preaching viewers a robust pious grounding for revolutionary commitments typically cast as secular. During the uprising Hania had gone to the Square several times behind her family's back to donate blood for the wounded. She judged Tahrir to "have brought out the best of us." But as soon as Mubarak stepped down, she went on, "we became the worst versions of ourselves. All those bad things that the regime had created over thirty years didn't go away, they got worse."

In particular, the year since the revolution had seen increasing violence against Christians across the nation, both by security forces and ordinary Muslims. In addition, prominent politicians and parties claiming an Islamic mantle had normalized anti-Christian rhetoric in their election campaigns and rallies. This was but an intensification of the religious strife that marked thirty years of authoritarian rule under Mubarak, further enabling the state's political repression under the guise of protecting "national unity," *al-wahda al-wataniyya*. The official rhetoric of national unity obscured the ways in which the toppled regime actually promoted the "sectarianization of Christians and Muslims into two distinct and segregated spheres," the result of which was to dramatically reduce everyday interaction between them and to increase mutual suspicion.[26] As the minority, Copts bore the brunt of this charged situation. State agencies and their official representatives not only repeatedly failed to stem vigilante attacks by Muslims against churches and Copt-owned businesses but also perpetuated their own forms of anti-Coptic violence, whether material or discursive.[27]

In response, civil rights advocates have long called for the secular reform of Egyptian legal structures, which they argue privilege Muslims and relegate

Copts and other religious minorities to second-class citizenship. Saba Mahmood has critiqued their efforts in light of critical theories of secularism, arguing that far from being the solution, secularism exacerbates sectarianism and reinscribes religious inequality as it makes "religion more, rather than less, important to the identity of the majority and minority populations."[28] Still, what stands out to me, based on my fieldwork with Islamic revivalists deeply concerned with inter-religious relations, is the way the state secularized such relations not by tacitly deeming religious identity referents important but by explicitly *refusing* to recognize the ways in which such referents might, in some circumstances, indeed provoke tension. Under Mubarak, state media coverage attributed conflicts between Muslims and Christians to anything *but* sectarian sentiment, insisting that such disputes were not rooted in religious passion but rather in land disputes, family feuds, even mental illness. And when religious difference was identified as a possible propeller of tension, it was framed as an external aberration, the work of foreign-funded extremists bent on destabilizing the country by stoking communal strife.[29]

The secularization of sectarianism—the papering over of the ways in which theological precepts underlay the ethical legitimacy of sectarianism as a principled Islamic differentiation for many Muslims—continued even with the election of an Islamist president in 2012. "Recalling the old regime," one local commentator argued, Morsi's government "looks everywhere but in anti-Christian prejudice for the causes of Muslim-Christian conflict." According to the official narrative, any inter-religious tensions were orchestrated by counterrevolutionary forces and did not reflect Egyptians' true theological sentiments.[30]

By contrast, my interlocutors worried constantly about the ways in which anti-Christian animus was being propagated under the guise of piety by television preachers such as Muhammad Hassan, Wagdy Ghoneim, and Abu Ishaq al-Huwayni, the luminaries of Salafi revivalism. In response to the question of whether "a Muslim has to hate non-Muslims," for example, Hassan argued on his Islamic television channel that it was an act of piety to cultivate feelings of *"bughd"* (hatred) and *"'adawa"* (enmity) toward non-Muslims. Such feelings are not contingent on the specific actions of non-Muslims but on their status as non-Muslims. As part of the doctrine of *bara'*, disavowal, non-Muslims had to be shunned, even if just within one's own heart. The uptick in violence against Christians across Egypt in the last decade of Mubarak's rule correlated, my interlocutors at Iqraa argued, with the spread of such Salafi ideas beyond the piety movement through satellite television. Still, for them, the solution to sectarian strife wasn't to promote secularism or to make religious identity matter less. Rather, it was to disrupt Salafi attitudes and doctrines toward non-Muslims by offering a theological alternative. In this way, Masoud's elaboration of love for Christians as an aspect of Islamic piety at the Sawy gathering was part of a broader revolution against Salafism within the piety movement that predated the Tahrir Square revolution.

The threat Salafism posed to inter-religious coexistence and solidarity in Egypt was a recurrent topic introduced by Hania in our conversations. She continually contrasted the amicable attitudes of the New Preachers toward "the other" to the adversarial ones of the Salafi preachers she grew up hearing first on her family's cassette deck and later on television. This contrast had practical stakes for her. Hania lived in Shubra, one of the capital's few neighborhoods where the number of Coptic residents almost equals Muslims. Hania described the Shubra Muslims she knew, including her own family, as having become "more and more Salafi" in their theological orientation in the decade before the revolution. Shubra is often idealized in popular media for its inter-religious conviviality and solidarity: On television dramas and on film, Muslims and Christians enthusiastically exchange greetings and food; decorate their streets together for Christmas and Ramadan; and frequent each other's stores and living rooms. These scripted scenes of friendships make for good television but were far from her neighborhood's acrimonious realities, Hania told me. Her father prohibited her from playing with the Coptic girls on her street and forbade his wife from visiting their mothers. And even if they weren't always followed, Salafi sermons prohibiting "unnecessary" interactions with non-Muslims and injunctions to cultivate feelings of enmity toward them had deleterious consequences for how Muslim families like hers viewed their Christian neighbors and the threat their proximity posed to their own "purity" as Muslims.[31]

Most disturbing for Hania was the ways in which the Salafi doctrinal prohibition of friendly feelings toward non-Muslims extended to political solidarity with them. So it was that even as Hassan, like several other prominent Salafi preachers, condemned the 2011 New Year's Eve suicide bombing of a cathedral in Alexandria—which killed two dozen worshippers as they were leaving midnight mass and is considered one of the precipitating causes of the Tahrir Square uprising—he nevertheless insisted that the moral concern motivating thousands of Muslims to hold teary vigils or act as human shields during church services negated the "fundamental religious pillar that love of God is inseparable from hatred of His enemies." Similarly, the Salafi preacher Muhammad Abd al-Maqsud, who is based in Alexandria, argued that the anti-sectarian slogan "Don't say *I am Muslim,* or *I am Christian*; just say *I am Egyptian*" that many Muslims chanted as an expression of solidarity corrupts Islamic faith; love of God cannot simultaneously exist alongside loving identification with "God's enemies."[32]

To be clear, it was not that these popular Salafi preachers promoted violence against Christians. To the contrary: they were clear God prohibited Muslims from physically harming non-Muslims under their "protection." But they were also clear that there were God-given parameters governing a Muslim's relationship to non-Muslims; these necessitated a cultivated attention to non-Muslims *as* non-Muslims and precluded feelings of affection. While it was incumbent on Muslims in Egypt, as the governing majority, to ensure the safety of Copts, God forbids feeling love toward them, Hassan said, just as He does smiling at them, let alone socializing with them.

Hania began questioning such attitudes when she matriculated to Cairo University. Like Amina, as a university student she was exposed to a much broader sociological and ideological swathe than her home life in Shubra allowed. While for Amina this instigated a questioning of secular liberal lifestyles, for Hania it was the beginning of a gradual provincialization of Salafi norms.

"I started to see that what I had been taught was pure Islam—like the niqab (face veil)—was actually just Saudi Wahhabi customs imposing themselves on us," she shared during one conversation she agreed I could record. "Before I went to university, I had this idea that anything that went against the dominant culture I learned at home had to be wrong. But then I found out all about these different opinions, they made me see that the world is not so black and white." At the same time, she went on, she felt deeply discomfited by her liberal and leftist professors' quick dismissal of religious revivalism—"of preaching, attending religious lessons, going to the mosque more"—in general. One of these professors, "my favorite one actually," even questioned the jurisprudential consensus that the hijab was a religious obligation, claiming that it was merely "a Semitic custom." Similar to Amina, for Hania it was during this disorienting time that she discovered Amr Khaled's *Call for Coexistence*, which aired just as she was starting university.

"It was like a new window opened in my mind and heart, it was like a breath of fresh air," Hania recalled. She appreciated how Khaled's *daʿwa* promoted a "culture of accepting the other," whether within the Muslim community or outside it. Khaled's program permitted her to not only "see from others' perspective" but to reassess the Salafi claim that her friendship with non-Muslims (and not-so-pious Muslims) necessarily corrupted her faith.[33] Most importantly, Khaled's message was a powerful one for Hania, as for Amina, because he showed how accepting the other didn't mean "losing the self." I asked her what she meant by this phrase. "To lose the self as a Muslim is to stop following God," she explained, "to stop obeying Him and to start just copying whatever the other is doing without thinking about it." Khaled's preaching, like that of the other New Preachers, was as critical of blind Western imitation as it was of blind rejection of all things Western, attempting to chart an Islamic "middle way" between these two poles.

During this period the question of what constitutes an Islamic interactional ethic toward difference became for Hania inextricable from the broader structural conditions that allowed Salafi norms such ascendancy within the Islamic Revival. Just as each week she looked forward to an episode of *Coexistence*, she "read religiously" each issue of *al-Dustor*, a newspaper edited by Ibrahim Eissa, then a journalistic hero within dissident circles for his criticism of state wrongdoing. Her political and religious reawakening were enmeshed as they reshaped her sensibilities about difference. Hania blamed sectarianism on the wide berth the Mubarak regime gave to a Salafi revivalism more interested in calling out heretical beliefs than political corruption. In doing so, the regime hit two birds with one stone: promoting secularism by giving piety "a bad name" by allowing Salafism to be its most public face while ensuring that the Muslim majority would be too busy worrying about the length of beards and the punctiliousness of prayers to protest decrepit hospitals and schools or stagnating wages and increasing grocery bills.[34]

Now, in this transitional period after the revolution, she felt that a similar dynamic was at work: counterrevolutionary regime remnants within the country's mainstream secular channels were giving Salafi antagonism toward Christians so much attention not because they cared about "the other" but because they wanted to stoke sectarianism and undermine the emergence of a New Egypt. Once again, watching programs by the New Preachers offered her a compelling alternative to both Salafi fanaticism and secular authoritarianism.

EXEMPLARY NON-MUSLIMS, *MARCH 2012*

"It is part of our tradition to learn from others, no matter their religion or beliefs," Emad, Iqraa's Cairo manager, explains as we get ready to leave the studio after another long evening of filming. We are discussing Salafi reactions to Hosny's *Ommar* program. As described in the previous chapter, this series aimed to ignite within the preacher's imagined middle-class audience of "ordinary people" a sense of their capacity to effect social change as a way of living up to the promise of a New Egypt. It did so by showcasing exemplary people who had a "positive impact" across a variety of domains, from human rights to medicine to technology. Several of these exemplars were not Muslim, such as the anti-apartheid leader Nelson Mandela and the pioneering heart transplant surgeon Magdy Yacoub, who was Coptic Christian. Still, despite their not being Muslim the program presented them as people who had lived up to the Qur'anic imperative of *i'mar*, of striving for the sake of others.

Ommar's relative indifference to religious difference earned the program opprobrium from Salafi revivalists, who objected to the show's premise that inspirational resources for godliness could be found beyond Qur'anic exemplars, the Prophet Muhammad, or the first generations of his Companions. Several such critics posted comments on the YouTube channel of Hosny's show and sent emails to the channel arguing that non-Muslims categorically cannot be role models (*qudwa*) for Muslims. Far from being Islamic, the inspirational capaciousness of *Ommar* opened the door to the grave sin of *al-tashabbuh bi-l-kuffar*, or the imitation of disbelievers.

The doctrine of *tashabbuh* prohibits emulating the manners, dispositions, and lifestyles of non-Muslims based on what Islamic Studies scholar Youshaa Patel calls a "maximalist" interpretation of the Prophet's saying that "whoever imitates a people becomes one of them." In the premodern period, many theologians construed this hadith as a descriptive statement rather than a proscription to refrain from imitation. With European colonialism in the nineteenth century, however, the hadith acquired critical overtones and was often taken as an admonition to not adopt "non-Muslim" names, habits, festivities, ways of dressing, and so on. Patel shows that many contemporary Salafis often add to this negative valence a literal reading in which the imitation of Christians, Jews, or other non-Muslims leads to, or is itself a form of, unbelief.[35]

Those holding such a view include Egyptian Salafi revivalists. For example, each year Salafi television preachers like Muhammad Ya'qub lament festivities such as Valentine's Day, when couples and families across Cairo wear red and gift each other flowers and teddy bears. Muslims observing Valentine's Day were not only engaging in a reprehensible imitation of non-Muslims but also committing *bid'a*, heretical innovations, since the only festivities permitted to Muslims by God were the two Eids.[36] Significantly, the doctrinal perils of *tashabbuh* extended to feelings of affection or esteem toward non-Muslims, intersecting with the theology of *bara'*. Salafi preachers like Muhammad Hassan had long warned that "admiration or appreciation of Christians and/or Jews will cause impurity (*najasa*) to lodge in one's own heart."[37] That Iqraa as an Islamic television channel was valorizing the "successful" life stories of individuals who were Christian and Jewish—and Hindu or maybe even atheist!—was an outrageous betrayal of its duty to enjoin virtue and forbid vice.

My interlocutors at Iqraa had a different sense of their religious mission as media producers. In their planning sessions for the *Ommar* series, producers looked for common ground across different cultural or historical contexts through evoking the ethical as a space of latent Islamic universalism. They would say things like "eighty percent of what we think of as Islamic values are in fact human values." At the same time, they were clear that those shared values—trustworthiness, for example, or justice—were nonnegotiable and unchanging because they were divinely enjoined.

"It is part of the greatness of this religion that it deals with differences in creed and differences in people's choices and opinions with mercy and mutual respect and civility (*adab*)," Emad said. Islamic ethics prohibited dealing with any person in an unethical way, even if they were an atheist, because every person was in the end one of God's creations, endowed with an innate inclination (*fitra*) to piety. That there could be non-Muslims who live up to Islamic values more than Muslims was possible because that ethical potential was ingrained in all humans by God. This is why, Emad explained during our conversation about Salafi criticisms of the series, the Azhari scholar Rifa'i al-Tahtawi declared upon returning from a visit to Europe that there he had found "Islam without Muslims." Not everyone understands this, Emad shook his head, and too many so-called pious people are too concerned with judging others as "un-Islamic" or not "real Muslims" when they should be looking at their own conduct. Furthermore, he argued that by denouncing as un-Islamic the positive appropriation of practices or ideas originally put forth by non-Muslims, Salafi theology narrows the historical openness and creative adaptability of Islam—which was, he went on, what had allowed Islam to spread across diverse societies in the first place. Whereas Salafi revivalists framed Muslims' emulation of non-Muslims as symptomatic of Western cultural colonization, for Hosny and his media team the idea that the "Islamic" was necessarily antithetical to everything "Western" was an overly defensive reaction to the trauma of colonialism that ironically enabled Western powers' continuing domination of Muslims in various ways. If a practice or an idea could lead to people's well-being, there should be no qualms about adopting and reworking it, even if it was originally a non-Muslim one or made Muslims appear similar to non-Muslims.[38]

Against the Salafi criticism of *tashabbuh*, Hosny defended the *Ommar* program through invoking other Prophetic sayings, such as the one about believers taking wisdom wherever they find it. The program's incorporation of contemporary non-Muslim exemplars—for example, one episode was devoted to the life story of Terry Fox, the Canadian athlete and amputee who raised funds for cancer research through running marathons—was not a nullification of its *da'wa* intent, but its elaboration in new forms. As described in chapter 2, the idea that godliness wasn't limited to Muslims or indeed to the Islamic tradition grounded my interlocutors' "promiscuous,"[39] that is, innovatively appropriative, attitude toward "foreign" ideas or customs. They were confident that most things deemed secular could be made compatible with Islam. Valentine's Day did not have to be about romance but rather about parental love, for example. The expression of such love was godly, and if it needed the form of Valentine's Day to propagate it effectively among contemporary Muslims, so be it.

Concluding our conversation, Emad argued that while of course Iqraa as an Islamic channel was "partisan" to the truth of Islam and desired to share this truth with Muslims and non-Muslims alike—"just like any religion wants"—preachers like Hosny did not have an obligation to convert non-Muslims. Muslims' own exemplary conduct created the conditions for non-Muslims to respect Islam, and perhaps to learn more about it beyond stereotypes. This is where the responsibility of Iqraa as an Islamic channel lay: in disrupting secular and non-Muslim stereotypes about piety informed by its dominant Salafi articulation, and in promoting an alternative conception of Islam that was ethical, inclusive, and inspirational. Otherwise, Emad said, "How can we judge people for not becoming Muslims when all they're being shown is a terrible Islam?"

In including non-Muslims as ethical exemplars on an Islamic preaching program, Hosny and his team prefigured a New Egypt beyond the sectarianism that had come to define the Mubarak years, when conflicts between ordinary Muslims and Coptic Christians increased dramatically. From my interlocutors' perspective, because Salafi preaching casts religious differences as battlegrounds between truth and falsehood, its notion of piety was antithetical to the interactional ethics of the New Egypt they wanted to cultivate through programs like *Ommar*.

This extended to off-screen practices as well. The channel did not, as a matter of policy or practice, discriminate against non-Muslims in hiring decisions. During my fieldwork several Coptic Christians were working there as well as American Jews. In fact, for a while some producers didn't know that I was Muslim. When I asked Emad if he had an extra prayer mat so that I could join evening prayers after one recording session, he exclaimed, "But I thought you were Christian!" He had assumed this because of my foreign last name and because I didn't wear hijab, a rarity for middle-class Muslim women, especially ones interested in Islamic preaching, during that period. I got the sense that Emad was a little disappointed that I was just another Muslim and so unlikely to be as moved by the power of the inclusive example he set as a gatekeeper at a prominent Islamic channel.

Perhaps noting my look of surprise at his surprise, Emad told me he aimed to hire "the best people" irrespective of religious identity; for him, this was not only the professional thing to do but also the Islamic one. The best production manager he ever worked with was Coptic, and he remembers a Muslim colleague in the industry asking him if he, as a Muslim, wasn't *awla*, more entitled, to the job; "I told him, 'No, the Copt is more entitled because he is more qualified.'" He reminded his colleague that the guide who led the Prophet to safety in Medina as he fled Mecca was not Muslim but a polytheist and that the Prophet entrusted him with this task because he was the best navigator. Emad lamented that even "educated people" among his friends and family voiced negative stereotypes about Copts as "sneaky" and only pretending to like their Muslim colleagues and classmates while secretly "conspiring" against them. Such stereotypes, he felt, went against the Islamic virtue of *insaf*, of fairness and even-handedness. "Of course, not all Christians are good, just like not all Muslims are good," he said. "You can find bad individuals from any religion, and you can find beneficial people (*'ummar al-ard*) from any religion."

Such disentangling of creedal distinctions from ethical potential was one way a theology of coexistence practically manifested itself within on-screen content and off-screen production practices of Iqraa as an Islamic channel. But it was not only tensions with non-Muslims that my New Preaching interlocutors hoped to redress with the theological imperative of coexistence: the revolutionary stakes of coexistence extended to Egyptian Muslims' own internal tensions and differences.

THE POLITICS OF PLURALISM, *APRIL 2012*

I am sitting with a group of about a dozen women in a classroom at the back of a large mosque complex, papers and pens out on our desks. In the front Dr. Soraya paces in front of the whiteboard as she gives us a basic primer on what believers could expect in the Afterlife. "Dr. Soraya" did not have a degree formally conferring that title, but the women of the study circle had bestowed it on her as a sign of their esteem. We listen attentively, the thick quiet of the windowless room broken up by muffled coughs and the whir of ceiling fans.

I had started attending Dr. Soraya's lessons in October 2010 with Reem, one of the first viewers of Islamic television preaching I met during fieldwork. Reem was looking to complement what she was learning on-screen from her favorite New Preachers with in-depth personal study, and this mosque complex, located in one of Cairo's more upscale neighborhoods, was recommended to her by an acquaintance. So it was that Dr. Soraya's arrival at the center in the distinctive Salafi ensemble of black face-veil, gloves, and cloak had abruptly ended Reem's excitement at taking lessons at this center. Her disappointment only increased when Dr. Soraya informed us that the main text for the course would be an abridgment of Muhammad Abd al-Wahhab's treatise *Kitab al-Tawhid*, the founding articulation of Saudi Arabia's Salafi-Wahhabi orientation. This orientation was antithetical to the pious sensibility Reem was cultivating and she didn't return to Dr. Soraya's class after that first lesson in 2010. Still, I decided to attend anyway whenever I could fit it into my fieldwork schedule; I felt it important as an anthropologist to have my own experiences, however limited, of Salafi teachings apart from their denigration by interlocutors like Reem. This aim delighted Dr. Soraya when I shared it with her. She welcomed my presence as both an opportunity to dispel "misconceptions" (*shubuhat*) around Salafism to a US-based researcher and to earn divine rewards by guiding me back, as a Muslim, to God's plain truth and away from the influence of the New Preachers who, she reminded me, as *ahl al-bid'a* claim to be following God and Prophet Muhammad while pursuing their own, all-too-human desires. The comparison of the foibles of the likes of Amr Khaled and the scriptural integrity of Salafi preachers would recur throughout Dr. Soraya's lessons and my presence probably contributed to its frequency.

It is now April 2012, almost a year and a half later. Toward the end of Dr. Soraya's lesson, the discussion shifts to the upcoming presidential election in June. The election had thirteen contenders representing diverse ideologies, from socialism to liberalism to Islamism to militarism, and was anticipated to be Egypt's first free and fair one. A few weeks before the first round of voting, there was even a US-style televised debate between two candidates considered to be the front-runners, Amr Moussa, former head of the Arab

League and self-described secularist who was running on a platform of stability and security, and Abdel Moneim Aboul Fotouh, a self-described "Islamic centrist" who had broken away from the Muslim Brotherhood and was running on a platform of bridging the secularist-Islamist divide. On the evening of May 10, I was glued to the television screen for three hours as the two men answered live questions posed by two broadcast journalists. This was the first public debate between presidential contenders not only for Egypt, but for the entire Arab region. Millions watched it. Still, many people I knew were worried that this newly unfettered political landscape would sow discord and confusion, especially when it came to the intersection of religion and politics. This included Dr. Soraya and the women of our study circle.

To protect us from unwittingly falling for the wrong kind of religious politics, Dr. Soraya parsed the linguistic markers of what she deemed Islamic versus un-Islamic ways of speaking. She picked her marker back up:

There are two kinds of people. There are those who say: "I see," "I consider that," or "In my opinion." [She wrote these phrases on the board as she explained this].

And then there are those who say: "the Prophet said" or "God said." [She underlined these phrases and crossed out the others.] This is correct knowledge, these are the God-fearing scholars, not the first.

I peered at the spiral notebook of the woman next to me—she had carefully copied the board, including the underlinings and the crossouts.

Dr. Soraya's categorizations recalled the Salafi shaykh al-Albani's oft-quoted statement that "the true scholar is the one who says 'God said, and the Messenger said' in all matters of religion and in all that he refers to concerning Islam. No one else is a scholar."[40] For adherents like Dr. Soraya, this is what made Salafism not a version or an interpretation *of* Islam, but simply the "true Islam": Salafi doctrines and practices were unequivocally and exclusively based on the Qur'an and the Prophetic Sunna, transparently apprehended.

This Salafi scriptural distinction, according to Dr. Soraya, extended to political speech. "The people of the 'in-my-opinion' camp are also the people who say things like 'religion has to become modern.' They will give you a fatwa to legitimate whatever you desire and pretend to give scriptural evidence for their position," she said. "They are like the secularists because they use their reason, they use their mashed-potato brains"—laughter tittered from desk to desk—"to reason with religion. But religion is submission to the text (*al-din taslim li-l-nass*)."

To speak about religion in a subjective manner—to say something like "in my opinion, Islam teaches . . ."—was to adopt a "secular" stance. Its secularity was characterized above all by the rendering of religion as a matter of reasoned human deliberation, of reasonable disagreement among humans. As described in chapter 3, the Salafi repudiation of the possibility of legitimate religious disagreement was based on an Athari epistemology of the Qur'anic text as self-evident in its meaning. This made disagreement not a virtue, as in the Ash'ari tradition, but a vice. Insofar as democracy hinged on the institutionalization of disagreement in the form of party pluralism, it was a fundamentally un-Islamic political system. The doctrine of *bara'*, of rejection, is important here. Examining the theological foundations of the Salafi stance against democracy, Ovamir Anjum points out that the Wahhabi expansion of the doctrine from non-Muslims to non-Salafi Muslims as well as to Muslims who ally with non-Muslims underlies the rejection of "a system in which a political party may uphold doctrines of disbelief or advocate ruling by laws other than God's."[41] True Muslims cannot acquiesce to such parties or individuals promoting such views or enter coalitions with them. Just as disagreement and differences of opinion were not intrinsic to the Islamic tradition, and in fact imperil it, so was democratic pluralism an obstacle to realizing the true freedom of enshrining divine commands as law. The fact that there were so many political parties, factions, and ideologies in the first place was a function of people using their own reasons and preferences as the basis for policies and proposals. For the Salafi movement, the institutionalization of such normative pluralism is what made democracy an inherently secular system.

In his rebuttal of Mustafa Hosny's Iqraa episode on the ethics of disagreement back in 2009, the Salafi preacher al-Huwayni had made this point.[42] He had argued that one of the biggest moral challenges facing the Muslim community today was that a variety of political parties were claiming the mantle of the Islamic while laying out different visions of governance, neglecting the fact that God Himself has already laid out how to govern in the Qur'an.

Al-Huwayni then turned to a discussion of the hadith of *al-firqa al-najiya*, or the saved sect. According to this hadith, the Muslim community will be divided into seventy-three sects, of which only one will escape the hellfire. The doctrine of the saved sect—which contemporary Egyptian Salafis understand themselves to be[43]—is important to Salafism's negative evaluation of disagreement.[44] During the Prophet's time, al-Huwayni went on, there was but one speech (*qawl wahid*). This uni-vocality continued under the leadership of the four rightly guided caliphs, a period when there were no disagreements among Muslims. In the Salafi historiography, disagreement only begins when human conjecture begins to supplant the clear meaning of the divine text, when Muslims under the influence of "foreign philosophies" begin to project their own whims and desires onto the text. Like Dr. Soraya, the Salafi preacher didn't blame secularists for the subversion of divine truth through human conjecture—after all, secularists didn't claim to care about the divine truth in the first place. The error was caused by some within the Islamic Revival, by what he called the "Islamic thinker," *al-mufakkir al-Islami*. The problem with these thinkers—he named Muhammad al-Ghazali, Yusuf al-Qaradawi, and Sayyid Qutb, all affiliated in some way with al-Azhar or the Muslim Brotherhood or both—is precisely that they are *thinkers*, "writing from their minds" (*bi-yiktibu min dimaghhum*), as opposed to hewing to the text. But the Qur'an, he reminded viewers, was sent down by God so that human beings would know what was categorically true and what was false.

From the New Preaching perspective, the Salafi rejection of disagreement had negative implications for coexistence among Muslims. Not only was the Qur'an open to multiple interpretations, my interlocutors argued, but God Himself valued multiplicity in His own self-disclosure. In his *Coexistence* program Amr Khaled had characterized the Qur'an as "a dialogical book" (*kitab hiwari*). In the Qur'an, Abraham differs with his son, as does Joseph with his brothers, with the text relaying their opposing views. "The opinion and the other opinion isn't heretical (*bid'a*)," Khaled concluded, "but a natural state of affairs."

The next time I saw Reem after the impromptu primer on the election, I shared with her what Dr. Soraya had said about what marks un-Islamic speech from Islamic speech. Reem agreed with her that there were indeed two kinds of people: those Muslims who can accept that that there are different kinds of Muslims with different opinions and peacefully coexist with them, and those Muslims who can't. She chastised me for continuing to "waste my time" with people incapable of entertaining the possibility that they could be wrong because they didn't accept that they were using their own "mashed potato brains" as much as anyone else.

"They make the words of their preacher just like the Qur'an—he can never be wrong," Reem told me. "They don't understand that what he is saying about politics can only ever be just his opinion, his personal perspective. They will hear this opinion and immediately adopt it as their own, as fact."

It wasn't that Reem felt it inappropriate that preachers should have something to say about politics. Like other New Preaching followers and producers, Reem was as convinced as the Salafi pietists I met that secularism was antithetical to Islam. When I asked Reem what she looked for in a president, the first thing she said was that he had to be religious, a man who "knows God." She was brought up to believe that religion is life itself (*al-din huwa al-hayah nafsuha*) in the sense that Islam governs all aspects of life. This conception allowed great latitude. You could do anything you wanted so long as it was within the parameters given by God, which were capacious. But, she clarified, that does not mean she would choose a president based on what he says *about* religion. The job of president calls for an expert in politics, not religion. As evidence, she recalled the Prophetic saying: "You know best the practical affairs of your world."

The story was that the Prophet had come across a group of men cross-pollinating their date palm trees and had remarked that this practice did not seem worthwhile. Hearing this, the men ceased and their yield suffered. When the Prophet asked about the newly sorry state of their date palms, they explained they had stopped their customary tending of the trees after what he had said. The Prophet then said that they knew better their worldly affairs. The oft-repeated interpretation of this tradition is that even the Prophet's opinion can be just that—an opinion that is not necessarily always correct. This idea is anathema to Salafi doctrine: "As for the Messenger, we follow him because of who he inherently is," al-Albani explains. "We do not question him if he says something."[45] When I mentioned this position to Reem, she quickly replied, echoing the New Preachers, that even the Qur'an itself—that is, even God—sanctioned multiple opinions. Contrary to Dr. Soraya's assessment, for Reem, reasoned deliberation—prefacing a remark with "I believe" or "in my view"—and holding space for a variety of opinions did not indicate a "secular" disposition but an Islamic one of coexistence, one that the New Egypt desperately needed.

After the election a few months later, Reem sent me the YouTube link of a mosque sermon by Amr Khaled that she had watched. In it Khaled laments that political disagreements were too often turning violent, even deadly. He blamed this not on Egyptian proclivities ("Are Egyptians just bad at disagreeing? I don't think so") but rather on Egypt's long history of authoritarianism.

"Dictatorship makes you unable to countenance disagreement," he argued, "because it only gives you one option." Prior to the revolution, Khaled's audience of twenty- and thirty-somethings had lived their entire lives under a single head of state: Mubarak's rule had started in 1981, the year I was born, and ended just before I marked my thirty-first birthday. The preacher spoke of a "long era of control" in which there could be "just one opinion," that of "the ruler, the teacher, or your father." And even in the mosque, he goes on to say, there is only one opinion allowed. "The shaykh doesn't give you all the options allowed so you can choose, just like the teacher tells you to just write down what he says, just like the ruler tells you what to think." This has created a culture of mono-thought, *fikr uhudi*. Dictatorial dispositions favor uniformity over diversity, the absolute over the contingent. But difference, *ikhtilaf*, is virtuous and desirable, especially right now as people work toward creating a New Egypt. Living together, *ta'ayush*, would require not agreement but an effort at understanding across difference. Muslims need to realize, Khaled argued, that difference is by divine design, a sign of God, for "if God had willed, He would have made you one community" (Qur'an 5:48). Just as God created a diverse world, He created the conditions for diverse interpretations of His revelation. Even the Qur'an itself, the preacher argued once again, is a deliberative book, *kitab hiwari*, presenting different points of view and experiences.

But tolerating difference is a difficult disposition to cultivate, the preacher reminded his audience. It would take some work: "Find three people who differ from you," he advised, "it could be about soccer or art or anything, and practice with them." Inspired, Reem made a list: her father, skeptical about the revolution, favoring stability; her colleague, wary of her efforts to "make science fun" at the school where they taught; her aunt, disbelieving that the Qur'an enjoins the hijab. She would, as Khaled advised in his sermon, "listen to them" and "try to understand why they think in this way." For her, this openness to difference, this coexistence, was a step toward the New Egypt.

This was also true for my interlocutors at Iqraa, who with the Tahrir uprising linked the theological idea of Islam as a moderate religion accepting of difference and disagreement to the revolutionary possibility of a democratic New Egypt. Posting on his website after voting in one of the referendums in 2011, Hosny wrote that, "like anything," democracy has its pros and cons, but overall what he has witnessed of democracy in Egypt after the revolution is "beautiful." He urged his followers to "hold on to this important and extraordinary experience" in political pluralism as a step in building the New Egypt. The inevitable ideological differences of democratic contest called not for refusal, *bara'*, but coexistence, *ta'ayush*.

"PARTICIPATION, NOT DOMINATION," *JUNE 2012–JUNE 2013*

On June 24, 2012, Mohamed Morsi, the Muslim Brotherhood candidate, was declared the winner of the presidential election against former aviation minister Ahmed Shafik by a margin of less than 2 percent. This narrow margin reflected how polarized Egyptians were, with Morsi limping to victory because of the tactical decision of many pro-revolution Egyptians to vote for him in the second round to keep Shafik, with his cozy ties to the old regime, out. The idiomatic phrase "squeezing a lemon" became a humorous way of characterizing this choice, referencing putting lemon juice on unsavory food to make it palatable.

For many, one important reason a vote for Morsi was so unappetizing was the Muslim Brotherhood's record of broken promises since Mubarak's toppling. Adopting a slogan of "participation not domination" to assuage anxieties that it would hoard power and exclude others from having a meaningful say in shaping the New Egypt, the eighty-five-year-old group had vowed not to run for more than one-third of parliamentary seats and not to try for the presidency. It reneged on both promises: its Freedom and Justice party ran for almost all available seats in the November 2011 parliamentary elections, securing a majority, and in April 2012 the party put forth Morsi, a senior Muslim Brotherhood leader, as its candidate for president. There was thus a widespread sense that the Muslim Brotherhood had proven itself to be untrustworthy and that exclusionary domination—not inclusive participation—was its real political ethos. While the Brotherhood's secular opponents were intransigent in their refusal to cooperate with the group on common policy problems, a noted scholar of the Islamist group observed that "there is no doubt that the Brotherhood's own actions reinforced the impression that it sought to monopolize power, which had the effect of undermining the very democratic institutions it claimed it sought to preserve."[46]

Among my interlocutors at Iqraa, there was particular concern with the sectarian implications of the group's evident disinterest in overcoming the country's partisan divides through more inclusive governance. Many worried that Salafi theological sensibilities toward "the other" were being given a platform by the Muslim Brotherhood in a bid to shore up support among Salafi-identifying voters and further marginalize its vocal "secular" critics.[47] Indeed, Morsi's first year did little to convince my interlocutors that he would, as he vowed, be "a president for all Egyptians." After the election, the Muslim Brotherhood and its Salafi allies dominated the process of drafting a new constitution. As they did in the March 2011 referendum, their supporters framed the December 2012 constitutional referendum in partisan religious terms: Muslims who were politically against passing the draft were tarred as "against Islam," while Christians were characterized as a "fifth column" secretly conspiring with Egypt's enemies to destabilize the country and foment chaos. One scholar characterized the rhetoric of Muslim Brotherhood leaders and supporters during the referendum campaign as "the most crude, offensive, and frankly ridiculous allegations of sectarian conspiracy that I have witnessed in an entire career of watching and studying Coptic-Muslim relations in Egypt."[48] Such sectarianism from Morsi's partisans was especially striking given that an important way in which the Muslim Brotherhood in the decades before the revolution had distanced itself from other Islamic groups, whether apolitical ones like the Salafis or armed ones like Islamic Jihad, was through its conciliatory rhetoric toward Christians, emphasizing their equal citizenship.[49] Over the next year, however, anti-Christian discourses only increased as Muslim Brotherhood supporters accused the Coptic Church itself, and not only ordinary Christians, of conspiring against Islam. Following violent clashes outside the Muslim Brotherhood's headquarters in March 2013, a poster on one of the organization's online forums asked, "Is this a war on creed? Is this a renewed version of the crusade against Islam? Is it a secular alliance with the Church to skin Egyptian society of the Islamic religion? ... Is it time for vigilance before the nation is stripped of its identity?"[50]

For Iqraa producers, the Muslim Brotherhood narrative that their political opponents were "against Islam" was as troubling as the Salafi claim to be "the saved sect." This exclusionary logic negated Tahrir Square's revolutionary ethos of coexistence and perpetuated a polarizing culture of "us versus them," of domination, not participation. Anger at such exclusivist discourse contributed to the decision by many of them to support the nationwide call in June 2013 for Morsi to step down and allow for new elections. Randa, the channel's head of translation, put it like this when I asked her why she planned to join the June 30 mobilization: "Islam isn't new to Egypt. It wasn't introduced into Egypt by the Brothers. In fact, the Brothers have tarnished the image of Islam. They do outrageous things and when we tell them that is not Islam, they call us infidels." From Randa's perspective, just as the Brotherhood aspired to political dominance, so it aspired to dominate the definition of Islam.[51]

Even those Islamic media producers I knew who felt that the June 30 mobilization had been coopted by counterrevolutionary forces and who supported Morsi finishing his term expressed reservations about his party's claim to represent Islam. Fikry, for example, wrote on his Facebook page a few weeks before the scheduled protests that while he "believed that the Islamic trend should exist in the political field," he refused to "sacralize the parties within this trend or treat them like they represent Islam. I am prepared to vote them out for being incompetent, and vote in non-Islamist parties if they are better able to govern." At the same time, he was adamant that criticism of the Muslim Brotherhood and allied Salafi parties shouldn't devolve into criticism of Islamic piety itself, as he felt it often did within secular liberal discourses. Just as it was important not to conflate Islamism with Islam, it was important not to attribute the political failures of Islamist parties to their declared commitment to Islam. The Salafi adversarial stances toward Christians and others getting much media attention during this time were a boon for counterrevolutionary regime remnants who wanted to stoke fears about Islamic revivalists of all stripes being exclusionary and sectarian.

This anxiety was shared by members of Hosny's team at the channel. Emad during this period put it like this: "I can never be convinced that Islam commands us to treat people who are different from us badly or unethically, even if that person belongs to a different religion or even decides to leave Islam." He concluded that if Muslims coming of age with the revolution continued to associate piety with hate and "rejecting the other," then he would have failed in his own ethical mission as an Islamic media producer. However, he insisted that secular liberal pundits and channels were also responsible for Egypt's "polarization" (*istiqtab*) by refusing any common ground with their political opponents. They too aspired to 'domination, not participation. Both camps, he told me, want "the freedom of one perspective (*hurriyat al-ra'y al-wahid*). They want freedom for themselves, and they want the other to be silent," he said. "That's no different from the previous regime." Secular liberals, as much as Islamists, needed to cultivate a culture of coexistence.

———

Coexistence struck multiple nadirs that summer. At a rally in Cairo Stadium that Morsi attended in his capacity as president on June 15, Muhammad Hassan implored Morsi to protect Egypt from the "corruption" of the Shia, referring to them with the Salafi nomenclature of *al-rafida*, or the rejectors.[52] While Shias are not a marked minority like Christians, with less than a million adherents in Egypt, this term is considered by many to be acutely sectarian, similar in its derogatory valence to the Salafi reference to non-Muslims as *al-kuffar*, the infidels. Religious difference became once again a political lightning rod. Standing on stage with Morsi sitting behind him, another famous Salafi preacher, Abd al-Maqsud, described the Shia as "filthy" (*anjas*) before supplicating God to "make June 30th a day of victory for Islam and Muslims and a day of defeat for the infidels and hypocrites."

A week later, on June 23, a mob attacked two dozen Shia Muslims while they were worshipping in Giza, killing four people, including the prominent leader of the small community, Hassan Shehata. Cellphone footage of a dead body being dragged through the dirt streets of the poor neighborhood by people shouting "God is great" was widely aired in the extensive news coverage of the attack. While mainstream channels drew a direct line between the attacks and the remarks by Salafi preachers at the rally, more detailed coverage on the ground suggested that tension had been building for months between the village's local Salafi preachers and their congregants and the minority Shia inhabitants, with reports of the former marching through the village a few weeks before chanting against the "heresy" of the latter. Coverage by major Salafi channels like al-Nas appeared to implicitly justify the killings by suggesting that the villagers were "understandably" enraged by Shia "insults" to the Prophet's family.

Morsi's office issued a statement condemning the attack as contrary to the "moderation" of Egyptians. For many, this was too little, too late: that the Muslim Brotherhood leader had allowed the Salafis to denigrate the Shia at the rally in the first place, and that his subsequent condemnation did not explicitly name the victims as Shia, was yet another indication of the emptiness of the Islamist group's promise that its candidate would represent "all Egyptians." The Muslim Brotherhood's complacency "with the divisive and inflammatory sectarian discourse of its [Salafi] allies," argued two critical scholars, was nothing short of a complicit "endorsement of violence against a rapidly expanding category of the 'other.'"[53]

Many of my interlocutors within New Preaching circles, whether producers or viewers, agreed. Instead of ushering in the New Egypt prefigured in Tahrir, Morsi and his supporters helped entrench divisions between those who identify as pious and those who do not, between Muslims and Christians, and between different kinds of Muslims. Muslim Brotherhood governance, they felt, had made it less possible for Egyptians to live with each other.

LIVING WITH EACH OTHER, *AUGUST 2013*

Amr Khaled faces the camera, the rolling hills and sunlit skies of southern Spain in frame behind him. It is the first episode of *Qissat al-Andalus* (*The Story of Andalusia*). Shot on location in historic towns and villages of the Iberian Peninsula, the series narrates key events in 800 years of Muslim medieval governance of Andalusia. Khaled evokes the history of Andalusia as a "magical mix" of three religions, Islam, Christianity, and Judaism, and three cultures, Arab, Amazigh, and Spanish. The preacher describes Andalusia as a place where people radically different from one another nevertheless managed to peacefully live with each other and together accomplish extraordinary things. As Eric Calderwood shows, this imagination of Andalusia as a past-place of exceptional coexistence has for centuries inspired artists and activists in the Arab world aspiring for a more tolerant future.[54] But while Andalusia's legendary *convivencia* is commonly identified as an Arab, not Muslim, phenomenon,[55] Khaled locates its "magical mix" squarely within an Islamic theological frame. The coexistence that characterized Andalusia at its civilizational height was, the preacher told his viewers, "a gift from God."

Highlighting that the current refusal of difference was a problem not only for Muslim-Christian relations but among Muslims themselves, Khaled argued that what "we urgently need in our country today is Andalusia's culture of coexistence," of *ta'ayush*. *Ta'ayush*, simply put, means "living with each other" (*n'ish ma'a ba'd*). Interactionally, that entails "respecting each other, listening to each other, and cooperating with each other." The New Preacher offered up the story of Andalusia as a "mirror for our own times," both cautionary and inspirational. When its denizens accepted their differences, they flourished; then they refused to coexist, and they faded. Will we learn from their mistakes? Khaled asked. Or will history repeat itself?

The series' thirty episodes were filmed in southern Spain during the polarizing year of Morsi's presidency. By the time it aired in Ramadan of 2013, the Muslim Brotherhood leader had been ousted and thousands of his supporters killed. In revenge, Christians had been killed and their churches, schools, businesses, and homes across the country attacked.[56] For New Preaching viewers, this shocking, blood-soaked turn of events made the series' theme of coexistence especially poignant.

Just as it did a decade earlier, Khaled's call for coexistence resonated with Hania, who regularly tuned in to the series that tragic summer. Like others identifying with the revolutionary "Third Trend" rejection of both Muslim Brotherhood and military rule, Hania had supported the June 30 protests but not the July 3 coup that followed. But even before that, as the political polarization worsened in the year after the revolution, as the competition for votes and seats drove politicians and their parties into more absolutist positions, as representatives of different ideological camps became self-caricatures, Hania was already connecting the theological imperative of "accepting the other" to the success of the revolution. For her, Andalusia's "magical mix" recalled the spirit of Tahrir Square and the capacity of ordinary people to determine their own fate, whether for good or ill. She felt that the New Preachers were the only Islamic figures truly concerned with how to practically recapture this revolutionary spirit in tumultuous times. Indeed, again and again, Khaled underscored on-air that coexistence is above all a question of practice: "It is not enough to say *But we love each other!* or *National unity!* whenever there is a problem. We need to do things together if we really want to live with each other."

Hania took this exhortation to coexistence as an everyday practice seriously. She had recently made a new friend, a Christian Catholic. With her, Hania entered a church for the first time in her life and she told me it was one of the most "Islamic" experiences she ever had. "I stayed with them for an hour as they prayed. It was a very moving experience," she shared in a phone conversation the summer of 2013. "When we can understand the other from the inside, from their core (*gawhar*), we can really love each other." The way she saw it, such personal interactions, and firsthand experiences of each other, across difference were not merely a precondition for revolutionary change, but also a revolutionary aim in and of themselves. To be sure, changing the policies that discriminated against Christians and holding accountable those who harmed them was important, but true coexistence could never be achieved if Muslims and Christians in Egypt didn't meaningfully interact with each other in daily life. The New Preachers' theological elaboration of coexistence mattered deeply to how Hania's pious commitment intertwined with her revolutionary commitment to building a New Egypt in whatever way she could.

Others I spoke with during that summer shared this assessment that coexistence as positive social interaction represented the first step out of the fear-based divisions the Mubarak regime had so expertly exploited and entrenched and that the Morsi regime had exacerbated. These included not only religious divisions but ideological ones. Several people I knew from fieldwork mentioned during this time their participation in initiatives aimed at promoting mutual understanding across ideological divides. For example, the Islamic life-coach Ahmed El Aawar helped facilitate what he called "deep democracy process work" between the liberal and Islamic camps. He explained that in contrast to the focus of "ordinary democracy" on winning votes, deep democracy is concerned with centering the inevitable diversity of perspectives around various issues. His role as a coach was to get people who were normally suspicious if not hostile toward each other to share their feelings and opinions with the goal of "letting us see ourselves and each other from different perspectives." He was adamant that the impact of such new awareness could be scaled up, that changing just one or two individuals at a time would make a real difference in the long term to changing everything.

Whether for Hania or Ahmed, the challenge of coexistence lay in the ethical effort of creating shared spaces, of looking for ways in which we are more alike than different. Similarly, the Islamic media producers I worked with at Iqraa were committed to actualizing their vision of the virtuous life in the world, but this vision was deliberatively expansive, the result of a broader commitment to create shared spaces (*misahat mushtaraka*) between those who identity as pious and those who do not.[57] Like with self-help, critical scholars tend to dismiss such sentiments as depoliticizing platitudes that obscure the structural work necessary to effect real change. But to a status quo built on exclusionary, zero-sum logics, even the rhetorical invocation of diversity and pluralism can seed the hope of an alternative future grounded in coexistence. Individual investments in coexistence, however small, can prefigure a better world in common. The struggle for the New Egypt begins within ourselves.

―――

Some have argued that the Arab Spring exposed "the absence of an Islamic political theology compatible with democratic transition" and the prevalence of an authoritarian one.[58] While New Preachers like Khaled did not systematically elaborate a doctrine of democracy—and a programmatic demand for democracy was absent from revolutionary calls for "bread, freedom and human dignity"[59]—they nevertheless linked theological precepts related to difference to the pious cultivation of proto-democratic habits befitting the New Egypt. Through their theology of coexistence, the New Preachers challenged Salafi doctrines of sectarian rejection while positioning a pious sensibility—not a secular one—as the foundational guarantor of interreligious harmony and solidarity.

Charles Hirschkind contends that injunctions not to let differences in faith sunder "the social fabric of our common citizenship" are secular in the sense that they position such differences as "markers of *private* distinction" and not of *"public* sociability."[60] This was the view of the Salafi preachers he researched. As mentioned earlier, Muhammad Hassan and other Salafi revivalists labeled the New Preachers "stealth secularizers," critiquing them for being insufficiently attuned to how the creedal differences between Muslims and non-Muslims must shape the principled refusal of social interactions. They also criticized the New Preachers for positing disagreement as essential to, as opposed to a threat to, the Islamic tradition. By contrast, for the New Preachers piety entailed friendship across religious difference and accepting the legitimacy of differing points of view. In this way, the concept of *ta'ayush* tied the challenge of Muslims and Christians living together to the challenges of Muslims' own internal diversity. This illustrates the ways in which the boundaries of the secular and the religious are theologically adjudicated and contested within the Islamic Revival, rendering their analytical identification impossible. By insisting that Islamic piety did not have to be an obstacle to inclusion and solidarity, Islamic media producers revolutionized deeply held religious convictions of what dispositions and actions are pleasing to God.

To be clear, coexistence wasn't a synonym for an ecumenism whereby all religious traditions are held to be "equally true" or essentially "the same." My interlocutors regarded the historical religion of Islam as the final revealed and most perfected one and took creedal differences, including those within it, seriously. But God does not will that all human beings be Muslim, or that all Muslims agree, and so we all must find a way to act in common despite not practicing and believing in common. Unlike secular notions of tolerance, this involved not finding a "neutral" nonreligious language from which to speak as a way of overcoming the social effects of religious difference, but rather of using religious language and imaginaries to meet ethical standards held in common despite religious difference. In this way the second part of the oft-quoted *ta'aruf* verse becomes important for my interlocutors: "Surely the most noble of you in the sight of God is the most righteous among you" (Qur'an 49:13). Comprehensibility and mutual knowing were not only divinely obligated goods in themselves but also ends to establishing the ethical conduct fostered by righteousness, by God-consciousness, whatever one's creed. As I have shown here, the search for ethical commensurability across creedal and ideological differences was rooted in a theological understanding of diversity as divinely sanctioned and, as such, part of a pious formation. Seeing how this is so complicates reductive binaries of secular Muslims who care about the rights and well-being of religious others and pious Muslims who seemingly do not.

These New Preaching elaborations resonated greatly with their followers, offering them a way to make ethical sense of the country's unfolding political dramas. Engy, a longtime New Preaching viewer, told me that their programs helped her understand that coexistence is the other side of freedom. Aspiring to freedom, she shared, can feel "very hard because it forces you to accept the existence of other even if you refuse what they are saying, even if what the other is saying goes against your own beliefs and ideas." The elusiveness of this freer New Egypt was already on Khaled's mind when he testified to seeing God in the Square in his television interview in February 2011. Just a week after Mubarak's toppling, Tahrir's radical spirit of coexistence seemed to be disintegrating as Egyptians resumed their old quarrels with each other. How can we live together with ideological foes, with religious difference, beyond endless vituperation and mutual animosity? How can we "see God" once again as we did in Tahrir?

In response, my interlocutors insisted on a deep connection between the Islamic and the revolutionary that leaves both open to multiple articulations. Islamic theology became a resource for living together with difference beyond both the postcolonial state's rhetoric of "national unity" and Salafi revivalism's sectarianizing assurances of "protection." In this way, the Islamic tradition is figured as a conversation in which non-Muslims can participate, not despite its distinctive theological suppositions, but because of them. The Qur'an, as a "universal message" from God addressed not merely to Muslims but to all human beings, allows for coexistence as an aspect of a divine creation.

The ways in which my interlocutors made sense of their work as Islamic media producers through the prism of *ta'ayush* illustrates the social life of theology not as abstract doctrine but as a lived practice of piety that informed their capacious understanding of what counts as Islamic media. Pietists' debates about the forms and ends of Islamic media intertwined with those about the forms and ends of a New Egypt.

Epilogue

"YOU HAVE TO WATCH THIS," ZAYNA WROTE TO ME IN 2014, ON THE eve of the third anniversary of the Egyptian revolution. "I watched it like fifty times already and still cry every time." I clicked on her Facebook message's link to Hamza Namira's music video "What Can I Say?" (*Wa Ulak Ay?*). Namira is a close friend of Hosny, and Zayna, like other members of the preacher's media team, had gotten to know the talented musician well through his collaboration with them on Iqraa productions. At the Islamic channel Namira's music exemplified ethical entertainment, *fann hadif*, that responded to social concerns within divinely permissible aesthetic parameters. In the wake of the 2011 uprising, Namira had also become for many of my interlocutors a revolutionary artist, *fannan al-thawra*, as he sang to crowds in Tahrir about a better tomorrow already here.

Namira's music video once again struck all the right chords for Zayna. Namira's lyrics and accompanying visuals speak of a nation deeply polarized and riven by violence and indifference: "What can I say? Where has the path of hatred led us?" A head-scarfed woman in a doctor's coat clutches the hand of a small girl as she dodges bullets; a spray can–wielding graffitist is water cannoned. "Our hope in our country has died. None of us is a stranger to loss or pain." A protester is tear-gassed after making the sign of the cross; a conscript cowers behind his Plexiglas shield, deflecting rocks.

Zayna felt that Namira's song had captured her feeling of overwhelming despair and her inability to speak in the bloody aftermath of the coup a year earlier. Her speechlessness was a function of an increasingly censorious state and its selection of which words would be rewarded and allowed publicity and which punished and silenced. But more distressingly for Zayna and some of her colleagues at Iqraa, speechlessness also was the result of an everyday animosity among friends and within families over reasons of state.

Indeed, the divisions Namira queried played out not only in staid newspaper headlines or satirical memes, not only in convictions or acquittals, not only in whose deaths were cheered or whose were mourned. They were also divisions that left family dinners unfinished, coffee dates canceled, phone numbers deleted, divorces threatened. This was the everyday ethical debris of Egyptians unable to live with one another. For Zayna and other Islamic media producers, Namira's single was a poignant refusal of polarization. And although it did not offer solutions, the song's reenactment of the iconography of the violence that unraveled the heady promise of 2011 was cathartic and, for many of my revivalist interlocutors, a revolutionary gesture.

Not everyone agreed with Zayna's positive assessment of the music video. The state banned all of Namira's music from the radio, citing his "opposition to the ruling regime in Egypt." Members of the Muslim Brotherhood also denounced the song. Backstage at his concert in Detroit in 2019, Namira explained to me that the Muslim Brotherhood and what he called the *dawlagiyya*—state apologists—didn't like the song for the same reason. In calling on Egyptians on "both sides" to recognize the pain of the other, it presented an equivalence that was from their perspectives false. But even beyond state and Brotherhood partisans, within the revolutionary circles that Namira would identify as his own, the song fell flat for similar reasons: to try to identify common ground or to cultivate empathy across divides was to legitimize the illegitimate grievances of "the other side."

"All of this kumbaya stuff is problematic if it doesn't address core power imbalances," one Egypt scholar wrote to me in a Facebook discussion when the song came out in 2014. "In fact, it is counterrevolutionary, despite whatever intentions might be behind it." As an example of a truly revolutionary stance, he directed me instead to a newly released song by Ramy Essam who, like Namira, also performed in Tahrir and was also banned from Egypt.

Far from appealing to a shared predicament, Essam's song sought catharsis in categorical division: "We are not them, nor them, nor them," he tells us. Meanwhile, a popular anti–Muslim Brotherhood song by Ali El Haggar, "We are one people, and you another," was just as categorical, its refrain relentlessly distinguishing an Egyptian self from its Islamist other: "We will never become you and you will never become us."

Such definitive declarations of belonging and difference exhibited a clarity and surety that was difficult to come by the year before. In the summer of 2013, following mass protests against the Muslim Brotherhood president Mohamed Morsi, the armed forces took over. The televised images of multitudes of flag-waving protesters that June looked strangely familiar, recalling those of the 2011 revolution that had forced Mubarak from power. The arc of the unfolding political drama, it seemed, was also strikingly similar: the people took to the streets peacefully; the president was unmoved, vowing to complete his term and threatening chaos if removed; the generals decided to side with the people; the revolution was saved.

But still everything felt mixed up. I had attributed my own confusion about what was happening to my distance—I was abroad at the time. But when I arrived back in Cairo the next month, I realized that most everyone seemed confused. In fact, many of my interlocutors looked to me for a clearer perspective precisely because I had been out of the country during the protests.

In the days after Morsi's ouster, Islamic television producers were talking and debating the extraordinary events of that summer as much as any other group of Egyptians. And like most people, they were unsure about what was transpiring and what it meant for them and the country. Moreover, they were as divided about the unfolding events as the viewers they hoped to reassure. One editor sounded subdued, tired, when I spoke with her on the phone.

"I don't know what to think," she said slowly. "I will sit with a pro-Morsi person and he will convince me. Then I will sit with an anti-Morsi person, and he will also convince me." She said that at the channel these three camps—the pro, the anti, the undecided—had each carved out a little space of the station for themselves. When I visited the channel the following week, the two distinct political camps, and the uncertain one in between, were apparent immediately. Those against the "coup" were congregating during their free time around a television tuned to al-Jazeera, while those for the "revolution" watched one of the private Egyptian channels together. In the meantime, a few unhappily drifted in and out of these two groups. One person in the uncertain, drifting group said that what saddened her the most was the fact that women on the floor were no longer all praying together as we used to. It has become very hard to have a simple conversation, she said in a half-whisper.

In the end, however, what distressed her the most was not the severed friendships and truncated collegiality, but the new risks that were becoming commonplace. Making the long commute to work every day had become a perilous obligation, with gunshots ringing out and fights erupting without warning. Her husband was walking to the mosque one evening, when a man, "a thug," suddenly appeared brandishing a knife and asked him, "What do you think of the Brothers?" Her husband noncommittally shrugged his shoulders because he was unsure which answer would save him the pain of the knife. His silence may have saved his life.

Indeed, if confusion was the problem, then silence might be the solution. In the face of the feverish polarizations among ordinary Egyptians that summer, including not just his own colleagues but also his viewers, Hosny decided that "maintaining silence" (*al-iltizam bi-l-samt*) was the only ethical stance available to him as a preacher. His producers contrasted the prudence of silence with the perils of speech. Speech in times of *fitna*, of strife and tumult among Muslims, risks making matters worse. Far from resolving uncertainty, words during polarized times could lead to more discord and doubt. They explained that the Prophet had forewarned of this: "There will be *fitna* which will render people deaf, dumb, and blind regarding what is right," he told his Companions. "Those who contemplate it will be drawn by it, and giving rein to the tongue during it will be like striking with the sword."

In both our scholarly and political imagination, silence is deplored as indicative of powerlessness and passivity. To be radical is above all to "speak truth to power." Nevertheless, across space and time examples abound of silence as an ethical and politically effective intervention, and even as a practice of opposing injustice.[1] There were important precedents for the power of silence in Islamic history familiar to my pious interlocutors. As H. A. Hellyer notes, "The avoidance of internecine discord and conflict is an important imperative within Sunni Islam. Such arguments are often accompanied by silence. In other words, in the interests of what they perceived as the greater good, scholars would not speak out against injustices around them—even though they recognized them as injustices."[2] In a time of confusion, of *fitna*, at a time when words are violence, it may be silence that can quell the discord incited by words.[3] For my interlocutors in Islamic television, the silence of the New Preachers could repair the fractures among their followers of "ordinary people," or at least it wouldn't make them worse. As the Iqraa producer Fikry put it: "We know our audience is very, very divided about what is going on." There was no consensus about whether the mass protests calling for Morsi to resign and for new presidential elections to take place were wise or necessary. Taking a "clear stance" would cost them half their audience. Whatever stance they adopted would be unacceptable to one or the other of the two most visible camps.

Like other producers, Fikry believed that Hosny's audience, whether those favoring Morsi finishing his term or those wanting him to resign early, or even those who were ambivalent, most needed a preacher who was above the partisan fray, a preacher who could maintain his moral credibility and the audibility of his words about godliness by refusing to speak about the "political scene" (*al-mashhad al-siyasi*). Political silence safeguarded against pious alienation. As the more cynical producers like Madame Nawal pointed out, silence also safeguarded their broadcast contracts with mainstream channels.

Indeed, the attempt to remain above the partisan fray incited widespread skepticism. In refusing to speak about what everyone else was speaking about, the New Preachers risked alienating everyone. For despite their principled silence, people found ample evidence that they were really "for the other side." Muslim Brotherhood supporters tarred them as hypocrites and military stooges. Brotherhood opponents interpreted their silence not as neutrality but as a lack of buy-in. Both camps called on the New Preachers to take a "clearer stance."[4] If you are not taking a side, the sentiment went, you were on the other side. And of course uncertainty tends to favor the powerful: if nothing can be definitively ascertained, no one can be held accountable, Morsi supporters pointed out.

But even those who had joined the protests against Morsi didn't appreciate the preacher's silence, characterizing it as an abdication of his pious responsibility to guide fellow Muslims to moral certainty in times of crisis. "The preacher by not speaking is not fulfilling his role," Hania complained to me in an email. She was joining the June 30 mobilization. "If religion as we are taught is more than just praying and fasting and fulfilling rituals, then why not speak when it matters the most, in times of crisis? Shouldn't the preacher be living people's problems, and helping them decide what is right and wrong?" She saw her favorite New Preachers' silence as an abdication of the revolutionary piety they promoted, turning them into the Salafi preachers they opposed, into those preachers who "limit" *da'wa* to ritual exhortation devoid of a "positive" impact on the world.

Mona—who, unlike Hania, felt that Morsi, however incompetent, should be subject to a vote in the next election, not forced out before—nevertheless also felt that the New Preachers' silence was ultimately unhelpful. Like many others, judging from the comments they left on Hosny's page, she did not interpret his public withdrawal, his refusal to comment directly on the events transpiring, as a gesture of attachment but rather as its opposite, as one of distancing. Indeed, Hosny's own claim to moral distinction as a preacher who shared the concerns of ordinary people was undermined by his attempt to reframe silence as the only moral path in troubling times. After all, many viewers found the New Preachers appealing precisely because they addressed "real problems," leading them to feel that such preachers were "just like them." This feeling of intimacy engendered the expectation that they would always have something to say on the matters preoccupying viewers.

"The job of the preacher is to share the anxieties of the people, not to lock himself up, isolate himself and pretend not to be there," Mona said. "We have to feel that he is living these moments with us—if this is a time of *fitna*, he should tell us how to deal with it. This is not dabbling in politics, but preaching!" Perhaps, she mused, the New Preachers were not saying anything because they, like so many of her family and friends, did not know what to say; right and wrong were so muddled right now. Still, she felt that this lack of ethical certitude, while understandable for ordinary people, was unbecoming of a preacher.

For their part, Hosny's producers worked hard to defuse the growing tide of public frustration among viewers by replying as much as possible to individual expressions of concern on Facebook. For example, in late July, after a deadly clash between protesters for and against Morsi, a member of Hosny's social media team posted a supplicatory prayer: "May God unite us, soften our hearts for each other, help us avoid hidden and visible *fitna*, lead us from injustice, and make our calamities a mercy." In reply, one user asked Hosny in a comment linked to the update: "Why don't you have a clear stance?"

A few hours later, a member of the team wrote as a comment to this comment: "Mister Mustafa believes in the principle of specialization, and that in every field there are experts and specialists." She directed the questioning user to a previous status update by Hosny dating from December 2012. That year had been a tumultuous one. The jockeying for power between the Islamist presidency, revolutionary activists, and entrenched members of the old regime often turned deadly, with clashes breaking out supporters and opponents of the different sides. In the meantime, more and more Egyptians, fearful and fatigued, muttered about "this wretched revolution." Against this backdrop, Hosny had written:

> I am not a politician and I am not qualified to comment on political matters. I will not be party to a political struggle. I love Egypt and my fellow Egyptians, and I will do my best in the midst of these contradictory and confusing events to reconcile the people of this country and to mediate between them. I will try to unite and not divide. I will try to be a preacher for building, not an agent for destruction. I will try to help in calming the situation not further igniting it.

The producers on Hosny's team reversed the negative moral assessment of not knowing through citing the Islamic jurisprudential concept of *tawaqquf*, or adopting a noncommittal or neutral stance on contentious matters when one does not know. Claiming ignorance should not be seen as a weakness on the part of the preacher, but as evidence of a sincerity of commitment to truth, especially during contentious times when truth is obscured and illegible. Within this logic, maintaining silence on politics was a moral obligation not only in times of *fitna*, but at all times for a person who has no "expertise" in politics.

Some viewers also agreed with this reasoning. On June 24, 2013, six days before millions took to the streets demanding Morsi's resignation and the end of Brotherhood rule, one viewer I knew wrote on her Facebook page that she "respects the preachers who are maintaining their silence. We are in this current predicament due to half-famous people feeling entitled to go on TV and give their opinions about matters they in truth know nothing about. When the Salafis and the Muslim Brotherhood used to speak politics in the name of religion, we were rightfully upset, so why do we want our own preachers to do that now? We love our preachers and our hearts are attached to them. Their words move us, making them responsible. So staying silent is the best course. Even the Prophet was silent when he felt that Muslims would end up fighting each other."

Still, in the days and weeks that followed, as the death toll rose, the arrests continued, the vitriol increased, followers begged Hosny in increasingly desperate comments on his official Facebook page to "take a stance!" (*khudd mawqif*). Some even wrote missives in his name and circulated them on social media. One was particularly poignant in its brevity: "My dear brothers and sisters, I have been silent because I am confused and I cannot believe what is going on and I do not know what to say."

―――

As the popular mobilization against Morsi devolved into a bloody crackdown, the New Preachers did break their silence to condemn the loss of life and the moral nonchalance toward it in the mainstream media.[5] "My God," Hosny wrote on his official Facebook page that night in August of the massacre of protesters in Rabi'a Square, a busy intersection in Cairo turned anti-coup sit-in. "My mind can't take all of this in and my heart is breaking from pain. I am in a state of total shock over the amount of blood being spilled. O God, I don't know what to say or what to think." Such feelings of powerlessness and pain, while shared by many, were often construed as acts of betrayal in the Manichean nation created by the triumphant fighting "the terrorists." They also fell short for Muslim Brotherhood supporters and some Salafi preachers who framed the stakes as being nothing less than Islam itself.

Indeed, when, two days after Rabi'a, Amr Khaled appeared on al-Jazeera, whose coverage of the events was highly sympathetic to the Muslim Brotherhood, the host immediately asked him to declare his "political stance." After the host continued to press the preacher, Khaled retorted: "Why do you insist on putting me back in politics? Let there be at least one person who remains outside of politics!" He went on: "I have been called names for my silence, but I remain silent. Because we still need to have someone who talks about ethical principles and maybe that is too idealistic, but I refuse to be pressured into taking a political position. Let me play my role as a preacher!"[6]

Of course, there is much pious precedent for political speech by preachers, especially in speech that challenges oppression. The Prophetic characterization of "a word of truth spoken to an unjust ruler" as the highest form of godly struggle was widely invoked that summer. To fail to speak out against injustice is to fail to discharge a fundamental obligation of piety. This was especially so for theologians at al-Azhar, the country's oldest bastion of Islamic teaching. "If you are a scholar and you accepted being in this position, then you should be willing to pay the price [for speaking the truth]," explained one former admirer of al-Azhar to a researcher. "Even if the price is really high. And even if I, as a layperson, can't pay that price, you should be able to because you are an 'alim [religious scholar]. You have double the responsibility."[7] Although the New Preachers not officially scholars, many have long felt that a "true preacher" is one with the "courage to speak the truth in the face of the very real danger of arrest and torture."[8]

In the long run, Hosny's team felt vindicated by the preacher's refusal to clearly take a side, never mind the name-calling and the motive-questioning. I called Zayna the day after she sent me the link to Namira's music video "What Can I Say?" on Facebook. By that point, we were both marking the third anniversary of the revolution far away from Egypt. We reminisced about our time at Iqraa and those extraordinary two years, and Zayna said she is glad that in the end Hosny listened to those like her and Emad and Fikry who advised him not to speak about politics. "Not speaking is going to anger some people, but not as much as speaking," she said. "If he speaks about the political situation, people who disagree will then be unable to hear what he has to say about God, which is much more important."

She reminded me of the catastrophic results of so many once-respected Islamic figures taking a clear stance—such as Egypt's mufti Ali Gomaa who urged soldiers in a leaked video to shoot Muslim Brotherhood members "like dogs," or Yusuf al-Qaradawi, who insisted that Morsi had only been disliked because he was a devout Muslim careful of his prayers and fasts, that his opponents had no real grievances. They had only made divisions among ordinary Egyptians much worse, contributing to the proliferation of an "either with them or against us" mentality, that either way "you" are against "us." This had had the effect that Iqraa producers had feared: turning people away from piety altogether and from the possibility of imagining a New Egypt through it. The "deliberate polyvalence" of silence, its capacity to avoid being pinned down to a "side," made it for many of my interlocutors a potent resource for drawing "the murky middle"—the New Preachers' middle-class viewers of ordinary people—toward a shared space in which it might be possible for them to live together with their differences.[9]

The avoidance of being pinned down to a side through silence could also call into question the inevitablilty of the Islamism of the Muslim Brothers and secularism as the only two viable political options for Egypt. Instead of subscribing to an either-or logic, many Islamic media producers I came to know during my fieldwork evinced an activist sensibility that tried to avoid the competing ideological claims of organized Islamist groups and their secular liberal counterparts of what the "New Egypt" should be like. Instead, they articulated a sociopolitical vision that, while incipient and not always coherent, was explicitly committed to the task of creating a shared space (*masaha mushtarika*) between Egyptians of different political orientations and moral sensibilities, including between those who identify themselves as pious and those who do not. This involved seeing Islam as providing a prescriptive framework for political practice while refusing exclusive partisan claims to it. As we have seen, this notion of a shared space was itself predicated on a particular theology of difference and coexistence, one that evaluated those qualities as goods internal to the Islamic tradition and not as threats to it.

For many, however, the very desire for a shared space was antithetical to the clarity that both political and pious purity demands. Radical politics, by definition, demand certainty and preclude compromise: there is no "on the other hand." Indeed, appeals to unity and coexistence can quickly be co-opted for counterrevolutionary purpose, to continue the unbearable present rather than build alternative futures. Still, the substantive ends of unity matter greatly to the actualization of the shared space as a revolutionary one. "Half our problems are because we don't listen to each other," Fikry told me on the third anniversary of the revolution. "And the other half because we don't respect each other." He hoped that Egyptians could find a way to see that everyone is complex, a little bit good, a little bad, and that if we could move beyond our mutual mistrust and hatred, we could still have a dream in common. Tending to the common good requires a more robust sense of "we." That's why Zayna, Fikry, and others at Iqraa found Namira's video so inspiring.

Their insistence as pious Muslim producers on creating the possibility of shared spaces, of an "us" and a "we," within Islamic media and the Islamic Revival more broadly foregrounds the ways in which revolutionary demands for dignity and social justice were not only political and economic, but also ethical demands that manifested themselves in everyday habits of interaction, in feelings about others, and in how one responded to inflicted hurt. With the curtailment of dissent in the decade since 2013, speaking the language of a shared space became a radical act, a way of working to realize the revolutionary demands for "bread, freedom, and social justice." Talk of solidarity and common action can seem at best naive amid the vitriol that marks much of public speech in Egypt today, and at worst complicit in occluding the pain of destroyed lives and loved ones. But for these Islamic media producers, it is the indifference of ordinary citizens to the silencing of those with whom they disagree, or dislike, that gives counterrevolutionary forces strength. Many of them were disturbed that so many Egyptians, including some of their friends and even close family members, could feel glee at reports of the killing or imprisonment of the "other side." Outrage should not be measured and doled out according to who is killing or who is being killed, they reasoned. From my interlocutors' perspective, the counterrevolution was an ethical failure on the part of individuals to enact, in their own interactions, alternatives to exclusionary logics. The politics of prefiguration went both ways.

In the face of bars and bullets, the self stubbornly remains a site of hopeful futurity, of possible redemption. Still, trying to create a shared space, let alone inhabiting it, can feel arduous and uncertain. It can feel wretched. To insist on nevertheless trying one's best is to overcome those who would make the "New Egypt" a more brutal version of the old.

The revolution within continues.

Acknowledgments

Many thanks are due here:

To my interlocutors in the world of Islamic television. Many of you remain anonymous in this work, but I hope that you will nonetheless recognize your insights, experiences, and aspirations in it. I continue to dream with you that a New Egypt is possible.

To NYU's Department of Anthropology, where I first started thinking about the social life of media in relation to the anthropology of Islam under the brilliant guidance of Faye Ginsburg, Michael Gilsenan, Angela Zito, Bruce Grant, and Lila Abu-Lughod, borrowed from Columbia. Each of them has profoundly shaped me as a scholar, teacher, and colleague in different ways. I also learned much from other NYU faculty on what it means to think and do anthropology in imaginative and ethical modes, in particular Tejaswini Ganti, Fred Myers, and Bambi Schieffelin. Cheryl Furjanic and Pegi Vail taught me the importance of making films that matter.

To my colleagues and friends at the University of Michigan, first in the Society of Fellows, later in the Department of Anthropology, who offered constructive criticism, inspiring ideas, and not least the comforts of ordinary conversation in extraordinary times. Ruth Behar, Melissa Burch, Luciana Chamorro, Jatin Dua, Amal Fadlalla, Kristzi Fehervary, Sherina Feliciano-Santos, Jennifer Hsieh, Judy Irvine, Webb Keane, Stuart Kirsch, Matt Hull, Alaina Lemon, Michael Lempert, Bruce Mannheim, Barb Meek,

Mike McGovern, Erik Mueggler, Alyssa Paredes, Damani Partridge, Liz Roberts, and Scott Stonington motivate me to try to be the best anthropologist I can by their excellent examples. Former departmental chair Andrew Shryock and current chair Kelly Askew's support for this book project was key to its start and completion. Melissa's friendship and solidarity on the tenure track kept me on track in innumerable ways, while Jatin and Scott showed the way. I couldn't have asked for better students and fellow travelers in the anthropology of the Middle East and North Africa than Özge Korkmaz, Roxana Maria Aras, Saquib Usman, Adeli Block, and Nesrien Hamid.

Beyond the anthropology department, I am fortunate at Michigan to be in the company of ethically and politically engaged scholars whose work is reshaping the study of contemporary Islam, the Middle East, and/or its diasporas: Su'ad Abdul Khabeer, Samer Ali, Hakem al-Rustom, Ummayah Cable, Juan Cole, Murad Idris, Charlotte Karem-Albrecht, Nancy Khalil, Aliyah Khan, Hossein Mostafa, and Renée Randall. Special thanks as well to Kathryn Babayan, Deidre de la Cruz, Abigail Dumes, Geoff Emberling, Michael Fahy, Susan Gilman, Don Lopez, Janet Richards, and Rebecca Wollenberg for their camaraderie and collaboration over the years. Life in Ann Arbor wouldn't be the same without Aliyah and Nancy's digital diversions and Abby's ambulatory ones.

To my fellow Writing Wizards for keeping me at my laptop through yet another "pomodoro" even when I really didn't want to: Dan Birchok, Jessie DeGrado, Hadil Ghonim, Devi Mays, Melissa Phruksachart, Swapnil Rai, Holly Singh, Alicia Ventresca-Miller, and so many others. Iram, Hila, and Saima, otherwise known as the "Gtown girls, " cheered me on every step of the way and cheered me up with fun getaways.

To the colleagues across different campuses and conferences who took the time over the many years of this project's life to comment with insight and generosity on bits and pieces of the ideas I develop in this book, as they progressed from informal musings to presentations to article drafts: Lori Allen, Febe Armanios, Walter Armbrust, Talal Asad, Evelyn Al-Sultany, Narges Bajoghli, Jon Bialecki, James Bielo, Amahl Bishara, John Bowen, Alireza Doostdar, Chihab El-Khachab, Sarah Eltantawi, Matthew Engelke, Katherine Ewing, Ayala Fader, Tessa Farmer, Naomi Haynes, Angie Heo, Hatim El-Hibri, Jeanette Jouili, Marwan Kraidy, Brian Larkin, Ashley Lebner,

Amira Mittermaier, Ram Natarajan, Wazhmah Osman, Aswin Punathambekar, Aaron Rock-Singer, Samuli Schielke, Emilio Spadola, Ted Swedenburg, Ana Maria Vinea, John Voll, Neha Vora, and Jessica Winegar.

Sherine Hamdy and James Hoesterey read the whole manuscript, their constructive and critical feedback making this a much better book. Their incisive contributions to scholarly understandings of contemporary Islam speak for themselves and inform much of my thinking. Here, I gratefully acknowledge their kind spirits.

Kate Wahl is the editor every first-time book author hopes for: methodical, prompt, and direct. I thank her and her team at Stanford University Press for steering this book from conversation to proposal to final draft. Karson Schenk has an amazing ability to give beautiful visual form to my half-baked ideas. I am delighted her art is on the cover of this book.

My fieldwork in Egypt was generously supported by the Wenner-Gren Foundation for Anthropological Research, the National Science Foundation, the Fulbright-Hays Program, and the Social Science Research Council. A year-long fellowship from the ACLS-Luce Program on Journalism, Religion and International Affairs in the 2021–22 academic year allowed me to complete a first draft of this book in the middle of a global pandemic.

To my family. If it weren't for the support of my parents, Urs Moll and Noha Maatouk, I never would have fulfilled my childhood dream of reading, writing, and thinking for a living.

Michael, thank you for believing in me more than I did in myself. That made all the difference. You know how much.

Zayn and Zadie: yes, Mama is finally done with The Book. You both light up the world and my heart. I dedicate this to you.

Notes

Preface

1. Noha El-Hennawy, "Ramadan Talk Show Questions Salafi Dogmas," *Egypt Independent,* August 21, 2011. Abu Isma'il was disqualified from the presidential race on a technicality in April 2012. On Abu Isma'il as the "incarnation of revolutionary Salafism," see Stéphane Lacroix and Ahmed Shalata, "The Rise of Revolutionary Salafism in Post-Mubarak Egypt," in *Egypt's Revolution,* ed. B. Rougier (New York: Palgrave Macmillan, 2016), 163–78. On the relationship between the new Salafi political parties and the long-standing Salafi *daʿwa* movement, see also Stéphane Lacroix, "Sheikhs and Politicians: Inside the New Egyptian Salafism," *Foreign Policy at Brookings* (Doha, Qatar, June 2012).

2. This and all subsequent citations of Qur'anic verses in English translation are from MAS Abdel Haleem, *The Qur'an: A New Translation* (Oxford: Oxford University Press, 2004), unless otherwise noted.

3. There was also a noticeable increase in legal "morality cases" after 2011, involving "the state's prosecution of individuals for their opinions, sexual behaviors, and religious beliefs." The legal grounding for these cases is the Islamic theological principle of *hisba,* whereby "Muslims are required to command right when it is not being observed and forbid wrong when it is being committed." Ahmed Ezzat, "Law and Moral Regulation in Modern Egypt: Hisba from Tradition to Modernity," *International Journal of Middle East Studies* 52, no. 4 (2020): 665, https://doi.org/10.1017/S002074382000080X.

4. During this period, a leading faction within al-Gama'a al-Islamiyya, the armed group responsible for assassinating President Anwar al-Sadat in 1981, renounced on theological grounds the legitimacy of violence for achieving an Islamic state through a series of historic publications aimed at "correcting misconceptions" within its ranks. For an English annotated translation and critical commentary, see Sherman Jackson, *Initiative to Stop the Violence—Mubadarat Waqf al-'Unf: Sadat's Assassins and the Renunciation of Political Violence* (New Haven, CT: Yale University Press, 2015).

5. Susan Harding, "Representing Fundamentalism: The Problem of the Repugnant Cultural Other," *Social Research* 58, no. 2 (July 1, 1991): 373–93.

6. Sherry B. Ortner, "Resistance and the Problem of Ethnographic Refusal," *Comparative Studies in Society and History* 37, no. 1 (January 1, 1995): 179, https://doi.org/10.1017/S0010417500019587.

7. Talal Asad, "The Idea of an Anthropology of Islam," Occasional Paper Series (Washington, DC: Center for Contemporary Arab Studies, Georgetown University, 1986).

8. Talal Asad, *Formations of the Secular: Christianity, Islam, Modernity* (Stanford, CA: Stanford University Press, 2003), 25.

9. Saba Mahmood, "Is Liberalism Islam's Only Answer?," in *Islam and the Challenge of Democracy*, by Khaled Abou El Fadl, ed. Joshua Cohen and Deborah Chaseman, A Boston Review Book (Princeton, NJ: Princeton University Press, 2004), 75.

10. I am not the first anthropologist to make this observation. Sindre Bangstad also characterized as a form of "ethnographic refusal" the Asadian refrainment from probing the exclusions and inconsistencies of anti- or nonsecular movements in contrast to the critical interrogation of secular formations. Sindre Bangstad, "Saba Mahmood and Anthropological Feminism after Virtue," *Theory, Culture & Society* 28, no. 3 (2011): 34, https://doi.org/10.1177/0263276410396914. In line with this critique, scholars beyond anthropology have argued that when it comes to Islamic movements, the Asadian hermeneutics of suspicion, which reads the reality of secular liberalism against the rhetoric of its declared ideals, "are abandoned for the hermeneutics of reclamation," which doesn't read Islamism against the grain but tries to recover its latent potentialities. Aamir Mufti, "The Aura of Authenticity," *Social Text* 18, no. 3 (Fall 2000): 92. Similarly, comparative literary theorist Sadia Abbas argues that the Asadian canon cannot conceive of secular progressive Muslim feminists "outside an economy of collaboration and treachery" with Western imperial ambitions, marking them as representative of "bad Islam" in contrast to the figure of the pious Muslim who seemingly exists outside such complicities. Sadia Abbas, *At Freedom's Limit: Islam and the Postcolonial*

Predicament (New York: Fordham University Press, 2014), 4. In an interview, Asad explained this critical asymmetry as a way of righting wrongs: Because liberals, whether in academia or in the media, seldom practice what they preach about the value of "think[ing] critically about imposed limits," they *"should* be made to feel uncomfortable." In Fadi Bardawil, "The Solitary Analyst of Doxas: An Interview with Talal Asad," *Comparative Studies of South Asia, Africa and the Middle East* 36, no. 1 (2016): 161, 163.

11. Saba Mahmood, *Politics of Piety: The Islamic Revival and the Feminist Subject* (Princeton, NJ: Princeton University Press, 2005), 192.

12. Sameh Selim, "Politics of Piety: The Islamic Revival and the Feminist Subject," *Jadaliyya* (blog), October 13, 2010, https://www.jadaliyya.com/Details/23539.

13. Samuli Schielke, "Second Thoughts about the Anthropology of Islam, or, How to Make Sense of Grand Schemes in Everyday Life," *Zentrum Moderner Orient Working Papers*, no. 2 (2010): 13, http://d-nb.info/1019243724/34.

14. Jon Bialecki, "Does God Exist in Methodological Atheism? On Tanya Luhrmann's When God Talks Back and Bruno Latour," *Anthropology of Consciousness* 25, no. 1 (2014): 38.

15. Talal Asad, "A Comment on Translation, Critique, and Subversion," in *Between Languages and Cultures: Translation and Cross-Cultural Texts*, ed. Anuradha Dingwaney and Carol Maier (Pittsburgh: University of Pittsburgh Press, 1995), 325–32.

Introduction

1. I use pseudonyms throughout this work unless a person requested that I identify them by their real name. I do not use pseudonyms for public figures making public statements, including the New Preachers, nor for public figures speaking to me in my capacity as a researcher and with the knowledge that the views they express may be reproduced and attributed to them in my writing.

2. Samia Mehrez, *Egypt's Culture Wars: Politics and Practice* (London: Routledge, 2008).

3. Saba Mahmood, *Politics of Piety: The Islamic Revival and the Feminist Subject* (Princeton, NJ: Princeton University Press, 2005); Charles Hirschkind, *The Ethical Soundscape: Cassette Sermons and Islamic Counterpublics* (New York: Columbia University Press, 2006); Hussein Agrama, *Questioning Secularism: Islam, Sovereignty and the Rule of Law in Modern Egypt* (Chicago: University of Chicago Press, 2012).

4. Walter Armbrust, "Islamists in Egyptian Cinema," *American Anthropologist* 104, no. 3 (2002): 922–31; Lila Abu-Lughod, *Dramas of Nationhood: The Politics of Television in Egypt* (Chicago: University of Chicago Press, 2005); Jessica Winegar,

Creative Reckonings: The Politics of Art and Culture in Contemporary Egypt (Stanford, CA: Stanford University Press, 2006).

5. Gregory Starrett, "The Varieties of Secular Experience," *Comparative Studies in Society and History* 52, no. 3 (2010): 634.

6. I use *producers* as a catchall term to describe the variety of roles and positions held by individuals working at Iqraa's Cairo branch in general and, more specifically, on Hosny's dedicated production team. Likewise, my use of *production process* includes not only the technical and creative work of television broadcast—directing and editing for example—but also the more diffuse and distributed labor of research, organization, and evaluation that is central to television production.

7. Hirschkind, *Ethical Soundscape*, 183.

8. "Revolution against Torture, Poverty, Corruption, and Unemployment" was the title of the mobilizing post published on the "We Are All Khaled Said" Facebook page. Set up to protest police brutality after a young man from Alexandria was killed in custody, this page was a key online node during the uprising.

9. To take a few examples, observers have described Muslim Brotherhood opponents in too-broad strokes as "liberals," "secular fundamentalists," and "Islamophobic," while characterizing those who joined the massive protests of Morsi's presidency as preferring "secular autocracy" to "Islamic democracy." For specific references, see Yasmin Moll, "The Future of Egyptian Democracy: Islamism beyond the Muslim Brotherhood," *The Immanent Frame*, August 29, 2014, https://tif.ssrc.org/2014/08/29/islamism-beyond-the-muslim-brotherhood/.

10. Azhari scholars were divided on the religious merits of television. Hatim remembers the outspoken preacher Shaykh Kishk forbidding the purchase of television sets and declaring Hatim, as the architect of state television, to be "in the hellfire" (153). In contrast, he recounts productive conversations with Shaykh Muhammad al-Ghazali about "new preaching styles" and media (305). The concerns about television weren't only religious: the education minister felt the money would be better spent on schools, and the agriculture minister worried that television would diminish farmers' productivity (146–48). Abd al-Qadir Hatim, *Mudhakkirat 'Abd al-Qadir Hatim, ra'is hukumat Harb Uktubir* [The memoirs of Abd al-Qadir Hatim, the leader of the October War administration] (Cairo: al-Hay'a al-'Amma li Qusur al-Thaqafa, 2016).

11. Jacquelene G. Brinton, *Preaching Islamic Renewal: Religious Authority and Media in Contemporary Egypt* (Berkeley: University of California Press, 2015).

12. Marc Lynch, "Watching al-Jazeera," *Wilson Quarterly* 29, no. 3 (2005): 36.

13. Philip Seib, "Preface," *Egyptian Revolution 2.0: Political Blogging, Civic Engagement and Citizen Journalism,* ed. Mohammed el-Nawaway and Sahar Khamis (New York: Palgrave Macmillian 2013), vii.

14. Some of the older producers remembered how Shaykh Saleh Kamel, Iqraa's Saudi owner, refused to bow to pressure from Mubarak-era officials to cancel Khaled's contract. Khaled was banned from public preaching within Egypt at the time that Iqraa was airing his programs in the early 2000s.

15. While officially committed to the neoliberal agenda of privatization dictated by the International Monetary Fund (IMF) and World Bank, the state during my fieldwork had a tactical attitude toward the Islamic satellite sector's various orientations, alternating between repudiation and accommodation.

16. Walter Armbrust, "Media Review: Al-Da'iyya (The Preacher)," *Journal of the American Academy of Religion* 82, no. 3 (September 1, 2014): 841–56, https://doi.org/10.1093/jaarel/lfu047.

17. Emilio Spadola, *The Calls of Islam: Sufis, Islamists and Mass Mediation in Urban Morocco* (Bloomington: Indiana University Press, 2014), 2. Spadola notes a parallel to developments within anthropological theorizations of religion and media. As part of a broader turn to media as a social practice [see the foundational volume, Faye D. Ginsburg, Lila Abu-Lughod, and Brian Larkin, eds., *Media Worlds: Anthropology on New Terrain* (Berkeley: University of California Press, 2002)], anthropologists of religion have considered practitioners' multifarious engagement with media forms and technologies. This book builds on this scholarship with a focus on Islamic television production. For introductions to the ethnographic literature, see David Morgan, ed., *Key Words in Religion, Media, and Culture* (New York: Routledge, 2008); Birgit Meyer, *Aesthetic Formations: Media, Religion, and the Senses* (New York: Palgrave Macmillan, 2009). For thoughtful reviews of the early literature in this now mature subfield, see Jeremy Stolow, "Religion and/as Media," *Theory, Culture & Society* 22, no. 4 (2005): 119–45; Patrick Eisenlohr, "Introduction: What Is a Medium? Theologies, Technologies, Aspirations," *Social Anthropology* 19, no. 1 (2011): 1–5; Matthew Engelke, "Religion and the Media Turn: A Review Essay," *American Ethnologist* 37, no. 2 (2010): 371–79; Charles Hirschkind and Brian Larkin, "Introduction: Media and the Political Forms of Religion," *Social Text* 26, no. 3 (2008): 1–9.

Arguably the most influential approach within this literature has been Birgit Meyer's analysis of religion *as* media. Meyer argues that positing religion as ineluctably tethered to its material and sensational forms moves the field beyond "Protestant views of religion" where "meaning, content and inward belief are privileged above media, form and outward behavior." Birgit Meyer, "Mediation and Immediacy: Sensational Forms, Semiotic Ideologies, and the Question of the Medium," in

A Companion to the Anthropology of Religion, ed. Janice Boddy and Michael Lambek (Hoboken, NJ: John Wiley and Sons, 2013), 314. Nevertheless, Charles Hirschkind criticizes the "religion as media" approach for embedding, not overcoming, a "Protestant theological sensibility" that revolves around a dichotomous distinction between internal experience and external expression. He argues that for Muslims, the Qur'an "does not mediate the traditions of Islam" but that the ways in which it is read, printed, circulated, and so on "are simply part of what is entailed in living as a Muslim." Charles Hirschkind, "Media, Mediation, Religion," *Social Anthropology* 19, no. 1 (2011): 90–93. This characterization is itself subject to Islamic theological adjudication. Instead of transcending or exposing the tacit theological sensibilities underpinning analytical understandings of religious mediation, this book focuses on how Muslims' own theologies matter to the lived experiences of the links between religion and media.

18. Leor Halevi, *Modern Things on Trial: Islam's Global and Material Reformation in the Age of Rida, 1865–1935* (New York: Columbia University Press, 2019).

19. Abd al-Latif Hamza, *Al-i'lam fi sadr al-Islam* [Media at the dawn of Islam] (Dar al-Fikr al-'Arabi, 1971).

20. Yasmin Moll, "The Idea of Islamic Media: The Qur'an and the Decolonization of Mass Communication," *International Journal of Middle East Studies*, 52, no. 4 (2020): 623–42.

21. Ilana Gershon uses the term "media ideologies" as an analytical shorthand for people's claims and assumptions about how communicative technologies work in the world. Ilana Gershon, "Media Ideologies: An Introduction," *Journal of Linguistic Anthroplogy* 20, no. 2 (2010): 283–93. Patrick Eisenlohr deploys the phrase "theologies of mediation" to refer to the tacit theological assumptions shaping the use and understanding of media technologies within religious settings. Patrick Eisenlohr, "Technologies of the Spirit: Devotional Islam, Sound Reproduction, and the Dialectics of Mediation and Immediacy in Mauritius," *Anthropological Theory* 9, no. 3 (2009): 285. My use of "theologies of mediation" synthesizes these two approaches by both underscoring the scriptural referents of media assumptions and claims and theology as the terrain for their internal contestation within Islamic television.

22. Webb Keane, *Christian Moderns: Freedom and Fetish in the Mission Encounter*, (Berkeley: University of California Press, 2007); Matthew Engelke, *A Problem of Presence: Beyond Scripture in an African Church* (Berkeley: University of California Press, 2007).

23. Meyer, "Mediation and Immediacy,"317.

24. The younger Hosny and Masoud both attended Amr Khaled's popular in-person religious seminars in the late 1990s and have credited him for launching

their interest in *daʿwa*. Lindsay Wise, "Interview with Moez Masoud, Host of ART's English-Language Islamic Talk Shows," *Transnational Broadcasting Studies* 15, September 1, 2005, available at https://www.arabmediasociety.com/interview-with-moez-masoud-host-of-arts-english-language-islamic-talk-shows/; Sarah Allam, "Al-Daʿiya Mustafa Hosny," *Al-Youm al-Sabiʿ*, September 9, 2010, https://bit.ly/3VaZ8vl. The term *al-duʿah al-judud* to refer to these men was popularized by book-length journalistic "exposés" in the early 2000s: Muhammad al-Baz, *Duʿah fi al-manfa: Qissat Amr Khalid w-al-Duʿah al-Judud Fi Misr* [Preachers in exile: The story of Amr Khaled and the New Preachers in Egypt] (Cairo: Al-Faris, 2004); Waʾil Lutfi, *Zaharit Al-Duʿah al-Judud* [The phenomenon of the New Preachers] (Cairo: General Book Authority, 2005).

25. Gretel C. Kovach, "Moderate Muslim Voice Falls Silent," *Christian Science Monitor*, November 26, 2002; Samantha Shapiro, "Ministering to the Upwardly Mobile Muslim," *New York Times*, April 30, 2006; Robin Wright, "Islam's Up-To-Date Televangelist: Amr Khaled Has Bridged the Religious-Secular with His Feel-Good Message," *Washington Post*, September 11, 2007; David Hardaker, "The Rise of the Anti-Osama," *Sydney Morning Herald*, November 18, 2007.

26. Episode 24 of *Insan Jadid (A New Person)*, al-Nahar channel, June 2016. Most of the programs I reference in this book I watched on television or while they were being recorded during my fieldwork. A few, like this one, I watched online on YouTube after my in-country research ended. YouTube links are not stable, as videos are frequently taken down—one study, cited in the reference below, puts the "half-life" of YouTube videos at 9–18 months. In this book I reference programs I watched online by episode number or title, series name, broadcast channel, and date so that interested readers can look them up. At the time of this writing, many (but not all) episodes of Hosny's programs from 2004 to the present are available on his official YouTube channel, https://www.youtube.com/MustafaHosnyOfficial. But it bears pointing out the obvious: YouTube, while useful for researching media and popular culture, is a commercial, user-generated video-sharing website, not an institutional repository of knowledge like a library collection or an archive. For a discussion of the difference in relation to academic research and teaching on music, see Dougan Kirstin, "'YouTube Has Changed Everything'? Music Faculty, Librarians, and Their Use and Perceptions of YouTube," *College and Research Libraries* 75, no. 4 (2014): 575–89.

27. Omid Safi, *Progressive Muslims: On Justice, Gender and Pluralism* (London: Oneworld, 2003), 16.

28. Recent ethnographic works examine in rich detail the reasoning and life-worlds of self-consciously nonpracticing Muslims, such as ex-Islamist students in Indonesia who aspire to make secular liberalism persuasive to other Muslims

through Qur'anic exegesis while abandoning ritual worship like prayer as superfluous, or Iraqi Kurds who deliberately turn away from the pursuit of piety as a moral aspiration while remaining attached to identifying as Muslims. Nur Amali Ibrahim, *Improvisational Islam: Indonesian Youth in a Time of Possibility* (Ithaca, NY: Cornell University Press, 2018); Andrew Bush, *Between Muslims: Religious Difference in Iraqi Kurdistan* (Stanford, CA: Stanford University Press, 2020).

29. John Bowen, *A New Anthropology of Islam* (Cambridge: Cambridge University Press, 2012), 60.

30. These debates scratch the surface of the fundamental theological question of a universal message from God addressed to all people for all time, but revealed in a particular language to a particular people at a particular time. Athari theology posits that the Qur'an's Arabic is the eternal and uncreated speech of God and in no way reflective of its seventh-century revelation. Ash'arism also posits that the Qur'an is uncreated, but makes a distinction between its linguistic form of Arabic words as an expression of God's speech, and God's speech in and of itself as a divine attribute. Elaborating on this difference, Halverson argues that unlike Atharism, Ash'arism semiotically historicizes the Qur'an in relation to its immediate recipients, seventh-century Arabs—"Had We revealed it as a non-Arabic Quran, they would have certainly argued, 'If only its verses were made clear in our language. What! A non-Arabic revelation for an Arab audience!'" (Qur'an 41:44)—and that this difference has broader sociopolitical ramifications. Jeffrey R. Halverson, *Theology and Creed in Sunni Islam: The Muslim Brotherhood, Ash'arism, and Political Sunnism* (New York: Palgrave Macmillan, 2010), 131–32.

31. Cited in Brett Wilson, "The Failure of Nomenclature: The Concept of 'Orthodoxy' in the Study of Islam," *Comparative Islamic Studies*, 2009, 3 no. 2: 178.

32. Talal Asad, *Genealogies of Religion: Discipline and Reasons of Power in Christianity and Islam* (Baltimore: Johns Hopkins University Press, 1993), 219.

33. Nathan Brown, *Arguing Islam after the Revival of Arab Politics* (Oxford: Oxford University Press, 2016), 121. Theology has been a neglected area of inquiry even with the textually focused field of Islamic Studies, artificially quarantined from the robust secondary literature on Islamic jurisprudence and ethics. Sabine Schmidtke argues that this oversight reflects a long-standing Western underestimation of "the place of reflection on doctrinal issues within the intellectual life of Muslim thinkers." Sabine Schmidtke, ed., *The Oxford Handbook of Islamic Theology*, Oxford Handbooks (New York: Oxford University Press, 2016), 5. On the pernicious "persistence of nineteenth-century assumptions about the marginality of abstract intellectual life in Islam," see also Tim Winter, ed., *The Cambridge Companion to Classical Islamic Theology* (Cambridge:

Cambridge University Press, 2008), 1. For an example of such persistence, see Francesca Aran Murphy, "Does Theology Exist Outside of Christianity?," October 19, 2017, https://www.firstthings.com/web-exclusives/2017/10/does-theology-exist-outside-of-christianity.

The neglect of substantive beliefs in favor of ritual practice when it comes to understanding Islam starts early. In my child's US public school unit on "world religions," for example, Islam was discussed solely in terms of its ritual obligations, the ever popular five "pillars" of *testifying, praying, fasting, almsgiving,* and *pilgrimaging*. By contrast, the units on other religions, whether Christianity, Hinduism, or Buddhism, presented some of their specific doctrines. An analogous treatment of Islam could have explained it to students in terms of its five fundamental beliefs: *in one God, in all of His messengers, His revealed books, His angels, and in the Day of Judgment*. These are so elemental that one scholar claims that "the core of Islamic theology is limited to [their] explanation and defence." MAS Abdel Haleem, "Qur'an and Hadith," in *The Cambridge Companion to Classical Islamic Theology*, 25. Yet even a cursory lesson about Islam overlooks theology in favor of ritual.

The utility of belief as a category is ripe for revisiting more broadly; on the potential of recovering belief as an analytic term in the anthropology of religion, see Matt Tomlinson, "Adventures in "Belief": Hearing an Old Concept in a New Key," *American Anthropologist* 125 (2023): 322–333.

34. Inspired by Joel Robbins's essay, "Anthropology and Theology: An Awkward Relationship?," *Anthropological Quarterly* 79, no. 2 (2006): 285–94, such engagement has taken diverse forms, from destabilizing the taken-for-granted secularity of anthropology's assumptions and methods by way of theological comparison and critique, to thinking about how anthropology might complicate and enrich theological frameworks, to anthropologically deferring to theological truth claims. For examples of this programmatic range, see J. Derrick Lemons, ed., *Theologically Engaged Anthropology: Social Anthropology and Theology in Conversation* (New York: Oxford University Press, 2018); Khaled Furani and Joel Robbins, "Introduction: Anthropology within and without the Secular Condition," *Religions* 51 (2021): 501–17; Joseph Webster, "Anthropology as Theology: Violent Endings and the Permanence of New Beginnings," *American Anthropologist* 124, no. 2 (2022): 333–44. For a spearheading consideration of the social life of Christian theology, see *The Social Life of Scriptures: Cross-Cultural Perspectives on Biblicism*, ed. James Bielo (New Brunswick, NJ: Rutgers University Press, 2009).

35. One anthropological critic attributes this ethnographic vagueness to Asad's theoretically driven textualism, which "hardly touches on the ways in which Muslims may disagree among themselves on what is and what is not Islamic practice, and how they differ in the interpretation of the correct way of observing their religious duties and in

the interpretation of those duties themselves." Abdellah Hammoudi, "Textualism and Anthropology: On the Ethnographic Encounter or an Experience in the Hajj," in *Being There: The Fieldwork Encounter and the Making of Truth*, ed. John Borneman and Abdellah Hammoudi (Berkeley: University of California Press, 2009), 31. A notable exception to the ethnographic thinness of internal debates within anthropological works on Egypt adopting the framework of Islam as a discursive tradition is Sherine Hamdy's *Our Bodies Belong to God: Organ Transplants, Islam and the Struggle for Human Dignity in Egypt* (Berkeley: University of California Press, 2012). Hamdy's examination of the social life of the theological idea that the body belongs to God illuminates both the entanglements of Islamic doctrines and ethics with bioethical frameworks and the contentions such entanglements provoke among differently positioned Muslims.

Beyond Egypt, John Bowen's *Muslims through Discourse: Religion and Ritual in Gayo Society* (Princeton, NJ: Princeton University Press, 1993) is a pioneering ethnography of competing scripturally informed understandings and practices of Islam, based on fieldwork in rural Indonesia. For an analogous sophisticated analysis of the social life of doctrinal critique and debate focused on contemporary Christianity, see Courtney Handman, *Critical Christianity: Translation and Denominational Conflict in Papua New Guinea* (Oakland: University of California Press, 2015).

36. Nadia Fadil and Mayanthi Fernando, "Rediscovering the 'Everyday' Muslim: Notes on an Anthropological Divide," *HAU Journal of Ethnographic Theory* 5, no. 2 (January 1, 2015): 76. For a programmatic critique of the "piety turn" from the vantage of everyday Muslim life, see Benjamin F. Soares and Filippo Osella, eds., "Islam, Politics, Anthropology," *Journal of the Royal Anthropological Institute* 15, special issue (May 2009). See also Samuli Schielke, "Second Thoughts about the Anthropology of Islam, or, How to Make Sense of Grand Schemes in Everyday Life," *Zentrum Moderner Orient Working Papers*, no. 2 (2010), http://d-nb.info/1019243724/34.

37. Lupti Ibrahim, "The Questions of the Superiority of Angels and Prophets between Az-Zamakhshari and al-Baydawi," *Arabica* 28, no. 1 (1981): 65–75.

38. Halverson, *Theology and Creed in Sunni Islam*, 20.

39. Yasir Qadhi, "Salafi-Ash'ari Polemics of the Third and Fourth Islamic Centuries," *Muslim World* 106, no. 3 (2016): 433–47. Qadhi identifies as each school's "most prominent medieval champions" the well-known theologians al-Ghazali and Ibn Taymmiya. These are household names within modern-day revivalist circles, and their texts are widely referenced. Contemporary Salafis disavow al-Ghazali as a heretic for his synthetic approach to Aristotelian philosophy while holding Ibn Taymiyya in high esteem for reviving what they see as the original creed of the Prophet. Nevertheless, the question of whether al-Ghazali's body of work was faithful to Ash'arism or exceeded its bounds is a much debated one in studies of Islamic theology. See Richard M.

Frank, *Al-Ghazali and the Ash'arite School* (Duke University Press, 1994) and Ahmed Dallal, "Review: Ghazali and the Perils of Interpretation," *Journal of the American Oriental Society* 122, no. 4 (2002): 773–87, for competing views. For the characterization of al-Ghazali as a dialogical "bricoleur" who "took neither the Hellenic sciences nor the Islamic sciences nor the Ash'ari theological school at face value," see Ebrahim Moosa, *Ghazali and the Poetics of Imagination* (Chapel Hill: University of North Carolina Press, 2006), 50. For accounts of the theological, political, and ethical debates Ibn Taymiyya's oeuvre has engendered among Muslims, including the pragmatics of its appeal to Salafi movements, see A. Kokoschka, ed., *Islamic Theology, Philosophy, and Law: Debating Ibn Taymiyya and Ibn Qayyim al-Jawziyya* (Berlin: de Gruyter, 2013); for an accessible overview of his influence on a variety of contemporary Islamic movements, see Jon Hoover, *Ibn Taymiyya* (New York: Simon and Schuster, 2019).

40. Aaron Spevack, "Egypt and the Later Ash'arite School," in *The Oxford Handbook of Islamic Theology*, ed. Sabine Schmidtke (Oxford: Oxford University Press, 2016), 105–15.

41. Al-Azhar also includes Maturidi theology and accepts the legitimacy of both Shia Ja'fari and Zaydi jurisprudential traditions. Matarudism is Sunni Islam's third main theological school, but it is not prevalent in Egypt; for an overview of its development, see Ulrich Rudolph, *Al-Maturidi and the Development of Sunni Theology in Samarqand* (Leiden: Brill, 2015). For how debates over the authoritativeness of hadiths relative to the Qur'an shaped Islamic theology into the twentieth century in Egypt, see Daniel Brown, *Rethinking Tradition in Modern Islamic Thought* (Cambridge: Cambridge University Press, 1999).

42. George Makdisi famously argued that the *ijaza* tradition inspired the degree system of the medieval European university. George Makdisi, *The Rise of Colleges: Institutions of Learning in Islam and the West* (Edinburgh: Edinburgh University Press, 1981).

43. Aria Nakissa, *The Anthropology of Islamic Law: Education, Ethics and Legal Intrepretation at Egypt's Al-Azhar* (Oxford: Oxford University Press, 2019).

44. John Walbridge, *God and Logic in Islam: The Caliphate of Reason* (Cambridge: Cambridge University Press, 2011).

45. Christopher Razavian, "Al-Azhar, Wasatiyah, and the Waqi'," in *Modern Islamic Authority and Social Change*, vol. 1, *Evolving Debates in Muslim Majority Countries*, ed. Bano Masooda (Oxford: Oxford University Press, 2018), 102–23.

46. Al-Azhar University is commonly depicted, whether by its religious opponents or academic commentators, as a state lackey promoting a government-friendly "secular" Islam. For their part, however, many Egyptian secularists attack the institution for being an illiberal breeding ground for the religious extremism it disavows.

See for example Maher Gabra, "The Ideological Extremism of Al-Azhar," *Fikra Forum*, May 3, 2016, https://www.washingtoninstitute.org/policy-analysis/ideological-extremism-al-azhar. Malika Zeghal complicates such reductive depictions by foregrounding the institution's complex internal diversity and power struggles from the 1960s to the present. Malika Zeghal, "The 'Recentering' of Religious Knowledge and Discourse: The Case of al-Azhar in Twentieth-Century Egypt," in *Schooling Islam: The Culture and Politics of Modern Muslim Education*, ed. Robert Hefner and Muhammad Qasim Zaman (Princeton, NJ: Princeton University Press, 2007), 107–30.

47. Vardit Rispler, "Toward a New Understanding of the Term Bidʿa," *Der Islam* 68, no. 2 (1991): 320–28; Maribel Fierro, "The Treatises against Innovations (Kutub al-Bidʿa)," *Der Islam* 69, no. 2 (1992): 204–36.

48. T. J. Winter, "The Poverty of Fanaticism," in *Islam, Fundamentalism, and the Betrayal of Tradition: Essays by Western Muslim Scholars*, ed. Joseph E. B. Lumbard, rev. ed. (Bloomington, IN: World Wisdom, 2009), 301–13.

49. David Dean Commins, *The Wahhabi Mission and Saudi Arabia* (New York: I. B. Tauris, 2009).

50. Al-Albani is an influential exponent of what some have called "quietist Salafism." This orientation is marked by its shunning of political affiliations and participation as illegitimate innovations that lead to internal discord. See Stéphane Lacroix, "Between Revolution and Apoliticism: Nasir al-Din al-Albani and His Impact on the Shaping of Contemporary Salafism," in *Global Salafism: Islam's New Religious Movement*, ed. Roel Meijer (New York: Columbia University Press, 2009), 58–80, for a biographical sketch and discussion of this influential figure, whose significance for contemporary Salafism is hard to overstate.

51. Henri Lauzière, *The Making of Salafism: Islamic Reform in the Twentieth Century* (New York: Columbia University Press, 2015).

52. Johanna Pink, *Muslim Qur'anic Interpretation Today: Media, Genealogies, and Intrepretive Communities* (Sheffield, UK: Equinox, 2019).

53. Emad Hamdeh, *Salafism and Traditionalism: Scholarly Authority in Modern Islam* (Cambridge: Cambridge University Press, 2021).

54. The differences and debates between the New Preachers and the Salafis can be located within the competing formations of Islamic reformism from the eighteenth century onward. For a comparison of Egypt's famous chief mufti and Azhari reformer Muhammad Abduh (1849–1905) and the Salafi reformer Muhammad Abd al-Wahhab (1703–1792), who came from what is now Saudi Arabia and played a key role in the formation of that country, see Samira Haj, *Reconfiguring Islamic Tradition: Reform, Rationality and Modernity* (Stanford, CA: Stanford University Press, 2009).

55. Salafi Muslims are not exceptional in their theological rejection of religious innovation, emphasis on ritual and doctrinal purity, and insistence of salvific exclusivism. Similar tendencies can be found among contemporary fundamentalist Protestant groups and ultra-Orthodox Jewish ones. See Joseph Webster, "Nor Shadow of Turning: Anthropological Reflections on Theological Critiques of Doctrinal Change," *Australian Journal of Anthropology* 33, no. 3 (2022): 360–82; Ayala Fader, *Hidden Heretics: Jewish Doubt in the Digital Age* (Princeton, NJ: Princeton University Press, 2020).

56. Salafism is globally associated with its Wahhabi incarnation and its "petrodollar" export through the funding of mosques, publications, associations, and other forms of outreach across the Muslim world by the Saudi state since the 1970s. While Egypt's most well-known Salafi preachers do claim to have spent time in Saudi Arabia in the company of its foremost Wahhabi clerics, the roots of Salafism in Egypt in stretch back to the colonial period, with the first Salafi association established in 1926. For a history of Egyptian Salafism from this period onward, see Aaron Rock-Singer, *In the Shade of the Sunna: Salafi Piety in the Twentieth-Century Middle East* (Berkeley: University of California Press, 2022); for an ethnography of Salafism as a lived practice, see Richard Gauvain, *Salafi Ritual Purity: In the Presence of God* (New York: Routledge, 2013) and, for a sensitive and insightful ethnographic account of Salafi healing modalities, Ana Maria Vinea, "What Is Your Evidence? A Salafi Therapy in Contemporary Egypt," *Comparative Studies of South Asia, Africa, and the Middle East*, 39, no. 3 (2019): 500–512.

On Salafi Wahhabism's elaboration and contestation within Saudi Arabia, see Madawi Al-Rasheed, *Contesting the Saudi State: Islamic Voices from a New Generation* (New York: University of Cambridge Press, 2006), and *Muted Modernists: The Struggle over Divine Politics in Saudi Arabia* (Oxford: Oxford University Press, 2015). For a historical and sociologically grounded critique of petrodollar narratives of the influence of Wahhabi Islam, see Michael Farquhar, *Circuits of Faith: Migration, Education, and the Wahhabi Mission* (Stanford, CA: Stanford University Press, 2017).

57. As Nathan Brown notes, "Encounters seem at times less designed to persuade each other than to listen to their own camp," resulting in "parallel preaching." *Arguing Islam*, 115, 188.

58. Hirschkind, *Ethical Soundscape*, 110.

59. Charles Hirschkind, "Experiments in Devotion Online: The YouTube Khutba," *International Journal of Middle East Studies* 44, no. 1 (2012): 11. An analytical distinction between the various orientations that constitute the "mosque movement" and their divergent histories is also absent in Mahmood's *Politics of Piety*, as various

scholars have pointed out. See Gauvain, *Salafi Ritual Purity*, 13; Sindre Bangstad, "Saba Mahmood and Anthropological Feminism after Virtue," *Theory, Culture & Society* 28, no. 3 (2011): 40.

60. Asad dismisses the oft-repeated suggestion that the object of ethnographic investigation should be Muslims and not Islam by arguing that the two are "conceptually inseparable" insofar as "arguments about what it means to be a Muslim ... are oriented towards a coherent understanding or appreciation of a divine revelation and the role of the messenger who made it available to mankind" (Basit Kareem Iqbal, "Thinking about Method: A Conversation with Talal Asad, " *Qui Parle* 26, no. 1, 2017: 43). But surely then it matters even more to our ethnographic understanding of "what it means to be Muslim" to investigate the profound differences in Islam's conceptualization across various Muslim groups. Such conceptualizations are the domain of theology broadly construed, as the anthropologist Abdul Hamid El-Zein pointed out as the anthropology of Islam was coalescing as a field in the late 1970s. El-Zein's rejection of the possibility of Islam as an analytical category has been misread as negating the possibility of analyzing Islam. Instead, he was interrogating the tacit theologies and ideologies that scholars often analytically smuggle into their categories to make sense of the diversity of Muslim beliefs and practices, a questioning that this book revalorizes. Abdul Hamid El-Zein, "Beyond Ideology and Theology: The Search for the Anthropology of Islam," *Annual Review of Anthropology* 6, no. 1 (1977): 227–54. In centering the social struggles that divergent theological conceptions of the Islamic tradition provoke among Muslims themselves and eschewing its analytic definition, this book is also inspired by historical anthropologist Michael Gilsenan's ahead-of-its-time meditation on "Islam" not as "a single, rigidly bounded set of structures determining or interacting with other total structures but rather a word that identifies varying relations of practice, representation, symbol, concept and worldview within the same society and between different societies." Michael Gilsenan, *Recognizing Islam: Religion and Society in the Modern Arab World* (New York: Pantheon Books, 1982), 19.

61. Talal Asad, *The Idea of an Anthropology of Islam*, Occasional Paper Series (Washington, DC: Center for Contemporary Arab Studies, Georgetown University, 1986), 15.

62. Ibid., 16.

63. Ibid., 16.

64. Asad, *Genealogies of Religion*, 236.

65. Talal Asad, "Modern Power and the Reconfiguration of Religious Traditions: An Interview with Saba Mahmood," *Stanford Electronic Humanities Review* 5, no. 1 (1996), https://web.stanford.edu/group/SHR/5-1/text/asad.html.

66. Edward Said, *Orientalism* (New York: Penguin, 1978).

67. The concept of Islam as a discursive tradition has been influential not just in anthropology but in Islamic Studies more broadly; see Ovamir Anjum, "Islam as a Discursive Tradition: Talal Asad and His Interlocutors," *Comparative Studies in South Asia, Africa and the Middle East* 27, no. 3 (2007): 656–72. It has also been subject to critique by Islamic Studies scholars who argue that Asad's reliance on "prescriptive," as opposed to "explorative," Islamic texts, has led to the marginalization of contradiction and contingency in his analytic concept of tradition. See for example Shahab Ahmed, *What Is Islam? The Importance of Being Islamic* (Princeton, NJ: Princeton University Press, 2016), 246–97. These criticisms appear to have been tacitly integrated by Asad and his interlocutors in recent reflections. In my view, the analytical centering of contradiction leads to the same impasses as the centering of coherence. Both introduce in the guise of theory a normative conception about what matters most to making scholarly sense of the Islamic tradition that is contested by participants in that tradition. My own interest is less in developing a better analytical concept of Islam and more in tracing my interlocutors' contestations over theological concepts of Islam.

68. Asad, "Modern Power," 1997.

69. In a later elaboration of the "Islamic concept of tradition," Asad notes his conversations with the Egyptian Azhari scholar Shaykh Usama Sayyid al-Azhari. Talal Asad, "Thinking about Tradition, Religion, and Politics in Egypt Today," *Critical Inquiry* 42 (2015): 173. Al-Azhari is one of the foremost defenders of Ashʿarism. For an English translation of his theological refutation of "extremist ideologies," see Usama al-Sayyid al-Azhari, *The Manifest Truth: A Refutation of Those That Manipulate Islam*, trans. Waleed Arafa (Abu Dhabi, UAE: Dar Alfaqih, 2017).

70. Quoted in Carrie Wickham, *The Muslim Brotherhood: Evolution of an Islamist Movement* (Princeton, NJ: Princeton University Press, 2015), 86.

71. Focusing on television production, this work builds on anthropological works based in Egypt that trace the complex reconfiguration of Islamic concepts and practices as they become intertwined with modern fields, such as developmentalism, bioethics, or psychology, to reference a few notable books in the anthropology of Egyptian Islam published in the last decade: Sherine Hafez, *An Islam of Her Own: Reconsidering Religion and Secularism in Women's Islamic Movements* (New York: New York University Press, 2011); Hamdy, *Our Bodies Belong to God*; Amira Mittermaier, *Dreams That Matter: Egyptian Landscapes of the Imagination* (Berkeley: University of California Press, 2010). Taken together, these works vividly illustrate how Muslims enact and claim what Lara Deeb in her work on Lebanon's Shia Revival has aptly called "an enchanted modern." Lara Deeb, *An Enchanted Modern: Gender*

and Public Piety in Shi'i Lebanon (Princeton, NJ: Princeton University Press, 2006). This has been of broad interest in the anthropology of Islam outside of Egypt as well. For some excellent recent examples across a range of countries and contexts just from the past decade, see Emilio Spadola, *The Calls of Islam*; Jeanette Jouili, *Pious Practice and Secular Constraints: Women in the Islamic Revival in Europe* (Stanford, CA: Stanford University Press, 2015); Su'ad Abdul Khabeer, *Muslim Cool: Race, Religion, and Hip Hop in the United States* (New York: NYU Press, 2016); James Bourk Hoesterey, *Rebranding Islam: Piety, Prosperity, and a Self-Help Guru* (Stanford, CA: Stanford University Press, 2016); Alireza Doostdar, *The Iranian Metaphysicals: Explorations in Science, Islam and the Uncanny* (Princeton, NJ: Princeton University Press, 2018); Daromir Rudnyckyj, *Beyond Debt: Islamic Experiments in Global Finance* (Chicago: University of Chicago Press, 2019); Narges Bajoghli, *Iran Reframed: Anxieties of Power in the Islamic Republic* (Stanford, CA: Stanford University Press, 2019).

72. Mahmood, *Politics of Piety*, 164.

73. Indeed, as Niloofar Haeri argues, even looking at the experiential affordances of different devotional acts within the same religious group keeps at bay scholarly generalizations like "'Islam is x; in Islam y.'" Niloofar Haeri, *Say What Your Longing Heart Desires: Women, Prayer, and Poetry in Iran* (Stanford, CA: Stanford University Press, 2020), 99. Yet academic arguments persist that some Islamic positions tacitly rehearse the secular epistemologies and norms they claim to repudiate.

74. Jessica Winegar, "Civilizing Muslim Youth: Egyptian State Culture Programmes and Islamic Television Preachers," *Journal of the Royal Anthropological Institute* 20, no. 3 (2014): 447.

75. This marks another inconsistency with the Asadian scholarship on the Islamic in relation to the secular. On the one hand, Islamic suppositions are said to be incommensurable with secular liberal ones. This is why, within this oeuvre, Islam is such a productive terrain for provincializing secular liberalism, the critical force of the contrast resting on treating all the various registers of piety as if they, like secular liberalism, had a singular grammar. On the other hand, within this scholarship, the religious and the secular are also analyzed not as incommensurable frameworks of meaning and action, but as shifting discursive categories with no predetermined content. This emphasis on the secular and religious not as fixed essences but as shifting and relational is in tension with the former claim that secular attachments come with intrinsic disciplines, practices, and behaviors that we can identity as such analytically, apart from their description as "secular" by the people holding them. "I take the secular to be," Asad writes, "a concept that brings together certain behaviors, knowledges, and sensibilities in modern life." Yet, he continues,

"The 'religious' and the 'secular' are not essentially fixed categories." Talal Asad, *Formations of the Secular: Christianity, Islam, Modernity* (Stanford, CA: Stanford University Press, 2003), 25. Bangstad notes this inconsistency as well. Sindre Bangstad, "Contesting Secularism/s: Secularism and Islam in the Work of Talal Asad," *Anthropological Theory* 9, no. 2, 2009: 188–208. Despite spirited protestations to the contrary, this approach leaves the "Islamic" an internally undifferentiated category of virtues, dispositions, and sensibilities that can be analytically set off from those of liberal secularism.

76. Egypt's revolution has also been extensively documented ethnographically. See in particular Samuli Schielke, *Egypt in the Future Tense: Hope, Frustration, and Ambivalence before and after 2011* (Bloomington: Indiana University Press, 2015); Sherine Hafez, *Women of the Midan: The Untold Stories of Egypt's Revolutionaries* (Bloomington: Indiana University Press, 2019); Walter Armbrust, *Martyrs and Tricksters: An Ethnography of the Egyptian Revolution* (Princeton, NJ: Princeton University Press, 2019); Rusha Latif, *Tahrir's Youth: Leaders of a Leaderless Revolution* (Cairo: American University in Cairo Press, 2022). Far from missing the revolution as usual during fieldwork (see Orin Starn, "Missing the Revolution: Anthropologists and the War in Peru," *Cultural Anthropology* 6, no. 1 (1991): 63–91), these anthropologists analyze its unfolding in almost real-time detail. In addition, other anthropologists of Egypt have traced how their interlocutors made different sense of the uprising and its aftermath through their own preexisting commitments and lived experiences. Farha Ghannam, "Meanings and Feelings: Local Interpretations of the Use of Violence in the Egyptian Revolution," *American Ethnologist* 39, no. 1 (2012): 32–36; Sherine Hamdy, "All Eyes on Egypt: Islam and the Medical Use of Dead Bodies Amidst Cairo's Political Unrest," *Medical Anthropology* 35, no. 3 (2016): 220–35; Mark Allen Peterson, "Re-Envisioning Tahrir: The Changing Meanings of Tahrir Square in Egypt's Ongoing Revolution," in *Revolutionary Egypt: Connecting Domestic and International Struggles*, ed. Reem Abou el-Fadl (London: Routledge, 2015); Jessica Winegar, "A Civilized Revolution: Aesthetics and Political Action in Egypt," *American Ethnologist* 43, no. 4 (2016): 609–22; Amira Mittermaier, *Giving to God: Islamic Charity in Revolutionary Times* (Berkeley: University of California Press, 2019).

77. Linda Herrera, *Revolution in the Age of Social Media: The Egyptian Popular Insurrection and the Internet* (London: Verso, 2014).

78. ABC News, "Egyptian Names Baby 'Facebook' for Site's Role in Revolution," February 21, 2011, https://abcnews.go.com/Technology/Egypt_Christiane _Amanpour/egyptian-names-baby-facebook-sites-role-revolution/story?id =12964978.

79. Nareman Amin, "Rebelling against the Ruler: Egyptian Youth and Azhari Scholars' Authority after the 2011 Uprising," *Islamic Law and Society*, 29, no. 3, (2022): 343–83; Usaama al-Azami, *Islam and the Arab Revolutions: The Ulama Between Democracy and Autocracy* (Oxford University Press, 2022).

80. Richard Gauvain, "Nothing Has Changed/Everything Has Changed: Salafi Daʿwa in Egypt from Rashid Rida to the 'Arab Spring,'" in *Culture of Daʿwa: Preaching in the Modern World*, ed. Itzchak Weismann and Jamil Malik (Salt Lake City: University of Utah Press, 2020), 79–95.

81. Wickham, *The Muslim Brotherhood*.

82. Malika Zeghal, "What Were the Ulama Doing in Tahrir Square? Al-Azhar and the Narrative of Resistance to Oppression," *Sightings: Martin Marty Center for the Advanced Study of Religion*, February 17, 2011, https://divinity.uchicago.edu/sightings/articles/what-were-ulama-doing-tahrir-square-al-azhar-and-narrative-resistance-oppression. See also Masooda Bano and Hanane Benadi, "Official Al-Azhar versus al-Azhar Imagined: The Arab Spring and the Revival of Religious Imagination," *Die Welt des Islams* 59, no. 1 (2019): 7–32.

83. Stéphane Lacroix and Ahmed Shalata, "The Rise of Revolutionary Salafism in Post-Mubarak Egypt," in *Egypt's Revolution*, ed. B. Rougier (New York: Palgrave Macmillan, 2016), 163–78.

84. Abdelrahman Ayyash, Amr ElAfifi, and Noha Ezzat, *Broken Bonds: The Existential Crisis of Egypt's Muslim Brotherhood, 2013–22* (New Century Foundation, 2023).

85. Take for example Wael Ghonim, who became the most public face of the revolution, especially in Western media coverage. Before he helped set up the Facebook page that led to hundreds of thousands converging in Tahrir Square on January 25 in a "Revolution against Torture, Poverty, Corruption, and Unemployment," before his emotional television appearance two weeks later after being detained by state security decisively shifted public opinion in favor of the protesters, he had launched a religious website called Islamway in the early 2000s. In doing so, he combined his deepening commitment to piety with his professional investment in technological outreach. Ghonim has described the New Preacher Amr Khaled as an "inspiration"; another New Preacher, Moez Masoud, is characterized as a "close friend." The pious sensibilities these preachers promoted—ones in which religious pluralism could be theologically legitimated, or social solidarity framed as an act of worship—influenced Ghonim both in the lead-up to and after the protests. Still, seasoned activists on the left were dismissive of Ghonim from the start; it was hard to imagine the pink Polo-clad Google executive as a hard-core revolutionary. See Benjamin Wallace-Wells, "The Lonely Battle of Wael Ghonim," *New York Magazine*, January

20, 2012. That Ghonim might admire Islamic preachers did nothing for his revolutionary creds.

86. Husam Tammam and Patrick Haenni, "Egypt: Islam in the Insurrection," *Religioscope*, February 22, 2011, https://english.religion.info/2011/02/22/egypt-islam-in-the-insurrection/.

87. "Q&A: Faith and Hope in Egypt," *Cairo Review of Global Affairs*, Spring 2011, https://www.thecairoreview.com/q-a/faith-and-hope-in-egypt/.

88. Samuli Schielke, *There Will Be Blood: Expecting Violence in Egypt, 2011–2013*, ZMO Working Papers, 11 (Berlin: Zentrum Moderner Oriente, 2014), https://nbn-resolving.org/urn:nbn:de:0168-ssoar-422946. For example, the March 2011 referendum—asking Egyptians to vote "yes" or "no" about whether the existing constitution should be just amended instead of rewritten entirely—crystallized most clearly the country's major divisions at the time: the military council, the Muslim Brotherhood, and Salafi groups supported amendment, while a diffuse coalition of vocal revolutionaries called for a new constitution altogether. The New Preachers were in the latter category, participating in a media campaign supporting the "no" vote, and criticizing the Salafi and Brotherhood characterization of the "yes" vote as a "vote for Islam."

89. Andeel, "Hamza Namira's Conservative Revolution," *Mada Masr*, December 17, 2014, https://madamasr.com/en/2014/12/17/feature/culture/hamza-namiras-conservative-revolution/.

90. Schielke, *Egypt in the Future Tense*, 212, 208.

91. Donald D. Donham, *Marxist Modern: An Ethnographic History of the Ethiopian Revolution* (Berkeley: University of California Press, 1999), as cited in Igor Cherstich, Martin Holbraad, and Nico Tassi, *Anthropologies of Revolution: Forging Time, People, and Worlds* (Oakland: University of California Press, 2020).

92. Cherstich, Holbraad, and Tassi, *Anthropologies of Revolution*, 9. In line with this approach, I have argued elsewhere for approaching the "revolutionary"—like the "Islamic"—as a *thick concept* in need of thicker description. Moral philosophers define thick concepts as at once descriptive and evaluative. Examples are "courageous" and "cruel": these moral concepts have a substantive heft that thin evaluations like right or wrong lack. They tell us something specific about the narrated action or attitude, not only how we should orient toward it. An anthropological reworking of thick concepts would recognize that what counts as courageous or cruel, as much as right or wrong, varies enormously not just across time and space but also within the same social formation. This sociological unevenness and cultural contingency make thick concepts analytical tricksters unsuitable for scholarly

abstraction aimed at second-order understanding, including theoretical comparison. Instead, the prismatic nature of thick concepts, their straddling of the descriptive and prescriptive, demands fine-grained attention to the knotty entwinements of expression and evaluation that make up charged moments of social life. Yasmin Moll, "Living through Thick Concepts in Revolutionary Egypt," *International Journal of Middle East Studies* 52 (2020): 493–97.

93. Gregory Starrett, *Putting Islam to Work: Education, Politics, and Religious Transformation in Egypt* (Berkeley: University of California Press, 1998), 245.

94. Julia Elyachar, "Before (and After) Neoliberalism," *Cultural Anthropology* 27, no. 1 (2012): 91.

95. Asef Bayat, *Revolution without Revolutionaries: Making Sense of the Arab Spring* (Stanford, CA: Stanford University Press, 2017), 173–75; Mona Atia, *Building a House in Heaven: Pious Neoliberalism and Islamic Charity in Egypt* (Minneapolis: University of Minnesota Press, 2013), 136–39; Schielke, *Egypt in the Future Tense*, 68.

96. Wendy Brown, *Undoing the Demos: Neoliberalism's Stealth Revolution* (Princeton, NJ: Princeton University Press, 2015), 40.

97. Yasmin Moll, "Building the New Egypt: Islamic Televangelists, Revolutionary Ethics and 'Productive' Citizenship," *Cultural Anthropology*, May 23, 2013, https://culanth.org/authors/yasmin-moll.

98. Brookings Institution, "Brookings Project on US Relations with the Islamic World: Remarks by Amr Khaled," Washington DC, May 11, 2007, 12, https://www.brookings.edu/wp-content/uploads/2012/04/20070511.pdf.

This response speaks to the frustrations of what James Ferguson calls the "politics of the anti" in analyses of neoliberalism. He asks, "What if politics is really not about expressing indignation or denouncing the powerful? What if it is, instead, about getting what you want?" James Ferguson, "The Uses of Neoliberalism," *Antipode* 41, no. S1 (2010): 167.

99. The entwining of individual reform with national change is common across a variety of Islamic movements, from Lebanon to Indonesia to Sudan. Deeb, *An Enchanted Modern*; Hoesterey, *Rebranding Islam*; Noah Salomon, *For Love of the Prophet: An Ethnography of Sudan's Islamic State* (Princeton, NJ: Princeton University Press, 2016). While today's left-leaning activists emphasize structural change, the yoking of collective change to self-transformation has long been characteristic of revolutionary movements on the left around the world, as even a cursory perusal of the historical record reveals. For example, in the 1960s and 1970s the Guinean revolutionary state aimed to form in citizens a durable socialist habitus through prescribing ways of dressing, speaking, and walking. Mike McGovern, *A Socialist Peace? Explaining the Absence of War in an African Country* (Chicago: University of

Chicago Press, 2017). Even avowedly atheistic revolutionaries linked political success to ethical transformation; for Vietnamese communists, for example, see Webb Keane, *Ethical Life: Its Natural and Social Histories* (Princeton, NJ: Princeton University Press, 2016), 216–40.

The sense that fundamental upheavals in entrenched institutions are necessarily entwined with fundamental changes in entrenched habits of thoughts and ways of interacting appears to be as much a secular progressive truism as a religious revivalist one.

100. Starrett, *Putting Islam to Work*.

101. Muhammad Qasim Zaman, "The Sovereignty of God in Modern Islamic Thought," *Journal of the Royal Asiatic Society* 25, no. 3 (2015): 389–418.

102. The Muslim Brotherhood itself reflects the diverse currents of Sunni revivalism, with some members deferring to the classical tradition institutionalized by al-Azhar and others veering more toward Salafism. This internal diversity is often overlooked in political contest. Carrie Wickham traces the ways in which the values and priorities of many leaders in the Muslim Brotherhood radically transformed over her twenty years of research from the 1990s to the lead-up to the revolution, provoking internal debate within the organization and the formation of competing factions. Wickham, *The Muslim Brotherhood*.

103. These accusations continue, as I discuss in the epilogue. For their part, Muslim Brotherhood–affiliated parliamentarians in the early 2000s protested Amr Khaled's ban from public preaching, but by the time of my fieldwork its members routinely accused him and other New Preachers of being covert American agents.

104. Hala Mustafa, quoted in David Hardaker, "Amr Khaled: Islam's Billy Graham," *The Independent*, January 4, 2006.

105. Allam, "Al-Daʿiya Mustafa Hosny."

106. Some have argued that *islamiyin* is an originally exonymic term, a back translation from the French *Islamisme*. A volume bringing together diverse reflections on the utility and history of "Islamism" as a term points out that Orientalists originally used Islamism like they did Hinduism—to describe the Muslim religion, before turning to "Mohammedanism." Islamism as interchangeable with "political Islam" has a much more recent history. Richard Bernstein and Abbas Barzagar, eds., *Islamism: Contested Perspectives on Political Islam* (Stanford, CA: Stanford University Press, 2009).

107. After the revolution, the increasing conflation of *islamiyin* with partisans of the Muslim Brotherhood lessened the term's currency even further. To be a participant in the Islamic Awakening wasn't necessarily to endorse the political agenda of the Muslim Brotherhood—a fact that was often lost on academic observers, the

group's secularist detractors, and the Muslim Brotherhood itself, which mistook the increased religiosity of the average Egyptian in the three decades leading up to the revolution as support for its political agenda. See Ayyash, ElAfifi, and Ezzat, *Broken Bonds*, 71–73.

108. Brian Larkin, "Binary Islam: Media and Religious Movements in Nigeria," in *New Media and Religious Transformations in Africa*, ed. Rosalind I. J. Hackett and Benjamin F. Soares (Bloomington: Indiana University Press, 2015), 67.

109. Yasmin Moll, "Al-qanawat al-fada'iyya al-Islamiyya wa akhlaqiyyat al-tarfih fi Misr," [Islamic satellite channels and the ethics of entertainment in Egypt], *al-Masry al-Youm*, April 21, 2010.

110. Yasmin Moll, "Special Report: What the Pew Poll on Egypt Really Means," *Cairo Review of Global Affairs*, May 2011.

Chapter 1

1. Stanley Cohen, *Folk Devils and Moral Panic: The Creation of the Mods and Rockers* (London: Routledge, 2011 [1972]).

2. Muhammad al-Baz, *Du'ah fi-l-manfa: Qissat 'Amr Khalid wa al-Du'ah al-Judud fi Misr* [Preachers in exile: The story of Amr Khaled and the New Preachers in Egypt] (Cairo: Al-Faris, 2004), 57. See also Al-Sayed Zaied, "Da'wa for Dollars: A New Wave of Muslim Televangelists," *Arab Insight* 2, no. 1 (2008).

3. Naomi Sakr, *Arab Television Today* (London: I.B. Tauris, 2007), 7. Sakr suggests that the 2000 privatization law provided well-timed stimulus for demand for slots on the new satellite provider, while Tanya Guaaybess argues that the private ownership of satellite channels resulted from a protracted legal battle mounted by liberal opposition leaders contesting the constitutionality of the prohibition of private—that is, non-state—television. Tanya Guaaybess, "Restructuring Television in Egypt: The Position of the State between Regional Supply and Local Demand," in *Mass Media, Politics and Society in the Middle East*, ed. Kai Hafez (Cresskill, NJ: Hampton Press, 2001).

4. For an insightful analysis of the range of content broadcast on satellite television and the debates the content engenders, see Marwan M. Kraidy and Joe F. Khalil, *Arab Television Industries, International Screen Industries* (London: Palgrave Macmillan, 2009) and Marwan M. Kraidy, *Reality Television and Arab Politics: Contention in Public Life* (Cambridge: Cambridge University Press, 2010); for a historical account of the rise of Christian satellite media in the region, see Febe Armanios, *Satellite Ministries: The Rise of Christian Television in the Middle East* (New York: Oxford University Press, forthcoming 2025).

5. Saleh Kamel, "Development of Islamic Banking Activity: Problems and Prospects," Islamic Development Bank Prize Winners' Lecture Series, no. 12 (Jeddah: Islamic Resarch and Training Institute, 1998), 23. Kamel's efforts to

develop Islamic alternatives to secular/Western economic institutions motivated his sponsorship of an annual symposium on Islamic economics. Running since 1981, each year the series gathers professors, researchers, theologians, financial experts, bankers, and heads of corporations dedicated to the idea of an alternative economic order that is "Islamic" to discuss the challenges and opportunities they faced. These discussions led to academic publications, policy recommendations, and fatwas. Kamel also helped institutionalize the idea of Islamic economics, endowing research centers at al-Azhar University in Egypt and King Abdulaziz University in Saudi Arabia. Like other large Gulf enterprises, the company endows lectureships in Islamic Studies at prestigious US universities, including Yale and Princeton, as a way of redressing long-standing Orientalist narratives about Islam and Muslims.

6. Leor Halevi, *Modern Things on Trial: Islam's Global and Material Reformation in the Age of Rida, 1865–1935* (New York: Columbia University Press, 2019), 117, 13.

7. This separation falls under critical scrutiny, a symptom more of secularization's fantasies than evidence of its realities. As Bill Maurer argues, "It is obvious to participants in alternative finance as it is to anthropologists that economics is a social convention." Bill Maurer, *Mutual Life, Limited: Islamic Banking, Alternative Currencies, Lateral Reason* (Princeton, NJ: Princeton University Press, 2005), 166–67. For both the Islamic bankers and secular cryptocurrency investors he writes about, the dual recognition of capitalism's real power and its social construction "carries with it the moral obligation to reconstruct and remake" its tools and structures for alternative ends.

8. Daromir Rudnyckyj, "Spiritual Economies: Islam and Neoliberalism in Contemporary Indonesia," *Cultural Anthropology* 24, no. 1 (2009): 104–41, https://doi.org/10.1111/j.1548-1360.2009.00028.x.

9. Charles Tripp, *Islam and the Moral Economy* (Cambridge: Cambridge University Press, 2006), 4.

10. Kamel, "Development of Islamic Banking Activity," 11.

11. Abd al-Latif Hamza, *Al-iʿlam la-hu tarikhuh wa madhahibuh* [Media: History and approaches] (Cairo: Dar al-Fikr al-ʿArabi, 1965).

12. Abd al-Latif Hamza, *Al-iʿlam fi sadr al-Islam* [Media at the dawn of Islam] (Dar al-Fikr al-ʿArabi, 1971), 6, 39.

13. Emilio Spadola, "The Call of Communication: Mass Media and Reform in Interwar Morocco," in *Middle Eastern and North African Societies in the Interwar Period*, ed. Ebru Boyar and Kate Fleet (Leiden: Brill, 2018), 99.

14. Ibrahim Imam, afterword to Hamza, *Al-iʿlam fi sadr al-Islam*.

15. Ibrahim Imam, *Al-iʿlam al-Islami, al-marhala al-shafhiyya* [Islamic media: The oral stage] (Cairo: Anglo-Egyptian Bookstore, 1980), 3–4.

16. Yasmin Moll, "The Idea of Islamic Media: The Qur'an and the Decolonization of Mass Communication," *International Journal for Middle East Studies* 52, no. 4 (2020): 623–42.

17. Abdul Qader Tash, "Islamic Satellite Channels and Their Impact on Arab Societies: Iqra Channel—A Case Study," *Arab Media and Society*, November 1, 2004, https://www.arabmediasociety.com/islamic-satellite-channels-and-their-impact-on-arab-societies-iqra-channel-a-case-study/. See also Abdulkader Tash, *Al-iʻlam al-Islami fi al-qanawat al-fadaʾiya* [Islamic media in the satellite channels] (Beirut: Dar al-Andalus, 2004).

18. Dubai Press Club, *Arab Media Outlook 2009–2013: Inspiring Local Content* (Dubai Press Club and Value Partners, 2010), https://irp.fas.org/eprint/arabmedia.pdf.

19. Lila Abu-Lughod, *Dramas of Nationhood: The Politics of Television in Egypt* (Chicago: Chicago University Press, 2005)

20. Timothy Mitchell, *Rule of Experts: Egypt, Techno-Politics, Modernity* (Berkeley: University of California Press, 2002).

21. Omar Dahi, "Understanding the Political Economy of the Arab Revolts," *Middle East Report* 259 (Summer 2011).

22. Mohammed Soliman, "Egypt's Informal Economy: An Ongoing Cause of Unrest, *Journal of International Affairs* 73, no. 2 (2020): 185–93. See also Joel Beinin, "Civil Society, NGOs, and Egypt's 2011 Popular Uprising," *South Atlantic Quarterly* 113, no. 2 (2014): 396–406, https://doi.org/10.1215/00382876-2644185.

23. Sakr, *Arab Television Today*.

24. Samia Mehrez, *Egypt's Culture Wars: Politics and Practice* (London: Routledge, 2008), 7. In an interview about Egypt's "culture wars," Mehrez, a noted literary theorist, negatively remarks on the apparent incongruity of her students at the American University in Cairo choosing to watch an Islamic channel like Iqraa. "Samia Mehrez, 'Egypt's Culture Wars: Politics and Practice,'" interview by Catherine David in a joint project by Haus der Kulturen der Welt and Europe in the Middle East—The Middle East in Europe, 2008, https://vimeo.com/137467613, accessed February 23, 2022.

25. Cited in Mamoun Fandy, *(Un)Civil War of Words* (Westport, CT: Praeger Security International, 2007), 44.

26. Shaykh Saleh Kamel, quoted in Naomi Sakr, *Satellite Realms: Transnational Television, Globalization and the Middle East* (London: IB Tauris, 2001), 47.

27. Abdullah Schliefer, "Does Satellite TV Pay in the Arab World Footprint? Exploring the Economic Feasibility of Specialized and General Channels," June 1, 2001. https://www.arabmediasociety.com/does-satellite-tv-pay-in-the-arab-world-footprint-exploring-the-economic-feasibility-of-specialized-and-general-channels/.

28. Patricia Kubala, "'You Will (Not) Be Able to Take Your Eyes Off It!': Mass-Mediated Images and Politico-Ethical Reform in the Egyptian Islamic Revival," in *Visual Culture in the Modern Middle East: Rhetoric of the Image*, ed. Christiane Gruber and Sune Haugbolle (Bloomington: Indiana University Press, 2013), 82–100.

29. Gregory Starrett, "The Political Economy of Religious Commodities in Cairo," *American Anthropologist* 97, no. 1 (1995), 64, https://doi.org/10.1525/aa.1995.97.1.02a00090.

30. Gamal Abdel Nasser, quoted in Malika Zeghal, "Religion and Politics in Egypt: The Ulema of al-Azhar, Radical Islam, and the State (1952–94)," *International Journal of Middle East Studies* 31, no. 3 (1999): 375.

31. Khaled Hroub, "Introduction: Religious Broadcasting; Beyond the Innocence of Political Indifference," in *Religious Broadcasting in the Middle East*, ed. Khaled Hroub (London: Hurst, 2012), 283. On Kamel as proxy, see Fandy, *(Un)Civil War of Words*, 44.

32. Daromir Rudnyckyj and Filippo Osella, eds., *Religion and the Morality of the Market: Anthropological Perspectives* (Cambridge: Cambridge University Press, 2017). See chapters by Benjamin F. Soares ("'Structural Adjustment Islam' and the Religious Economy in Neoliberal Mali") and Filippo Osella ("'A Poor Muslim Cannot Be a Good Muslim': Islam, Charitable Giving, and Market Logic in Sri Lanka"), and Sarah Tobin, *Everyday Piety*, 5.

33. Naomi Haynes, *Moving by the Spirit: Pentecostal Social Life on the Zambian Copperbelt* (Berkeley: University of California Press, 2017), 1.

34. Mona Atia, *Building a House in Heaven: Pious Neoliberalism and Islamic Charity in Egypt* (Minneapolis: University of Minnesota Press, 2013); Aaron Rock-Singer, "Neoliberal Daʿwa: The Egyptian New Preachers (al-Duʿa al-Judud) and the Restructuring of Transnational Religious Preaching and Practice," in *Culture of Daʿwa: Preaching in the Modern World*, ed. Itzchak Weismann and Jamil Malik (University of Utah Press, 2020).

35. Halevi, *Modern Things on Trial*.

36. Ahmed Abu Haiba, quoted in Ursula Lindsey, "The New Muslim TV: Media-Savvy, Modern, and Moderate," *Christian Science Monitor*, May 2, 2006.

37. While the political proclivities of critical scholars, including anthropologists, tend to evaluate modern market systems as amoral if not ethically detrimental, "at issue in indigenous critiques of money is often not so much its alienating and corrosive effects per se as its unequal distribution. Not the presence of money *in general* but its absence *for us*," as Webb Keane notes. Webb Keane, "Markets, Materiality and Moral Metalanguage," *Anthropological Theory* 8, no. 1 (2008): 29.

38. Amira Mittermaier, *Giving to God: Islamic Charity in Revolutionary Times* (Berkeley: University of California Press, 2019).

39. Nada Moumtaz, *God's Property: Islam, Charity, and the Modern State* (Berkeley: University of California Press, 2021), 25.

40. Abdulkader Tash, "Hal nahtaj ila qana fada'iyya Islamiyya?" [Do we need an Islamic satellite channel?], in *Al-thaqafa wa-l-i'lam wa-ma baynahuma* [Between culture and media] (Jeddah: Sharikat al-Madina al-Munawwara, 1997), 100–102.

41. Abdulkader Tash, "Al-tarbiyya am san' al-bada'il?" [Virtuous self-cultivation or creating alternatives?], in *Qadaruna an nakuna Islamiyin* [Our fate is to be Islamic] (Riyadh: Dar 'Alam al-Kutub, 1993), 80.

42. In August 2013 Suwaidan, who had several programs of his own on Resala, was fired by Alwaleed following his critical on-air comments about the ouster of the Muslim Brotherhood leader Morsi from Egypt's presidency the month before.

43. Faye D. Ginsburg, Lila Abu-Lughod, and Brian Larkin, eds., *Media Worlds: Anthropology on New Terrain* (Berkeley: University of California Press, 2002).

44. Tejaswini Ganti, "Sentiments of Disdain and Practices of Distinction: Boundary-Work, Subjectivity, and Value in the Hindi Film Industry," *Anthropological Quarterly* 85, no. 1 (2012): 9.

45. David Kloos, "Experts beyond Discourse: Women, Islamic Authority, and the Performance of Professionalism in Malaysia," *American Ethnologist* 46, no. 2 (2019): 162–75.

46. These quotes are from a special issue of the secularist magazine *Rose al-Youssef* dedicated to exposing "the danger" posed by religious channels, including Arab Christian ones. October 29, 2010.

47. John Thornton Caldwell, *Production Culture: Industrial Reflexivity and Critical Practice in Film and Television* (Durham, NC: Duke University Press, 2008), 5.

48. Narges Bajoghli, *Iran Reframed: Anxieties of Power in the Islamic Republic* (Stanford, CA: Stanford University Press, 2019).

49. See, for example, Adel Iskandar, "Media as Method in the Age of Revolution: Statism and Digital Contestation," in *The Oxford Handbook of Contemporary Middle Eastern and North African History*, ed. Amal Ghazal and Jens Hanssen (Oxford: Oxford University Press, 2020), 342–64, https://doi.org/10.1093/oxfordhb/9780199672530.013.4.

50. Patrick Haenni and Husam Tammam, "Chat Shows, Nashid Groups, and Lite Preaching: Egypt's Air-Conditioned Islam," *Le Monde diplomatique*, September 2003, 3 https://mondediplo.com/2003/09/03egyptislam.

Chapter 2

1. For an interdisciplinary examination of innovation in relation to Islam, see Mehran Kamrava, ed., *Innovation in Islam: Traditions and Contributions* (Berkeley: University of California Press, 2011).

2. James Bourk Hoesterey, *Rebranding Islam: Piety, Prosperity, and a Self-Help Guru* (Stanford, CA: Stanford University Press, 2016).

3. Mathew Engelke, *God's Agents: Biblical Publicity in Contemporary England* (Berkeley: University of California Press, 2013), 68, 27. For an ethnography of US evangelical investments in developing immersive forms of biblical entertainment, see James Bielo, *Ark Encounter: The Making of a Creationist Theme Park* (New York: New York University Press, 2018).

4. Charles Hirschkind, *The Ethical Soundscape: Cassette Sermons and Islamic Counterpublics*, Cultures of History (New York: Columbia University Press, 2006), 183.

5. Iqraa's inaugral Saudi director Tash wrote extensively on this theme; see for example "Thaqaftna al-zatiyya bayn al-asala wal-targhib" [Our culture between authenticity and westernization], in *Al-thaqafa wal-i'lam wa-ma baynahuma* [Between culture and media] (Jeddah: Sharikat al-Madina al-Munawwara, 1997), 7–14.

6. Khaled Abou El Fadl, *Reasoning with God: Reclaiming Shar'iah in the Modern Age* (Rowman & Littlefield, 2013), 49–55; Christopher Razavian, "Al-Azhar, Wasatiyah, and the Waqi'," in *Modern Islamic Authority and Social Change*, vol. 1, *Evolving Debates in Muslim Majority Countries*, ed. Masooda Bano (Edinburgh: Edinburgh University Press, 2018), 102–23.

7. Dale Eickelman and Jon Andersen, eds., *New Media in the Muslim World: The Emerging Public Sphere*, 2nd ed. (Bloomington: Indiana University Press, 2003).

8. Nabil Echaibi, "Hyper-Islamism? Mediating Islam from the Halal Website to the Islamic Talk-Show," *Journal of Arab and Muslim Media Research* 1, no. 3 (2008); Aaron Rock, "Amr Khaled: From Da'wa to Political and Religious Leadership," *British Journal of Middle Eastern Studies* 37, no. 1 (2010): 15–37, https://doi.org/10.1080/13530191003661104.

9. To be sure, Al-Azhar's scholars see their role of being "custodians of change" as necessitating a focus on mastering contemporary media technologies and messaging strategies. Muhammad Qasim Zaman, *The Ulama in Contemporary Islam: Custodians of Change* (Princeton, NJ: Princeton University Press, 2002).

10. Dale Eickelman, "'Mass Higher Education and the Religious Imagination in Contemporary Arab Societies,'" *American Ethnologist* 19, no. 4 (1992): 643–55.

11. Brinkley Messick, "Genealogies of Reading and Scholarly Cultures of Islam," in *Cultures of Scholarship*, ed. S. C. Humphreys (Ann Arbor: University of Michigan Press, 1997): 387–408.

12. Aria Nakissa, *The Anthropology of Islamic Law: Education, Ethics and Legal Intrepretation at Egypt's Al-Azhar* (Oxford: Oxford University Press, 2019), 266.

13. One of those shaykhs was Salem Abdel Galil, then a newly minted PhD from Al-Azhar's *da'wa* faculty who served as the deputy minister of religious endowments from 2007 to 2012. Galil went on to have a popular television program of his own giving fatwas on Azhari channel. This privately funded channel was started by the Azhari shaykh Khaled al-Guindi in 2009 and was not officially affiliated with al-Azhar. Another was the Azhari Sufi preacher Awad al-Munqush, who was born in Libya.

14. Historically there existed different types of Islamic preachers: the *khatib* (sermon-giver, often appointed by the ruler), the *wa'iz* (admonisher), the *mudkhakkir* (reminder), and the *qass* (storyteller). The latter three were called "free preachers" as they were not affiliated with a mosque like the *khatib*. Richard Antoun, *Muslim Preacher in the Modern World: A Jordanian Case Study in Comparative Perspective* (Princeton, NJ: Princeton University Press, 1989), 69. In the contemporary period, *da'iya* has become a catchall term subsuming these historical distinctions. Patrick Gaffney, "The Changing Voices of Islam: The Emergence of Professional Preachers in Contemporary Egypt," *Muslim World* 81, no. 1 (1991).

15. Rachel Heiman, Carla Freeman, and Mark Leichty, eds., *The Global Middle Classes: Theorizing through Ethnography*, School for Advanced Research Advanced Seminar Series (Santa Fe: University of New Mexico Press, 2012). For an in-depth ethnographic analysis of the intersection of class and Muslim piety, see Sarah Tobin, *Everyday Piety: Islam and Economy in Jordan* (Ithaca, NY: Cornell University Press, 2016).

16. In Sharon Otterman, "Fatwas and Feminism: Women, Religious Authority, and Islamic TV," *Arab Media and Society* June 1, 2006, https://www.arabmediasociety.com/fatwas-and-feminism-women-religious-authority-and-islamic-tv/.

17. Wa'il Lutfi, *Zaharit Al-Du'ah al-Judud* [The phenomenon of the New Preachers] (Cairo: General Book Authority, 2005).

18. Jessica Winegar, "Civilizing Muslim Youth: Egyptian State Culture Programs and Islamic Television Preachers," *Journal of the Royal Anthropological Institute* 20, no. 3 (2014): 455, https://doi.org/10.1111/1467-9655.12116.

19. Patrick Haenni and Husam Tammam, "Chat Shows, Nashid Groups, and Lite Preaching: Egypt's Air-Conditioned Islam," *Le Monde diplomatique*, September 2003, https://mondediplo.com/2003/09/03egyptislam.

20. Asef Bayat, "Piety, Privilege and Egyptian Youth," ISIM Newsletter 10, no. 1 (2002): 23.

21. Mark Allen Peterson, *Connected in Cairo: Growing Up Cosmopolitan in the Modern Middle East,* Public Cultures of the Middle East and North Africa (Bloomington: Indiana University Press, 2011); James B. Hoesterey, "Prophetic Cosmopolitanism: Islam, Pop Psychology, and Civic Virtue in Indonesia," *City & Society* 24, no. 1 (2012): 38–61, https://doi.org/10.1111/j.1548-744X.2012.01067.x. See also Tobin, *Everyday Piety.*

22. Ien Ang, *Desperately Seeking the Audience* (London: Routledge, 1991), 6.

23. Brian Larkin, "Ahmed Deedat and the Form of Islamic Evangelism," *Social Text* 26, no. 3 (2008): 104–5, https://doi.org/10.1215/01642472-2008-006.

24. Beth Baron, *The Orphan Scandal: Christian Missionaries and the Rise of the Muslim Brotherhood* (Stanford, CA: Stanford University Press, 2014), 196. See also Nile Green, *Terrains of Exchange: Religious Economies of Global Islam* (New York: Oxford University Press, 2014).

25. See Karin van Nieuwkerk, *Performing Piety: Singers and Actors in Egypt's Islamic Revival* (Austin: University of Texas Press, 2013); Lara Deeb and Mona Harb, *Leisurely Islam: Negotiating Geography and Morality in Shi'ite South Beirut* (Princeton, NJ: Princeton University Press, 2013); Su'ad Abdul Khabeer, *Muslim Cool: Race, Religion, and Hip Hop in the United States* (New York: NYU Press, 2016).

26. Hirschkind, *Ethical Soundscape.*

27. Michael Warner, "Publics and Counterpublics," *Public Culture* 14, no. 1 (2002): 49–90.

28. Ayala Fader, *Hidden Heretics: Jewish Doubt in the Digital Age* (Princeton, NJ: Princeton University Press, 2020).

29. Richard Gauvain, *Salafi Ritual Purity: In the Presence of God* (New York: Routledge, 2013), 90.

30. Aaron Rock-Singer, *In the Shade of the Sunna: Salafi Piety in the Twentieth-Century Middle East* (Berkeley: University of California Press, 2022), 104.

31. Joas Wagemakers, "The Enduring Legacy of the Second Saudi State: Quietist and Radical Wahhabi Contestations of *al-Wala' Wa-l-Bara',*" *International Journal of Middle East Studies* 44, no. 1 (2012): 93–110, https://doi.org/10.1017/S0020743811001267.

32. Karim Tartoussieh, "Pious Stardom: Cinema and the Islamic Revival in Egypt," *Arab Studies Journal* 15, no. 1 (2007): 30–43.

33. Episode 6, *Sihr al-Dunya,* Iqraa, July 2012.

34. Hirschkind, *Ethical Soundscape,* 92.

35. Hans Wehr, "Bhr," in *A Dictionary of Modern Written Arabic (Arabic-English)*, ed. J. Milton-Cowan (Wiesbaden: Otto Harrassowitz, 1979).

36. Chihab El Khachab, *Making Film in Egypt: How Labor, Technology and Mediation Shape the Industry* (Cairo: American University in Cairo Press, 2021), 191.

37. Marshall McLuhan, *Understanding Media: The Extensions of Man* (New York: Signet Books, 1964), 309–12.

38. Abd al-Halim Sayyid and Mikhael Hifz Allah, *Al-Nas wa-l-tilifiziyun* [People and television] (Cairo: Anglo-Egyptian Bookstore, 1963), 6, 14. This Egyptian book's toggling between the sensory capacities of the medium's technical features and the social effects of its broadcast content anticipated still-ongoing debates about whether it is the technology or the humans who create and wield it that matter most when it comes to understanding media effects. While McLuhan classically argued that "the medium is the message"—that technological properties determine interaction irrespective of content—cultural studies scholar Raymond Williams, for instance, made a case against "a self-directing technology" removed from "social and cultural definition." Raymond Williams, *Television: Technology and Cultural Form* (Collins/Fontana, 1974), 137.

While the definitive social history of television in Egypt has yet to be written, scholars of the modern Middle East have started to pay more attention to the everyday life of techno-communicative innovations in the region across various time periods. On the cassette, for example, see Andrew Simon, *Media of the Masses: Cassette Culture in Modern Egypt* (Stanford, CA: Stanford University Press, 2022).

39. Kristina Nelson, *The Art of Reciting the Qur'an* (University of Texas Press, 1985).

40. The Qur'an's self-referentiality with respect to its communicative qualities has informed theological debates from the ninth century to the present. These concern the interplay of form and meaning, *jism* and *m'ana*, in constituting its miraculous inimitability, its *i'jaz*. Nasr Hamid Abu-Zayd, "The Dilemma of the Literary Approach to the Qur'an," *Alif* (Cairo, Egypt), no. 23 (2003): 8, https://doi.org/10.2307/1350075. "And if you are in doubt about what We have revealed to Our servant, then produce a surah like it," God challenges (Qur'an 2:23). The doctrine of *i'jaz* underpins the widespread social sensitivity in Egypt to the imitation or adoption of Qur'anic addressive forms or references in creative projects, with such attempts at times deemed heretical by religious authorities. Samuli Schielke, "Is Prose Poetry a Conspiracy against the Noble Qur'an? Poetics, Humans, and God in Contemporary Egypt," *Historical Social Research / Historische Sozialforschung* 44, no. 3 (169) (2019): 101–26.

41. On technologies of voice, see Jacques Derrida, "'Above All, No Journalists!,'" in *Religion and Media*, ed. Hent de Vries and Samuel Weber (Stanford, CA: Stanford University Press, 2001), 56–93. On listening as essential to moral conduct, Hirschkind, *Ethical Soundscape*, 39.

42. Patrick Eisenlohr, *Sounding Islam: Voice, Media, and Sonic Atmospheres in an Indian Ocean World* (Berkeley: University of California Press, 2018).

43. Jacquelene G. Brinton, *Preaching Islamic Renewal: Religious Authority and Media in Contemporary Egypt* (Berkeley: University of California Press, 2015), 180–98. Brinton's intervention is part of an emerging body of work that explicitly aims to explore "seeing Islamically," focusing on the social lives of images—and the productive provocations that often attend them—in relation to diverse Islamic formations around the world. For the phrase "seeing Islamically," see Kristin Scheid, "Over the Shoulder: Looking at Islamic Visuality, Projected Scandals, and Muslim Visibility," in *Provocative Images in Contemporary Islam*, ed. David Kloos, Mark Westmoreland, Leonie Schmidt, and Bart Barendregt (Leiden University Press, 2023), 141. At the same time, as Christiane Gruber and Sune Haugbolle argue in their landmark volume on visual culture in the Middle East, it would be remiss to posit a distinctively "Muslim" mode of visuality because "even the most self-consciously 'purified' and 'Islamic' imagery often borrows from the more recent products of modern Euro-American visual culture." Christiane Gruber and Sune Haugbolle, "Introduction: Visual Culture in the Modern Middle East," in *Visual Culture in the Modern Middle East: Rhetoric of the Image*, (Bloomington: Indiana University Press, 2013), xxii.

44. Yasmin Moll, "Islamic Televangelism: Religion, Media and Visuality," *Arab Media and Society*, 2010.

45. For example, building on the notion of an Islamic counterpublic, Karin van Nieuwkerk argues in her in-depth examination of the field of ethical entertainment in Egypt that aural media may be a "more fruitful foundation" for cultivating piety in that, unlike visual media, aural media are more resistant to "los[ing] their religious references and becom[ing] mainstream." Van Nieuwkerk, *Performing Piety*, 272. However, the desire to go mainstream was a constitutive one for the sort of piety my interlocutors promoted, informing the ethics of their professional investments in the visual.

46. This is akin to what Webb Keane calls the "iconoclastic impulse" of Protestant reformers whereby "pictures should only convey visual information," not "stir feelings." Webb Keane, "Freedom and Blasphemy: On Indonesian Press Bans and Danish Cartoons," *Public Culture* 21, no. 1 (2009): 59. This valorization of minimalism extends to recitations of the Qur'an itself. Michael Frishkopf shows how the Wahhabi-Salafi style deliberately reduces melodic embellishment to sonically emphasize

an "unmediated directness," while censuring as *bid'a* the long association in Egypt between Qur'anic recitation and musical traditions—a synergy that enabled the professionalization of recitation as artistic pursuit. Michael Frishkopf, "Mediated Qur'anic Recitations and the Contestation of Islam in Contemporary Egypt," in *Music and the Play of Power in the Middle East, North Africa, and Central Asia*, ed. Laudan Nooshin, (Burlington, VT: Ashgate, 2009), 107. That the rejection of aesthetic innovation extends beyond visual practices to oral ones like recitation suggests a broader Salafi "semiotic ideology." For an explication of this term, see Webb Keane, "On Semiotic Ideology," *Signs and Society* 6, no. 1 (2018): 64–87, https://doi.org/10.1086/695387.

47. Birgit Meyer, "Mediation and Immediacy: Sensational Forms, Semiotic Ideologies, and the Question of the Medium," *Social Anthropology* 19, no. 1 (February 1, 2011), 29–30, https://doi.org/10.1111/j.1469-8676.2010.00137.x.

48. Amr Khaled, *Al-Iman wa al-'asr: Ru'ya jadida fa'ala li dawr al-din fil-hayah* [Faith and the age: A new dynamic vision for the role of religion in life] (Cairo: Sama for Publishing and Distribution, 2015), 36.

49. Issa Boullata, "Sayyid Qutb's Literary Appreciation of the Qur'an," in *Literary Structures of Religious Meaning in the Qur'an* (Richmond, Surrey: Curzon Press, 2000), 356.

50. Hirschkind, *Ethical Soundscape*, 154–56.

51. Moll, "Islamic Televangelism."

52. Episode 16, *'Ala Khuta al-Habib,* Iqraa, October 2005.

53. Christopher Pinney, *"Photos of the Gods": The Printed Image and Political Struggle in India* (London: Reaktion Books, 2004).

54. Maurice Chammah, "Cosmopolitan Islamism and Its Critics: Ahmed Abu Haiba, 4Shbab TV, and Western Reception," *Arab Media and Society*, March 30, 2010.

55. This aspiration was hampered by the reality that most of the funding for his television projects came from Saudi sources favoring a more conservative approach. For an in-depth profile of Abu Haiba and the challenges he faced putting into practice his idea of "ethical entertainment," see van Nieuwkerk, *Performing Piety*, 261–267. Abu Haiba's travails with Gulf capital are also the subject of the documentary *Pop Goes Islam*, directed by Ismail Elmokadem, 52 min. (Alegria Productions, 2011).

56. Ahmed Abu Haiba, quoted in Ursula Lindsey, "The New Muslim TV: Media-Savvy, Modern, and Moderate," *Christian Science Monitor*, May 2, 2006.

57. From the magazine *Rose al-Youssef* [in Arabic], November 2, 2006, https://www.linga.org/international-news/MTQ2MA, accessed January 29, 2024.

58. These televised tears provoked ambivalence in even the most dedicated New Preaching viewers, leading them to wonder about the artifice of the pious sentiment they embodied. Yasmin Moll, "Televised Tears: Artifice and Ambivalence in Islamic

Preaching," *Comparative Studies of South Asia, Africa and the Middle East* 41, no. 2 (2021): 153–65.

59. Moez Masoud, "Interview with Moez Masoud, Host of ART's English-Language Islamic Talk Shows," *Transnational Broadcasting Studies* 15, November 2, 2005.

60. See van Nieuwkerk, *Performing Piety*.

61. Hirschkind, *Ethical Soundscape*.

62. "Disappearing medium," from Meyer, "Mediation and Immediacy"; printing as problematic, Brinkley Messick, *The Calligraphic State: Textual Domination and History in a Muslim Society* (Berkeley: University of California Press, 1993). On digitizing the printed Qur'an, Natalie Suit, *Qur'anic Matters: Material Mediations and Religious Practice in Egypt* (London: Bloomsbury Academic, 2020). On debates about religious mass mediation in relation to gender, Dorothea Elisabeth Schulz, *Muslims and New Media in West Africa: Pathways to God* (Bloomington: Indiana University Press, 2012). See also Leor Halevi, *Modern Things on Trial: Islam's Global and Material Reformation in the Age of Rida, 1865–1935* (New York: Columbia University Press, 2019). Some Islamic revivalist groups like the Tablighi Jamaat in Pakistan abjure all forms of technological mediation, arguing that only face-to-face preaching can truly promote piety. Arsalan Khan, "Islam and Pious Sociality: The Ethics of Hierarchy in the Tablighi Jamaat in Pakistan," *Social Analysis* 60, no. 4 (2016).

63. Samira Haj, *Reconfiguring Islamic Tradition: Reform, Rationality and Modernity* (Stanford, CA: Stanford University Press), 7. See also Omnia El Shakry, "Inwardness: Comparative Religious Philosophy in Modern Egypt," *Journal of the American Academy of Religion* 90, no. 2 (2022), 454, https://doi.org/10.1093/jaarel/lfaco32; Talal Asad, "Modern Power and the Reconfiguration of Religious Traditions: An Interview with Saba Mahmood," *Stanford Electronic Humanities Review* 5, no. 1 (1996), https://web.stanford.edu/group/SHR/5-1/text/asad.html.

64. Hirschkind, *Ethical Soundscape*, 34.

Chapter 3

1. Jeffrey Kenney, *Muslim Rebels: Kharijites and the Politics of Extremism in Egypt* (Oxford: Oxford University Press, 2006), 4.

2. Abdulkader Tash, "Hal nahtaj ila qana fada'iyya Islamiyya?" [Do we need an Islamic satellite channel?], in *Al-thaqafa wa-l-i'lam wa-ma baynahuma* [Between culture and media] (Jeddah: Sharikat al-Madina al-Munawwara, 1997), 100.

3. Samira Haj, *Reconfiguring Islamic Tradition: Reform, Rationality and Modernity* (Stanford, CA: Stanford University Press, 2009), 87; see also Mohamed Sherif, *Ghazali's Theory of Virtue* (Albany: State University of New York Press, 1975), 33–38.

4. Abdulkader Tash, "'An 'al-tatarruf,' mara ukhra" [On 'extremism,' once more], in *Qadaruna an nakun Islamiyin* [Our fate is to be Islamic] (Riyadh: Dar 'Alam al-Kutub, 1993), 213–17.

5. Episode 13, *Sihr al-Dunya*, Iqraa, July 2012.

6. Richard Gauvain, *Salafi Ritual Purity: In the Presence of God* (New York: Routledge, 2013).

7. Mamoun Fandy, *(Un)Civil War of Words* (Westport, CT: Praeger Security International, 2007). Iqraa producers were well aware of this perception, with the channel's translators feeling that they had to be very careful with their subtitling choices as compared to their colleagues in regular channels because the channel's programs were regularly targeted by MEMRI, a neoconservative Zionist company that sends, free of charge, selected clips from Arabic media to American news outlets and the US Congress in order "to elaborate a narrative of Arab societies as extremist, anti-Semitic and a threat to western democracies." Mona Baker, "Reframing Conflict in Translation," in *Critical Readings in Translation Studies*, ed. Mona Baker (New York: Routledge, 2010), 120. On the channel's subtitling strategies, see Yasmin Moll, "Subtitling Islam: Translation, Mediation, Critique," *Public Culture* 29 no. 2 (2017): 333–61.

8. Salwa Ismail, "Producing 'Reformed Islam': A Saudi Contribution to the US Projects of Global Governance," in *Kingdom without Borders: Saudi Arabia's Political, Religious and Media Frontiers*, ed. Madawi Al-Rasheed (London: Hurst; New York: Columbia University Press, 2009), 114, 130.

9. Saba Mahmood, "Secularism, Hermeneutics, and Empire: The Politics of Islamic Reformation," *Public Culture* 18 no. 2 (2006): 329, https://doi.org/10.1215/08992363-2006-006.

10. Abdulkader Tash, "Al-tatarruf al-dini" [Religious extremism], in *Qadaruna an nakun Islamiyin* [Our fate is to be Islamic] (Riyadh: Dar 'Alam al-Kutub, 1993), 210–11.

11. Sherali Tareen, "The Problems and Perils of Translating Sufism as 'Moderate Islam,'" in *Modern Sufis and the State*, ed. Katherine Pratt Ewing and Rosemary Corbett (Columbia University Press, 2019), 175–176.

12. This could also be true of groups that receive Western state funds. Stephen Jones shows how the Radical Middle Way, a British Muslim initiative, was not simply a state tool of discipline and surveillance that created a form of religion that it then "imposed" on British Muslims, even if it did receive funding from the UK government after the 2005 bombings in London. Rather, it grew out of the constellation of ideas, practices, and networks within the British Muslim community that crystallized in the 1990s around the community magazine *Q-News*. This magazine was an important platform for local Muslim activists and leaders critical of British foreign policy and worried about Islamophobia and institutionalized discrimination

against Muslim citizens. Many of its contributors were also critical of the religious discourses circulating within their own communities. Stephen Jones, "New Labour and the Re-Making of British Islam: The Case of the Radical Middle Way and the 'Reclamation' of the Classical Islamic Tradition," *Religions* 4 (2013): 550–66. Both the New Preachers Amr Khaled and Moez Masoud were involved with the Radical Middle Way as visiting speakers.

13. Episode 1, *Ahla Hayah*, Iqraa, January 2011.

14. Charles Hirschkind, *The Ethical Soundscape: Cassette Sermons and Islamic Counterpublics* (New York: Columbia University Press, 2006), 34.

15. Uriya Shavit and Ofir Winter, "Sports in Contemporary Islamic Law," *Islamic Law and Society* (2011): 250–80.

16. Samuli Schielke, "Second Thoughts about the Anthropology of Islam, or, How to Make Sense of Grand Schemes in Everyday Life," *Zentrum Moderner Orient Working Papers*, no. 2 (2010): 13, http://d-nb.info/1019243724/34; Samuli Schielke, "Being Good in Ramadan: Ambivalence, Fragmentation, and the Moral Self in the Lives of Young Egyptians," *Journal of the Royal Anthropological Institute* 15, S1 (2009): 24–40.

17. Nadia Fadil and Mayanthi Fernando, "Rediscovering the 'Everyday' Muslim: Notes on an Anthropological Divide," *HAU Journal of Ethnographic Theory* 5, no. 2 (2015): 61, 67, https://doi.org/10.14318/hau5.2.005. As Lara Deeb has argued in relation to this debate, "What constitutes the realm of piety in the first place" is above all an ethnographic question. Lara Deeb, "Thinking Piety and the Everyday Together: A Response to Fadil and Fernando," *HAU Journal of Ethnographic Theory* 5, no. 2 (2015), 94. My point is that it is also a theological one. For example, Fadil and Fernando (p. 70) argue that "the efficacy of norms is not only determined by their realization but also by conscious and unconscious discursive and affective attachments to them, irrespective of one's 'actual' practices." But the question of attachment versus practice is a matter of theological contention among revivalists themselves. For Hosny, a godly person might not be praying regularly but is trying to. This theology of godliness is anathema to Salafi revivalists, for whom, to be Muslim it is not enough to aspire to prayer, or to concede its divine efficacy and obligatory nature—one has to actually pray.

The question of how to understand creedal status in light of habitual miscreance is not a minor one, either. It played a major role in the formative period of Islamic theology as it ultimately revolved around competing conceptions of the character of God, as Sherman Jackson has discussed. Sherman Jackson, *On the Boundaries of Theological Tolerance in Islam* (Oxford: Oxford University Press, 2002). Did God see ongoing sin as reconcilable with ongoing attachment to Him? Or did one preclude the other? In their programs, the New Preachers advanced the first conception by openly speaking about their own histories of struggling with temptation and uncertainty as part of a persuasive strategy of normalizing the fragility of faith and its practice, and thus drawing more "ordinary people" to God. For their part, Salafi preachers criticized such intimate self-disclosure as itself sinful. While doubt may be the other side of faith, it shouldn't be spoken about publicly but mitigated through enhanced ritual discipline and constant remembrance of the hellfire.

18. Wilfred Cantwell Smith, *On Understanding Islam: Selected Studies* (The Hague: Mouton,1981), 15–16.

19. Saba Mahmood, *Politics of Piety: The Islamic Revival and the Feminist Subject* (Princeton, NJ: Princeton University Press, 2005), 49.

20. Amr Khaled, "Hubb Allah li-l-'abd, silsilat islah al-qulub" (Cairo: Al-Nour for Media Production and Distribution, 2001), CD-ROM.

21. William Chittick, *In Search of the Lost Heart: Explorations in Islamic Thought* (Albany: SUNY Press, 2012).

22. John Renard, *Friends of God: Islamic Images of Piety, Commitment, and Servanthood* (Berkeley: University of California Press, 2008).

23. Amr Khaled, *Al-Iman wa al-'asr: Ru'ya jadida fa'ala li dawr al-din fil-hayah* (Cairo: Sama for Publishing and Distribution, 2015), 208.

24. Episode 7, *Uhibbika Rabbi*, Iqraa, August 2011.

25. And not only on their programs; see for example the newspaper editorial by Moez Masoud, "Al-din . . . hijab?" [Religion . . . a barrier?], *al-Masry al-Youm*, February 11, 2010.

26. Episode 1, *Madrasat al-Hubb*, Iqraa, August 2010.

27. Mahmood, *Politics of Piety*.

28. Saba Mahmood, "Rehearsed Spontaneity and the Conventionality of Ritual: Disciplines of Salat," *American Ethnologist* 28, no. 4 (2001): 843.

29. Tim Winter, ed., *The Cambridge Companion to Classical Islamic Theology*, Cambridge Companions to Religion (New York: Cambridge University Press, 2008), 222.

30. On "God's ethics," see William Chittick, "The Ambiguity of the Qur'anic Command," in *Between Heaven and Hell: Islam, Salvation and the State of Others*, ed. Mohammad Hassan Khalil (Oxford: Oxford University Press, 2013), 82. Salafis object to this phrase, a key aspect of Sufi theological ethics, as heretical; see for example https://salafcenter.org/7586/. Yet while denouncing Sufism as *bid'a* and disavowing al-Ghazali as a reprehensible heretic for his synthetic approach to ancient Greek philosophy, Salafi practitioners still took for granted as "Islamic" al-Ghazali's Aristotelian paradigm of virtue ethics. Gauvain, *Salafi Ritual Purity*, 74–82. See also Richard Gauvain, "Egyptian Sufism under the Hammer: A Preliminary

Investigation into the Anti-Sufi Polemics of 'Abd al-Rahman al-Wakil (1913–1970)," in *Sufis and Salafis in the Contemporary Age*, ed. Lloyd Ridgeon (London: Bloomsbury, 2015).

31. Bruce Lawrence, *Who Is Allah?* (Chapel Hill: North Carolina University Press, 2015), 67.

32. William Chittick, *In Search of the Lost Heart: Explorations in Islamic Thought* (Albany: SUNY Press, 2012), 23.

33. This push to cultivate "ethics" in everyday interpersonal life may be compared with a turn within the anthropology of ethics toward "ordinary ethics." See Michael Lambek, ed., *Ordinary Ethics: Anthropology, Language, and Action.* (New York: Fordham Press, 2010); Veena Das, "Ordinary Ethics," in *A Companion to Moral Anthropology*, ed. Didier Fassin (Oxford: Wiley-Blackwell, 2012), 133–49. For a recent edited volume that situates this turn within a broad range of contemporary anthropological approaches to ethics, see James Laidlaw, ed., *The Cambridge Handbook for the Anthropology of Ethics* (Cambridge: Cambridge University Press, 2023).

34. Talal Asad, *Genealogies of Religion: Discipline and Reasons of Power in Christianity and Islam* (Baltimore: Johns Hopkins University Press, 1993).

35. Gregory Starrett, *Putting Islam to Work: Education, Politics, and Religious Transformation in Egypt* (Berkeley: University of California Press, 1998), 151.

36. While Western scholars have reached a critical consensus that to ascribe to Islamic rituals symbolic meaning is necessarily to distort pious Muslims' own concern with correct practice, medieval Islamic theologians engaged in lively dispute about whether prescribed rituals had "deeper" and "wider" significance or whether their punctilious performance was all that was called for by God. See Marion Katz, "The Study of Islamic Ritual and the Meaning of Wudu'," *Der Islam* 82, no. 1 (2005): 106–45. Drawing a neat conceptual secular-religious divide between a stress on ritual as apt performance versus as a conventional form with deeper significance obscures these theological disagreements.

37. Gauvain, *Salafi Ritual Purity*, 128.

38. Episode 46, *Khada'ukka fa-Qalu*, Iqraa, November 2009.

39. John Walbridge, "The Islamic Art of Asking Questions: 'Ilm al-Ikhtilaf," *Islamic Studies* 41, no. 1 (2002): 75. In a later work, Walbridge shows how the medieval institutionalization of the acceptability of contending truths went beyond jurisprudence and included variant readings of the Qur'an, multiple canonical collections of hadiths, and diverse philosophical reflections on the nature of reality. John Walbridge, *God and Logic in Islam: The Caliphate of Reason* (Cambridge: Cambridge University Press, 2011).

40. Paul Heck, *Skepticism in Classical Islam: Moments of Confusion* (New York: Routledge Press, 2013); Mohammad Fadel, "The True, the Good and The Reasonable: The Theological and Ethical Roots of Public Reason in Islamic Law," *Canadian Journal of Law and Jurisprudence* 21, no. 1 (2008): 5–69.

41. Robert Gleave, *Islam and Literalism: Literal Meaning and Interpretation in Islamic Legal Theory* (Edinburgh: Edinburgh University Press, 2012), 194.

42. Emad Hamdeh, "Qur'an and Sunna or the 'Madhhabs'? A Salafi Polemic against Islamic Legal Tradition," *Islamic Law and Society* 24, no. 3 (2017): 219, 226.

43. Bernard Haykel has argued that a great deal of contemporary Salafism's global appeal lies in its insistence that ordinary Muslims, assuming a proper doctrinal formation, can directly apprehend the Qur'anic truth through their own reading. Bernard Haykel, "On the Nature of Salafi Thought and Action," in *Global Salafism: Islam's New Religious Movement*, ed. Rojel Meijer (Oxford: Oxford University Press, 2013). The Salafi critique of the madhab tradition for erecting an unnecessary barrier between believers and God's word is radically inclusive in the sense that it subverts the hierarchies historically regulating the production of religious knowledge. Jonathan Brown points out that while this is a common rhetorical stance in polemics against the authority of the classical madhab system, it is not necessarily followed in practice. Salafis constantly defer to what they recognize as scholarly authorities, "the people of knowledge" (*ahl al-'ilm*), and discourage ordinary Muslims from attempting to extract correct meaning from the text themselves. Jonathan Brown, "Is Islam Easy to Understand or Not? Salafis, The Democratization of Interpretation, and the Need for the Ulama," *Journal of Islamic Studies* 26, no. 2 (2015).

44. Simon Coleman, "When Silence Isn't Golden: Charismatic Speech and the Limits of Literalism," in *The Limits of Meaning: Case Studies in the Anthropology of Christianity*, ed. Matthew Engelke and Matt Tomlinson (New York: Berghahn, 2006), 39–63; Vincent Crapanzano, *Serving the Word: Literalism in America from Pulpit to the Bench* (New York: New Press, 2000).

45. Recently, some scholars have analyzed this insistence on Qur'anic univocality and the singularity of truth as symptomatic of Salafism's tacit absorption of the secular modernist epistemologies it so vehemently disavows. In contrast, premodern Islam was more pluralistic and less exclusivist, characterized by what Thomas Bauer calls a "culture of ambiguity." Thomas Bauer, *A Culture of Ambiguity: An Alternative History of Islam*, trans. Hinrich Biesterfeldt and Tricia Tunstall (New York: Columbia University Press, 2021); see also Azmi Bishara, *On Salafism: Concepts and Contexts* (Stanford, CA: Stanford University Press, 2022). This historical analysis agrees with the internal evaluations of self-described *wasati* scholars, who have long characterized the Salafi rejection of interpretive pluralism and its institutionalization in the

madhab system as a radical rupture in Islamic theological history. At the same time, other scholarship on premodern Islam illustrates that the exclusivist intolerance of competing interpretations is not peculiar to modern Salafism—such intolerance and its perceived detrimental effects on the Muslim community in the twelfth century preoccupied al-Ghazali, who sought to "define the boundaries within which competing theologies can coexist in mutual recognition of each other, i.e., as 'orthodox.'" Sherman Jackson, *On the Boundaries of Theological Tolerance in Islam* (Oxford: Oxford University Press, 2002), 5.

46. Noah Salomon, "The Salafi Critique of Islamism: Difference and the Problem of Islamic Political Action in Contemporary Sudan," in *Global Salafism: Islam's New Religious Movement*, ed. Rojel Meijer (Oxford: Oxford University Press, 2013), 156.

47. At times, however, producers made what in hindsight were spectacularly wrong calls. In 2011, Iqraa International, a sister channel to Iqraa, was launched by the Cairo branch with ambitions to eventually broadcast in seven languages. During my fieldwork, the new channel was mostly relying on dubbing and subtitling into English and French selections from the original Iqraa's Arabic programs, but had debuted a limited amount of original programming in English. I had attended a few of the brainstorming sessions leading up to the channel's launch and, as with the original Iqraa, the different English-speaking preachers proposed to host programs that reflected the gamut of orientations existing within Muslim communities in the West, from Sufism to Islamism to Salafism. From the latter, Iqraa International hired an Australian preacher named Musa Cerantonio who was starting to make a name for himself on social media and the global Salafi lecture circuit. Iqraa International's team had judged him to be moderate, but this began to change as Cerantonio started preaching the necessity of establishing a single caliphate for the Muslim community even by force. In 2012, the situation reached a climax as Cerantonio, after multiple attempts by producers to get him to tone it down, was literally chased out of the building. Cerantonio would go on to international infamy as a stalwart supporter of the caliphate declared in Iraq and Syria by the violent militant group the Islamic State. See Graeme Wood, *The Way of the Strangers: Encounters with the Islamic State* (New York: Random House, 2017), 88–139.

48. Talal Asad, *The Idea of an Anthropology of Islam*, Occasional Paper Series (Washington, DC: Center for Contemporary Arab Studies, Georgetown University, 1986), 16.

49. Kahlway was an outspoken advocate for the right of Muslim women to initiate divorce and Saleh often discussed her struggle to get al-Azhar to recognize the right of qualified women scholars like herself to issue fatwas. Sharon Otterman, "Fatwas and Feminism: Women, Religious Authority, and Islamic TV," *Arab Media*

and Society, June 1, 2006, https://www.arabmediasociety.com/fatwas-and-feminism-women-religious-authority-and-islamic-tv/. Nevertheless, this pioneering generation of female Islamic television preachers explicitly renounced "feminism" as a Western import. As Ellen McLarney has shown, their sensibility reflects "less a feminist theology for Islam than a gendered one." Ellen McLarney, *Soft Force: Women in Egypt's Islamic Awakening* (Princeton, NJ: Princeton University Press, 2015), 6.

50. Tatiana Rabinovich, "Mediated Piety in Contemporary Syria: Women, Islam, and Television," *Feminist Media Studies* 13, no. 5 (2013): 819–29.

51. Azza Khattab, "Damned If You Do, Damned If You Don't?, " *Egypt Today*, September 2003.

52. Patricia Kubala, "'You Will (Not) Be Able to Take Your Eyes Off It!': Mass-Mediated Images and Politico-Ethical Reform in the Egyptian Islamic Revival," in *Visual Culture in the Modern Middle East: Rhetoric of the Image*," ed. Christiane Gruber and Sune Haugbolle (Bloomington: Indiana University Press, 2013), 82–100.

53. In an interview on the Salafi channel al-Hikma that aired July 17, 2009, al-Huwayni objected to the appearance of women preachers on television even if they covered their faces, arguing that such mass-mediated public preaching was categorically forbidden to women, who should limit themselves to teaching "their sisters" about religion face-to-face.

54. Raihan Ismail, "Al-Azhar and the Salafis in Egypt: Contestation of Two Traditions," *Muslim World* 113 (Summer 2023): 260–80.

55. Aaron Rock-Singer, "The Salafi Mystique: The Rise of Gender Segregation in 1970s Egypt," *Islamic Law and Society* 23 (2016): 279–305.

56. Zareena Grewal, *Islam Is a Foreign Country: American Muslims and the Global Crisis of Authority* (New York: New York University Press, 2014).

57. Sarah El Masry, "A Polarised Media: Religious Satellite Channels," *Daily News Egypt*, April 13, 2013, 4.

58. Hussein Agrama, *Questioning Secularism: Islam, Sovereignty and the Rule of Law in Modern Egypt* (Chicago: University of Chicago Press, 2012).

59. Hussein Ali Agrama, "Reflections on Secularism, Democracy, and Politics in Egypt," *American Ethnologist* 39, no. 1, (2012): 26–31, https://doi.org/10.1111/j.1548-1425.2011.01342.x.

60. Marc Lynch, "Trashing Transitions: The Role of Arab Media after the Uprisings," in *Revisiting the Arab Uprisings: The Politics of a Revolutionary Moment* (Oxford: Oxford University Press, 2018), 95.

61. While Amr Khaled didn't run for president, at the end of May 2012, as the results for the first round of voting for the presidential election were announced pitting the Muslim Brotherhood candidate Morsi against the Mubarak regime insider

Shafik, Khaled founded a new party that he positioned as an alternative to both "political Islam" and secularism. He resigned as its head—and renounced "political life"—following the July 2013 ouster of Morsi from the presidency.

62. On the Western trope of moderate Islam, Mahmood Mamdani, *Good Muslim, Bad Muslim: America, the Cold War and the Roots of Terror* (New York: Pantheon Books, 2004); Arun Kudnani, *The Muslims Are Coming! Islamophobia, Extremism, and the Domestic War on Terror* (London: Verso, 2014). On Egyptian state media and the production of "good Islam," Lila Abu Lughod, *Dramas of Nationhood: The Politics of Television in Egypt* (Chicago: Chicago University Press 2005).

63. Giovanni Bonacina, *The Wahhabis Seen through European Eyes (1772–1830): Deists and Puritans of Islam* (London: Brill, 2015), 173–176, 31–34.

64. Malika Zeghal, "On the Politics of Sainthood: Resistance and Mimicry in Postcolonial Morocco," *Critical Inquiry* 35, no. 3 (2009): 587–610. This positive framing of Wahhabism was also shared by some anti-colonial Muslim intellectuals; for example, the Egyptian Azhari graduate Hafiz Wahba, who would become a Saudi citizen and diplomatic envoy, argued in 1929 that the religious orientation is "a veritable re-creation of the Enlightenment brought about by the Protestant reformation in Europe." Khaled Abou El Fadl, *Reasoning with God: Reclaiming Shari'ah in the Modern Age* (Lanham, MD: Rowman & Littlefield, 2014), 184. More research is needed on the engagement of Islamic theologians with the emergence of Protestantism in Europe and their own evaluations of different forms of Christianity in comparison to Islam. For example, the influential Islamic reformist and Egypt's former chief mufti Muhammad Abduh lauded the Protestant Reformation, with its emphasis on individual reason over institutional dogma, as a welcome "Islamization" of Christianity, arguing that "the Protestant Reformation was Islamic in its structure and purpose." Suzanne Elizabeth Kassab, *Contemporary Arab Thought: Cultural Critique in Comparative Perspective* (New York: Columbia University Press, 2010), 266.

65. Hisham Aidi, *Race, Empire and the New Muslim Youth Culture* (New York: Pantheon Books, 2014), 239–41.

66. Deepa Kumar, "The Right Kind of 'Islam,'" *Journalism Studies* 19, no. 8 (2018): 1079.

67. Mahmood, "Secularism, Hermeneutics, and Empire," 329.

68. Ibid., 344.

69. Bauer, *A Culture of Ambiguity*, 76.

70. In Hamid Redissi, "The Refutations of Wahhabism in Arabic Sources, 1745–1932," *Kingdom without Borders: Saudi Political, Religious and Media Frontiers*, ed. Madawi Al-Rasheed (New York: Columbia University Press, 2008), 161.

71. Madawi Al-Rasheed, *Contesting the Saudi State: Islamic Voices from a New Generation* (New York: University of Cambridge Press, 2006). These debates among Muslims can also take on a foreign policy cast. For example, James Hoesterey traces the efforts of Indonesian diplomats and religious scholars to promote the country as the locus of "moderate Islam" not merely in the West but in the Middle East as well. These efforts are often self-consciously critical of the Salafi Wahhabi tradition historically promoted by Saudi Arabia across the Muslim world. James Hoesterey, "Saints, Scholars, and Diplomats: Religious Statecraft and the Problem of 'Moderate Islam' in Indonesia," in *Religious Pluralism in Indonesia* (Ithaca, NY: Cornell University Press, 2021), 185–206. For its part, even as it becomes more politically repressive, Saudi Arabia has over the past decade publicly pivoted to an explicit embrace of "moderate Islam" that, in contravention of long-standing Wahhabi strictures, permits female driving, relaxes gendered dress codes, and allows music concerts and movie festivals.

72. Bettina Gräf, "The Concept of *wasatiyya* in the Work of Yusuf al-Qaradawi," in *Global Mufti: The Phenomenon of Yusuf al-Qaradawi*, ed. Bettina Gräf and Jakob Skovgaard-Petersen (New York: Columbia University Press, 2009).

73. Ron Shaham, "The Rhetoric of Legal Disputation: Neo-Ahl al-Hadith vs. Yusuf al-Qaradawi," *Islamic Law and Society* 22 (2015): 114–41.

74. Raymond William Baker, *Islam without Fear: Egypt and the New Islamists* (Cambridge, MA: Harvard University Press, 2009). See also Raymond William Baker, *One Islam, Many Muslim Worlds: Spirituality, Identity, and Resistance across Islamic Lands* (New York: Oxford University Press, 2015).

75. Carrie Wickham, *The Muslim Brotherhood: Evolution of an Islamist Movement* (Princeton, NJ: Princeton University Press, 2015), 83. Ahead of parliamentary elections in 2013, al-Wasat tried to forge a "political, electoral and cultural" alliance between secular and Islamically oriented political parties to "restore national cohesion away from any polarization." "Wasat Party Calls for Islamist Electoral Alliance," *Al-Ahram Gate*, January 15, 2013.

76. Manar Shorbagy, "The Egyptian Movement for Change—Kefaya: Redefining Politics in Egypt," *Public Culture* 19, no. 1 (2007): 195. In *Egypt's Long Revolution*, Maha Abdelrahman traces how the writings of the intellectuals, journalists, and lawyers associated with the New Islamists and later Kefaya on citizenship, equality, and pluralism were significant resources for democracy advocates in the two decades leading up to the 2011 revolution. Maha Abdelrahman, *Egypt's Long Revolution: Protest Movements and Uprisings* (London: Routledge, 2014), https://doi.org/10.4324/9781315762265. Still, while acknowledging that Kefaya's "cross-ideological dissenting posture" helped model a new kind of politics, Mona El-Ghobashy cautions

against reading its protests as a dress rehearsal for Tahrir given the Mubarak regime's success in "evict[ing] the possibility of revolution from thought and deed." Mona El-Ghobashy, *Bread and Freedom: Egypt's Revolutionary Situation* (Stanford, CA: Stanford University Press, 2021), 76, 82.

77. Talal Asad, "Thinking about Religion, Belief, and Politics," in *The Cambridge Companion to Religious Studies,* ed. Robert Orsi (Cambridge, UK: Cambridge University Press, 2011), 55–56.

Chapter 4

1. Samuel Lee Harris, "Development through Faith: The Ma'adi Life Makers and the Islamic Entrepreneurial Subject" (master's thesis, Georgetown University, April 28, 2008).

2. Mona Atia, *Building a House in Heaven: Pious Neoliberalism and Islamic Charity in Egypt* (Minneapolis: University of Minnesota Press, 2013), 155. Similarly, Samuli Schielke argues that Amr Khaled is a "neoliberal piety counselor" and that the Islamic revivalist emphasis on "self-discipline shows a striking resonance with the neoliberal shift of governance from public responsibility to self-responsibility and self-care." Samuli Schielke, *Egypt in the Future Tense: Hope, Frustration, and Ambivalence before and after 2011* (Bloomington: Indiana University Press, 2015): 68, 79.

3. See for example Micki McGee, *Self-Help, Inc.: Makeover Culture in American Life.* (Oxford: Oxford University Press, 2005).

4. James Bourk Hoesterey, *Rebranding Islam: Piety, Prosperity, and a Self-Help Guru* (Stanford, CA: Stanford University Press, 2016), 22. Neoliberalism's meaning is unsettled, whether among critical scholars or devoted policy advocates, but most agree that at minimum it entails an ideological conviction that free market economies are superior to state-controlled ones and that the state has little responsibility of care for the quality of life of its citizens. On its unsettled ethnographic meaning, see Stephen Collier, "Neoliberalism as Big Levathian, Or . . . ? A Response to Wacquant and Hilgers," *Social Anthropology* 20, no. 2 (2012): 186–95. See also Tejaswini Ganti, "Neoliberalism," *Annual Review of Anthropology* 43, 2014: 89–104.

5. Andrew March, *The Caliphate of Man: Popular Sovereignty in Modern Islamic Thought* (Cambridge, MA: Harvard University Press, 2019).

6. Some anthropologists have criticized such interpretations for appropriating in a pious register the anthropocentric biases of modern Western epistemologies (see, for example, Anand Taneja, "Saintly Animals: The Shifting Moral and Ecological Landscapes of North India," *Comparative Studies of South Asia, Africa and the Middle East* 35, no. 2 (2015): 204–21. Yet the notion of human beings as God's caliphs informed the programmatic calls by Muslim scholars in the Western academy

for "Islamic anthropology" as a liberatory alternative to secular anthropology. For a theological elaboration, see Merryl Wyn Davies, *Knowing One Another: Shaping Islamic Anthropology* (London: Mansell, 1988), 88–98. For a discussion of *khalifa* in relation to this quest for an "Islamic anthropology," see Yasmin Moll, "Can There Be a Godly Ethnography? Islamic Anthropology, Epistemic Decolonization and the Ethnographic Stance," *American Anthropologist* 125, no. 4 (2023): 746–60.

7. William C. Chittick, "Worship," in *The Cambridge Companion to Classical Islamic Theology*, ed. Tim Winter (New York: Cambridge University Press, 2008), 218–36.

8. Abdel Haleem's translation is "Allah would never change a people's state of favour until they change their own state of faith." I have used the more common translation of "condition."

9. Samira Haj, *Reconfiguring Islamic Tradition: Reform, Rationality and Modernity* (Stanford, CA: Stanford University Press, 2009), 119.

10. Roxanne L. Euben, *Enemy in the Mirror: Islamic Fundamentalism and the Limits of Modern Rationalism* (Princeton, NJ: Princeton University Press, 1999).

11. Episode 1 of *Ommar al-Ard*, Iqraa, January 2012.

12. Kimberly Hart, *And Then We Work for God: Rural Sunni Islam in Western Turkey* (Stanford, CA: Stanford University Press, 2013); Jeanette Selma Jouili, *Pious Practice and Secular Constraints: Women in the Islamic Revival in Europe* (Stanford, CA: Stanford University Press, 2015), 34.

13. Jessica Winegar, "A Civilized Revolution: Aesthetics and Political Action in Egypt," *American Ethnologist* 43, no. 4 (2016). Winegar shows how such political actions encoded middle-class aesthetics of "order" and "civilization." Such aesthetics were naturalized by my interlocutors as part of a theological ontology through the Prophetic saying "God is Beautiful and loves beauty." This hadith is often cited by Muslim artists as broadly inspirational and legitimizing their endeavors as "Islamic" in the face of Salafi-oriented criticisms of pictorial representation as religiously forbidden. See Kenneth George, *Picturing Islam: Art and Ethics in a Muslim Lifeworld* (Sussex, UK: John Wiley and Sons, 2010).

14. David Graeber, *Possibilities: Essays on Hierarchy, Rebellion, and Desire* (Oakland, CA: AK Press, 2007); Stine Krøijer, *Figurations of the Future: Forms and Temporalities of Left Radical Politics in Northern Europe* (New York: Bergahn, 2020).

15. Carrie Wickham, *Mobilizing Islam: Religion, Activism, and Political Change in Egypt* (New York: Columbia University Press, 2002), 120.

16. On the political in the quotidian, Khaled Fahmy, "Opening Politics' Black Box: Reflections on the Past, Present and Future of Egypt's Revolution," in *Shifting Sands: The Unravelling of the Old Order in the Middle East*, ed. Raja Shehadah (London:

Profile Books, 2015), 81. On the DIY spirit, Jack Schenker, "Egypt's Uprising Brings DIY Spirit out on to the Streets, " *Guardian,* May 19, 2011, https://www.theguardian.com/world/2011/may/19/egypts-uprising-diy-art-cairo-streets.

17. See for example Ahmed Abu Haiba, "Islamic Media and the Shaping of an Arab Identity," *Perspectives* 3, no. 2 (February 2011). This assessment may be shared by scholars. While not mentioning New Preaching programs like *Lifemakers* specifically, Mohammed Bamyeh, a political sociologist of Egypt, notes the fact that "mutual help and solidarity networks could be easily mobilized in the direction of revolutionary activity at the right moment was abundantly clear in 2011, as millions of previously non-political citizens, who had never joined a demonstration before, found it second nature to trust each other in the novel task of becoming revolutionary subjects." Mohammed Bamyeh, "The Rise and Fall of Postcolonial Charisma," *Arab Studies Quarterly* 45, no. 1 (2023): 71.

18. Nicole Aschoff, *The New Prophets of Capital* (London: Verso, 2015), 14.

19. Stephen Covey, *The Seven Habits of Highly Successful People* (New York: Simon and Schuster, 1989), 16.

20. Ibid., 18.

21. Malcolm Gladwell, *The Tipping Point: How Little Things Can Make a Big Difference* (New York: Little, Brown, 2000), 19.

22. Stephen Covey, *The Divine Center: Why We Need a Life Centered on God and Christ and How We Attain It* (Salt Lake City: Deseret Book Company, 1982), 240.

23. As Sandra Dolby argues in her history of US self-help literature, the genre's "notion of the 'obligated self' encourages a kind of introspection and programmatic effort reminiscent of traditional Christian regimens," as does the sense that "individuals must have their own house in order before they can sally forth to serve the community." Sandra Dolby, *Self-Help Books: Why Americans Keep Reading Them* (Urbana: University of Illinois Press, 2005), 21–22.

24. Hoesterey, *Rebranding Islam.*

25. R. J. Morris, "Samuel Smiles and the Genesis of Self-Help; The Retreat to a Petit Bourgeois Utopia," *Historical Journal* 24, no. 1 (1981): 89–109.

26. Timothy Mitchell, *Colonising Egypt,* Cambridge Middle East Library (Cambridge: Cambridge University Press, 1988), 109.

27. Arthur Zarate, "The American Sufis: Self-Help, Sufism, and Metaphysical Religion in Postcolonial Egypt," *Comparative Studies in Society and History* 61, no. 4 (2019): 864. Zarate argues that al-Ghazali saw in American self-help a powerful critique of the top-down social engineering of Nasser's state socialism. Like the leaders of other leftist revolutions [Webb Keane, *Ethical Life: Its Natural and Social Histories* (Princeton, NJ: Princeton University Press, 2016): 216–40], Nasser held up ethical self-fashioning as

key to revolutionary success. In a memorable speech a few years after toppling the colonial-backed monarchy, Nasser explained that "building the new Egypt relies on the adequate development of the latent potentialities with which the Creator has endowed this raw material [of the human].... Building factories is easy, building hospitals and schools is possible but building a nation of men is a hard and difficult task." In Eva Garzouzi, *Old Ills and New Remedies in Egypt* (Cairo: Dar Al Maaref, 1957), 6. According to Zarate, al-Ghazali was concerned that Nasser's socialist revolution had become too authoritarian in its quest for total transformation, moving beyond the economic and political spheres to take aim at people's everyday habits and ethics, the privileged domains of Islamic theologians and preachers such as himself.

28. Amira Mittermaier, *Giving to God: Islamic Charity in Revolutionary Times* (Berkeley: University of California Press, 2019), 76.

29. Dietrich Jung, Marie Petersen, and Sara Sparre, *Politics of Modern Muslim Subjectivities: Islam, Youth, and Social Activism in the Middle East* (Palgrave Macmillan, 2014).

30. Video uploaded on YouTube November 16, 2012. https://www.youtube.com/watch?v=Waa4e6sEfRc.

31. Arjun Appadurai, "Deep Democracy: Urban Governmentality and the Horizon of Politics," *Public Culture* 14, no. 1 (2002): 21–47.

32. Janine Clark, *Islam, Charity, and Activism: Middle-Class Networks and Social Welfare in Egypt, Jordan, and Yemen* (Bloomington: Indiana University Press, 2004).

33. For a compelling ethnography of poor Egyptians' struggles to access water, see Tessa Farmer, *Well Connected: Everyday Water Practices in Egypt* (Baltimore, MD: Johns Hopkins University Press, 2023).

34. Joel Beinin and Marie Duboc, "Workers' Social Movement on the Margin of the Global Neoliberal Order, Egypt 2004–2012," in *Social Movements, Mobilization, and Contestation in the Middle East and North Africa*, 2nd ed., ed. Joel Beinin and Frédéric Vairel (Stanford, CA: Stanford University Press, 2013), 250. Also see Joel Beinin, "Civil Society, NGOs, and Egypt's 2011 Popular Uprising," *South Atlantic Quarterly* 113, no. 2, 2014: 396–406.

35. Schielke, *Egypt in the Future Tense*, 116.

36. Vickie Langohr, "Too Much Civil Society, Too Little Politics: The Case of Egypt and the Arab Liberalizers," *Comparative Politics* 36, no. 2 (January 2004): 181–204. For a comprehensive critical discussion of this literature and an alternative view of NGOs' "technomoral politics," ethnographically focused on India, see Erica Bornstein and Aradhana Sharma, "The Righteous and the Rightful: The Technomoral Politics of NGOs, Social Movements, and the State in India," *American Ethnologist* 43, no. 1 (February 2016): 76–90.

37. Amira Mittermaier, "Trading with God: Islam, Calculation, Excess," in *A Companion to the Anthropology of Religion*, ed. Michael Lambek and Janice Boddy (John Wiley and Sons, 2013), 275.

38. Andrea Muehlebach proposes something similar in relation to her research on socialist and Catholic charitable practices in Italy. Volunteerism allows her interlocutors to form a "moral neoliberal" of care and community that sharply contrasts with the instrumental relationality of market neoliberalism, even as the withdrawal of state welfare under the latter is what makes their volunteer efforts so valuable in the first place. She argues that the simultaneity of critique and complicity at the heart of volunteerism invites attention to neoliberalism as a "force that can contain its own negation." Andrea Muehlebach, *The Moral Neoliberal: Welfare and Citizenship in Italy* (Chicago: University of Chicago Press, 2012), 25.

39. Miriam Cooke, "Zaynab Al-Ghazali: Saint or Subversive?," *Die Welt des Islams* 34, no. 1 (1994): 1–20.

40. Wendy Brown, "Resisting Left Melancholia," *Boundary* 2, 1999.

41. Christina Scharff, "The Psychic Life of Neoliberalism: Mapping the Contours of Entrepreneurial Subjectivity," *Theory, Culture and Society* 33, no. 6 (2016): 107–22.

42. Adel Abdel Ghafar, "Educated but Unemployed: The Challenges Facing Egyptian Youth" (Doha, Qatar: Foreign Policy at Brookings, 2016), https://www.brookings.edu/wp-content/uploads/2016/07/en_youth_in_egypt.pdf.

43. Jeffrey T. Kenney, "Selling Success, Nurturing the Self: Self-Help Literature, Capitalist Values, and the Sacralization of Subjective Life in Egypt," *International Journal of Middle East Studies* 47, no. 4 (2015): 668–669, 676, 673–674, https://doi.org/10.1017/S0020743815000926.

44. Sara Ahmed, "Selfcare as Warfare," *Feminist Killjoys* (research blog), August 25, 2014, https://feministkilljoys.com/2014/08/25/selfcare-as-warfare/.

45. Lauren Berlant, *Cruel Optimism* (Durham, NC: Duke University Press, 2011).

46. Ahmed, "Selfcare as Warfare."

47. This includes within contexts in which neoliberalism is ideologically embraced, such as in the United States. Writing on the "microvision of justice" underlying efforts to meet the immediate needs of marginalized communities, Ruha Benjamin argues that "it may tempting to dismiss these efforts as small, fleeting, and inconsequential, as we're still taught to only appreciate that which is big and grand, official, and codified." Ruha Benjamin, *Viral Justice: How to Grow the World We Want* (Princeton, NJ: Princeton University Press, 2022), 15–16.

Chapter 5

1. Many protesters chanted, "The people and the army are one hand" during the uprising. For a discussion of the revolutionary sense that the military had a moral obligation to overthrow the regime on behalf of "the people," see Noah Feldman, *The Arab Winter: A Tragedy* (Princeton, NJ: Princeton University Press, 2021). Khaled was interviewed by Mahmoud Sa'ad, one of the first TV anchors to resign from state television during the uprising.

2. Amira Mittermaier, "Invisible Armies: Reflections on Egyptian Dreams of War," *Comparative Studies in Society and History* 54, no. 2 (2012): 392–417.

3. Laure Guirguis, *Copts and the Security State: Violence, Coercion and Sectarianism in Modern Egypt* (Stanford, CA: Stanford University Press, 2017), 170.

4. Nadine Sika, "Dynamics of a Stagnant Religious Discourse and the Rise of New Secular Movements in Egypt," in *Arab Spring in Egypt: Revolution and Beyond*, ed. Bahgat Korany and Rabab El-Mahdi (Cairo: American University in Cairo Press, 2012).

5. Slavoj Zizek, "For Egypt, This Is the Miracle of Tahrir Square," *Guardian*, February 10, 2011, https://www.theguardian.com/global/2011/feb/10/egypt-miracle-tahrir-square.

6. Joas Wagemakers, "The Enduring Legacy of the Second Saudi State: Quietist and Radical Wahhabi Contestations of *al-Wala' Wa-l-Bara'*," *International Journal of Middle East Studies* 44, no. 1 (2012): 93–110, https://doi.org/10.1017/S0020743811001267.

7. Noah Salomon, "The Salafi Critique of Islamism: Difference and the Problem of Islamic Political Action in Contemporary Sudan," in *Global Salafism: Islam's New Religious Movement*, ed. Rojel Meijer (Oxford: Oxford University Press, 2013). Notably, the revolutionary sharing of public space had also been grounds for the Salafi criticism of Egypt's 1919 uprising against the British colonial occupation. While popularly celebrated for the participation of Egyptians from all walks of life, whether men or women, Muslims or Christians, the prominent turn-of-the-century Salafi leader Hamid al-Fiqi had criticized the revolutionary co-presence of men and women as inevitably leading to "'brazenness' (*tabarruj*), a quintessentially non-Muslim (but very Western) quality" and the co-presence of Muslims and Christians as violating the doctrinal mandate of *bara'* that Muslims "keep a distance from Christians." Richard Gauvain, "Nothing Has Changed/Everything Has Changed: Salafi Da'wa in Egypt from Rashid Rida to the 'Arab Spring,'" in *Culture of Da'wa: Preaching in the Modern World*, ed. Itzchak Weismann and Jamil Malik (Salt Lake City: University of Utah Press, 2020), 92.

8. Hussein Agrama, *Questioning Secularism: Islam, Sovereignty and the Rule of Law in Modern Egypt* (Chicago: University of Chicago Press, 2012), 27.

9. Charles Hirschkind, "Beyond Secular and Religious: An Intellectual Genealogy of Tahrir Square," *American Anthropologist* 39, no. 1 (2012): 50, https://doi.org/10.1111/j.1548-1425.2011.01346.x.

10. Pamela Klassen and Courtney Bender, "Introduction: Habits of Pluralism," in *After Pluralism: Reimagining Religious Engagement*, ed. Pamela Klassen and Courtney Bender (New York: Columbia University Press, 2010), 8, 14, 17.

11. Raja Abillama, "'The Love That Muslims Have for Mary': Secularism and Christian-Muslim Coexistence in Lebanon," *Comparative Studies of South Asia, Africa and the Middle East* 42, no. 1 (2022): 56.

12. Such theological contestations tend to be overlooked within the broader scholarship on coexistence in the region. Arguing that "every history of sectarianism is also a history of coexistence," Ussama Makdisi shows how both the conventional Western narrative that religious violence is inherent to the region and the Arab counternarrative that inter-religious harmony was the norm until the advent of European colonialism simplify the histories of struggle for political inclusion in the region. His focus, however, is on secular nationalist attempts to develop an "ecumenical frame" inclusive of the region's religious diversity. Ussama Makdisi, *The Age of Coexistence: The Ecumenical Frame and the Making of the Modern Arab World* (Berkeley: University of California Press, 2019), 1.

13. Yusuf rose to worldwide fame in 2003 with his music video *Al-Muʿulim* [*The Teacher*] about the Prophet Muhammad, marking for many the creation of the first "Islamic music video." Christian Pond, "The Appeal of Sami Yusuf and the Search for Islamic Authenticity," *Arab Media and Society*, June 1, 2006, https://www.arabmediasociety.com/the-appeal-of-sami-yusuf-and-the-search-for-islamic-authenticity/.

14. Interview of Sami Yusuf with Lamees El-Hadidy on *Huna al-ʿAsima*, CBC channel, aired February 28, 2012.

15. Mariz Tadros, "Sectarianism and Its Discontents in Post-Mubarak Egypt," *Middle East Report*, no. 259 (Summer 2011): 26–31, https://merip.org/2011/06/sectarianism-and-its-discontents-in-post-mubarak-egypt/.

16. For elaboration, see Khalid's doctoral thesis on the "concept of coexistence." Amr Khalid, "Aspects of Islam and Social Coexistence: The Case of Britain" (University of Wales Trinity Saint David, 2010), https://repository.uwtsd.ac.uk/id/eprint/1979/.

17. For an example of a Salafi refutation of the idea of "accepting the other," see https://salafcenter.org/273/.

18. Various clips of this interview were available on YouTube during my fieldwork; the one I quote from here was a nine-minute one titled "The Truth of Tareq al-Suwaidan [according to] Wagdy Ghoneim."

19. Episode 23, *Daʻwa li-l-Taʻayush*, Resala, October 2007.

20. Wendy Brown, *Regulating Aversion: Tolerance in the Age of Identity and Empire* (Princeton, NJ: Princeton University Press, 2008): 25–47. See Theresa Bejan for an examination of the Christian theological history of secular concepts of tolerance and its close cousin civility. She shows how these liberal mainstays were forged within early modern Christian experiences of sectarianism between Protestants and Catholics as well as evangelical competition among the former. Theresa Bejan, *Mere Civility: Disagreement and the Limits of Toleration* (Cambridge, MA: Harvard University Press, 2017).

21. The other advertised speakers were Amr Hamzawy, liberal professor turned parliamentarian; Yusri Foda, the investigative television journalist whose coverage of the Tahrir protests and on-screen grilling of government officials earned him a loyal viewership among revolutionaries; Ahmed Harrara, a protester who lost both of his eyes to police snipers; Mohamed Sobhy, an actor known for his family-friendly comedies who was leading with Amr Khaled and Wael Ghonim a project investing in Cairo's "informal slums" (*ʻashwaiʼyat*); Mustafa al-Nagger, an ex–Muslim Brotherhood member and founder of the Al-Adl party, which aimed to forge a "third way" between secularism and Islamism; and Abdul Rahman Yusuf, a renowned poet who was also the somewhat estranged son of the Muslim Brotherhood–leaning theologian Yusuf al-Qaradawi.

22. Febe Armanios, "Remembering Abouna Makary, Coptic Priest Loved by Egypt's Evangelicals," *Christianity Today*, February 4, 2022.

23. This woman became known in international media as the "the blue-bra girl" and locally as "the dragged girl." For a trenchant analysis, see Sherine Hafez, "Bodies That Protest: The Girl in the Blue Bra, Sexuality, and State Violence in Revolutionary Egypt," *Signs: Journal of Women in Culture and Society* 40, no. 1 (Autumn 2014), https://doi.org/10.1086/676977.

24. The New Preachers' emphasis on loving friendship with non-Muslims can be located within a broader Ashʻari reconsideration of "the way in which thicker relationships of moral concern with non-Muslims might be part of a comprehensive conception of an Islamic good life." Andrew F. March, "Sources of Moral Obligation to Non-Muslims in the 'Jurisprudence of Muslim Minorities' (*Fiqh al-Aqalliyyat*) Discourse," *Islamic Law and Society* 16, no. 1 (2009): 46.

25. Masoud had coauthored a *New York Times* editorial three weeks earlier calling for civilian rule, https://www.nytimes.com/2012/01/05/opinion/sunday/tahrir-squares-gains-threatened-by-egypts-interim-rulers.html.

26. Angie Heo, *The Political Lives of Saints: Christian-Muslim Mediation in Egypt* (Berkeley: University of California Press, 2018), 204.

27. Guirguis, *Copts and the Security State*.

28. Saba Mahmood, *Religious Difference in a Secular Age: A Minority Report* (Princeton, NJ.: Princeton University Press, 2016), 15.

29. Elizabeth Monier, "The 'Mediation' of Muslim-Christian Relations in Egypt: The Strategies and Discourses of the Official Egyptian Press during Mubarak's Presidency," *Islam and Christian-Muslim Relations* 23, no. 1 (2012): 31–44.

30. Tadros, "Sectarianism and Its Discontents in Post-Mubarak Egypt."

31. For an account of Shubra Salafi discourses about the "purification" of the neighborhood from religious others, see Richard Gauvain, *Salafi Ritual Purity: In the Presence of God* (New York: Routledge, 2013). Reacting against an Islamic Revival they experienced as adversarial, church leaders in Shubra also strove to "protect" Coptic youth "from culturally and socially mixing with Muslims." See Mina Ibrahim, "The Invisible Life-Worlds of a Coptic Christian," *Middle East—Topics & Arguments* 13 (2019): 90.

32. Muhammad Abd al-Maqsud, "Loving Infidels from Jews and Christians is a Cause of the Corruption of Hearts" [in Arabic], 2011, https://ar.islamway.net/lesson/106070/.

33. Egyptian Copts who watched this program appreciated Khaled's message of respect and inclusion. Some even felt that the program reflected a Christian influence with its stress on God's love. Personal communication with Febe Armanios, April 21, 2021.

34. Documents gleaned from Cairo's state security headquarters following its storming in March 2011 by protesters appear to show that leading Salafi figures had direct relations with the security agency. Samuli Schielke, "State Security Leaks, and a Theory of Anxiety," *A Book of Unfinished Theories* (blog), March 7, 2011, https://samuliegypt.blogspot.com/2011/03/state-security-leaks-and-theory-of.html. This does not mean of course that they were prescriptively complicit in its machinations.

35. Youshaa Patel, "'Whoever Imitates a People Becomes One of Them': A Hadith and Its Interpreters," *Islamic Law and Society*, no. 25 (2018): 359–426.

36. Valentine's Day was problematic for many Salafis because of its link to a Christian saint and because it was associated with romantic love outside the bounds of marriage, but the doctrine of *tashabbuh* extended to everyday practices that were in and of themselves morally neutral. A good example of this is clapping. Salafi scholars argued that Muslims had to develop an alternative way of applauding not because clapping violated Islamic norms but because it was how Westerners customarily showed appreciation. Like other Ash'ari theologians, Abou El Fadl diagnoses such reasoning as a symptom of a broader "stagnation" of Islamic thought in which the "Islamic" is a priori antithetical to the Western. Khaled Abou El Fadl, *Reasoning with God: Reclaiming Shari'ah in the Modern Age* (Lanham, MD: Rowman & Littlefield, 2014), 88.

37. Gauvain, *Salafi Ritual Purity*, 246.

38. This reasoning is analogous to the concept of *maslaha* within Islamic jurisprudence, which centers people's well-being as a vehicle of legal innovation. Felicitas Opwis, *Maslahah and the Purpose of the Law: Islamic Discourse on Legal Change from the 4th/10th to 8th/14th Century* (Leiden: Brill, 2010).

39. For the concept of "promiscuous publics," see Brian Larkin, "Ahmed Deedat and the Form of Islamic Evangelism," *Social Text* 26, no. 3 (2008): 101–21, https://doi.org/10.1215/01642472-2008-006.

40. Emad Hamdeh, "Qur'an and Sunna or the 'Madhhabs'? A Salafi Polemic against Islamic Legal Tradition," *Islamic Law and Society* 24, no. 3 (2017): 236.

41. Ovamir Anjum, "Salafis and Democracy: Doctrine and Context," *Muslim World* 106 no. 3,(2016): 468

42. "Al-radd 'ala Mustafa Hosny" [Refuting Mustafa Hosny], al-Nas channel, aired 2009.

43. Gauvain, *Salafi Ritual Purity*.

44. See Salomon, "The Salafi Critique of Islamism," 152–166.

45. Hamdeh, "Qur'an and Sunna or the 'Madhhabs'?", 288.

46. Carrie Wickham, *The Muslim Brotherhood: Evolution of an Islamist Movement,* (Princeton, NJ: Princeton University Press, 2015), 292.

47. See Stéphane Lacroix ("Sheikhs and Politicians") for an in-depth discussion of these political parties and their relations to the long-standing Salafi *da'wa* movement. For a detailed look at the often erratic relationship between the Salafi *da'wa* movement and the Muslim Brotherhood during the revolution, see Abdelrahman Ayyash, Amr ElAfifi, and Noha Ezzat, *Broken Bonds: The Existential Crisis of Egypt's Muslim Brotherhood, 2013–22* (New Century Foundation, 2023). Still, some ordinary Salafis didn't make much of the historically significant doctrinal and political distinctions between the Islamist group and their own orientation. "The differences aren't that great. We're happy to see the Muslim Brotherhood win," one Salafi supporter told an inquiring anthropologist before the elections. "We can work with them. We want the same thing." Walter Armbrust, *Martyrs and Tricksters: An Ethnography of the Egyptian Revolution* (Princeton, NJ: Princeton University Press, 2019), 150.

48. Paul Sedra, "The Brotherhood's Politics of Fear and Division," *Egypt Independent*, December 23, 2012, https://www.egyptindependent.com/brotherhood-s-politics-fear-and-division/.

49. Rachel Scott, *The Challenge of Political Islam: Non-Muslims and the Egyptian State* (Stanford, CA: Stanford University Press, 2010).

50. Translation in English posted on *mbinenglish* (blog) May 25, 2013, https://mbinenglish.wordpress.com/page/2/. An administrator for this blog explains that it

"features English translations of awful statements of a sectarian, conspiratorial, or bonkers nature that the Muslim Brotherhood (MB) intends for domestic consumption only." Sarah Carr, "On Sheep and Infidels," *Jadaliyya*, July 8, 2013, https://www.jadaliyya.com/Details/29011. For an eyewitness account of the Mokattam clashes, see Ali Abdel Mohsen, "A Day at the Moqattam Clashes," *Egypt Independent*, March 23, 2013, https://egyptindependent.com/day-moqattam-clashes/. It is important to stress that some tried to challenge this sectarianism from within the structures of the Muslim Brotherhood. In 2012, Abu Haiba, Amr Khaled's debut producer, was hired as the director of Misr25, the Muslim Brotherhood's short-lived television channel. I interviewed him in September as he was moving into his new office. He told me that he hoped to take the channel "away from the Muslim Brotherhood even if they remain the owners" and take it in a *wasati* direction. This involved above all making its content less partisan and more inclusive. "This channel is going to be all about accepting the other (*qubul al-akhir*)," he said.

51. As Hisham Hellyer has pointed out, such critiques of the Islamist group by self-identifying pious Muslims were at times characterized as "Islamophobic" by Western scholars supportive of the Muslim Brotherhood, who were quick to read into this critique the fear-based mongering about the dangers of Islamism that animate much of US right-wing discourses about Muslims. H. A. Hellyer, *A Revolution Undone: Egypt's Road beyond Revolt* (London: C. Hurst, 2016), 176–78.

52. The rally convened under the banner of "supporting Syria"—that is, supporting the Sunni rebels fighting against the regime of Bashar al-Asad, who comes from a minority Shia sect—but the chants of the attendees and comments from speakers focused on supporting Morsi. A recording of the rally is available on YouTube: www.youtube.com/watch?v=4gv_is7hO-o; accessed November 23, 2023.

53. Sherine Seikaily and Adel Iskandar, "Between Inaction and Complicity: The Shi'a and the Brotherhood," *Jadaliyya* (blog), June 29, 2013, https://www.jadaliyya.com/Details/28874/Between-Inaction-and-Complicity-The-Shi%E2%80%98a-and-the-Brotherhood.

54. Eric Calderwood, *On Earth or In Poems: The Many Lives of Al-Andalus* (Berkeley: University of California Press, 2023).

55. Ibid., 47.

56. "Egypt: Mass Attacks on Churches," Human Rights Watch, August 21, 2013, https://www.hrw.org/news/2013/08/21/egypt-mass-attacks-churches.

57. Nor were grassroots efforts at finding common ground limited to Egypt. In the 2000s in Saudi Arabia, a coalition of diverse reformists, including former Islamists, liberals, Sunnis, and Shias, sought democratic change within an Islamic context, challenging Wahhabi orthodoxy by insisting that political change was

inextricable from religious transformation. Calling themselves "al-wasatiyyun," or the centrists, they gained notice with a series of petitions and manifestos and even found some royal support. Arguing that democratization did not necessarily entail secular Westernization, they aimed to bridge the gap between Islamists and liberals by stressing mutual understanding and common principles. See Stéphane Lacroix, "Between Islamists and Liberals: Saudi Arabia's New Islamo-Liberal Reformists," *Middle East Journal* 58, no. 3 (Summer 2004): 345–65; and Madawi Al-Rasheed, *Muted Modernists: The Struggle over Divine Politics in Saudi Arabia* (Oxford: Oxford University Press, 2015).

58. Ebrahim Moosa, "Political Theology in the Aftermath of the Arab Spring: Returning to the Ethical," in *African Renaissance and the Afro-Arab Spring*, ed. Charles Villa-Vicencio, Erik Doxtader, and Ebrahim Moosa (Washington, DC: Georgetown University Press, 2015), 104.

59. Feldman, *The Arab Winter*.

60. Charles Hirschkind, *The Ethical Soundscape: Cassette Sermons and Islamic Counterpublics*, Cultures of History (New York: Columbia University Press, 2006), 211.

Epilogue

1. Part of this epilogue appeared in my 2020 essay "Living Through Thick Concepts in Revolutionary Egypt" published in *The International Journal of Middle East Studies* and is adapted here with permission.

The anthropology of silence is a small but evocative field; for an overview, see Ana Dragojlovic and Annemarie Samuels, "Silence," in *The Open Encyclopedia of Anthropology*, ed. Felix Stein (2023), https://doi.org/10.29164/23silence. Silence as a practice of pious discipline and an act of moral protest is found across religious traditions, and is perhaps most associated in the scholarly record with Quakerism thanks to Richard Bauman's classic study. Richard Bauman, *Let Your Words Be Few: Symbolism of Speaking and Silence among Seventeenth-Century Quakers* (New York: Cambridge University Press, 1983).

Ethnographic research has focused on silence as a communicative practice in nondevotional contexts as well. As famously detailed in Basso's work on the Western Apache, for example, whether and when to "give up on words" is related to one's uncertain relationship to others of ambiguous status, such as strangers. Keith Basso, "'To Give Up on Words': Silence in Western Apache Culture," in *Language and Social Context*, ed. Pier Paolo Giglioli (Baltimore: Penguin Books, 1972), 67–86. In Michael Jackson's study of the West African Bambara, silence furthers social solidarity: "Speech disperses the world, say the Bambara; silence restores wholeness. Speech burns the mouth; silence heals it. Speech builds the village; silence regenerates the world." Michael Jackson, "The Prose of Suffering and the Practice of Silence," *Spiritus* 4 (2004): 56. A classic feminist essay on gender and silence in anthropology is that of Susan Gal, "Between Speech and Silence: The Problematics of Research on Language and Gender," in *Toward a New Anthropology of Gender*, ed. M. di-Leonardo (Berkeley: University of California Press, 1990). The linking of the speaking subject to courageous truth, and thus to a claiming of one's own power to speak truth to power, is elaborated by Foucault through the concept of parrhesia, commonly defined as fearless speech. As Harri Englund notes, parrhesia "binds the person to his or her statement and to nothing and no one else." Harri Englund, "The Front Line of Free Speech: Beyond Parrhêsia in Finland's Migrant Debate," *American Ethnologist* 45, no.1 (2018): 102. Such fearless speech is risky, not just for the safety of the speaker, but also for their social bonds with others.

2. H. A. Hellyer, *A Revolution Undone: Egypt's Road beyond Revolt* (London: C. Hurst, 2016), 188–89. The twelfth-century theologian al-Ghazali expounded on the virtue of deliberate silence when the social effects of speaking were mixed, arguing that it is better to avoid harm by remaining silent. It was the way of Hasan, one of the Prophet's grandsons, who had "a forbearing position, designed to avoid making an already bad situation worse for the community at large. It involves engaging in prudent silence in the face of an unjust ruler" (p. 204). This position resembles the position taken by many that summer, not just by the New Preachers but also by Islamic figures across different orientations and groups, from al-Azhar's highest-ranking official, Ahmed el-Tayeb, to famous Salafi preachers such as Muhammad Hassan and Ismail al-Muqaddam. Even the secular revolutionary camp remained largely silent.

3. Lauren Berlant is helpful to think with here. She reframes silence as possessing the potential to "expose the corruption of, or toxic noise within, political speech, as well as to measure the perverse relation between ideals of the political and the practice of politics." "When," she asks, "is public withdrawal a gesture seeking to sustain attachment and attain repair, and what does that have to do with trying to incite conscience in others, forcing them to experience affectively the political condition of being out of control in the middle of managing the world?" Lauren Berlant, *Cruel Optimism* (Durham, NC: Duke University Press, 2011), 229, 231.

4. This has continued for many more years. In 2019, an official complaint was filed by the lawyer Samir Sabry against Hosny accusing him of harboring pro–Muslim Brotherhood sympathies. The evidence was episodes of *Ommar* where he discussed Zaynab al-Ghazali, a dissident Islamist tortured under the Nasser regime. On his program *90 Minutes* on El-Mehwar channel on August 27 that same year, the

secularist television pundit Muhammad al-Baz said that if Hosny wasn't "actually from the Muslim Brotherhood," he needs to have a "clear speech against the terrorist group" as opposed to speaking in "ethical generalities" since his viewers are "those most likely to fall for the Brotherhood." In 2021, al-Baz also accused Moez Masoud of trying "to revive the Muslim Brotherhood." Reda Galal, "Al-Baz: Moez Masoud yusʿayid ʿala al-ihya' al-rabiʿ lil-Ikhwan bil tariqa al-naʿima wal-latifa [Moez Masoud is helping the fourth revival of the Brotherhood with a soft and friendly manner], *Akhbar al-Youm*, July 7, 2021.

5. After the shooting of pro–Muslim Brotherhood protesters on July 27, Moez Masoud, for example, issued a Facebook statement that day on the inviolability of blood "no matter who it belongs to" and calling for a "speedy investigation and bringing the perpetrators to justice." He also argued that "in this time of great passion and anger we have to give each other the benefit of the doubt and not frame the current political struggle as a struggle over Islamic identity; we should act on the ethics of the noble Prophet." In August, however, various versions of a video featuring Amr Khaled went viral on social media under different headings, including "Amr Khaled issues a fatwa authorizing the killing of protesters." Despite such titles, at no point in the thirty-four seconds featuring Khaled does he call for the killing of protesters. In a post on August 25 on his Facebook page, Khaled said that there had been two contradictory rumors circulating in relation to this video: that he supported violence against protesters and that he had founded a movement called "The Brotherhood against Violence." He denied both and explained that the video was made before the "current events" to support Egyptian soldiers defending Sinai. This statement was similar in its denial of a specific endorsement of violence to that of another preacher who appeared in the video, the Azhari scholar and former deputy in the Ministry of Religious Affairs Salem Abdel Galil, who pointed out that some of his family members had been in Rabi'a. Nathan Brown, "The Brotherhood Withdraws into Itself," *POMEPS Briefings: Rethinking Islamist Politics*, February 11, 2014, 19–23. Nevertheless, most commentary on this video persists in claiming that all its participants supported the August 14 massacre in the Muslim Brotherhood encampment.

6. This same exchange—almost verbatim—would happen ten years later on the Saudi channel al-Arabiya, which is generally antagonistic to the Muslim Brotherhood. When on July 31, 2021, the host of the program *Su'al Mubashir* (*Direct Question*) asked Amr Khaled about his relationship to the Muslim Brotherhood and his reaction to June 30, he replied: "I won't accept to talk about politics." When the host persisted, Khaled temporarily went off-camera, asking, "Why do you want to harm me? I don't want to talk about these issues. You are harming me by insisting."

7. In Nareman Amin, "Rebelling against the Ruler: Egyptian Youth and Azhari Scholars' Authority after the 2011 Uprising," *Islamic Law and Society*, 29, no. 3 (2021): 381.

8. Charles Hirschkind, *The Ethical Soundscape: Cassette Sermons and Islamic Counterpublics*, Cultures of History (New York: Columbia University Press, 2006), 47.

9. As Nomi Dave argues, "Silence ... represents not just the denial or lack of voice, but a particular strategy of communication and being in an authoritarian state." She shows how silence for the Guinean musicians she worked with was a mode of existing within a highly fraught and unpredictable political scene. "Silence thus does not simply mean an un-thought void or submission, but rather a deliberate polyvalence, an involute space in which to purposefully avoid being pinned down." Nomi Dave, "The Politics of Silence: Music, Violence and Protest in Guinea," *Ethnomusicology* 58, no. 1 (2014): 2, 19.

Index

Aawar, Ahmed El, 188–90, 249
Abdelrahman, Maha, 310n76
Abduh, Muhammad, 183, 309n64
Abdullah, Khalid, 125
Abillama, Raja, 217
Abul-Magd, Kamal, 167
Abu-Lughod, Lila, 62–63
acceptance of the other (*qubul al-akhir*), 215, 220–21
adab al-ikhtilaf (ethics of disagreement), 147, 148–49, 150
'*adawa* (enmity), 107, 227
advertising, 52, 86–88
Agrama, Hussein, 217
Ahla Hayah (*The Best Life*) (television series), 135
ahl al-bid'a (people of innovation), 24, 92, 196, 236
ahl al-'ilm (people of knowledge), 306n43
Ahmed, Sara, 211

'Ala Khuta al-Habib (*On the Path of the Beloved*) (television series), 115–16
al-'aql (reason), 22
al-Arabiya, 324n6
al-Asad, Bashar, 321n51
al-Ash'ari, Abu Hasan, 22, 318n23
al-Awa, Salim, 167
al-Azhar, 21, 30, 31, 95, 96–97, 154
Al-Azhar University, 279n46, 291n5
Albani, Nasir al-Din al-, 23, 149, 240, 280n50
al-Baz, Farouk, 181
al-Baz, Muhammad, 324n4
al-Dustor (newspaper), 230
al-Fiqi, Hamid, 316n7
al-firqa al-najiyya (saved sect), 23–24, 106–7, 145, 149, 239
al-Ghazali, Muhammad, 58, 143–44, 192, 239, 278n39, 279n39, 313n27, 323n2
al-Ghazali, Zaynab, 197–98, 323n4

al-Guindi, Khaled, 296n13
al-Habash, Rufaida, 153
al-Hadith, Ahl, 150
al-Hekma, 80
al-Huwayni, Abu Ishaq, 23, 77, 80, 123–24, 149, 227, 238–39, 308n53
Al-'Ilm wa-l-Iman (*Science and Faith*) (television series), 74–75
al-Jazeera, 12–13
al-Khattab, Umar ibn, 3–4, 28, 146, 161–62
al-Maqsud, Muhammad Abd, 229, 245
al-Misri, Mahmud, 150
al-mufakkir al-Islami (Islamic thinker), 239
Al-Mu'ulim [*The Teacher*] (Yusuf), 317n13
al-muzlumin (poor/downtrodden), 173
al-Nagger, Mustafa, 318n20
al-Nahar, 206
al-Nas, 78, 79–80
al-nass (revelation), 22, 26, 149
al-Qaradawi, Yusuf, 58, 129, 166–67, 239, 262
al-raqa'iq, 119
Al-Takfir wal Hijra, 108
al-tanmiya al-dhatiya (self-development), 188
Al-Tariq al-Sah (*The Right Path*) (television series), 74
al-tashabbuh bi-l-kuffar (imitation of disbelievers), 231–32
al-wahda al-wataniyya (national unity), 226
al-Wahhab, Muhammad Abd, 23, 164, 166, 236
al-wala' wa-l-bara' (loyalty and disavowal), 107, 217

al-Wasat, 167–68, 310n75
al-wasatiyyun (the centrists), 322n56
Amer, Du'aa, 153
American University in Cairo, 177–79
Andalusia, 246–48
Ang, Ien, 100
Anjum, Ovamir, 238
anxiety, 138
'aql, al- (reason), 22
Arabiya, al-, 324n6
Arab League, 54
Arab Media Corporation (AMC), 55
Arab Radio and Television (ART), 54–55, 64–65, 69
Arabsat, 54, 70
Arab Spring, 1, 9, 249. *See also* Tahrir Square; 2011 revolution
Aristotle, 4
art, 108–9
Asad, Bashar al-, 321n51
Asad, Talal, 19, 26, 145, 168, 284–85n75
Ash'ari, Abu Hasan al-, 22, 318n23
Ash'arism (Ash'arite), 20–25, 27, 276n30
Atharism (Athari), 20–25, 27, 276n30
athletics, 136–37
Atia, Mona, 174
attachments, 20
audience: concerns of, 122–23; as disconnected, 100; of Mustafa Hosny, 98–103, 122–23, 194; of the New Preachers, 2, 16, 31, 98–103
Awa, Salim al-, 167
Awaken the Giant Within (Robbins), 191
Azhar, al-, 21, 30, 31, 95, 96–97, 154
Azhari, 296n13
Azhar University, Al-, 279n46, 291n5

Bajoghli, Narges, 83
Bamyeh, Mohammed, 313n17
bara' (refusal), 221–22, 238, 316n7
battle of Badr, 157–58
Bauer, Thomas, 165, 306n45
Baz, Farouk al-, 181
Baz, Muhammad al-, 324n4
beauty, 312n13
before-and-after advertising strategy, 87–88
Bejan, Theresa, 318n19
belief: *bid'a* and, 23, 24; discursive tradition and, 26; heretical, 230; Islamic, 17, 277n33, 282n60; love and, 140; loyalty and, 210; moderation in, 72, 130, 132; neglect of, 277n33; practice and, 19, 21; privatized, 216, 224; Protestant, 273n17; Salafi, 107, 145; secularism and, 29; unity of, 277n33
belonging, 255
Benjamin, Ruha, 315n47
Berlant, Lauren, 323n3
The Best Life (*Ahla Hayah*) (television series), 135
bid'a (heretical innovation), 106, 147
Bishry, Tarek el-, 167
bi-yiktibu min dimaghhum (writing from their minds), 239
Bollywood film industry, 78
Bonacina, Giovanni, 164
Boullata, Issa, 114
Bowen, John, 18
Brinton, Jacquelene, 113
bromo, 49–50
Brown, Jonathan, 306n43
Brown, Nathan, 281n57
Brown, Wendy, 223–24

bughd (hatred), 107, 227
Bukra Ahla (*Tomorrow Will Be Better*) (television show), 188
Burckhardt, Frederick, 164

Calderwood, Eric, 247
Caldwell, John, 82
calibration (*dabt*): capital, 53, 54, 60, 68, 73, 76; defined, 52; ethical, 84; of financial capital, 60; godly, 53–54; of Iqraa, 56, 61, 72–73; of moral capital, 60; of piety, 84; of political economy, 83–84; of professionalism, 83–84; of Qur'anic logic, 60; of resources, 53–54; risks of, 52–53; successful, 68
caliph (*khalifa*), 172, 177, 180–92, 311–12n6
A Call for Coexistence (*Da'wa li-l-Ta'ayush*) (television series), 220–21, 230, 239
capitalism: buffer against, 70; crony, 63; entwinements of, 56–57; neoliberalism, 196; protection from, 76; shaping of, 52; supremacy of, 73
Carnegie, Dale, 192
Catholicism, 248, 315n38
CBC, 75
Cerantonio, Musa, 307n47
change, tradition and, 26
Christians/Christianity, 19, 130, 213, 227, 228, 243, 247. *See also* Coptic Christians; Muslim-Christian solidarity
civic initiatives, as form of worship, 173
clapping, 319n35
Class A and Class B Plus, 98–103, 111, 136, 194

coexistence (*ta'ayush*): acceptance of the other (*qubul al-akhir*) and, 220–21; challenge of, 249; criticism of, 222; culture of (*thaqafit al-ta'ayush*), 220, 223, 247; defined, 215, 250; New Preachers and, 249–50; as positive social interaction, 248; recentering of, 217; religious laxity (*tamyi' al-din*) and, 222; scholarship of, 317n12; as side by side, 223–24; social life of, 217–18; tolerance and, 223
Cohen, Stanley, 52–53
colonialism, 317n12
committed (*multazim*), 143
community service, 173
continual transformation, 18
Coptic Christians, 167, 175, 226, 234, 244
cosmopolitan, 98–103
counterpublic, 9, 103–9
courage, 197–98, 212, 287n92
Covey, Stephen, 189–91
creative innovation (*ibda'*), 90, 91–92, 127
creativity, in religious outreach, 18
culture wars, 6

dabt (calibration). *See* calibration (*dabt*)
Dallah al-Baraka, 55, 56, 60, 69
damaging divide (*fagwa*), 93
Dave, Nomi, 325n9
da'wa: as advertising, 86–87; as boring, 177; characteristics of, 8, 16; dazzling, 110–23; direct, 8, 51, 60, 103, 110, 177; divine dynamism and, 90; dollars for, 53; innovative, 135; as marketing, 86; of New Preachers, 109; new ways of doing, 92–93; piety and, 8; political economy and, 53; as revolution, 109; Salafi preachers' influence over, 97; self-help and, 191–92; as too conventional, 103; truth-telling in, 149
Da'wa li-l-Ta'ayush (*A Call for Coexistence*) (television series), 220–21, 230, 239
dazzlement (*ibhar*): defined, 110–11; examples of, 115–16; *i'mar* and, 201–2; intimate innovations and, 117–23; by New Preachers, 115; power of, 198; process of, 111; of the Qur'an, 113, 114; strategies of, 115; visual piety and, 112–17
Deeb, Lara, 283n71
democratic/democracy: dissent, 12; dreams, 13; election and, 158; ethos, 168; habits of, 249; Hosny on, 242; Islamic, 321–22n56; people's authority in, 182; pluralism, 238
depoliticization, 186
despair, 199
Developers of the World (*Ommar al-Ard*) (television series). *See Ommar al-Ard* (*Developers of the World*) (television series)
Diab, Amr, 99
dictatorship, 241
difference: acceptance of, 131, 215, 220–21, 223, 242, 247; affirmation of, 216; celebration of, 32; coexistence across, 44, 104, 168, 223, 235, 242, 262; in community, 131, 146; connection across, 219; co-presence across, 217; as cosmological reality, 221; as divine, 214, 215–16, 221, 224, 241; doctrinal, 19; ethical,

28, 44, 162; hospitality to, 22; hostility toward, 161; ideological, 242; internal, 11; interpretive, 147, 149; love across, 226; maintaining, 222; making a, 35; in media, 51, 61; as mercy, 131, 146, 149–50; Muslim, 27; Muslim-Christian, 141, 225–26, 247; mutual engagement in, 215, 224, 248; in piety and fanaticism, 180; political, 44; reframing, 150; religious, 8, 216, 217, 218, 221, 226, 227, 231, 233, 234, 245; secular-religious, 9, 25–30, 216, 250–51; social interaction across, 223; solidarity across, 213; in structure and culture, 199–200; theological, 20, 22, 45, 262; tolerating, 131, 216, 223, 241–42; unification in, 10, 150
different spirit (*ruh mukhtalifa*), 213
Direct Question (*Su'al Mubashir*) (television show), 324n6
disagreement (*ikhtilaf*), 147–50
disappearing medium, 16, 126
disbelief, 199
discursive tradition, 26–27, 93, 128, 131, 213, 278n35, 283n67
distance, metaphor of, 121–22
The Divine Center (Covey), 190–91
divine/divinity: accountability, 53, 196; commands, 238; difference, 251; mercy, 27; obligation, 70; parameters, 7, 29, 51, 131, 135, 219; recompense, 76; revelation, 6, 16, 28, 59, 112, 113, 114, 128, 131, 149, 167; rewards, 236; self-disclosure, 53; sovereignty, 28, 199; standards, 52; submission to, 22; truth, 239. *See also* God; Qur'an
division, 253–54

Dolby, Sandra, 313n23
Dream (private channel), 63
dreaming, 178, 202–6
Dustor, al- (newspaper), 230

economy, separation from religion, 57. *See also* capitalism; neoliberalism
education, 193–94
Effat, Emad, 225
Egypt: affective landscape of, 11; building the new, 314n27; colonial period of, 56; conditions of, 134; conditions of, under Mubarak, 185, 187–88; connectedness in, 99; culture wars of, 6; dreaming for, 202–6; economic challenges of, 5–6, 193; economic growth of, 63; election in, 158, 236–37, 242–43, 287n88; ethical crisis in, 178; imbalance of society in, 142; polarization (*istiqtab*) in, 245; political rule in, 31; public speech in, 263; referendum in, 158; "the country is now ours" concept in, 185. *See also* New Egypt
Egyptian Movement for Social Change (Kefaya (Enough)), 167–68, 310–11n76
Egyptian Radio and Television Union (ERTU), 54, 62
Eickelman, Dale, 95
Eisenlohr, Patrick, 274n21
Eissa, Ibrahim, 230
El Aawar, Ahmed, 188–90, 249
el-Bishry, Tarek, 167
elections, 1, 158, 236–37, 242–43, 287n88
El Fadl, Abou, 319n35
Elfiky, Ibrahim, 210
el-Ghobashy, Mona, 310–11n76

El Haggar, Ali, 255
Elmessiri, Abdelwahab, 167
Emara, Nadia, 153
Englund, Harri, 323n1
enmity (*'adawa*), 107, 227
entertainment: as cultural language, 92; *da'wa* reduction and, 19, 33, 61; dazzlement and, 8, 18, 111; as empty, 81; ethical (*fann hadif*), 50, 81, 105, 108, 253; features of, 109; financing for, 76; Hosny on, 109; incorporation of, 34; influence of, 109; leisure and, 135–36; of the New Preachers, 92, 105–6, 108; objections to, 78–79, 92, 106, 123, 136; religion and, 125; secular, 51, 118, 136; types of, 54; virtue and, 51; Western, 124–25. *See also* media/mass media
Essam, Ramy, 254–55
ethics: aptness of, 94; dilemmas of, 15–16; of disagreement (*adab al-ikhtilaf*), 147, 238; of engagement, 6; in entertainment (*fann hadif*), 50, 81, 105, 108, 253; as foundation, 161; of God, 144; of interaction, 145–46, 162, 230, 234; of Islam, 135, 171, 233; loving friendship as, 225; in marketing, 86; of music, 207; of the New Preachers, 38; as other-oriented, 174; piety and, 33, 36, 141–46 (*See also* piety); political, 4; potential of, 162; in practice, dilemmas of, 11; of the revolution, 11, 33–38, 45; revolutionary, 166–68, 178, 225; of self-help, 174, 177, 191; of self-transformation, 35; *ta'arruf* (mutual engagement) as, 104, 105, 215, 216; in transformation, 188; of *waq'iya* (reasonableness), 94

Facebook, 30
Faculty of Media (Cairo University), 13
Fader, Ayala, 106
fadfada (heartfelt confiding), 119, 205–6
Fadil, Nadia, 137
Fadl, Abou El, 319n35
fagwa (damaging divide), 93
faith (*iman*), 21
fanaticism, 64, 93, 130, 138, 180, 231
fann hadif (purposeful art/ethical entertainment), 50, 105, 253
Fernando, Mayanthi, 137
Fiqi, Hamid al-, 316n7
firqa al-najiyya, al- (saved sect), 23–24, 106–7, 145, 149, 239
fitra (God-given nature), 109, 135–36, 161, 173, 233
Foda, Yusri, 318n20
folk devils, 52–53
Fotouh, Abdel Moneim Aboul, 237
Fox, Terry, 233–34
fragmentation (*tafakkuk*), 150
France, Islamic representation in, 184
Freedom and Justice Party, 243
friendship (*mawadda*), 225
Frishkopf, Michael, 299–300n46

Galil, Salem Abdel, 296n13, 324n5
Ganti, Tejaswini, 78
garments, social significance of, 137
Gershon, Ilana, 274n21
Ghazali, Muhammad al-, 58, 143–44, 192, 239, 278n39, 279n39, 313n27, 323n2
Ghazali, Zaynab al-, 197–98, 323n4
Ghobashy, Mona el-, 310–11n76
Ghoneim, Wagdy, 107–8, 222, 227
Ghonim, Wael, 196, 286n85, 318n20

ghuluw (religious fanaticism), 130, 131
Gilsenan, Michael, 282n60
Gladwell, Malcolm, 190
Gleave, Robert, 148–49
globalization, 58
God: accountability of, 53; as al-Wadud, 139; attributes/nature of, 20, 22, 131, 141, 143; beauty and, 312n13; calling people to, 96; command from, 108; consciousness of, 142; as creator, 140, 173, 183, 215–16, 221, 241; emotional image of, 144; ethics of, 144; giving to, 71; governance and, 238–39; hope in, 201; judgment of, 178, 194; love for, 17, 87, 124, 152, 162; love for worship by, 139; love of, 127, 135, 138–41, 229; mandate from, 182–83; mindfulness to, 55; as Originator, 91; as owner of all things, 14, 70, 182; parameters of, 51, 131, 135, 219; permission from, 240–41; piety for, 33 (*See also* piety); punishment from, 139, 140–41; in the Qur'an, 90, 165; as really Real, 52; rebranding of, 92; recompense of, 76; relationship with, 118, 119, 138, 139, 140; repentance to, 121; revelation from, 59, 112–13, 114, 128, 146, 149, 216–17, 251; sin and, 121; as ultimate resource, 211; will of, 216, 241; worship of, 173
God-given nature (*fitra*), 109, 135–36, 161, 173, 233
godliness (*rubbubiyya*), 143–44
Gomaa, Ali, 129, 262
Graf, Bettina, 166–67
Grewal, Zareena, 154
Gruber, Christiane, 299n43
Guaaybess, Tanya, 290n3

Guindi, Khaled al-, 296n13
Gym, Aa, 92, 99, 191

Habash, Rufaida al-, 153
Hadith, Ahl al-, 150
Haeri, Niloofar, 284n73
Haggar, Ali El, 255
Haiba, Ahmed Abu, 68, 117–19, 145–46, 321n49
Hamdy, Sherine, 278n34
hamimiya (intimacy), in media, 117–23
Hamsho, Sirin, 153
Hamza, Abd al-Latif, 15, 58–59
Hamzawy, Amr, 318n20
haram (earnings), 91, 208
Harrara, Ahmed, 318n20
Hart, Kimberly, 184
Hassan, Muhammad: concerns regarding, 227; on corruption, 245; criticism of, 81; on New Preachers, 250; popularity of, 23, 25, 77, 123; on Salafi, 78–81; silence and, 323n2; on women drivers, 154
hatred (*bughd*), 107, 227
Haugbolle, Sune, 299n43
Haykel, Bernard, 306n43
Haynes, Naomi, 66
heart, 118, 140
heartfelt confiding (*fadfada*), 119, 205–6
Hekma, al-, 80
Hellyer, Hisham, 257, 321n50
Help Club, 177–79
hijab, 153–54
Hinduism, 289n106
Hirschkind, Charles, 25, 105–6, 128, 217, 250, 274n17
Hoesterey, James, 99, 176, 310n71

hope, 199
Hosny, Mustafa: on 2011 revolution, 31–32; advertising for, 129; *Ahla Hayah (The Best Life)*, 135; on al-Nahar, 206–7; audience of, 98–103, 122–23, 194; background of, 17, 85; beliefs of, 2; on beneficial impact, 184; on *bid'a*, 147; callers into series of, 202–6; characteristics of, 7, 122; on collaboration, 108; on continual transformation, 18; control of, 82–83; on courage, 198; on creation, 183; on creativity, 94; criticism of, 38, 148, 324n4; defense of, 108; on disagreement (*ikhtilaf*), 147–48; on diversity, 146; on entertainment, 109; entertainment understanding of, 92; on face-to-face learning, 95; *fadfada* (heartfelt confiding) and, 205–6; focus of, 6–7, 12, 34; goals of, 127–28; on godly behavior, 303n17; on godly people, 105; on heart worship, 140; on his identity, 94; on his purpose, 38; on Islam, 95, 136, 138; *Khada'ukka fa-Qalu (They Tricked You and Said)*, 146–48; media goals of, 110; mission of, 96; on moderation (*wasati*), 133; on Muslim Brotherhood, 37; as New Preacher, 2; *Ommar al-Ard (Developers of the World)*, 175, 181, 183–84, 185–88, 194, 197–201, 203–6, 231–35; Ommar al-Ard (voluntary association) of, 195–96; optimism of, 175; overview of, 2; personal life of, 4; photograph collection of, 180–81; physical features of, 122; on piety, 184–85; on politics, 160–62, 259; popularity of, 17, 39, 85, 86, 97, 204–5; production of, 10; production team of, 152; questions for, 4–5; on the Qur'an, 94; on religion, 184; revolution with viewers and, 215; on *rubbubiyya* (godliness), 143, 144; on Salafi preachers, 7–8; on Salafism, 96; salary of, 86; *School of Love*, 144; seminar of, 1, 3–4; show format of, 96, 103–4, 127–28; silence and, 256, 258–59, 260; on starting with yourself, 187–88; target audience of, 194; "Technology and Godliness" seminar of, 89–90, 91, 103, 104–5; on translation, 98; *Uhibbika Rabbi (I Love You My Lord)*, 140; viewer interaction and, 203–6; *Worldly Enchantments*, 109, 131; YouTube channel of, 275n26

How to Stop Worrying and Start Living (Carnegie), 192

human beings: authority of, 182; creation of, 140, 183; distinctness of, 182; diversity of, 146, 221; as God's caliphs, 172, 177, 311–12n6; God's mandate to, 182–83; *i'mar* responsibility of, 183; leaving a mark by, 182; love of God to, 139; nature of, 136; pluralism of, 216; purpose of, 173, 190; social obligation of, 183; supremacy of, 182; theological ontology of, 182

human innovation, limitations of, 91

Huwaidi, Fahmi, 167

Huwayni, Abu Ishaq al-, 23, 77, 80, 123–24, 149, 227, 238–39, 308n53

INDEX   335

i'adit ihya' al-thawra guwwana (revive the revolution within ourselves), 225–26
ibda' (creative innovation), 90, 91–92, 127
ibhar (dazzlement). *See* dazzlement (*ibhar*)
Iblis, 199
ideal avatar, 100–101
idolatry, 113–14
ijazas, 96
'Ilm wa-l-Iman, Al- (*Science and Faith*) (television series), 74–75
I Love You My Lord (*Uhibbika Rabbi*) (television series), 140
iltizam bi-l-samt, al- (maintaining silence), 256
Imam, Ibrahim, 59, 60
iman (faith), 21
i'mar (impact): adaptation of self-help for promoting, 176; cultivating godliness through, 184; dazzlement (*ibhar*) and, 201–2; defined, 172, 184; ethical, 208–9; as everyday practice, 185; *khalifa* (caliph) and, 182–83; obligation for, 173; piety as, 184; responsibility of, 183; ritual worship and, 184; self-cultivation as foundation of, 184; self-help and, 174; starting with yourself for, 185–88; verse regarding, 183; widening of, 183
i'mar al-ard, 208
imitation of disbelievers (*al-tashabbuh bi-l-kuffar*), 231–32
imperialism, 25, 58, 167, 222
impiety, doors to, 136–37
impurity, 124–25

incommensurable value, religion and economics as domains of, 53
Indonesia, 310n71
innovation: in Ash'arism, 27; in *da'wa*, 135; defined, 9; as godly attribute, 127; importance of staying new and, 123–28; in Islamic theology, 23; limitations of, 91; of New Preachers, 92; perils of, 123–28; through television, 92; tradition and, 94–98
inspiration, power of, 198
International Monetary Fund (IMF), 63, 273n15
internet, 63, 106
interpretive pluralism, 306–7n45
inter-religious harmony, 317n12
intimacy (*hamimiya*), in media, 117–23
Iqraa: advertising of, 84, 86, 129–30; aim of, 83; Arab Spring and, 13; audience-seeking atmosphere of, 100, 120; benefits of, 207; billboards of, 84, 86; as bridge, 81; broadcasting hours of, 74; budget of, 52; calibration of, 56, 61; capitalism and, 52; celebration at, 174; changes to, 206; characteristics of, 12–13, 206; concerns regarding, 64, 80; content of, 51; criticism of, 13, 61, 65, 66; dazzling by, 109; employees of, 55; ethical policy of, 161; field research at, 39–50; financial challenges of, 73–77; financial structure of, 70, 73; focus of, 7, 37–38, 51, 84–85; funding for, 70; *i'mar* and, 174; impacts of, 208–9; importance of, 132–33, 208–9; inclusion in, 150; inclusion of women at, 152–56; as Islamic channel, 51; location of, 65; as media

Iqraa: advertising (*cont.*)
alternative, 64; media content of, 60–61; MEMRI and, 302n7; mission statement of, 130; as moderate (*wasati*) channel, 130, 150, 158; moderation of, 13, 22; moral seriousness of, 71; non-discrimination in, 234–35; obduracy (*tazammut*) and, 130; origin of, 54–55, 60; overview of, 5, 11–14; physical conditions of, 68–69; pledge of, 55; politics and, 156–62; popularity of, 39; professional distinctions and, 77–81, 157; programming changes of, 33–34, 150; recalibration of, 72–73; relevance of, 174; retention challenges of, 209; revolutionary goal of, 109; *The Right Path* (*Al-Tariq al-Sah*) on, 74; *Science and Faith* (*Al-'Ilm wa-l-Iman*) (television series) on, 74–75; significance of, 208–9; slogan of, 60–61; target viewers of, 102; tolerance (*tasammuh*) and, 130; viewer interaction and, 203–6; voting policy of, 158–59; waqf of, 76. *See also specific shows/series*

Iqraa conference, 57–58

Iqraa International, 307n47

islah (reform/making right), 121

Islam: as analytical category, 282n60; anthropology of, 25–30; anxiety in, 138; boredom in, 136; Christianity as compared to, 19, 130; communication concerns of, 58; as communicative call, 15; as community of the middle way (*ummatan wasatan*), 130; conspiracy of silence around, 59; conversion to, 234; creative adaptability of, 233; democratizing of, 95; as discursive tradition, 26–28, 93, 128, 283n67; disposition in, 135; ecumenical, 132; ethical objections in, 207–8; extremism in, 132–33; foundational nature of, 72; gendered evaluations and exclusions in, 154; imbalance of society in, 142; individualizing of, 95; as making new again, 16–19; marketing of, 86–87; as media, 14–16; as natural religion, 135; orthodoxy and, 19; Protestant Reformation and, 132; purification of, 24; rebranding of, 92, 176, 191; recreation of the present in, 18; religious fanaticism (*ghuluw*) and, 130; returning self-help to, 188–92; ritual excellence in, 138; as saved sect (*al-firqa al-najiyya*), 106–7; secularism and, 284n75; sensational forms of, 114; stagnation of, 319n35; transmission of, 95; unity (*wahda*) in, 150; as universal, 97; Westernization and, 72, 124–25, 130, 138, 163. *See also* Muslims

Islamic anthropology, 311–12n6

Islamic Awakening (*al-sahwa al-islamiyya*), 38

Islamic economics, 291n5

Islamic media: characteristics of, 7; as conventional, 51, 52; criticism of, 13; debates regarding, 5; as expansive, 61; funding for, 68–73; idea of, 57–61; as mass communication subfield, 59–60; moral panics about, 61–68; piety and, 37; satellite signals of, 12; stereotypes of, 51; as unconventional, 51

Islamic preachers, 296n14. *See also* Salafi preachers

Islamic Revival, 9, 25, 72, 131–32, 133, 142
Islamic television, 53, 66, 77
Islamic television preachers: beliefs of, 2; control of, 82; criticism of, 13–14; exhortations from, 25; financial focus of, 67; focus of, 25; funding for, 68; incomes of, 14; influence of, 1–2; skepticism regarding, 65–66; technology use of, 91. *See also* Salafi preachers
Islamic thinker (*al-mufakkir al-Islami*), 239
Islamism, 289n106. *See also* Islam
islamiyin, 37–38, 289n106
Islamophobia, 302n12, 321n50

Jazeera, al-, 13
Jesus, 90
Jobs, Steve, 180
Jones, Stephen, 302n12
Jordan, 66
Jouilli, Jeanette, 184
judgment, 140
June 30 mobilization, 244

Kahlway, Abla al-, 152–53, 307n49
Kalam min al-Qalb (*Words from the Heart*) (television series), 117–19
Kamel, Shaykh Saleh, 54–57, 60, 64, 66, 69, 71, 73, 273n14, 291n5
Kamil, Mustafa, 191–92
Keane, Webb, 293n37, 299n46
Kefaya (Enough [Egyptian Movement for Social Change]), 167–68, 310–11n76
Kenney, Jeffrey, 210
Khachab, Chihab El, 111

Khada'ukka fa-Qalu (*They Tricked You and Said*) (television series), 146–48
Khaled, Amr: 2011 revolution and, 31; Ahmed El Aawar and, 190; *'Ala Khuta al-Habib* (*On the Path of the Beloved*), 115–16; at American University in Cairo, 177–79; banning of, 37, 273n14, 289n103; *Bukra Ahla* (*Tomorrow Will Be Better*), 188; on coexistence, 220–21, 222; criticism of, 123–24, 134–35, 216–17, 324n5; *Da'wa li-l-Ta'ayush* (*A Call for Coexistence*), 220–21, 230, 239; departure from Iqraa by, 209; on dictatorship, 241; on difference, 241–42; focus of, 34; influence of, 102–3, 274–75n24, 286n85; on Iqraa, 12; *Lifemakers* (*Sunna' al-Hayah*), 34, 35, 103, 173, 187; on love of God, 138–40; on Muslim Brotherhood, 324n5, 324n6; as neoliberal piety counselor, 311n2; as New Preacher, 2; on Pact of Medina, 221; piety of privilege and, 99; political agenda of, 35; on politics, 162, 241–42, 261, 308–9n61; popularity of, 17, 25, 116; project of, 318n20; *Qissas min al-Qur'an* (*Stories from the Qur'an*), 116; *Qissat al-Andalus* (*The Story of Andalusia*), 246–48; on Qur'an dazzlement, 114; on revolutionary ethics, 178; self-transformation and, 174; on silence, 261; statement of, 87; on Tahrir Square, 213, 214–15, 251; *Until They Change Themselves*, 190; work of, 34
khalifa (caliph), 172, 177, 180–92, 311–12n6

Kharijites, 130
khatib (sermon-giver), 296n14
Khattab, Umar ibn al-, 3–4, 28, 146, 161–62
King Abdulaziz University, 291n5
Kishk, Shaykh, 272n10
Kitab al-Tawhid (Wahhab), 236

Ladin, Osama bin, 165
Larkin, Brian, 40, 104
LBC, 77
Lebanese secularism, 217
leisure activities, 136–37
Leithy, Amr el-, 96
Lifemakers (Sunna' al-Hayah) (television program), 34, 35, 103, 173, 187
Lifemakers groups, 192–93
Lifemakers NGO, 196
lived relevance, 37
love: for Egypt, 185; as emulation, 124, 137; in friendship, 225; for God, 17, 87, 124, 152, 162; of God, 127, 138–41, 229; as godly, 234; *Madrasat al-Hubb (School of Love)* (television series), 89, 142, 144; in music, 219; in ordinary youth, 119; piety and, 133; for the Prophet, 184; in protesting, 214; purpose of, 135; in religious difference, 226, 228; for the revolution, 225; romantic, 319n35; sin and, 108; types of, 152; worship and, 162
love (*mahabba*), 225
love of God, 138–41
loving friendship, in Tahrir Square, 225
loyalty and disavowal (*al-wala' wa-l-bara'*), 107, 217
Lutfi, Wa'il, 99
Lynch, Marc, 161

madhab system, 23, 149, 306n43
Madison, James, 4
Madrasat al-Hubb (School of Love) (television series), 89, 142, 144
mahabba (love), 225
Mahmood, Saba, 142, 165, 227
Mahmud, Mustafa, 74
maintaining silence (*al-iltizam bi-l-samt*), 256
Makdisi, George, 279n42
Makdisi, Ussama, 317n12
Malcolm X, 180
Mandela, Nelson, 180–81, 231
Maqsud, Muhammad Abd al-, 229, 245
March, Andrew, 182
Marina, 99, 100
Masoud, Moez: 2011 revolution and, 31, 32; background of, 120–21; criticism of, 324n4; departure from Iqraa by, 209; focus of, 34; on Iqraa, 12; on Muslim Brotherhood shooting, 324n5; as New Preacher, 2; popularity of, 17, 97; at "The Revolution: Past, Present and Future," 224–26; *Tariq al-Sah (The Right Path)* (television series), 74, 120; *Thawra 'ala al-Nafs (The Revolution Within)*, 10–11, 188
Maspero Massacre, 175
Masry, Mahmoud al-, 129
mass mobilization, inspiration from, 213
Matarudism, 279n41
Maurer, Bill, 291n7
maven, 190
mawadda (friendship), 225
MBC, 73, 77
McLuhan, Marshall, 111–12
Media at the Dawn of Islam (Hamza), 58–59

media funding, as charitable giving, 68–73
media/mass media: capitalism of, 52; conventional, 110; corruption of, 71; defined, 58; as direct *da'wa*, 51; disappearing, 16, 126; dramas of nationhood in, 62–63; ethnography of, 83; harnessing power of, 16; ideologies, 274n21; legalization of privately funded, 63; mainstreaming impact of, 206–9; media as the message in, 298n38; Ministry of National Guidance for, 62; political economy in, 83; potential of, 71–72; processes of, 78; religion and, 16, 273–74n17; religious autodidacticism and, 95; as religious imperative, 59; revolutionary potential of, 62; revolutionizing, 51; self-representation, self-critique, and self-reflection of, 82; as subfield of Islamic studies, 59–60; technologies of, 15; transformative potential of, 59
media producers, revolutionizing ideals of, 51
MEMRI, 302n7
Meyer, Birgit, 16, 114, 126, 273n17
"The Middle," 167
middle-class aesthetics, 312n13
minimalism, 299–300n46
Ministry of National Guidance, 62
Misri, Mahmud al-, 150
Mitchell, Timothy, 191
Mittermaier, Amira, 194, 196
moderation: equilibrium, 130–31
moderation (*wasati, wasatiyya*): defined, 133; establishment of, 33; ethical piety and, 141–46; foundational matters of, 131; function of, 33; in Islamic Revival, 133; limitations of, 131; love of God and, 138–41; many lives of, 162–66; as many truths, 146–51; in mission statement of Iqraa, 130; natural, 134–38; origin of, 166–68; overview of, 131; in piety, 140; politics and, 156–62; possibilities of, 133; promotion of, 133–34; as revolutionary ethos, 166–68; scholarship regarding, 132; true *versus* fake, 131; Western norms and interests regarding, 133; women's inclusion and, 151–56
moral panic, 52–53, 66
Morsi, Mohamed: candidacy of, 308–9n61; concerns regarding, 243, 244, 262; condemnation by, 246; election of, 9, 242; government under, 227; mobilization against, 260; pleas to, 245; protests against, 255
Moses, 90
mosque movement, 281–82n59
Moumtaz, Nada, 70
Moussa, Amr, 236–37
Mubarak, Husni: alternative media narratives under, 62; conditions of Egypt under, 185, 187–88, 202, 234, 241; following 2011 revolution, 1; privatization push of, 63; resignation of, 9, 31, 158, 166, 174
Muehlebach, Andrea, 315n38
mufakkir al-Islami, al- (Islamic thinker), 239
Muhammad (Prophet), 57, 90, 157–58, 197
multazim (committed), 143
Munqush, Awad al-, 296n13

Muqaddam, Ismail al-, 323n2
music, 136; *Al-Muʿulim* [*The Teacher*], 317n13; ethics and, 207; of Hosny, 91, 104–5; impact of, 136; impurity and, 124; innovation and, 92; love in, 219; of *Madrasat al-Hubb* (*The School of Love*), 89–90; of *Qissas min al-Qur'an* (*Stories from the Qur'an*), 116; religion and, 125; videos, 6, 64, 73, 108, 127, 145, 253–54, 261, 317n13; "What Can I Say?" (*Wa Ulak Ay?*), 253–54, 261; as worship, 219
Muslim Brotherhood: broken promises of, 242–43; campaign of, 3; complacency of, 246; concerns regarding, 37, 243; criticism of, 10, 262; demonstrations from, 31; distancing by, 243–44; electoral ambitions of, 37; grassroots initiatives of, 186; *islamiyin* and, 289–90n107; "The Middle" and, 167; on New Preachers, 257; opponents of, 272n9; political Islamism and, 168; Qur'an 13:11 and, 183; relationships with, 198; Salafi and, 320n46; sectarianism and, 321n49; shooting of, 324n5; stance of, 30–31; Sunni revivalism and, 289n102
Muslim-Christian solidarity, 213, 214, 217, 219–24, 225, 229
Muslims: Christian conflicts with, 227; as community of the middle way (*ummatan wasatan*), 130; conflicts of, 234; discrimination against, 302–3n12; imbalance of categories of, 142; as living together with Christians, 213; what it means to be, 282n60. See also Islam

Muʿtazila, 21–22, 150
mutual engagement (*taʿarruf*), 104, 105, 215, 216
muzlumin, al- (poor/downtrodden), 173

Nagger, Mustafa al-, 318n20
Nahar, al-, 206
Namira, Hamza, 253–55, 261
narcissism of minor differences, 26
Nas, al-, 78, 79–80
nass, al- (revelation), 22, 26, 149
Nasser, Gamal Abdel, 62, 66, 313–14n27
national unity (*al-wahda al-wataniyya*), 226
Nawal, Madame, 102–3, 257
nearness, metaphor of, 121–22
neoliberalism, 34–35, 66, 174, 176, 196, 311n4, 315n47
New Egypt, 175, 180, 198, 251. See also Egypt
new information order, 58
New Islamists, 167, 310n76
New Preachers: on 2011 revolution, 36; acceptance of change by, 93; acceptance of the other and, 215; advertising for, 86–87; artistic productions of, 105; Ashʿarism and, 21, 22; audience of, 2, 16, 31, 98–103; becoming, 84–88; on *bidʿa*, 93; on change, 18; characteristics of, 2, 17, 85–86; compensation for, 86; counterpublic and, 9; on creativity, 18; criticism of, 29, 37, 53, 66, 95, 96–97, 99, 105–6, 107–8, 123–26, 128, 257–58; *daʿwa* of, 109, 115; dazzlement by, 115; DIY spirit of, 187; elaborations of, 131–32; election viewpoint of, 287n88;

entertainment forms of, 92–93; ethical approach of, 38; evangelical strategy of, 191; exhortation of, 22; focus of, 6–7, 17, 22; hope through, 6; innovation of, 92; on Islam's universalism, 97–98; lament of, 33; life raft from, 100; lived relevance of, 37; on loving friendship with non-Muslims, 318n23; mission of, 109; moderation (*wasati*) and, 133–34; overview of, 2; as people of innovation (*ahl al-bid'a*), 24; personal sharing by, 120–21; piety and, 36, 131, 250; political rhetoric of, 3, 287n88; popularity of, 2, 204–5; promiscuity of, 105–6; pro-revolutionary stance of, 31–32; purpose of, 11; Qur'anic inimitability of, 90; recreation viewpoint of, 93; relevance of, 22; on religion and politics, 38; religion as commodity to, 53; remaining Islamic by, 9; on resonant reconfiguration, 18; as revolutionaries, 32; risks of, 257; ritualism of, 145; Salafi preachers as compared to, 228–29; secularism and, 29; self-help and, 174, 186–87, 210; silence of, 45, 257–60; sin and, 303–4n17; spiritual role of, 97–98; as stealth secularizers, 250; *taswir fanni* (imaging modes) of, 115; as televangelists, 67–68; theology of coexistence of, 249–50; voting policy of, 158–59; warning against, 92–93. See also *specific persons; specific programs*

Nilesat, 54, 61
9/11 attacks, 132, 163–65
1919 uprising, 316n7

90 Minutes (television show), 323–24n4
non-Muslims, 107, 231–35, 318n23

objectification of the religious imagination, 95
obstacles, overcoming, 200–201
Ommar al-Ard (Developers of the World) (television series): *al-tashabbuh bi-l-kuffar* (imitation of disbelievers) and, 231–35; brainstorming for, 183–84; Cody's story on, 197–201; focus of, 203; key takeaway of, 183; origin of, 175, 181; planning sessions for, 194; purpose of, 194; selection process of, 181–82; starting with yourself concept on, 185–88; viewer interaction on, 203–6
Ommar al-Ard (voluntary association), 195–96, 210–11
On the Path of the Beloved ('Ala Khuta al-Habib) (television series), 115–16
ordinary youth: as audience, 175; competing for attention of, 111; instilling love in, 119; interviews with, 197; Salafism and, 8; as seeking, 98–103
Orientalism, 27
orthodoxy, 19
other-orientation, 10
others help, self-help as, 192–96

Pact of Medina, 221
parrhesia, 323n1
"participation, not domination," 242–46
partisan agnosticism, 195
Patel, Youshaa, 232
people of innovation (*ahl al-bid'a*), 24, 92, 196, 236

people of knowledge (*ahl al-'ilm*), 306n43
Peterson, Mark Allen, 99
piety: as accommodating, 124; advertising and, 52; attachment and, 20; beyond the counterpublic, 103–9; calibration of, 84; centering of, 98; citizenly care and, 184; for Class A and Class B Plus, 136; in *da'wa* movement, 8; discipline and, 44; enmity (*'adawa*) as, 227; ethical, 33, 36, 141–46; excellence at, 29; fanaticism (*tashaddud*) versus, 180; friendship with God and, 139; hatred (*bughd*) as, 227; Help Club and, 177; image (*taddayun sura*), 144; as *i'mar*, 184; inclination to, 233; of Islamic media production, 37; in Islamic Revival, 131–32; love and, 133; love of God and, 140–41; moderation (*wasati*) in, 140; movement of, 90; natural, 134–38; neoliberalism and, 174; of New Preachers, 36, 131, 250; numerical (*taddayun raqami*), 144; as other-centered, 33, 185; on pedestal, 121; of privilege, 99; purpose of, 180; as repelling, 91; revolutionizing, 91, 131, 133, 141, 175, 182, 258; ritual worship and, 8, 33, 51, 72, 143, 144; in Salafi, 24, 25, 39–40, 110, 134, 137, 142; as self-centered, 185; in self-cultivation, 33, 72; self-discipline and, 184; selling, 86–87; silence and, 322n1; in social activism, 33; of social engagement, 10; of solidarity, 10; of *tadayyun fitri*, 179; visual, 112–17; volunteerism and, 196; worship and, 141, 143–44, 276n28

pluralism, 235–42, 306–7n45
polarization (*istiqtab*), 245
political awareness, 193
political economy, 83–84
political silence, 257
politics, 156–62, 238–39, 262–63
poor/downtrodden (*al-muzlumin*), 173
popular culture, connectedness to, 99
preachers. See Islamic television preachers; New Preachers; Salafi preachers
prefiguration, 186
Princeton University, 291n5
private channels, 54, 63
privatization, 63, 64, 290n3
professional distinctions, 77–81, 83–84
promiscuous publics, 103–4
prophetic cosmopolitanism, 99
prosperity gospel, 66
Protestant Reformation/Protestantism, 119, 132, 164–65, 218, 224, 273n15, 281n55, 299n46, 309n64
purification, 143–44
purposeful art/ethical entertainment (*fann hadif*), 50, 105, 253

Qaradawi, Yusuf al-, 58, 129, 166–67, 239, 262
qawl wahid, 239
Qissas min al-Qur'an (*Stories from the Qur'an*) (television series), 116
Qissat al-Andalus (*The Story of Andalusia*) (television show), 246–48
Q-News (magazine), 302n12
qubul al-akhir (acceptance of the other), 215, 220–21
Qur'an: assumption regarding, 165; boredom and, 112–13; as commodity,

65; dazzlement of, 113, 114; as God's message/newspaper, 15, 58–59, 128; governance requirements in, 238–39; Hosny's viewpoint regarding, 94; inimitability of, 90; as knowing too well, 90–91; logic of, 60; media angle of, 59; miraculous nature of, 18; printing of, 126; self-referentiality of, 298n38; *taswir fanni* (imaging modes) of, 114; technologies regarding, 126; understandability of, 149; as universal message, 251; univocality of, 306n45; visuality of, 114, 115
Qur'an 13:11, 183, 191
Qutb, Sayyid, 114, 183, 239

Rabi'a Square, 260
Radical Middle Way, 302n12
radio, television as compared to, 111–12
Ramadan, 147
raqa'iq, al-, 119
reason (*al-'aql*), 22
reform/making right (*islah*), 121
refusal (*bara'*), 221–22, 238, 316n7
religion: before-and-after advertising strategy for, 88; as boring, 127; boundaries of, 9, 93–94, 125; as commodity subject, 65, 82; corruption of, 124; creativity in, 18; economic separation with, 57; ethics and, 141–46; impurity of, 124–25; inventing a new, 27; as life itself (*al-din huwa al-hayah nafsuha*), 240; as media, 14–16, 273–74n17; media and, 16; political economic structures and, 66; politics and, 159–60; reconstruction of, 66; silence in, 322n1; wealth and, 87
religious autodidacticism, 95

religious fanaticism (*ghuluw*), 130, 131
religious laxity (*tamyi' al-din*), 124, 222
religious violence, 317n12
repentance (*tawba*), 121
repudiation, 107
Resala, 49–50, 52, 77–81, 194–95, 196
revealed text (*al-nass*), 22, 26, 149
revive the revolution within ourselves (*i'adit ihya' al-thawra guwwana*), 225–26
"The Revolution: Past, Present and Future," 224–26
revolution/revolutionary: within, 45; consciousness of, 13, 175; *da'wa* as, 109; disposition, 205; ethics, 45, 166–68, 178, 225; failure as, 201; of Islam, 17; of Islamic media, 29–30, 51, 53, 61, 77, 99, 117, 173, 216; love for, 225; of media, 62; of piety, 91, 131, 133, 141, 175, 182, 258; of politics, 182; religiously, 30–33; rhetoric of, 63; sense of, 32; transformation, 180, 202, 205, 216. *See also* 2011 revolution
The Revolution Within (*Thawra 'ala al-Nafs*) (television program), 10–11, 188
Rida, Rashid, 15
The Right Path (*Al-Tariq al-Sah*) (television series), 74, 120
rituals/ritualism: *i'mar* (impact) and, 184; of New Preachers, 145; overview of, 145, 305n36; piety and, 8, 33, 51, 72, 143, 144; purpose of, 184; of Salafi/Salafism, 37, 138, 140, 145–46; self-cultivation, 142, 184, 186; social apathy and, 180; worship, 8, 51, 142, 144, 145, 162, 184–85, 303n17

Robbins, Joel, 277n34
Robbins, Tony, 191
Rock-Singer, Aaron, 107
rubbubiyya (godliness), 143–44
Rudnyckyj, Daromir, 57
ruh mukhtalifa (different spirit), 213

Sabry, Samir, 323n4
sadaqa, 69
Sadat, Anwar al-, 62, 63
Salafi preachers: characteristics of, 25, 34; criticism from, 105–6, 123–26, 128; criticism of, 118; focus of, 24; influence of, 97; Islamic truism and, 9; Mustafa Hosny's viewpoint regarding, 7–8; New Preachers as compared to, 228–29; opening by, 24; politicism of, 34; rebuttals of, 123; in Saudi Arabia, 281n56; secularism and, 29; on self-disclosure, 304n17; on sin, 120–21; stylings of, 94–95; themes of, 140–41; theology of *bid'a* of, 92–93; warning from, 30, 92–93, 113–14
Salafi revivalists, 232, 233
Salafi/Salafism: on 1919 uprising, 316n7; *bid'a* interpretation of, 93, 106; characteristics of, 3, 8, 24, 78, 281n55; criticism from, 148; criticism of, 8, 10, 80, 110, 118, 145, 165–66; defined, 16; on diversity, 150; following 9/11 attacks, 163–65; funding for, 80; global appeal of, 306n43; inclusion of women at, 152; on innovation, 128; interpretive pluralism and, 306–7n45; Islam as natural religion to, 136–37; Islam as ritual excellence in, 138; on leisure activities, 136–37; literalism of, 165; loyalty and disavowal (*al-wala' wa-l-bara'*) doctrine and, 217; on madhab tradition, 306n43; moral superiority of, 108; movement of, 23–24; Muslim Brotherhood and, 320n46; on Muslim-Christian solidarity, 229; on pant length, 137; partisanship of, 159; piety and, 24, 25, 39–40, 110, 134, 137, 142; pluralism and, 168; popularity of, 7, 80; preachers on, 78–79; programming policy of, 150–51; quiet, 280n50; Qur'an interpretation by, 149; rebuttal of, 216; recreation viewpoint of, 93; refusal (*bara'*) doctrine of, 221–22; religious outreach and, 18; revivalism of, 25; ritualism of, 138, 140, 145–46; as saved sect (*al-firqa al-najiyya*), 107, 145, 149, 239; separatism in, 108; shifting status of, 163–65; slogan of, 79; spiritual distinction of, 237–38; state security and, 319n33; threat from, 228; tolerance in, 307n45; on tradition, 109, 123; undermining of, 7; as unnatural, 137–38; Valentine's Day and, 319n35; violence against Christians and, 228; Wahhabism of, 23, 125, 281n56, 166, 299–300n46 (*See also* Wahhabism)
Saleh, Suad, 152–53
Salman, Mohammad bin, 71
Salomon, Noah, 150
Sameh, Maurice, 119, 224–26
Satan, 199
satellite television: concerns regarding, 80; content of, 65; legalization of, 63; need for, 72; origin of, 54; political

economy of, 53, 63; religious channels as minor players in, 61; socially corrosive effects of, 64
Saudi Arabia, 61, 164–65, 321–22n56
saved sect (*al-firqa al-najiyya*), 23–24, 106–7, 145, 149, 239
Sawy Cultural Wheel, 89, 91, 103
Schielke, Samuli, 32, 137, 311n2
School of Love (Madrasat al-Hubb) (television series), 89, 142, 144
Science and Faith (Al-'Ilm wa-l-Iman) (television series), 74–75
sectarianism, 216, 227, 230
secularism: attachment and, 20; boundaries of, 9, 93–94; compatibility with Islam and, 234; defined, 28–29; Egyptian revivalist understanding of, 28; Islam and, 284n75; Muslim-Christian solidarity and, 217; opposition to, 10; religion as subjective in, 238; sectarianism and, 227; understanding of, 159–60
secular-religious difference, 25–30, 93–94, 284–85n75
self-cultivation (*tahdib al-nafs*), 144, 184
self-development (*al-tanmiya al-dhatiya*), 188
self-discipline, 311n2
self-fashioning, 313–14n27
self-help: colonial context of, 191–92; context of, 191–92; criticism of, 199, 210; *da'wa* and, 191–92; *i'mar* and, 174; literature, 175–76, 186, 210, 313n23, 313n27; of New Preachers, 174, 186–87; as others help, 192–96; to recreate Islamic media, 176–77; as resource, 211; returning to Islam, 188–92; significance of, 191; starting with yourself concept in, 186–88
Self-Help (Smiles), 191
Self-Help Society, 191
self-transformation, 174, 212
Selim, Khalid, 89–90, 103, 104–5
separatism, 108
The 7 Habits of Highly Effective People (Covey), 189–90
Shafik, Ahmed, 242
Sha'rawi, Huda, 198
Sha'rawi, Shaykh, 12, 113
Shari'a and Life (television show), 167
Sharif, Safwat al-, 62
Shehata, Dr. Sherif, 194–95
Shehata, Hassan, 245–46
Shias, 21, 245–46
silence: *al-iltizam bi-l-samt* (maintaining silence), 256; deliberate, 323n2; function of, 323n2; maintaining silence (*al-iltizam bi-l-samt*), 256; of the New Preachers, 45, 257–60; overview of, 322–23n1; political, 257; potential of, 323n3; significance of, 256–57, 325n9
sin, 120–21, 135, 140, 303–4n17
Sirsawi, Mazin, 125, 148–49
Smiles, Samuel, 191
Smith, W. C., 19, 138
Sobhy, Mohamed, 196, 318n20
social change, 186
social media, 30
Spadola, Emilio, 14–15
specialization, 259
spirit of Tahrir, 36. *See also* Tahrir Square
Star Academy (television show), 77
Starrett, Gregory, 6, 145

starting with yourself concept, 185–88
stewardship, 182
Stories from the Qur'an (Qissas min al-Qur'an) (television series), 116
The Story of Andalusia (Qissat al-Andalus) (television series), 246–48
storyteller (*qass*), 296n14
storytelling, power of, 151–52
structural transformation, 11
Su'al Mubashir (Direct Question) (television show), 324n6
suffering, 198
Sufi, 139
Sufism, 163, 304n30
suicide bombing, 228–29
Su'ud, Safa' Abu al-, 64–65
Suwaidan, Tareq el-, 76–77, 219
Syria, 321n51

ta'arruf (mutual engagement), 104, 105, 215, 216
ta'ayush (coexistence). *See* coexistence (*ta'ayush*)
tadayyun fitri, 179
tafakkuk (fragmentation), 150
tahdib al-nafs (self-cultivation), 144, 184
Tahrir Square: as asecular, 217; celebration in, 178; conflicting interpretation regarding, 217; ethics of, 174–75, 185; friendship of, 224–31; as godly space, 214; hope in, 199; love in, 214, 225; as outside of religion, 217; political sensibility and, 217; revive the revolution within ourselves (*i'adit ihya' al-thawra guwwana*) and, 225–26; revolutionary ethics in, 178; significance of, 10, 36, 157, 171, 188, 214; skit regarding, 171–72; small acts of care in, 171; spirit in, 213, 248, 251; sublime moment of, 214; as un-Islamic, 217; unity in, 10; violence in, 220. *See also* 2011 revolution
Tahtawi, Rifa'i al-, 233
Takfir wal Hijra, Al-, 108
Talal, Alwaleed Bin, 50
tamyi' al-din (corruption of religion), 124
tamyi' al-din (religious laxity), 222
tanmiya al-dhatiya, al- (self-development), 188
Tariq al-Sah, Al- (The Right Path) (television series), 74, 120
tasammuh (tolerance), 130, 223, 241–42
Tash, Abdulkader, 58, 60, 61, 72, 130–31, 132–33
tashabbuh bi-l-kuffar, al- (imitation of disbelievers), 231–32, 319n35
tawba (repentance), 121
Tayeb, Ahmed el-, 97, 323n2
televangelists/televangelism, 67–68, 118–19
television: as addictive, 112; concerns regarding, 272n10; immersive quality of, 114; innovation of, 92; as involving medium, 112; as magical, 112; mainstream, 206–9; as not radio, 110, 111–12, 126; social history of, 298n38; spatial-temporal compression by, 116; visual piety and, 112–17
textualism, 276n35
Thawra 'ala al-Nafs (The Revolution Within) (television program), 10–11, 188
theology: anthropology and, 26–30, 282n60, 303n17; of attention, 136; of impact, 173, 184, 212; of mediation,

16, 92, 274n21; of moderation, 131, 168; neglected area of inquiry, 276–77n33; of refusal (*bara'*), 217; social life of, 8, 11, 19–20, 26; two main extant schools of Sunni, 20–24
They Tricked You and Said (Khadaʿukka fa-Qalu) (television series), 146–48
Third Trend, 247
tolerance (*tasammuh*), 130, 223, 241–42
Tomorrow Will Be Better (Bukra Ahla) (television show), 188
tradition, 26, 27–28, 94–98
Tripp, Charles, 57
truth, as contingently conveyed, 90
Turkey, 184
Twitter, 30
2000 privatization law, 290n3
2011 revolution: celebrations following, 174; chants during, 316n1; conditions following, 226; defined, 1; effects of, 10; election following, 1; ethics of, 33–38; feeling, 197–202; as a feeling, 202; as hypermediated, 30; purpose of, 10; as secular, 214; social media impact on, 30; women as attending, 43, 154–55. *See also* Tahrir Square

Uhibbika Rabbi (I Love You My Lord) (television series), 140
Until They Change Themselves (television series), 190

Valentine's Day, 232, 234, 319n35
van Nieuwkerk, Karin, 299n45
viewer interaction, 203–6

violence, 175, 245–46
virtues, 145–46
visual break, 197
visual piety, 112–17
volunteerism, 192–93, 196, 315n38. *See also specific organizations*

Wahba, Hafiz, 309n64
wahda al-wataniyya, al- (national unity), 226
Wahhab, Muhammad Abd al-, 23, 164, 166, 236
Wahhabism: characteristics of, 25; customs of, 229; expansion of doctrine of, 238; literature of, 166; minimalism and, 299–300n46; mission of, 125; overview of, 164; positive framing of, 309n64; Salafi preachers and, 281n56
wala' wa-l-bara', al- (loyalty and disavowal), 107, 217
waqf, 69, 70, 71, 76
Wasat, al-, 167–68, 310n75
wasati, wasatiyya (moderation). *See* moderation (*wasati, wasatiyya*)
wasatiyyun, al- (the centrists), 322n56
wealth, 87
Westernization, 72, 124–25, 138, 163
"What Can I Say?" (*Wa Ulak Ay?*), 253–55, 261
Wickham, Carrie, 186, 289n102
Winegar, Jessica, 29, 312n13
Winter, Tim, 143
Words from the Heart (Kalam min al-Qalb) (television series), 117–19
World Bank, 273n15
Worldly Enchantments (television series), 109, 131

worship, 184; community service as, 173, 182; devotional, 141; God's love for, 139; heart, 140; love and, 162; music as, 219; obligation for, 183; piety and, 141, 143–44, 276n28; purpose of, 173; ritual, 8, 51, 142, 144, 145, 162, 184; self-help and, 176; solidarity as, 286n85
writing from their minds (*bi-yiktibu min dimaghhum*), 239

Yacoub, Magdy, 181, 231
Yale University, 291n5
Ya'qub, Muhammad, 23, 77, 78–80, 123, 134, 159, 232
Yassin, Shaykh, 181
YouTube, 275n26
Yusuf, Abdul Rahman, 318n20
Yusuf, Sami, 219–20

Zarate, Arthur, 313n27
Zein, Abdul Hamid El-, 282n60
Zizek, Slavoj, 214

Stanford Studies in Middle Eastern and
Islamic Societies and Cultures

Lara Deeb and Sherene Seikaly, editors

Unruly Labor: A History of Oil in the Arabian Sea   2024
ANDREA WRIGHT

The Incarcerated Modern: Prisons and Public Life in Iran   2024
GOLNAR NIKPOUR

Elastic Empire: Refashioning War Through Aid in Palestine   2023
LISA BHUNGALIA

Colonizing Palestine: The Zionist Left and the Making of the Palestinian Nakba   2023
AREEJ SABBAGH-KHOURY

On Salafism: Concepts and Contexts   2023
AZMI BISHARA

Revolutions Aesthetic: A Cultural History of Ba'thist Syria   2022
MAX WEISS

Street-Level Governing: Negotiating the State in Urban Turkey   2022
ELISE MASSICARD

Protesting Jordan: Geographies of Power and Dissent   2022
JILLIAN SCHWEDLER

Media of the Masses: Cassette Culture in Modern Egypt   2022
ANDREW SIMON

States of Subsistence: The Politics of Bread in Contemporary Jordan   2022
JOSÉ CIRO MARTÍNEZ

Between Dreams and Ghosts: Indian Migration and Middle Eastern Oil   2021
ANDREA WRIGHT

Bread and Freedom: Egypt's Revolutionary Situation   2021
MONA EL-GHOBASHY

Paradoxes of Care: Children and Global Medical Aid in Egypt 2021
RANIA KASSAB SWEIS

The Politics of Art: Dissent and Cultural Diplomacy in Lebanon, Palestine, and Jordan 2021
HANAN TOUKAN

The Paranoid Style in American Diplomacy: Oil and Arab Nationalism in Iraq 2021
BRANDON WOLFE-HUNNICUTT

Screen Shots: State Violence on Camera in Israel and Palestine 2021
REBECCA L. STEIN

Dear Palestine: A Social History of the 1948 War 2021
SHAY HAZKANI

A Critical Political Economy of the Middle East and North Africa 2020
JOEL BEININ, BASSAM HADDAD, AND SHERENE SEIKALY, EDITORS

Showpiece City: How Architecture Made Dubai 2020
TODD REISZ

Archive Wars: The Politics of History in Saudi Arabia 2020
ROSIE BSHEER

Between Muslims: Religious Difference in Iraqi Kurdistan 2020
J. ANDREW BUSH

The Optimist: A Social Biography of Tawfiq Zayyad 2020
TAMIR SOREK

Graveyard of Clerics: Everyday Activism in Saudi Arabia 2020
PASCAL MENORET

Cleft Capitalism: The Social Origins of Failed Market Making in Egypt 2020
AMR ADLY

The Universal Enemy: Jihad, Empire, and the Challenge of Solidarity 2019
DARRYL LI

Waste Siege: The Life of Infrastructure in Palestine 2019
SOPHIA STAMATOPOULOU-ROBBINS

For a complete listing of titles in this series, visit the Stanford University Press website, www.sup.org.

The authorized representative in the EU for product safety and compliance is:
Mare Nostrum Group B.V.
Mauritskade 21D
1091 GC Amsterdam
The Netherlands
Email address: gpsr@mare-nostrum.co.uk

KVK chamber of commerce number: 96249943

The authorized representative in the EU for product safety and compliance is:
Mare Nostrum Group
B.V Doelen 72
4831 GR Breda
The Netherlands

www.ingramcontent.com/pod-product-compliance
Lightning Source LLC
Chambersburg PA
CBHW031752220426
43662CB00007B/377